EX LIBRIS
Hugo
Adam
Bedau

# CONSCIENCE AND CASUISTRY IN EARLY MODERN EUROPE

# IDEAS IN CONTEXT

Edited by Richard Rorty, J. B. Schneewind, Quentin Skinner
and Wolf Lepenies

The books in this series will discuss the emergence of intellectual traditions and of related new disciplines. The procedures, aims and vocabularies that were generated will be set in the context of the alternatives available within the contemporary frameworks of ideas and institutions. Through detailed studies of the evolution of such traditions, and their modification by different audiences, it is hoped that a new picture will form of the development of ideas in their concrete contexts. By this means, artificial distinctions between the history of philosophy, of the various sciences, of society and politics, and of literature, may be seen to dissolve.

Titles published in the series:

Richard Rorty, J. B. Schneewind and Quentin Skinner (eds.), *Philosophy in History*
J. G. A. Pocock, *Virtue, Commerce and History*
M. M. Goldsmith, *Private Vices, Public Benefits: Bernard Mandeville's Social and Political Thought*
David Summers, *The Judgment of Sense*
Anthony Pagden (ed.), *The Languages of Political Thought in Early-Modern Europe*
Laurence Dickey, *Hegel: Religion, Economics and the Politics of Spirit, 1770–1807*
Margo Todd, *Christian Humanism and the Puritan Social Order*
Lynn S. Joy, *Gassendi the Atomist: Advocate of History in an Age of Science*

This series is published with the support of the Exxon Education Foundation.

This book is published as part of the joint publishing agreement established in 1977 between the Fondation de la Maison des Sciences de l'Homme and the Press Syndicate of the University of Cambridge. Titles published under this arrangement may appear in any European language or, in the case of volumes of collected essays, in several languages.

New books will appear either as individual titles or in one of the series which the Maison des Sciences de l'Homme and the Cambridge University Press have jointly agreed to publish. All books published jointly by the Maison des Sciences de l'Homme and the Cambridge University Press will be distributed by the Press throughout the world.

Cet ouvrage est publié dans le cadre de l'accord de co-édition passé en 1977 entre la Fondation de la Maison des Sciences de l'Homme et le Press Syndicate de l'Université de Cambridge. Toutes les langues européennes sont admises pour les titres couverts par cet accord, et les ouvrages collectifs peuvent paraître en plusieurs langues.

Les ouvrages paraissent soit isolément, soit dans l'une des séries que la Maison des Sciences de l'Homme et Cambridge University Press ont convenu de publier ensemble. La distribution dans le monde entier des titres ainsi publiés conjointement par les deux établissements est assurée par Cambridge University Press.

# CONSCIENCE AND CASUISTRY IN EARLY MODERN EUROPE

EDITED BY
## EDMUND LEITES

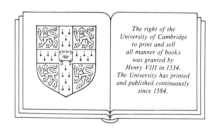

The right of the
University of Cambridge
to print and sell
all manner of books
was granted by
Henry VIII in 1534.
The University has printed
and published continuously
since 1584.

CAMBRIDGE UNIVERSITY PRESS

CAMBRIDGE

NEW YORK  NEW ROCHELLE  MELBOURNE  SYDNEY

EDITIONS DE LA MAISON DES SCIENCES DE L'HOMME

PARIS

Published by the Press Syndicate of the University of Cambridge
The Pitt Building, Trumpington Street, Cambridge CB2 1RP
32 East 57th Street, New York, NY 10022, USA
10 Stamford Road, Oakleigh, Melbourne 3166, Australia
and Editions de la Maison des Sciences de l'Homme
54 Boulevard Raspail, 75270 Paris Cedex 06

© Maison des Sciences de l'Homme and Cambridge University Press 1988

First published 1988

Printed in Great Britain at the University Press, Cambridge

*British Library cataloguing in publication data*
Conscience and casuistry in early modern
Europe. – (Ideas in context).
1. Casuistry   2. Ethics, European – History
I. Leites, Edmund   II. Series
171'.6   BJ1441

*Library of Congress cataloguing in publication data*
Conscience and casuistry in early modern Europe
edited by Edmund Leites.
p.   cm. – (Ideas in context)
Includes index.
ISBN 0 521 30113 0
1. Ethics – Europe – History – 17th century. 2. Ethics – Europe –
History – 18th century. 3. Conscience. 4. Casuistry. I. Leites,
Edmund, 1939–   . II. Series.
BJ301.C63   1988
171'.6'094–dc19   87–19716CIP

ISBN 0 521 30113 0

ISBN 2 7351 0185 1 (France only)

*For John Dunn and Justin Leites*

There is a solid bottom everywhere. We read that the traveller asked the boy if the swamp before him had a solid bottom. The boy replied that it had. But presently, the traveller's horse sank up to the girths, and he observed to the boy, 'I thought you said that this bog had a hard bottom.' 'So it has', answered the latter, 'but you have not got half way to it yet.' So it is with the bogs and quicksands of society; but he is an old boy that knows it.

Henry David Thoreau, *Walden*

# Contents

# Contributors

JOHN BOSSY is Professor of History in the University of York. He is the author of *The English Catholic Community, 1570–1850* (1976) and *Christianity in the West, 1400–1700* (1985).

JEAN DELUMEAU is Professor at the Collège de France, holding the Chaire d'Histoire des Mentalités Religieuses dans l'Occident Moderne. His books include *La Peur en Occident, XIV<sup>e</sup>–XVIII<sup>e</sup> siècles* (1978), which is soon to appear in English, and *Le Péché et la peur, XIII<sup>e</sup>–XVIII<sup>e</sup> siècles* (1983).

H.-D. KITTSTEINER is the author of *Naturabsicht und Unsichtbare Hand* (1980). He has published a number of papers on the philosophy of history, Walter Benjamin, and the history of conscience in the seventeenth and eighteenth centuries, on which he is at present writing a book.

EDMUND LEITES is Professor of Philosophy at the Graduate School of Queens College of the City University of New York. He is the author of *The Puritan Conscience and Modern Sexuality* (1986).

MARGARET SAMPSON is Lecturer in History at the University of Queensland. She has published articles on Australian history and is at present studying the relation of seventeenth-century English political thought to ideas of property and marriage.

JOHANN P. SOMMERVILLE is a Fellow of the Royal Historical Society and author of *Politics and Ideology in England, 1603–1640* (1986).

RICHARD TUCK is a Fellow of Jesus College, Cambridge, where he is Director of Studies in History. His publications include *Natural Rights Theories* (1979).

JAMES TULLY is Associate Professor of Political Science and Philosophy at McGill University. His most recent book, of which he is the editor, is *Meaning and Context: Quentin Skinner and his Critics* (1987).

# INTRODUCTION

## EDMUND LEITES

The contributors to this volume are philosophers, historians, and political theorists from Great Britain, Canada, the United States, Australia, France, and Germany. In spite of the diversity of disciplines and national traditions, their contributions show a remarkable convergence on three themes: changes in the modes of moral education in early modern Europe, the emergence of new relations between conscience and law (particularly the law of the state), and the shared continuities and discontinuities of both Roman Catholic and Protestant moral culture in relation to their medieval past.

The late nineteenth-century American historian Henry Charles Lea saw the history of conscience in early modern Europe as the liberation of conscience in Protestant lands from the authority of priests and casuists, who had built their power upon 'the weakness of those unable to bear their burdens, unable to trust themselves'.[1] A number of contributors to this volume, however, question whether the early modern period did see the emergence of new practices and ideas which 'freed' the individual conscience from social and political control. In the first chapter James Tully argues that a new practice of governing conduct was formed in the early modern era which was a direct attack upon conscience, its aim being the creation of habits that would replace conscience as a governing element of action. He relies largely, but by no means exclusively, on a wide variety of works by John Locke to describe the new constellation of moral ideas and practices, which he calls 'penal'.

Tully sees a close connection between changes in dominant conceptions of epistemology and changing beliefs about how morality is to be taught, learned, and enforced. The new way of governing, he

[1]  Henry Charles Lea, *A History of Auricular Confession and Indulgences in the Latin Church* (3 vols., Philadelphia, Lea Brothers and Company, 1896), vol. II, p. 456.

1

writes, depends upon the conviction that assent or belief is not governed by a natural human attraction to the truth, but by acquired dispositions or habits which are created by the social environment. It is in this manner, Tully says, that Locke accounts for the religious wars which were such a prominent feature of the sixteenth and seventeenth centuries. To free people from thought formed by custom, fashion, and the claims of authority of religious elites, Locke proposes the mental technique of suspending one's judgment and examining the grounds for and against any proposition before assenting to it. The force of the argument and the weight of the evidence can then be the criteria on which one's beliefs are formed. There is no innate disposition to truth, but if these criteria are applied in the context of a suspension of belief, mankind will get as close to the truth as humanly possible. The trouble is that neither the methods of suspension and examination nor the rational criteria for the assessment of evidence and granting of assent are natural or innate in Locke's view. Rationality is itself an acquired disposition that is created by the social environment. Tully therefore argues that an adequate and free judgment for Locke is as much a consequence of external manipulation as the crude hatreds that fuel religious wars.

This account of the mode by which beliefs are formed, Tully argues, is analogous to a new constellation of ideas about conduct. Just as Locke believes there is no innate attraction to the truth, so he believes that there is no innate inclination to goodness. It, too, is made up of acquired habits created by the social environment. The lack of innate connection between the human will and the moral truth is all the more drastic in Locke because of his 'voluntarism' concerning the will of God. The divine will which determines what is right and wrong is, to Locke's mind, not a function of any rationality to which God himself submits. One cannot assume that human rational conceptions of right and wrong correspond to God's will, and in any case, as Locke repeatedly says, human reason cannot demonstrate that a purely rational conception of good is backed up by divine sanctions. This, however, is what makes God's will a law for mankind.

This voluntarism is combined by Locke, in the latter half of the 1670s, with hedonism, the doctrine that what governs choice in conduct is attraction to pleasure and avoidance of pain. Humanity can be brought into a steady compliance and willing harmony with God's law, then, only if it finds that the balance of pleasure and pain makes compliance worthwhile. It is, however one's *current* uneasiness or pain which is the source of one's choices, not absent and far-off goods. The knowledge of hell, Locke points out, is not always enough to bring the human will into compliance with God's, or else men who know very well what is in store for them would behave better than they do.

The uneasiness associated with particular choices is learned, not innate. The present pain one may commonly feel at giving up a good in present possession for the sake of a greater future good is itself an acquired habit that can be broken, according to Locke. In Tully's view, Locke therefore finally arrives at a programme for the refashioning of the human will which is drastically coercive. In all phases of life, practices must be established which will make one feel sufficient present pain in the desire or intention to violate God's law to guarantee a habitually law-abiding will. Locke is far from being a champion of the liberty of conscience. The coercive methods of social and moral reform which Locke proposed to apply to the poor illustrate, Tully says, Locke's willingness to use the law of the state as an instrument of moral education. The penalties of the law, including death, are to be used to create the regular and law-abiding self which is now a familiar feature of the modern Western world. For Tully, this reveals no true freedom of conscience.

Sampson stresses both the continuities and discontinuities in the changing treatments of conscience and moral reasoning in seventeenth-century England. Many of the crucial elements of Dutch and English political and legal theory of the seventeenth century were directly borrowed from Catholic casuistry. Ideas central to the probabilist doctrines of Roman Catholic casuistry were also alive in English law. In fact, they became more important to English legal practice as the century developed. The antagonism of lawyers and political theorists against the casuists was nonethelss deep. As the casuists' opponents saw it, divines should not meddle in the daily life of mankind by determining for particular cases what was permissible or forbidden. For many of the defenders of the common law during the Interregnum, that determination was the task of lawyers. They were to be the casuists of English society. The clergy had a different job: to encourage people to form their characters on the basis of the love of God and their neighbour. Similarly, Grotius and Locke envisaged an entirely educative role for the divines. They were not to be judges, relying on the penal power of the law, but teachers. Law, Locke wrote, works by force, but the task of religion is to make men true Christians in their hearts. It has the task of spiritual and moral education, which was more a matter of the formation of the selves than it was the precise determination of the bounds of Christian liberty.

Sampson agrees with Tawney's thesis that the claim of religion to guide conscience in economic affairs had vanished by the reign of James II, but she sees this as an outcome of the general campaign on the part of lawyers and political theorists to monopolize the science of casuistry (in its broad sense as the application of general principles to particular cases) and to relegate the clergy to the role of teachers of moral and spiritual values. The very groups, however, who fought to deny church casuistry a role in the regulation of daily life borrowed much of its teachings for their own casuistical endeavours.

In my own contribution to this volume, I argue that the opposition to church casuistry in seventeenth-century England owed much to the belief in utility of individual autonomy – the conviction that when it came to moral and spiritual matters, people were served best by being left to direct themselves. Autonomy was seen as furthering the formation of a more adequate moral and spiritual self because the use of one's own judgment in the choice of actions and beliefs was held to be necessary for the development of character in adults. However correct the casuists may have been in their conclusions, they were seen as hindering (or, at least, not furthering) the end of spiritual and moral education because they took the task of judgment away from the individual himself. The casuistry of English common law, however, did not commonly receive the same critique because it was not seen as impeding the formation of a moral and pious self. Unlike casuistry it made no claims to regulate the character of our conduct through conscience, but tried to control behaviour directly through penal sanctions. The casuistry of the English courts was ultimately compatible with seventeenth-century ideas of the necessity of autonomy in the moral growth of adults. This does not mean (and here I disagree with Tully) that the claims of conscience and autonomy which were so forcefully advanced in seventeenth-century England were in the end no more than a devious mode to create an even more powerful social and state control of the individual. Ideas of moral character, as expressed in conduct, could and did oppose the actual requirement of law. A concern for the harmonization of law and character has therefore been one legacy of seventeenth-century English moral and political philosophies.

Delumeau also sees a discontinuity between the medieval and the early modern eras in the realm of moral education. The church gave up its accommodation of popular and age-old magical practices and replaced it by a sustained and marked effort to eradicate these customs. The pure religion of the elite was imposed upon the masses. This relatively recent process of Christianization cut across the division between Protestant and Roman Catholic. Both were involved in the same programme of conversion. Penal repression was one chief mode, but another, equally important, was education. The medieval clerical attitude was that people would be saved in spite of their ignorance as long as they did not rebel against the church, by virtue of their good will and the prayers of the clergy. Both Protestant and Catholic now argued that religious ignorance led to damnation. The new attitude required that Christian doctrine and proper modes of conduct be taught to the masses, particularly to the rural population, which for so long had been left untutored.

The attempt to make the rural population, even in the secret details of their daily life, thoroughly conscious of God and eternity was a massive challenge. It is Delumeau's contention that the Protestant and Roman Catholic pedagogies meant to serve this purpose did not fundamentally differ. They tried to create and intensify the fear of hell and at the same time relied upon the newly powerful state to enforce beliefs and practices through its own penal mechanisms. The result was that by 1700, true and salvific religion was seen as a choice of the hearts and minds of individuals, yet nearly everyone regularly attended church, something never previously achieved.

Delumeau is nonetheless well aware of the gap between pastoral ambition and actual results. Travelling people who lived outside the framework of the parish and migrants from rural areas to the city where there was no parish to welcome them were barely touched by the church's interior mission. For other reasons as well, the old rural magical ways survived. Both clergy and laity often grew tired of the unending emphasis on the fear of the hereafter, a fatigue which weakened their piety to the extent that it depended on that fear. The power of the clergy over the laity, which was sustained by the superior education to which the cleric could lay claim, was weakened by the increase in the number of educated laymen, the extension of secular learning to new regions, and the increased independence, in terms of learning and power, of the educated city-dweller. The result was that the church more and more turned for support to the very rural areas which centuries earlier had been seen as no less pagan than the Indies.

Divisions over serious ethical questions in early modern Europe did not always parallel the division between Protestant and Catholic,

as Sommerville shows in his study of the casuists' treatment of lies.
Nineteenth-century Protestant attacks against Roman Catholic
casuistry, like Pascal's polemic against the Jesuits, supposed that the
judgments of the casuists which were offensive to the mind of the
plain and honest man had been developed to make lax moral
behaviour morally acceptable. The doctrine of mental reservation,
according to which it would not be a lie to make a spoken assertion
which one believes to be false and believes will deceive one's hearer
if one adds in thought some words which will make the whole truthful
was, as Sommerville shows, in fact developed in order to reconcile
the strict ban on lying, which had its authority from Augustine, with
such duties as saving lives and preserving secrets. The persecution of
Catholics in Protestant countries may account for the popularity of
the doctrine in the years around 1600, but it was not invented for the
benefit of Catholic priests under interrogation. Their equivocation,
however, did bring the theory to the attention of both Protestant
and Catholic laymen. Catholic vernacular writings had stressed the
virtue of honesty, but the contrary ideas which had been developed
by the casuists to solve difficult theoretical problems and which had
been argued for in scholarly Latin volumes were now made available
to a large mass of people who lacked the casuist's education.
Catholics and Protestants alike found the doctrine of mental reservation thoroughly offensive. An embarrassment to the church, it
was finally condemned by Pope Innocent XI in 1679.

It was by no means the case, however, as enemies of the Jesuits
repeatedly said in the seventeenth century, that mental reservation
was a doctrine and practice peculiar to the Jesuits. There were
Jesuits who opposed it and, in fact, there was no distinct Jesuit moral
code. Moreover, there were important Protestants who argued that
lying could sometimes be justified, including Hugo Grotius and
Jeremy Taylor. Casuistry was a phenomenon that was as much
Protestant as Catholic in the seventeenth century and the divisions
between casuists on ethical questions did not correspond to the
boundaries between these two religious worlds.

Although casuistry was an active force in seventeenth-century
Protestantism, it has not survived in the modern Protestant world as
it has in Roman Catholicism. Kittsteiner argues that casuistry went
out of fashion in Protestant Germany because conscience itself
asserted its independence from the casuists' mode of reasoning.
Kant claimed that when conscience was truly grounded in morality it
could resolve its cases quickly, correctly, and unequivocally. In the
older idea of conscience, however, upon which casuistry based its

claims to authority, conscience was constantly in danger of doing something wrong. It was not simply an entity within, but was outside the self in the form of revealed divine law. Religious people understood conscience to include both that law and the complex science and accumulated wisdom developed by the church concerning its interpretation. No wonder, then, that in doubtful matters they would turn to those more experienced in thinking and morals for aid.

Kittsteiner (agreeing with Delumeau) says, however, that the bulk of the European population from the Middle Ages to the seventeenth century were not religious in this ethical sense. They did not know the statutes and precepts of the church and seldom made any attempt to gain a knowledge of them or to ask experts for advice. The great casuistical summas of the seventeenth century – meant to instruct the clergy who were in turn to instruct the laity – were in fact part of a massive attempt at the ethical Christianization of Europe.

This attempt to introduce biblical norms into the interpretation of daily conduct was linked to a ministry of fear, which stressed the idea that eternal life was not to be obtained by a few prayers shortly before death, but by a true morality embedded in daily conduct. In spite of its spiritual claims, Kittsteiner argues, seventeenth-century casuistry did nonetheless commonly attempt to accommodate itself to the demands of earthly survival. The casuists sometimes referred to Thomas Aquinas, who said that in cases of misery, the goods ordained for subsistence had to be accessible to everyone. In this, the casuists were not alone. Penal codes also recognized desperate circumstances as modifying the statutes and penalties protecting property.

The casuists permitted the individuality of desperate circumstances to create exceptions to the general rule. The individual, in certain respects, took precedence over the general. Kittsteiner points out that matters were very different in Kant's ethics, where the individual had to do whatever was necessary to sustain the rule of law. The change in the idea of what constituted true moral reason was as well a shift in the content (and social context) of morality. Casuistry, in fact, characteristically understood the plight of those who could not survive if they did not steal from the rich in directly economic terms. It was a question of the relations between rich and poor, not of a relation between an individual and a system of law (which in turn served property and encouraged commerce).

The attack against casuistry in the name of morality, according to

Kittsteiner, was, however, a good deal more than a defence of bourgeois forms of property and exchange. Casuistry had been flexible enough, in spite of its pretensions to syllogistic form, to modify the balance between the world and salvation according to the changing situation. In pre-capitalist societies, the difference between relatively prosperous times and times of distress was so great that the casuists had to take account of the difference in their practical ethics. Whatever the accommodation, casuists always tried to connect life in its givenness to questions about the right way to salvation. In the conscience advocated by Kant, there was a move away from a concern to justify oneself before God towards an emphasis on one's responsibility to society. A thorough respect for the outward forms of legality was not connected by Kant to outward penal sanctions so much as it was to the idea of duty and law as inner springs of conduct. Kittsteiner adds, however, that the moral law which created a link between inward moral feeling and outward legality did not represent bourgeois society as it was, but as it should be. There was an implicit but powerful antagonism towards things as they were in the apparently bourgeois form of Kant's thought. Inspired by the idea of a society in which every rational creature is an end in itself, the moral law was intimately linked to the hope and belief in the possibility of a better society. This, above all, is what distinguishes the ethics of Kant and his descendants from the casuists, who attempted to create a practical connection between the world of the spirit and the world as it actually was.

Bossy, like Delumeau, sees a pattern of change common to both the Protestant and Roman Catholic worlds of early modern Europe. For the most part, the moral system taught in medieval Western Christianity was constituted by the Seven Deadly Sins, but after the sixteenth century, a different moral system, the Ten Commandments, was universally taught throughout Western Christianity, whether Roman Catholic or Protestant. In this change of systems, Bossy argues, Christians had acquired a morality which gave greater emphasis to the worship of God, less emphasis to one's obligations to one's neighbour, and in both matters was more precise, more penetrating, and more binding. Bossy argues that this change was not a consequence of the Reformation, although the Protestant emphasis on Scripture did advance the cause of the Ten Commandments. In quite a lot of the West, the transition from one scheme to the other had occurred before the Reformation. The adoption of the Decalogue by the Council of Trent was as much an expression of the

movement towards the new system as was its universal adoption by
the Reformers.

Advocacy of the Decalogue began with the thirteenth-century
schoolmen, but their scheme was not generally communicated by
the clergy to the laity. There were a number of practical and
theoretical difficulties which blocked the scholastics' project, one of
which was the useful role which the Seven Sins could play in the
calculation of one's moral account, an account-keeping which was
encouraged by the requirement of annual confession. Much before
Luther, Jean Gerson advanced the cause of the Ten Commandments, giving them effective vernacular expression and integrating
them into a general scheme of Catholic piety which included the
practice of confession. His innovations were particularly influential
in Germany. In spite of Luther's insistence on Scripture, Bossy
notes, it is still surprising that he was the vehicle for the final victory
of the Decalogue, since he might more naturally have been among
those who resisted it. From an early date, however, perhaps even
before his break with Rome, he had abandoned the Seven Sins in
favour of an ethics built on the Ten Commandments. He was, of
course, well aware of their 'legal' character and in fact saw them as
properly supported by the penal powers of secular authority.

This change in moral systems and moral education had some surprising results, Bossy argues. Under the old scheme, the Devil was
seen as an anti-type of Christ, but under the new, with its emphasis
on worship, he became the anti-type of the Father, the source and
object of all idolatry and false worship. This led in turn to a change in
the idea of witchcraft. Under the Seven Sins, witchcraft was the
offence of causing malicious harm to one's neighbour by occult
means; under the new scheme, it was an offence against the first
commandment. Witches were now Devil-worshippers. In both
Roman Catholic and Reformation Christianity, obedience to
parents (and by extension, to other authorities) also underwent a
change, not so much in meaning as in importance. It was not an
obligation that had received much notice in the exposition of the
sins.

Although the philosophically systematic moral and political
theorists of the seventeenth century owed much to the ideas of
medieval scholastics and casuists, they were clearly doing something
new. In what respects, however, were they different? In the concluding contribution to this volume, Tuck argues that there was a crucial
break in the history of the philosophical ethics in the seventeenth

century, marked above all by the emergence of a group of theorists
who took as one of their main tasks the development of a
philosophically sensitive answer to the scepticism of both classical
antiquity and their own time. Mersenne proposed a programme for
the refutation of scepticism which recognized the force of sceptical
arguments and aimed to transcend them. This was a programme,
Tuck argues, which Descartes, Gassendi, and Hobbes all tried to
carry out. The core of Mersenne's programme was the argument that
each science had a set of indisputable *a priori* principles on which a
science could be built in spite of the inadequacy of the senses. What
Tuck argues is that Hobbes developed an analogous programme for
ethics and politics.

The seventeenth-century sceptic denied the existence of secure
means for establishing the truth of any proposition in natural
science. Perceptions were relative, as were morals. Tuck sees
Grotius as taking the first steps towards the refutation of scepticism
in moral matters by a 'transcendental' argument: however much
diversity there was among moralities, all societies had to possess certain moral principles, or else they could not exist. There had to be,
behind the variety, a universal though minimal moral core. This
argument, with its distinctly anti-sceptical purpose, marked Grotius
off from earlier moral and political theorists to whom he is in other
respects similar. He did not, however, support his argument with
extensive philosophical underpinning, which is just what Tuck
thinks Hobbes did do. He designed a transcendental argument to
support the possibility of a science of *both* nature and morals.

Hobbes agreed with the sceptics that there was no necessity that
one's perception of things was of what the things were in themselves.
He took up as well Descartes's more general doubts about whether
there was any material reality at all behind any of one's perceptions
(although he did not accept Descartes's resolution of this doubt). To
surmount these challenges to the possibility of knowledge of the
material world, Hobbes developed the argument that the reality of
the change in our perceptions, which the sceptics did not doubt,
could only be caused by motion – and motion could only be conceived of by supposing the existence of material bodies which
operated on one another. This answered Descartes's challenge. To
this, Hobbes added a philosophy of science or knowledge in which
he asserted that although there can be many causal accounts relying
on the motion of bodies that could account for changes in perception, it is sufficient for science if the perceptions could be brought
about by the ascribed cause and that cause could not be shown to

bring about something which was not the case. Hobbes developed, as did Descartes, a scheme in which sceptical elements were incorporated into a philosophy which nonetheless permitted the construction of systems of knowledge.

In morals, Tuck argues, Hobbes did the same. He agreed with the sceptic that everyone calls 'good' that which pleases him and 'evil' that which displeases him, but went on to argue that this was compatible with the possibility of an ethical science. Grotius' argument that there had to be certain moral rights and duties embedded in the variety of moralities that societies adopt, otherwise they would not exist, was just what Hobbes needed. It paralleled his arguments concerning the reality of the material world. Hobbes did modify the content of Grotius' doctrines in such a way as to make them unacceptable to Grotius himself, but Tuck argues that at least some of these modifications came about because Hobbes took greater interest in some of the challenges of sceptical epistemology.

It is not surprising, given the scope of this volume, that there is considerable diversity of interpretation and perspective. What is more significant, however, is the remarkable convergence of these essays on a common set of themes and issues. The perception that early modern European developments in conscience, moral education, and law are coordinated phenomena in both the Protestant and Roman Catholic worlds is perhaps the most important of these. There is considerable disagreement about what sort of coordination this was, but there is enough agreement on the terms and issues to lead one to expect fertile debate in the years to come.

The PSC-CUNY Research Award Program of the City University of New York and the American Council of Learned Societies supported the travel and research necessary to prepare this collection. Two French institutions who have long been hospitable to foreign scholars, la Fondation de la Maison des Sciences de l'Homme and l'Ecole des Hautes Etudes en Sciences Sociales, were also most helpful. I thank Clemens Heller, Director of the Maison, and François Furet, former President of the Ecole, for their hospitality. I am also grateful to Quentin Skinner for his help in the preparation of this volume.

# 1

◁ ════════════════════════════════════════ ▷

## Governing conduct

JAMES TULLY

## INTRODUCTION

This is a working chapter.[1] The claims it embodies are provisional and tentative. The hypothesis laid out in the chapter is that a new practice of governing conduct was assembled in the period from the Reformation to the Enlightenment. My aim is to describe this ensemble of power, knowledge, and habitual behaviour at the point, 1660–1700, when its relatively enduring features consolidated, and from the perspective of one person who described, evaluated, and partly constructed it: John Locke. This mode of governance links together probabilistic and voluntaristic forms of knowledge with a range of techniques related to each other by a complex of references to juridical practices. Its aim is to reform conduct: to explain and then deconstruct settled ways of mental and physical behaviour, and to produce and then govern new forms of habitual conduct in belief and action. Finally, this way of subjection, of conducting the self and others, both posits and serves to bring about a very specific form of subjectivity: a subject who is calculating and calculable, from the perspective of the probabilistic knowledge and practices, and the sovereign bearer of rights and duties, subject to and of law from the voluntaristic perspective. The whole ensemble of knowledge, techniques, habitual activity, and subject I will provisionally call the juridical government.

Aspects of this have been studied by Michel Foucault in *Surveiller et punir: naissance de la prison* (1975). He isolated and distinguished two complexes of power and knowledge, the juridical and the disciplinarian.[2] The former assembled around the spread of secular and

---

[1] In memory of Michel Foucault.
[2] For comparisons and contrasts of these two forms of power and knowledge see Michel Foucault, *Discipline and Punish*, tr. Alan Sheridan (New York, Vintage Books, 1979), pp. 177–83; and 'Two lectures', in Michel Foucault, *Power/ Knowledge*, ed. Colin Gordin (New York, Pantheon Books, 1980), pp. 92–108.

Canon Law from the twelfth century and the latter around the dispersion of techniques of discipline and normalizing from the early seventeenth century. There are important similarities, that would repay close study, between these two concepts and Gerhard Oestreich's distinction between constitutionalism and social discipline in *Neostoicism and the Early Modern State*, and this in turn is based on an older dichotomy used by Friedrich Meinecke and Otto Hintze.[3] Foucault's concern was to show how the disciplines, both as bodies of knowledge – the sciences of man – and as practices of fostering and administering individual and collective life, are, by the nineteenth century, heterogeneous with respect to juridical knowledge and practices. My concern is, rather, to show the tangled nest of relationships between these two before their separation. I want to suggest that the techniques, functions, and forms of knowledge, centered on the norm or statistical regularity, of the disciplines emerged out of the expanded demands placed on the older juridical complex in the mercantile age.

By placing the juridical features of early modern thought and action in the centre of my study I seek to revive and question the thesis advanced by Nietzsche in the second essay of *On The Genealogy of Morals*.[4] He argued that any genealogy of the modern subject, who is both calculable in his behaviour (and so the object of the explaining social sciences and their administrative practices) and sovereign, the bearer of rights and responsibility (and so the subject of the political, legal, and moral sciences and their legal and political practices), must predominantly refer to the secular and church penal practices of the early modern period. I want to explore some of the complexities of this thesis by focusing on the late seventeenth century; and, secondly, to question his conclusion that the product of this long process is the conscience. If my study is correct, just the opposite is true. The new practice of governing was an attack on the conscience, as both too radical and too submissive, and an effort to create habits that would replace the conscience and guide conduct.

This government by reform was put into practice in response to four problems of governability in the early modern period. The first three problems were how to govern the labouring classes; what form of rule would end the civil and religious wars that swept Europe for

---

[3] Gerhard Oestreich, *Neostoicism and the Early Modern State* (Cambridge, Cambridge University Press, 1982).
[4] Friedrich Nietzsche, 'Second essay: guilt, bad conscience and the like', in *On the Genealogy of Morals*, tr. Walter Kaufmann and R. J. Halliday (New York, Vintage Books, 1969).

100 years and claimed 30 per cent of the population; and how to administer global relations of commercial exploitation, colonization, and military power. The fourth problem provided the means to organize the other three into an overall political strategy. In 1648 the consolidating early modern states faced each other as independent and sovereign powers in a situation of uncertainty and military-commercial competition. This predicament of balance of powers, as it was called, marks the threshold of modernity. The Anglo-Dutch war showed that war could now be global and that it would be primarily concerned with the commercial interests of states, not with religion. To compete it was necessary to construct a vast military-diplomatic ensemble capable of protecting and extending commercial relations. The key to this 'power' was, as everyone argued, the enhancement of the wealth and strength of the nation. This required a way of solving the first three problems: so to govern trade, manufacturing, labour, religion, and so on as to bring about riches and strength, which, in turn, would increase military power. The formation of the welfare-warfare state was thus a response to the strategic situation, as many contemporaries noted:[5]

But some nations having departed from the ancient simplicity of living contented with productions of their own countries and having by navigation and trade, raised themselves to wealth, power and increase of inhabitants; it thereupon grew necessary for other nations to fall into like methods, lest otherwise they should have been a prey, as well as a derision to them whom trade hath rendered mighty and opulent.

Mercantilism is the name we give to government policies that sought to solve the problems in all four areas and to coordinate them by means of the law.[6] However, it involved more than an extension and intensification of the law: it marked, and sometimes masked, the transition to the new practice of governing. If the juridical apparatus is partly a response to these problems of governability it is also the way in which new types of knowledge were employed in dealing with these problems.

The religious wars that swept Europe were partly a response to and partly the carrier of the rule of faith controversy. This was the great struggle over the true faith that rapidly deepened to an intellectual battle over the grounds for rational belief or assent in matters of

---

[5] C.K., *Some seasonable and modest thoughts partly occasioned by, and partly concerning the East Indian Company* . . . (Edinburgh, 1696). Cited in Lawrence A. Harper, *The English Navigation Laws: a Seventeenth Century Experiment in Social Engineering* (New York, Columbia University Press, 1939), p. 233.

[6] For a survey of mercantilism see Eli Heckscher, *Mercantilism*, tr. M. Shapiro, ed. E. F. Soderlund, 2nd edition (2 vols., London, Allen and Unwin, 1955 (1st edition 1931)).

faith. This was the most important question in a person's life not only because it involved eternal salvation or damnation, but also because the answer could bring persecution or the duty to take up arms in this world. This radical questioning of the foundations of belief spread throughout European knowledge, or linked up with independently provoked questioning in other areas of knowledge. The revival of scepticism aided these processes, which, by the end of the sixteenth century, had undermined the orthodox certainties and ushered in a general sceptical or legitimation crisis. In throwing into question the regimes of knowledge that had supported traditional ways of governing in politics, church, and university, the intellectual crisis delegitimated the ways of governing that were under siege on the battlefields as well.

Politically, the centre of this crisis was the presupposition that it was the role of government to bring about the good life; to propagate the true faith and inculcate virtue. Yet, as everyone from Montaigne onwards realized, this was the cause of religious and civil wars, for there were three conflicting views concerning the true faith. The seventeenth century provided a solution to this problem of what kind of government is possible if diversity in religious-moral belief is ineradicable. The answer, from Lipsius to Locke, was that the objective of government is preservation of life, not religion. Every school from natural law to scepticism could agree on this. Preservation was thus articulated in three ways as the objective of the early modern state: preservation of the population from internal and external attacks by war and war-preparation; preservation of the life, subsistence, discipline, and health of the population; and preservation of the rights and duties of subjects compatible with or derivable from the underlying objective of the preservation of life. Another way of putting this is to say that every political tradition came to terms with *raison d'état* practice in the seventeenth century, seminally with Lipsius, Grotius, and Harrington. This modern political project, where life itself is wagered on our political technology, is the informing principle of mercantile practice.

The dissolution of the legitimation crises in other areas of knowledge coalesced around new criteria of rational belief that Richard Popkin has termed 'constructive scepticism'.[7] This com-

---

[7] Richard Popkin, *The History of Scepticism from Erasmus to Spinoza*, revised edition (Berkeley, University of California Press, 1979), pp. 129–50. Popkin does not take into account the role of voluntarism in the formation of constructive scepticism. For a consideration of constructive scepticism as a response to the broad crisis, see Theodore R. Rabb, *The Struggle for Stability in Early Modern Europe* (Oxford, Oxford University Press, 1973), and Marc Raeff, *The Well-Ordered Police State: Social and Institutional Change through Law in the Germanies and Russia 1600–1800* (New Haven, Yale University Press, 1983).

prises two distinctive types of knowledge: probabilistic and voluntaristic. These were employed in a multiplicity of ways in the policies of the early modern states, from Montchretien to Petty, and so came to be constitutive of the new practice of government. Indeed, one of the reasons why a consensus began to emerge around the new epistemological foundations, by the time of Boyle, Locke, and Newton, was that these two types of knowledge gradually became invested in a host of practices of the consolidating state.

Locke is a good guide to the juridical way of governing because he was involved in the problems of governability, as a member of the Board of Trade, and of knowledge, as a philosopher.[8] This chapter is therefore centered on Locke's work, and is divided into four sections: governing belief, governing action, three practices of governing, and the penalized self.[9]

## GOVERNING BELIEF

The first feature of the new way of governing is the rejection of any theory that assent or belief is governed by a natural disposition (or telic faculty) to the true or the good. This theory of a natural conscience is replaced by an account of the conscience as a completely non-dispositional power of judgment, and of the mind as a blank tablet, indifferent to true and false, good and evil. Belief then ought to be governed by a new criterion, the weight of the evidence, but, as Locke argues, it is in fact governed by acquired dispositions.

The two questions concerning the grounds that ought to govern assent, and what in fact does govern it, dominate the 150-year intellectual struggle of the Reformation. As I have mentioned, it was not only the question of what one must believe in order to be saved; because most sects believed theirs to be the true religion and that it was a primary Christian duty to take up arms to defend and extend their religion, there was also the political-military question of life and death. Several other factors contributed to this legitimation crisis: the effects of global conquest, the revolutionary changes in science, the developments in the mechanical arts, and so on. However, the religious wars and the multifaceted repercussions in the realm of knowledge seem to me to be the major provocation which rendered assent and its foundations problematic. The

---

[8] Locke served on the Board of Trade from October 1673 to December 1674 and from May 1696 to 1700.
[9] My greatest debt in this chapter is to Ed Hundert and his classic article, 'The making of *homo faber*: John Locke between ideology and history', *Journal of the History of Ideas* (1972), 3–22.

seventeenth-century quest for certainty and grounds for assent, from clear and distinct ideas to innateism, is a response to this problem in all areas of knowledge.[10]

Locke's *Essay Concerning Human Understanding*, as well as the second draft (*Draft B*), is addressed explicitly to this issue:[11] 'to search out the Bounds between Opinion and Knowledge; and examine by what measures, in things, whereof we have no certain knowledge, we ought to regulate our Assent, and moderate our Persuasions'. Also, Locke's interest began with the specific religious and moral question of assent and gradually developed to comprise, and in a sense invent, a general epistemological context covering all areas of knowledge.[12] Further, the criteria of assent advanced in the *Essay* constitute the solution to the crisis.[13] The criteria, and the concept of assent itself, are foundational for the modern concept of rational belief. They now govern our mental conduct in science, law, history, and religion, to cite the conclusion of the most recent research.[14] This is partly because the *Essay* was so influential in the Enlightenment, but also because it is a survey of the way in which the reconceptualization of assent was taking place in these other fields. Most important of all, the new account of assent forms part of the juridical practice of governing, and it contains its own mechanism of dissemination, as I will presently show.

The theories under attack in the *Essay* are teleological, dispositional or participant accounts of assent. They hold that there are either innate ideas (knowledge) or innate dispositions that predispose us to assent to the true or the good and dissent from the false

---

[10] For the concept of legitimation crisis that I use here see James Tully, 'The pen is a mighty sword', *British Journal of Political Science*, 13 (1983), 489–509.

[11] John Locke, *An Essay Concerning Human Understanding*, ed. Peter Nidditch (Oxford, Clarendon Press, 1975), 1.1.3. Compare John Locke, *Draft B of Locke's Essay Concerning Human Understanding*, ed. Peter Nidditch (Sheffield, University of Sheffield, 1982), 2, p. 37.

[12] The early drafts of the *Essay*, A and B, were written for a group of friends who met at Exeter House in 1670–1 to discuss problems of 'religion and morality', as James Tyrrell noted in the margin of his copy of the *Essay* next to Locke's reference to these meetings in the Epistle to the reader (*Essay*, p. 7). As Locke explains, the religious and moral questions could not be solved until the epistemological questions of assent were settled.

[13] This is the conclusion of the study by Henry G. van Leeuwen, *The Problem of Certainty in English Thought 1630–1690* (The Hague, Martinus Nijhoff, 1963); and, earlier, Paul Hazard, *The European Mind: 1680–1715*, tr. J. Lewis May (Harmondsworth, Middlesex, Penguin, 1973); and, of course, Voltaire, 'Treizième lettre', in *Lettres philosophiques*, ed. F. A. Taylor (Oxford, Basil Blackwell, 1976), pp. 39–45.

[14] Barbara Shapiro, *Probability and Certainty in 17th Century England* (Princeton, Princeton University Press, 1983); Douglas Patey, *Probability and Literary Form: Philosophic Theory and Literary Practice in the Augustan Age* (Cambridge, Cambridge University Press, 1984), pp. 27–35.

or evil; these are standardly in propositional form. These inclinations may require sensation or even ratiocination to activate them, but they are independent of and prior to either. Almost all the immediate critics of Locke's attack on the theory of innate ideas reassert it in one form or another, with John Norris, the Malebranchean occasionalist, excepted. Innumerable examples could be cited from religious and philosophical literature prior to the publication of the *Essay*, as John Yolton has shown.[15]

In many respects the best presentation of the dispositional theory is the *Treatise Concerning Eternal and Immutable Morality* by Ralph Cudworth, the leading Cambridge Platonist. It was written prior to the *Essay* and published posthumously in 1739. It is a refutation of a *tabula rasa* theory of the mind. Cudworth's target is of course the non-dispositionalists prior to Locke: Thomas Hobbes, Walter Charleton, Nathaniel Culverwel, Samuel Parker, and, primarily, Pierre Gassendi, who had launched a famous assault on the dispositional theory of Lord Herbert of Cherbury.[16] However, let me cite Henry Lee, because his response to the *Essay*, *Anti-Scepticism*, is one of the best guides to precisely what the blank tablet hypothesis displaced. Published in 1702, it is a detailed commentary on and refutation of the *Essay*. He writes:[17]

the *Soul* of man is so framed by the Author of Nature, as not to be equally disposed to all sorts of perceptions, to embrace all propositions with an *indifferency*, to judge them true or false; but *antecedently* to all the Effects of Custom, Experience, Education or any other *Contingent* Causes, it is *limited* to perceive by certain external Motions or Impressions, is necessarily *inclined* to believe some Propositions *true*, others *false*; some actions *good*, others *evil*: and so is not altogether like a *rasa tabula*, on which you may set any impression indifferently . . . Because it's presupposed with such inclinations and dispositions . . .

The innate knowledge or disposition provides the foundation for knowledge and especially for moral knowledge. A person assents to a proposition *because* he or she is naturally inclined towards truth and goodness, just as a stone naturally tends to its natural home, the

[15] John Yolton, *John Locke and the Way of Ideas* (Oxford, Oxford University Press, 1956). John Norris's book is *Cursory Reflections upon a book call'd An Essay Concerning Human Understanding* (1690).
[16] Thomas Hobbes, *Leviathan* (1651), chaps. 1–6; Walter Charleton, *Physiologia Epicuro-Gassendo-Charletonia, or a Fabrick of Science Natural, upon the hypothesis of atoms* (1654), bk 3, chap. 15; Nathaniel Culverwel, *Of the Light of Nature*, ed. John Brown (Edinburgh, 1857), chap. 11, pp. 121–41; Samuel Parker, *A Free and Impartial Censure of the Platonick Philosophy* (1666); Pierre Gassendi, *Syntagma Philosophicum*, in *Opera Omnia* (1658), vol. I, pp. 90–3; Edward Lord Herbert of Cherbury, *De Veritate*, tr. M. H. Carre (Bristol, 1937). For the English non-dispositionalists, see Yolton, pp. 30–48. For Gassendi's response to Lord Herbert see Popkin, pp. 151–9.
[7] Henry Lee, *Anti-Scepticism* (1702), p. 5.

earth. As in all forms of teleological explanations, the action, assent, is explained by its natural tendency to a certain result or end, true beliefs. Leibniz's commentary provides good examples of teleological explanations.[18]

There were two general types of teleological theories of assent. The individualist and politically subversive one was put forward by some puritans and radicals, especially during the English Civil War period. Here, the natural conscience is a dispositional faculty with which one judges the moral goodness or evil of one's actions. Yet conflicting moral and religious beliefs are conscientiously held. Therefore, how does one distinguish an erring conscience from a true one? The radical puritan's answer is that those with a regenerate conscience do not err because the grace or spirit of God moves their assent from within and, secondly, they know that they are regenerate or elect by virtue of an inner assurance or grace. The conscience is thus sovereign and cannot be subordinated to any authority or authoritative external criteria. As Catholic opponents would say, these radical Protestants had set up their conscience as a new pope. This radical puritanism is similar in kind to the equally subversive animistic, hermetic, and pantheistic political and scientific movements that justified belief by reference to an inner force, and rejected accepted criteria. These movements were all called enthusiastic because they appealed in different ways to a God within. They were subversive because they undermined appeals to accepted authority, advanced a radical kind of subjectivity, and legitimated the right of the people to speak and act for themselves.[19]

[18] G. W. Leibniz, *New Essays on Human Understanding*, tr. Peter Remnant and Jonathan Bennett (Cambridge, Cambridge University Press, 1981), 79, 80, 84, 86.

[19] The classic treatment of these radicals is Christopher Hill, *The World Turned Upside Down* (Harmondsworth, Middlesex, Penguin, 1972). For the animistic scientific movement, see M. C. and J. R. Jacob, 'The Anglican origins of modern science: the metaphysical foundations of the whig constitution', *Isis*, 71 (1980), 251–67; David Kubrin, 'Newton's inside out: magic, class struggle and the rise of mechanism in the west', in Harry Woolf, ed., *The Analytic Spirit* (Cornell, Cornell University Press, 1981), pp. 96–122; and Carolyn Merchant, *The Death of Nature, Women, Ecology and the Scientific Revolution* (San Francisco, Harper and Row, 1981). For the establishment attack on the radical dispositionalists as 'enthusiastic', see Morris Berman, *The Reenchantment of the World* (New York, Bantam, 1981), chaps. 1–2; M. Heyd, 'The reaction to enthusiasm in the seventeenth century', *Journal of Modern History*, 53 (1981), 258–80; Michael Spiller, 'Concerning natural and experimental philosophie', in *Meric Casaubon and the Royal Society* (The Hague, Martinus Nijhoff, 1980); Frederic Burnham, 'The More–Vaughan controversy: the revolt against philosophical enthusiasm', *Journal of the History of Ideas*, 35 (1974), 33–49; and Brian Easlea, *Witch-hunting, Magic and the New Philosophy 1450–1750* (New Jersey, Humanities Press, 1980), pp. 89–154. For the radical puritan doctrine of the conscience, see William Perkins, *A Discourse of Conscience*, in *William Perkins: 1558–1602, English Puritanist*, ed. T. F. Merrill (1966), pp. 31–2, 61; William Ames, *Conscience with the Power and Case Thereof* (London, 1639), bk 11, p. 10.

'Enthusiasm' was used in a pejorative sense, and a massive intellectual assault was waged on all its forms, especially after 1660. Locke attacked this radical theory as early as 1660, and he added a chapter on enthusiasm to the fourth edition of the *Essay*. It is based on arguments he had worked on over a twenty-five-year period. The motivation for publication may have been the revival of pantheistic radicalism around John Toland and Locke's desire to disassociate his kind of radicalism from it.[20] As he describes it, 'firmness of persuasion is made the cause of believing, and confidence of being in the right, is made an argument for truth'.[21] He argues that it is a purely subjective and so non-verifiable ground of assent. As always, Locke's concern is that enthusiasm could be used to justify persecution of religious dissent.[22] This separates Locke from the mainstream Anglican and latitudinarian refutations of enthusiasm, which were used to justify persecution of the enthusiasts (nonconformists).[23] This campaign was so successful that the charge of enthusiasm could be used to discredit any appeal to a 'subjective' criterion of assent. Even Descartes's 'clear and distinct ideas' and Leibniz's teleology were branded as enthusiastic.[24]

If this type of theory, that God or immanent gods govern assent directly, was too subversive, the second type of theory was too submissive. In this traditional view, the conflicting yet firmly held beliefs that have plunged Europe in war are governed by bad customs and education.[25] Although assent naturally tends to true

---

[20] For Locke and Toland, see below, pp. 56–8.

[21] *Essay* 4.19.12. For Locke's early work on enthusiasm see 'On Enthusiasme' (1682), MS. Locke f. 6, p. 205, in R. I. Aaron and J. Gibb, *An Early Draft of Locke's Essay* (Oxford, Clarendon Press, 1936), pp. 119–21. Locke's earliest political writings, the two Latin and English manuscripts in support of monarchical absolutism (1660–1), are in response to a radical dispositional defence of toleration on the basis of the sovereignty of natural conscience by Edward Bagshawe in *An Essay in Defence of the Good Old Cause* (1660). See John Locke, *Two Tracts on Government*, ed. Philip Abrams (Cambridge, Cambridge University Press, 1968). I have discussed this in my introduction to John Locke, *A Letter Concerning Toleration* (Indianapolis, Hackett Publishing Company, 1983). See also John Colman, *John Locke's Moral Philosophy* (Edinburgh, Edinburgh University Press, 1983), pp. 9–29; and Edmund Leites, 'Conscience, casuistry and moral decision: some historical perspectives', *Journal of Chinese Philosophy*, 2 (1974), 41–58.

[22] *Essay* 4.19.12.

[23] I therefore demur at the tendency to assimilate Locke's political and religious thought and action to that of the latitudinarians. See Neil Wood, *The Politics of Locke's Philosophy* (Berkeley, University of California Press, 1983). Locke and Shaftesbury were revolutionary defenders of toleration of nonconformity, not latitudinarians. See my introduction to *A Letter Concerning Toleration* and the literature referred to there.

[24] See Steven Shapin, 'Of gods and kings: natural philosophy and politics in the Leibniz–Clark disputes', *Isis*, 72 (1981), 187–215; Easlea, pp. 158–64.

[25] Cf. John Locke, *Two Tracts*, p. 160.

beliefs, this tendency can be deflected and overridden by bad mental habits acquired by custom or education. Therefore, an authority is required to guide the pupil to the truth and to educate him so his innate disposition develops into good operative mental habits.[26]

The innate and dispositional theories underpinning established religion and morality are the sole target in the early *Draft B* of the *Essay*. By the time of the *Essay* the same strategy is used to refute any form of innateism, including the Aristotelian-scholastic sciences of the universities.[27] The two standard arguments of universal assent and ready assent are shown to be false – and, even if they are true, they do not prove innateness.[28] Locke's main argument, however, is that the appeal to custom and education to explain why some fail to assent to propositions others take to be innate puts the authority in the dispositional theory in the same position as the individual in the enthusiast theory. That is, the proponent of a certain set of first principles will have no criteria to appeal to except their innateness, yet this is what is in question.[29]

Locke's strategy for undermining this 'established opinion' and so 'pulling up the old foundations of knowledge and certainty' is the following.[30] He denies that there is a distinction between assent based on innate principles and dispositions and assent based on custom and education. Principles or ideas and dispositions that are said to be innate are, in fact, the *product* of custom and education. By being called 'innate' or 'divine' and 'first principles' they are

[26] This is reasserted by Locke's major critics: Henry Lee, *Anti-Scepticism*, pp. 4–12; Edward Stillingfleet, *Discourse in Vindication of the Doctrine of the Trinity . . .* (1696, 1697 (2nd edition)), chapter 10; William Sherlock, 'A digression concerning connate ideas or inbred knowledge', in *A Discourse Concerning the Happiness of the Good Man and the Punishment of the Wicked in the Next World* (1704), pp. 124–65; Thomas Burnet, *Remarks upon an Essay Concerning Humane Understanding* (1697). (Two further sets of *Remarks* followed in 1697 and 1699.)

[27] *Essay* 1.2, 4.7.

[28] *Essay* 1.2. I demur at Yolton's suggestion that Locke does not attack innate dispositions but only innate ideas (*John Locke*, p. 53). It is clear from *Essay* 1.2.5–10, 22 that Locke explicitly attacks the dispositional view as well. Yolton seems to rely on Locke's comment on Thomas Burnet's *Third Remarks upon an Essay Concerning Humane Understanding* (1699): 'I think noe body but this Author who ever read my book could doubt that I spoke only of innate ideas for my subject was the understanding and not of innate power . . .' (Noah Porter, 'Marginalia Locke-a-na', *New England and Yale Review*, 7 (1887), 33–49, 45. It is clear from the context (pp. 38, 44) that this 'faculty' or 'power' is just the non-dispositional power of judgment Locke uses throughout the *Essay* and his other writings. Compare Colman, p. 51.

[29] *Essay* 1.3.20. *Draft B*, 7, pp. 57–8. Compare Locke's identification of dispositionalism with enthusiasm in his marginal comments on Burnet's *Third Remarks* (Porter, p. 38). See also Colman, p. 57; and R. S. Woolhouse, *Locke* (Minneapolis, University of Minnesota Press, 1983), pp. 16–26.

[30] *Essay* 1.2.1, 1.4.23.

insulated from examination and taken on 'trust' or on 'authority'.[31]
This concept of 'trust' is of course the central target of the *Essay*.[32]
Children are taught them 'as soon as they have any apprehension',
and their teachers 'never suffer those propositions to be otherwise
mentioned, but as the Basis and Foundation, on which they build
their Religion or Manners'. In this way they come to be taken for
granted and to 'have the reputation of unquestionable, self-evident
and innate Truth'.[33] They become riveted in the understanding.[34]
Not only principles and dispositions to believe become entrenched
in this way, but also a whole 'hypothesis' such as the Aristotelian-
scholastic one.[35] The innateist or dispositional hypothesis itself
became established by custom and education, and is then used to justify taking certain principles on trust.[36]

Therefore custom, education, and fashion in fact govern assent.
This is just the surface of Locke's analysis of governing assent. The
actual techniques of education and custom will be discussed below
since they are employed in the new practice of governing. The investigation of the factors that do govern assent, as opposed to those that
ought to, was carried out by Locke throughout his lifetime. This was
part of a widespread analysis of *de facto* grounds of assent that accompanied the legitimation crisis in Europe.

Thus, the dispositional 'hypothesis' is an established form of
knowledge and it, in turn, supports authorities or elites in religion,
science, and politics. This political perspective is, as Leibniz
comments, the major argument against dispositionalism and it is a
constant theme in Locke's writings.[37] The classical summary is at
1.4.24:[38]

And it was of no small advantage to those who affected to be Masters and
Teachers, to make this the Principle of *Principles*, That Principles must not
be questioned: For having once established this Tenet, That there are innate
Principles, it put their Followers upon a necessity of receiving some
Doctrines as such; which was to take them off from the use of their own
Reason and Judgement, and put them upon believing and taking them upon
Trust, without further examination: in which posture of blind Credulity,
they might be more easily governed by, and made useful to some sort of
men, who had the skill and office to principle and guide them. Nor is it a
small power it gives one man over another, to have the Authority to be the

---

[31] *Draft B*, 8–10, pp. 58–65; *Essay* 1.3.20–7, 4.7.11, 4.20.18.
[32] *Essay*, Epistle, p. 7, 1.3.24, 27, 1.4.23, 4.20.17.   [33] *Essay* 1.3.22.
[34] John Locke, *Draft A of Locke's Essay Concerning Human Understanding*, ed. Peter
     Nidditch (Sheffield, University of Sheffield, 1980), 42, pp. 148–9, *Essay* 4.20.9.
[35] *Draft A*, 42, pp. 150–1, *Essay* 4.20.11.
[36] *Draft B*, 10, pp. 61–5, *Essay* 1.3.26, 1.4.24, 1.2.1, 4.7.11.
[37] Leibniz, *New Essays*, 74, 107.   [38] Compare *Draft B*, 13, pp. 72–3.

Dictator of Principles, and Teacher of unquestionable Truths; and to make a Man swallow that for an innate Principle, which may serve to his purpose, who teacheth them.

Both the 'natural conscience' and the innate dispositions are hence exposed as dispositions acquired by education and the workings of custom.

As early as 1660 Locke began to analyse how religious elites, especially Anglicans and Catholics, used the innateist approach to gain power, dominate the laity, and justify the suppression of dissent by persecution.[39] The one hundred years of war were caused by religious and political elites using allegedly dispositional knowledge to justify the inculcation of conflicting principles in their followers, including the duty to take up arms to defend and spread the true faith.[40] As Locke summarizes:[41]

And he that shall deny this to be the method, wherein most men proceed to the assurance they have, of the truth and evidence of their principles, will, perhaps, find it a hard matter any other way to account for the contrary tenets, which are firmly believed, confidently asserted, and which great numbers are ready at any time to seal with their blood.

The genealogy of belief formation, summarized at 1.3.22–6, therefore begins to explain the central problem of the Reformation period: the situation of contradictory beliefs held with confidence and resolution and a readiness to go to war to defend them. Developing such a comprehensive explanation is one of the major aims Locke set himself in the *Essay*.[42]

The intellectual weapon Locke advances to destroy these established bodies of knowledge and power in religion, politics, and science is 'suspension and examination'; that is, to suspend the judgment and examine the grounds for and against any proposition before assenting to it. This is what the dispositional theory blocks, and so it serves as a 'false foundation' to legitimate unquestioning acceptance of

---

[39] *Two Tracts*, pp. 118–19, 158–61, 210; and Tully's introduction, *A Letter Concerning Toleration*, pp. 1–16.

[40] *Two Tracts*, pp. 158–61; *A Letter Concerning Toleration*, pp. 42–3.

[41] *Essay* 1.3.27, *Draft B*, 10, p. 64.

[42] *Essay* 1.1.2, *Draft B*, 2, p. 38. A similar genealogy is developed in *Draft A* in the discussion of assent (42, pp. 148–57), as I noted above. This forms the basis of *Essay* 4.20.7–18 (see below). It is not reproduced in *Draft B*, but it is reworked in 'Study', MS. Locke f. 2, pp. 87–90, 91–3, 95–6, 97–100, 100–1, 114–17, 118–22, 124–40 (beginning on 26 March 1677). Reprinted in Peter King, *The Life and Letters of John Locke* (2 vols., London, H. Colburn and R. Bentley, 1830), vol. 1, pp. 171–203, pp. 188–92. For a similar analysis of Locke's radical attack on innate ideas see John Biddle, 'Locke's critique of innate principles and Toland's deism', *Journal of the History of Ideas*, 37, 3 (July–September 1976), 411–22.

authority.[43] 'Suspension and examination' *versus* 'trust and authority'
is the intellectual demand of the Reformation, cutting across
religious lines.[44] The *Essay* opens with this formula, but it receives its
most famous statement in what is one of the most reworked sections
of book 1: 'The great difference that is to be found in the Notions of
Mankind is from the different use they put their faculties to, whilst
some (and those the most) taking things upon trust, misemploy their
power of assent, by lazily enslaving their minds, to the Dictates and
Dominion of others, in Doctrines, which it is their duty carefully to
examine; and not blindly, with an implicit faith, to swallow.'[45]

The early critics of the *Essay* charged that it undermined religion
and morality. These critics were Anglicans, and what they meant was
that it undermined established religion.[46] As we have seen, this is
true, and it was in fact Locke's intention. The few people who defended
the *Essay* were dissenters like Samuel Bold.[47] However, the critics
based their charge on a much more fundamental claim. In sweeping
aside the old foundations, Locke had swept aside all foundations. If
the mind were not disposed in some way to the truth or the good,
then it must be indifferent, and so all our knowledge is the product
of custom and education. This argument of *indifferency*, and hence of
relativism, is advanced by almost all of Locke's critics. As Henry Lee
states it:[48] 'The true state of the question seems to me this, whether
the minds of men are so framed, as to be just like white paper,
equally capable of any letters or characters, indifferently disposed to
believe any proposition true or false, any actions good or bad?'
Locke is our best guide to the transition to new foundations of

[43] *Essay*, Epistle, p. 10.
[44] For a recent and perceptive discussion of this constitutive intellectual contest of
  the Reformation see Walter Rex, *Essays on Pierre Bayle and Religious Controversy* (The
  Hague, Martinus Nijhoff, 1965), especially pp. 9–42.
[45] *Essay* 1.4.22. For Locke's drafts of this famous sentence, see R. I. Aaron, *John Locke*
  (Oxford, Clarendon Press, 1972 (1937)), p. 59.
[46] For the response to the *Essay*, see H. O. Christophersen, *A Bibliographical Introduction to the Study of John Locke* (Oslo, 1930); and Kenneth MacLean, *John Locke and the
  Literature of the Eighteenth Century* (New York, Russell and Russell, 1962); and
  Yolton, 1956.
[47] Samuel Bold, *Some Considerations on the Principle Objections and arguments which have been
  published against Mr Locke's Essay* (1699).
[48] Henry Lee, *Anti-Scepticism*, p. 12. Compare William Sherlock, *A Discourse*, pp. 161–2,
  where he accuses Locke of promoting atheism: 'for if all the knowledge we have of
  God, and of Good and Evil, be made by ourselves, atheists will easily conclude that
  is only the effect of education and superstitious fears; and satisfy themselves that
  they can make other notions, more for the ease and security of life'. James Lowde,
  *A Discourse Concerning the Nature of Man* (1694), pp. 54–5. Most of the criticisms
  brought against Locke had already been made by Cudworth, and the non-
  dispositional theory placed in the context of the revival of Greek atomism (*A
  Treatise*, bk 4, pp. 127–35, 214–22, 286–7).

knowledge in the seventeenth century because he accepts this radical indifferency, 'for white paper receives any character', and attempts to construct a new governor of assent.[49]

Having swept away the epistemological foundations of the *ancien régime*, in both its radical and conservative variants, Locke reconstructs belief on the blank and indifferent *tabula rasa* that remains. He considers two solutions. The first is advanced by the latitudinarians and the experimental scientists and is accepted in a broad range of disciplines by the late seventeenth century, as Henry van Leeuwen and Barbara Shapiro have shown. Locke ultimately rejects it and, as we shall see, develops a different explanation of how assent is governed.

The first solution is that if belief is not governed by innate tendencies, because there are no such occult forms *in re*, then assent is, or at least ought to be, governed by and proportional to the grounds that can be adduced in its support after a thorough examination. The 'force of the better argument' and 'the weight of the evidence' are the external criteria, accessible in theory to all, on which rational belief is grounded and by which it is governed. As Locke summarizes this new concept of rationality:[50]

the mind if it will proceed rationally, ought to examine all the grounds of probability, and see how they make more or less, for or against any probable proposition, before it assents to or dissents from it, and upon due balancing the whole, reject, or receive it, with a more or less firm assent, proportionably to the preponderancy of the greater grounds of probability on one side or the other.

Two changes have taken place here relative to the dispositional view. First, the faculty of judgment, which makes the probability calculations, has been cleansed of any telic properties. It is a purely non-dispositional power of judging that is indifferent to the object of judgment; void of intrinsic causal efficacy.[51] It is, as Leibniz notes, the revival of the nominalist concept of a faculty: a power which could not in itself have a necessary causal tendency, as the Aristotelian-scholastic had posited, because this would bind God's omnipotence.[52] Locke's whole attack on 'faculties' is a rejection of the Aristotelian-scholastic concept of a teleological faculty and the reworking of a nominalist concept of faculty as an indifferent capacity.

[49] *Essay* 1.3.22.   [50] *Essay* 4.16.5.
[51] Locke possessed this concept of judgment as early as 1660, when he described the conscience as nothing but the power to judge the good or evil of one's actions. See *Two Tracts*, p. 138, *Essay* 1.3.8, 4.14.4; Porter, pp. 35, 38. Compare Colman, pp. 12–26; and Lee, *Anti-Scepticism*, p. 5.
[52] Leibniz, *New Essays* 174 (comment on 2.21.6).

The second change is that almost all our beliefs are viewed as probable as opposed to certain.[53] A few propositions remain that are
certain, and here a person gives full and ready assent. However, the
'ready assent', and so the certainty, is based on either the comparison of the subject and predicate of a proposition, as in *A* is *A*
(intuition) or in the comparison of one proposition with another, as
in strict entailment (demonstration). This small class of propositions
comprises knowledge in the proper sense of the word. Once the
component ideas are understood and the comparison is made, assent
is ready, certain, and involuntary.[54] However, the vast majority of
reasoning is concerned not with certain knowledge but with 'belief'
or 'opinion'; that is, 'knowledge' (as I will continue to use the term in
this wider sense) that is only probable.[55] Here, assent cannot be
based on a comparison of the ideas themselves, but rather 'something extraneous to the thing I believe', and the grounds cannot
induce certainty, but only degrees of assurance.[56]

[53] Compare Margaret Osler, 'John Locke and the changing ideal of scientific
knowledge', *Journal of the History of Ideas*, 31 (1970), 1–16.
[54] *Essay* 1.2.18, 4.2.1–9, 4.7.2, 4.7.10. Note that certainty depends on comparison,
not on 'self-evidence' or 'clear and distinct' ideas; Locke thus tries to avoid a subjective, Cartesian criterion.
[55] *Essay* 1.1.5, 4.14–15.
[56] *Essay* 4.15.4. This and the following sections of book 4 of the *Essay* that I refer to
here follow fairly faithfully *Draft A*, 32–42. The main sources of Locke's ideas of
probable assent are almost certainly Robert Boyle and Pierre Gassendi. Locke's
account of probability in *Draft A* is similar to Gassendi's account of criteria of
assent in part 1 of *Syntagma Philosophicum* (1658). Locke apparently did not own
*Syntagma*, but he quoted from it, and he did own Thomas Stanley, *The History of
Philosophy* (4 vols, 1655–62), vol. 3 of which contains *Syntagma*. (See Richard Kroll,
'The question of Locke's relation to Gassendi', *Journal of the History of Ideas*, 45, 3
(July–September 1984), 339–61.) It is also possible and indeed highly probable
that Locke was familiar with the work on probable assent in England when he
wrote *Draft A* (1670): William Chillingworth, *The Religion of Protestants* (1633); John
Tillotson, *Rule of Faith* (1666); Joseph Glanvill, *The Vanity of Dogmatizing* (1661),
and *Scepsis scientifica* (London, 1665).
John Wilkins, *Of the Principles and Duties of Natural Religion* (1675) is too late for
*Draft A* yet very similar on assent. Richard Burthogge, *Organum Vetus & Novum or a
discourse of reason and truth* (1678), is probably the closest to Locke. He went on to
defend Locke in *An Essay Upon Reason and the Nature of Spirit* (1694). Boyle's main
works on probable assent were published after 1670: *Some Considerations about the
Reconcileableness of Reason and Religion* (1675); *A Discourse of Things above Reason* (1677).
However, as early as 1667 Locke noted Boyle's praise of Gassendi (MS Locke,
f. 14) (see E. A. Driscoll, 'The influence of Gassendi on Locke's hedonism', *International Philosophical Quarterly*, 12 (1972), 87–110, 87–9). These authors are discussed by van Leeuwen and Shapiro. Richard Tuck also discusses a group of writers
who introduced probability into political writing in England in the 1640s (*Natural
Rights Theories* (Cambridge, Cambridge University Press, 1979), pp. 101–18). Both
Leibniz and Lee suggest that Locke's views on assent and other issues were influenced
by Gassendi. See further below, and Margaret Osler, 'Providence and divine will in
Gassendi's views on scientific knowledge', *Journal of the History of Ideas*, 44, 4
(October–December 1983), 549–60, 560; Gabriel Bonno, 'Les Relations intellec-

The criteria of probable belief, or 'grounds of probability', are twofold. The first is conformity with what we already know, in Locke's strong sense, have observed, or have experienced. The second is reliance on the 'testimony of others, vouching their observation and experience'. The criteria in accordance with which their testimony is to be judged are the following:[57]

1. The number. 2. The Integrity. 3. The Skill of the Witnesses. 4. The Design of the author, where it is a Testimony out of a Book cited. 5. The consistency of the parts, and the circumstances of the relation. 6. Contrary testimony.

A proposition is judged relative to these criteria and the proportional degree of assent given to it, 'from full assurance and confidence, quite down to conjecture, doubt and distrust'.[58]

The concept of probability that is introduced here dominates the *Essay*. The *Essay* in fact is a celebration that this form of knowledge 'is sufficient to govern all our concernments'.[59] The type of probability is epistemological: judging reasonable degrees of belief relative to the evidence or grounds. It is not aleatory probability concerned with statistical regularities of natural or human phenomena. The epistemological concept was used in the early modern period from the thirteenth century onwards in an increasing number of disciplines. The use of both types of probability increased in the first part of the seventeenth century and, in addition, Blaise Pascal formulated a theory of probability.[60] From a dispersion of early modern sources probabilistic reasoning came to predominate in a wide range of disciplines by the late seventeenth century, gradually changing them into their modern forms. However, one context that must be considered central is the rule of faith controversy. In the thousands

tuelles de Locke avec la France', *University of California Publications in Modern Philosophy*, 38 (1955), 37–264, 237–42.
　Other possible sources of Locke's concept of probability are: Cicero, *Academica* II. 20–48 (Cicero's defence of Carneades' constructive scepticism); Sextus Empiricus, *Outlines of Pyrrhonism*, first published in early modern Europe in 1562 and available to Locke in Stanley, *History of Philosophy*; and [Pierre Nicole and Antoine Arnault,] *La Logique ou l'art de Penser* (Paris, 1662), bk. 4, chaps. 13–16. For the early modern influence of *Academica*, see Charles Schmitt, *Cicero Scepticus* (The Hague, Martinus Nijhoff, 1972); for Empiricus, see Popkin 1969.
[57] *Essay* 4.15.4.　[58] *Essay* 4.15.2.
[59] *Essay* 1.1.5, not in *Draft B*. This signals that a demonstrable ethic is not a necessary part of his moral theory.
[60] Ian Hacking, *The Emergence of Probability* (Cambridge, Cambridge University Press, 1984 (1975)). For a corrective to Hacking's hypothesis that the emergence of the *concept* of probability marked an abrupt discontinuity see below concerning the role of voluntarism in widening the scope of probability, and Patey, pp. 266–73.

of pamphlets and books that constitute this debate, these criteria are partly formed and employed to justify rational religious belief. Specifically, a consensus gradually developed around the assumption that faith is belief, not knowledge, and that these criteria make it reasonabale to believe that Revelation is the word of God, based on the testimony of witnesses and the evidence of miracles.[61]

Secondly, these criteria undercut any appeal to authority in the old sense of the word, as Locke immediately points out.[62] In casuistry, a belief is probable because it is not demonstrable, and so authorities had advanced different and sometimes contradictory opinions about it. The authority weighs the various authoritative opinions and applies them to particular cases (as in, for example, the Jesuit doctrine of probabilism).[63] But this whole schema came under severe strain with the sceptical crisis, as can be seen in the remarkably sceptical and unsure *Ductor Dubitantium or the rule of conscience* by Jeremy Taylor.[64] The new criteria mitigated the threat of extreme scepticism, as Popkin has argued. It also forced the enthusiast to regulate his assent by these criteria and so relinquish his certainty and admit 'reasonable doubt'. But the price for this was that any putative claim to authority could itself be examined and scrutinized by these criteria. The leading latitudinarians were willing to pay this price, however, because it toppled the basis of certainty in religious belief that had led to confrontation and placed all the different sects in the realm of opinion and 'latitude'. They assumed that it would thus be unreasonable not to conform to a simplified and more liberal Anglicanism.[65] Locke, although he accepted and refined these criteria from the predominantly latitudinarian context, as van Leeuwen has shown, drew exactly the opposite conclusion. Precisely because certainty in religious belief is not possible on these criteria, it would be unreasonable to force dissenters to conform.[66]

---

[61] *Essay* 4.18–19 summarizes the consensus. Compare 'Faith and Reason', MS Locke f. 1, pp. 412–32, in W. von Leyden, ed. *John Locke: Essays on the Laws of Nature* (Oxford, Clarendon Press, 1954), pp. 274–81. The important studies by Popkin, van Leeuwen, and Shapiro have barely scratched the surface of this controversy.

[62] *Essay* 4.15.6.

[63] See Patey, pp. 58–61; and C. W. Slights, *The Casuistical Tradition* (Princeton, Princeton University Press, 1981); Hacking, pp. 18–30.

[64] Jeremy Taylor, *Ductor dubitantium or The Rule of Conscience*, in *The Whole Works of Jeremy Taylor* (10 vols., London, 1751 (1970 reprint)), vols. 9–10. For the importance of Taylor see H. Baker, *The Wars of Truth: Studies in the Decay of Christian Humanism* (1952); Robert Hoopes, 'Voluntarism in Jeremy Taylor and the Platonic tradition', *The Huntington Library Quarterly*, 13 (1950), 341–54; Leites (1974).

[65] For a similar argument see Heyd.

[66] *Essay* 4.16.4. This sceptical justification of toleration is the main theme of *The Third Letter Concerning Toleration*, thus separating Locke decisively from the latitudinarians.

The rule of faith controversy is not, however, foundational for the development of this kind of reasoning. The controversy is carried on in terms drawn from legal reasoning and practices of early modern Europe. The conscience it conceptualized as an inner tribunal, the court of appeal and so on, and the criteria are drawn from juridical discourses and practices. In addition, when the experimental scientists in and around the Royal Society employ these criteria, reference is often made to trial and judicial reasoning. The central concepts of this probable form of reasoning – 'evidence', 'proof', 'probability', and 'testimony' – were gradually constructed in the context of the spread of the inquisitorial methods of justice throughout Europe from the condemnation of the trial by battle of 1215 to the great codification in the French ordinance of 1670.[67] In England, where the accusatory system lived on after 1215 in the jury trial, concepts of evidence, testimony, and probability developed in and around the non-jury, inquisitorial institutions of the law. In the 1670s, there was an important and unsuccessful attempt to impose these criteria on the jury in the Bushel case.[68] This perhaps marks the transition of the old idea of the jury as partial witnesses, drawn from the neighbourhood of the crime, to the modern, quasi-inquisitorial view of the jury as impartial judges of the evidence. The most systematic treatment of these criteria prior to Locke's *Essay* in England is the work of Sir Matthew Hale, the leading legal theorist of the Restoration. The first modern theory of evidence is written by a lawyer, Baron Geoffrey Gilbert (1674–1726), and is based on the criteria laid out in the *Essay*.[69] Therefore, although this form of reasoning begins to be applied in all fields of knowledge and is universalized by Locke in England and Bayle on the continent, its concepts are drawn from the reasoning and practices of the inquisitorial institutions of early modern Europe.[70] It is not surprising

[67] A. Esmein, *A History of Continental Criminal Procedure with Special Reference to France* (Boston, Little, Brown, 1913), pp. 183–288. For one aspect of the development of probability in a juridical context see John H. Langbein, *Torture and the Law of Proof* (Chicago, University of Chicago Press, 1977).

[68] This trial could hardly have been of more importance to Locke since the jury, against the entreaty of the judge, acquitted William Penn and William Mead of the charge of unlawful assembly under the anti-dissent Conventicle Act. The jury were imprisoned and fined but then acquitted by Chief Justice Vaughan. For the importance of this case, see J. B. Thayer, *A Preliminary Treatise on Evidence at the Common Law* (Boston, Harvard University Press, 1898), pp. 166–70.

[69] Geoffrey Gilbert, *The Law of Evidence* (1756). For Gilbert's importance and his relation to Locke, see Theodore Waldman, 'Origins of the legal doctrine of reasonable doubt', *Journal of the History of Ideas*, 20, 3 (June–September 1959), 289–316.

[70] For Pierre Bayle in this context see Ed James, 'Pierre Bayle on belief and evidence', *French Studies*, 27 (1973), 395–404. In 1699 John Craig attempted to quantify Locke's criteria of probable assent: 'A calculation of the credibility of human testimony', *Philosophical Transactions of the Royal Society*, 21 (1699), 359–65.

that Richard Burthogge calls Locke's probable reasoning 'judicial assent' and Locke refers to it as *Argumentum ad Judicium*.[71]

Locke's first analysis of probable reasoning is that assent is necessarily governed by the grounds of probability that are available and in accordance with which judgment is made. This made belief involuntary, like knowledge and perception, and Locke used it in this way to justify toleration.[72] However, as he corrected himself in *Draft A*, belief must be in some sense voluntary, or ignorance and error would not be faults, and infidelity would not be a sin.[73] It is at this point that he introduced the power to suspend one's assent and examine the grounds for it. The concept, almost surely adapted by Locke from Gassendi, is the foundation of intellectual liberty or freedom of thought.[74] Once the examination is carried through, assent still necessarily closes with, and in proportion to, the available grounds of probability. It is, as he says, 'the nature of the understanding constantly to close with the more probable side': 'a man, who has weighed them, can scarce refuse his assent to the side on which the greater probability appears'.[75] This is so not because the judgment is partial or internally related to the truth. The judgment is impartial and external to it. Rather, it is the new mechanical properties, the 'weight' of the evidence, and the 'force' of the argument that cause assent. The manifest probabilities govern assent by acting as 'inducements' and 'motives'.[76]

There is an important Enlightenment ideal here: once our beliefs are carefully examined in the light of rational criteria we will come to agree. The old superstitions and authorities will give way to an age of reason. However, as a result of his analysis, Locke is forced to reject this hypothesis on four grounds. First, the great majority, because of their conditions of work, cannot examine the proofs of their beliefs. Secondly, often those who have the ability are not able to exercise it owing to political repression, as with the Huguenots. Thirdly, people may have the opportunity yet lack the will, usually out of laziness.[77]

The fourth and most important reason for wrong assent is that even when the probabilities 'are plainly laid before them', some people give their assent 'to the less probable opinion'.[78] This happens because they have the 'wrong measures of probability'. These are of

---

[71] Burthogge (1694), p. 44; *Essay* 4.17.22.
[72] John Locke, *An Essay Concerning Toleration* (1667), MS. Locke C. 28, fols. 21–32, fol. 21–2.    [73] *Draft A*, 42, p. 156; *Essay* 4.20.16.
[74] See Kroll 1984 and Bonno, pp. 241–2.    [75] *Essay* 4.20.15.
[76] *Essay* 4.15.4, 4.20.1.    [77] *Essay* 4.20.1–6.    [78] *Essay* 4.20.7.

four types: the first is taking an opinion as a first principle, as knowledge, and thus as a certain criterion for judging other beliefs. This is, of course, our old friend the innate principle, riveted in the understanding, and Locke repeats how custom and education establish it there.[79] The second wrong measure is a whole 'wrong hypothesis', again fixed in the understanding in the same way. Here Locke's target is the Aristotelian-scholastic professors, whose conceptual framework will allow a different role for grounds of probabilities.[80] The third wrong measure of probability is a 'prevailing passion'. For example, 'Let never so much Probability hang on one side of a covetous man's reasoning; and money on the other; and it is easie to foresee which will out-weigh.'[81] The fourth and most insidious wrong measure of probability is, not surprisingly, authority. By 'authority' Locke means the general phenomenon of the Reformation of yielding one's assent to the beliefs of one's political or religious group:[82] 'I mean, giving up our assent to the common received opinions either of our Friends, or Party; Neighbourhood or country. How many men have no other ground for their tenets than the supposed honesty, or learning, or number of those of the same profession.'

Locke realizes in the course of this analysis, which takes place over twenty-five years, that these arguments refute his initial claim that assent is mechanically governed by the external proofs. As John Passmore has argued, from his examples Locke is forced to realize that these four non-rational factors can govern assent even in the face of the manifest right measures of probability.[83] This is true in all four cases, although the prevailing passion case is the most obvious: 'Tell a man passionately in Love that he is jilted; bring a score of witnesses of the falsehood of his mistress, 'tis ten to one but three kind Words of hers, shall invalidate all their testimonies.'[84]

Therefore, the modern rationalist's belief that the weight of the evidence and the force of the better argument will govern our belief once we have critically examined is false. These are just what they appear to be: mechanical metaphors with no causal efficacy. Assent is governed by non-rational factors; by passion, custom, and education. Locke tries to save the rationalist assumption in this old part of the *Essay* from which I have been quoting, by saying that people

[79] *Essay* 4.20.8–10.    [80] *Essay* 4.20.11.    [81] *Essay* 4.20.12.
[82] *Essay* 4.20.17. This is again identified as the cause of the division of the world into warring religious factions (4.15.6).
[83] John Passmore, *Locke and the Ethics of Beliefs*, Dawes Hicks Lecture, British Academy, 1978. I am indebted to this fine piece of analysis even though I disagree with parts of it.

who give in to these wrong measures have not really examined.[85] But
this is contradicted by his own examples. Richard Burthogge
attempted to save the theory by arguing that the mind has a natural
disposition not to assent to incongruous propositions in virtue of 'a
certain sensible reluctance' or 'pain' annexed to it.[86]

Some time between 1671 and 1677 Locke abandoned the idea that
assent would be automatically governed by the probabilities that we
have seen him struggling with in the oldest part of the *Essay*. In a
manuscript in 1677 he constructed his alternative: for the mind to be
governed by the right measures of probabilities, it is necessary to
develop an artificial inclination or passion to suspend, examine, and
assent in accordance with the correct grounds. Men must be
educated to 'covet truth', to develop a 'love' or passion for it.[87] This
is then added to the fourth edition of the *Essay* in book 4, chapter 19,
*Of Enthusiasm*, contradicting the claims of the old chapter 20, which
repeats the early *Draft A*. Assent is governed by passions, and thus he
'that would seriously set upon the search of Truth, ought in the first
place to prepare his mind with a love of it'. The one mark of having
acquired this passion for truth is 'not entertaining any proposition
with greater assurance than the Proofs it is built upon will warrant'.
Now, there is no mention that to do otherwise after examination
might be 'impossible', as before. Rather, all the 'surplusage of
assurance' beyond what the proofs warrant 'is owing to some other
affection, and not to the love of truth'.[88]

Locke's project from this point on was to develop an educational
practice that would form mental 'inclinations' or 'relish' to examine
and assent in accordance with the probable proofs, i.e. with the new
form of reasoning. This is laid out in the *Conduct of the Understanding*,
intended as a chapter of the *Essay* but published posthumously, and
*Some Thoughts Concerning Education*. This 'passion' or 'love' is in fact a
kind of mental habit, acquired by education and capable of

---

[85] *Essay* 4.20.18.
[86] Burthogge 1694, pp. 39–40.
[87] 'Study', March 1677 (n. 42 above). Locke was in France from 1675 to 1679 hiding
from arrest and probable execution for his first public call for revolution, *A Letter
from a person of quality to his friend in the country* (1675). In this French period Locke
changed his views on a number of central issues, including the determinants of
assent, and then incorporated these into the second to fifth editions of the *Essay*.
There is a second Gassendi connection here as a result of Locke meeting François
Bernier, Gassendi's able disciple. See F. Bernier, *Abrégé de la Philosophie de Gassendi*
(1678). For this relationship see Driscoll and Bonno. In addition, Locke began to
assimilate the ideas of Pierre Nicole and Pascal during this period (see below). Locke's
pre-1675 analysis of the role of custom and education remains with the
latitudinarian and Baconian context studied by van Leeuwen and Wood.
[88] *Essay* 4.19.1.

withstanding and eroding the habits formed by the old education, which were falsely claimed to be innate.


## GOVERNING ACTION

The attack on the old way of governing physical behaviour and the construction of a new governor are analogous to the treatment of mental behaviour. The dispositionists held not only that men are disposed to assent to the good and to dissent from evil, but also that they are disposed to act towards good and away from evil. This behavioural disposition, as with its mental counterpart, could be deformed by bad customs and education, giving rise to vicious habits, and thus the same justification for practical guidance by teaching, penance, and discipline followed. Practical principles were thus distinguished from speculative principles by the fact that once they were assented to they tended to influence one's conduct. As Henry Lee stated it:[89]

> The true question is whether human nature be not so constituted by the provident author of it, as to be more inclined to the observance of some rules of action, for the promoting of their own and the happiness of all mankind, than to the breach of them. Or, in other words, whether all men or any one man is free from all sense of duty, and indifferent to all sorts of action.

Locke, like the anti-dispositionalists before him, argues that there are no innate practical principles and no innate dispositions to act in accordance with them or, as against Burnet, no disposition to assent to and tend towards good acts directly.[90] Again, this was taken to undermine religion and morality, and to encourage atheism.[91] The account of conduct put forward by Locke is a synthesis of two powerful traditions in the seventeenth century: voluntarism and hedonism. I call this synthesis penalism for reasons that will become obvious. Ralph Cudworth argued that these two traditions provided the intellectual framework for the revolution in thought and action he observed occurring around him.[92] Locke's role was to build on earlier syntheses, especially by Pierre Gassendi, Samuel Pufendorf,

---

[89] Lee, *Anti-Scepticism*, p. 12. Compare: Leibniz, 90; Lowde, preface; John Sergeant, *Solid Philosophy asserted against the Fancies of the Ideists*, (London, 1697), p. 224; Burnet, *Third Remarks*, pp. 4, 7–8.
[90] *Draft B*, 4–8; *Essay* 1.3; *Essays on Laws of Nature*, pp. 137–45.
[91] Lee, p. 17; Burnet, p. 4. Compare Yolton, pp. 29, 39, 68.
[92] Cudworth, books 1–2, pp. 1–75.

and Robert Boyle, to construct both an explanation of conduct and an apparatus for governing conduct.[93]

Voluntarism or Ockhamism and Intellectualism or Thomism are the two major theological traditions of the early modern period.[94] Intellectualism is a synthesis of Aristotelian and Christian thought. Its seminal and classical presentation is the *Summa theologiae* of Saint Thomas Aquinas. Aquinas emphasized God's reason and intellect over his will and omnipotence. God created the universe in accordance with reason and thus it is a rational and purposive order governed by the law of reason or eternal law. In addition, God created Aristotelian essences, causes, or forms which incline things towards their ends; that is, acting in harmony with eternal law. It is possible by reason to know the nature or essence of things and from these definitions to demonstrate the necessary relations among things and so to understand the relational and purposive order of nature.

In 1277 a number of propositions drawn from Aristotle and positing necessary relations in nature were condemned in Paris and Oxford. A similar anti-Aristotelian move had been made a century earlier in Islamic theology. This condemnation can be taken as a rough starting-point for early modern voluntarism. It was formed initially in opposition to Intellectualism in the generation after Aquinas, by Duns Scotus and William of Ockham. The central tenet of voluntarism is that Revelation clearly states that the Christian God created the world out of nothing; it is a creation, not a product made in accordance with anything. The emphasis is on God's omnipotence and his free will, not his reason. Therefore, to say that God created the world in accordance with reason, either in the Platonic sense of an independently existing order, or in Aquinas'

93  For Gassendi's voluntarism, see Osler (1983) and for his hedonism L. T. Sarasohn, 'The ethical and political philosophy of Pierre Gassendi', *Journal of the History of Philosophy*, 20, 3 (July 1982), 239–61. For Pufendorf's voluntarism see *The Law of Nature and Nations* (1672), ed. J. Barbeyrac, tr. B. Kennett (London, 1729), 2.3.20, and Leibniz's response, in 'Opinion on the principles of Pufendorf' (1706), in *The Political Writings of Leibniz*, tr. Patrick Riley (Cambridge, Cambridge University Press, 1972), pp. 64–77. For Boyle's voluntarism, see *A Free Inquiry into the Vulgarly Received Notion of Nature*, in Robert Boyle, *The Works*, ed. T. Birch, intr. D. McKie (6 vols., Hildesheim, Georg Olms, Verlagsbuchhandlung, 1965), vol. 5, pp. 158–255. See J. E. McGuire, 'Boyle's conception of nature', *Journal of the History of Ideas*, 33 (1972), 523–42; and Eugene M. Klaaren, *Religious Origins of Modern Science* (Grand Rapids, Michigan, Eerdmans, 1977).

94  For these two traditions see Francis Oakley, 'Medieval theories of natural law: William of Ockham and the voluntarist tradition', *Natural Law Forum*, 6 (1961), 65–84, and *The Political Thought of Pierre D'Ailly: The Voluntarist Tradition* (New Haven, Yale University Press, 1964); Steven Ozment, *The Age of Reform 1250–1550* (New Haven, Yale University Press, 1980), pp. 22–73.

sense of God creating a rational order which then embodies necessity, is to limit God's omnipotence. The universe is a contingent creation of God's will. Any necessary laws or natures would equally limit God's omnipotence and free will. Thus, God acts directly on nature, which is made up solely of his creatures and the order he wills on them.

It follows that 'nature' is simply contingently related particulars and the 'laws of nature' are observed regularities which God could change any time. There can be no *a priori* knowledge of the necessary and immanent relations in nature, because these do not exist. Knowledge of 'nature' must be *a posteriori* observation of individuals and generalizations. These generalizations will be 'hypotheses' that describe the regularities and, because the relations among things are contingent, they will be probable, not certain. Thus, the voluntarist tends to be nominalist and empiricist. Knowledge of kinds will be of what Locke calls their 'nominal essences'; of observed correlations of properties.

A number of remarkable studies in the post-war period have shown that the revival of voluntarism during the Reformation provided the intellectual foundations for the birth of modern science in the seventeenth century.[95] At the centre of this movement are Pierre Gassendi and Robert Boyle, the two major influences on Locke. In addition, the features of voluntarism that I have listed run through the writings of the members of the Royal Society, especially John Wilkins and Joseph Glanvill.[96] The Leibniz–Clarke correspondence is a classic confrontation between an intellectualist and Clarke's defence of Newton's voluntarism.[97] The practical consequence of the displacement of intellectualism by voluntarism is the elevation of use, as opposed to understanding, as the goal of science. 'Understanding' is no longer possible because there is no rational, *a priori* order to understand. Secondly, certain knowledge is beyond our reach because there are no necessary relations that our knowledge identifies. It follows that our knowledge is predominantly

---

[95] Michael Foster, 'The Christian doctrine of creation and the rise of modern natural science', *Mind*, 43 (1934), 446–68 and 'Christian theology and modern science of nature II', *Mind*, 45 (1936), 1–28 are the seminal articles. Francis Oakley, 'Christian theology and the Newtonian science: the rise of the concept of the laws of nature', *Church History*, 30, 4 (December 1961), 433–57; McGuire 1972; Osler 1983 and 'Descartes and Charleton on nature and God', *Journal of the History of Ideas* (September 1979), 445–56; Klaaren 1977. The best full-length study is R. Hooykaas, *Religion and the Rise of Modern Science* (Edinburgh, Scottish Academic Press, 1984 (1972)).

[96] Glanvill, *Scepsis scientifica*, pp. 211–12; John Wilkins (1675), chapter 11.

[97] See McGuire 1972 and Shapin 1981.

probable, in the two senses of *likely to occur*, as in natural regularities, and *likely to be true*, as in epistemic probability. Thus the spread of voluntarism is an important factor in the development of probability. Coupled with the seventeenth-century sense of mediocrity, due to loss of understanding and certainty, is an equally strong countervailing feeling of being able to use and control nature.[98] Although this is usually identified with Bacon it should, I believe, be placed in this broader context. The sense of God's omnipotence and man's mediocrity can be seen clearly in the analysis of 'hypothesis' in writers like Joseph Glanvill and Robert Boyle.[99] These writings as well stress the goal of use and control, and Boyle's manuscript on hypothesis articulates the modern identification of explanation and prediction. This whole theme of use *versus* understanding is addressed by Locke in a 1677 manuscript and then woven into the fabric of the *Essay*.[100]

The intellectualist tradition also provides the basis for the view that man has an innate disposition to assent and act in accordance with reason; that is, with natural law. Men have, as Aquinas classically stated it, 'a certain share in the divine reason itself from which they derive a natural inclination to such actions and ends as are fitting'.[101] It is this kind of theory that we have seen Locke's critics put forward. Some actions are intrinsically good or evil and man is naturally inclined towards the former and away from the latter. For the voluntarist, on the other hand, good and evil cannot be necessary properties of actions because this would limit God's freedom. Good and evil are rather external evaluations of actions relative to a law or standard. 'Evil is', as Ockham classically stated, 'nothing other than doing something opposite to that which one is obliged to do.'[102] What one is obliged to do is obey the will of God

[98] See, especially, Merchant 1981, pp. 164–236, and Hooykaas 1972, pp. 67–75.
[99] Glanvill 1665, pp. 211–12; Robert Boyle, in Richard Westfall, 'Some unpublished Boyle papers relating to scientific method', *Annals of Science*, 12 (1956), 63–73, 107–17. For the voluntarist conception of hypothesis see Robert Kargon, *Atomism in England from Hariot to Newton* (Oxford, Clarendon Press, 1966), pp. 106–18. For Locke on hypothesis, see *Essay* 4.12.9–15 and Osler 1970; L. Laudan, 'The nature and sources of Locke's views on hypothesis', in *Locke on the Human Understanding*, ed. I. C. Tipton (Oxford, Oxford University Press) 1977, pp. 149–62.
[100] 'How far and by what means the will works upon the understanding and assent', MS Locke f. 2 pp. 42–55, in R. I. Aaron and Gibb, *An Early Draft of Locke's Essay* (Oxford, Clarendon Press, 1936), pp. 84–90. The justification for studying the understanding with which the *Essay* opens is that the understanding gives man 'Advantage and Dominion' over nature (1.1.1). He then moves on to attack the possibility of understanding and to advance use (1.1.5–6). Compare 4.12, 4.14.2 and Wood, pp. 94–121. [101] Aquinas, *Summa Theologiae*, 1a-2ae qu. 93, art. 1, *resp.*
[102] William of Ockham, *Super Quatuor Libros Sententiarum* II, qu. 5 H.

expressed in divine law. Obligation to divine law is based on its being God's will, not on its being rational, as with Aquinas. Secondly, because there is no necessary and rational moral order in which we participate by virtue of our reason, the way to know divine law is through Revelation, where God has revealed his will. God could even change the definition of good and evil if he willed. However, this would be an expression of his absolute power (*potentia absoluta*), like miracles. Customarily, he governs by his ordinary power (*potentia ordinata*), and this is the reason for the regularity in our moral and natural universe. He has even created us in such a way that our powers of probable reasoning can play some role in discovering divine law. But this is a different concept of reason from that of the Thomists, and it is a contingent and not necessary feature of the universe.

This ethical voluntarism complemented the spread of epistemic and ontological voluntarism in both Protestant and Catholic theology during the Reformation. It is articulated by the young Grotius, Samuel Pufendorf (who is attacked by Leibniz), Jeremy Taylor, Robert Sanderson, Walter Charleton, Pierre Gassendi, Robert Boyle, Richard Cumberland, Thomas Hobbes, and Nathaniel Culverwel, among others.[103] The religious motivation here is particularly clear in a work such as Nathaniel Culverwel's *Of the Light of Nature* (1657). He attacks the whole intellectualist tradition as embodying the sin of pride. God has imprinted no innate ideas or dispositions in man, nor does man share in any way, especially through his reason, in God's divine reason. The mind is a 'blank sheet' and all our knowledge is based on simple observation. Man does not participate in God's essence, which is unknown and omnipotent. Man is as the vessel to the potter: all of mankind could be annihilated without touching God's essence. Man, and even the soul, is 'infinitely distant from him'.[104] Similar voluntaristic themes are present in Boyle's writings. Cudworth summarized the voluntarists in this way:[105]

---

[103] Hugo Grotius, *De Jure Praedae* (1868 (1604)), chap. 2; Jeremy Taylor, *Ductor Dubitantium*, in *Works*, vol. 9, pp. 333–40; Robert Sanderson, *De Obligatione conscientiae* (1660), 4th lecture, pp. 5–6; Walter Charleton, *The Darknes of Atheism Dispelled by the Light of Nature* (1652), chap. 10, p. 1; Robert Boyle, *Some Considerations about the Reconcileableness of Reason and Religion*, in *Works*, vol. 4, pp. 151–91, p. 162; Thomas Hobbes, *Leviathan* (1651), bk. II, chaps. 30–1; Richard Cumberland, *A Treatise on the Law of Nature*, tr. J. Maxwell (London, 1672), p. 320. A fuller account is given by Oakley 1961. J. McGuire and Herschel Baker, *The Wars of Truth* (Cambridge, Harvard University Press, 1952). Also, see nn. 93, 95 above.
[104] Culverwel, pp. 125–40.
[105] Cudworth, pp. 9–11.

divers Modern Theologers do not only seriously, but zealously contend . . . *That there is nothing Absolutely, intrinsecally, and Naturally Good and Evil, Just and Unjust, antecedently to any positive Command or Prohibition of God; but that the Arbitrary will and Pleasure of God,* (that is, an Omnipotent Being devoid of all Essential and Natural Justice) *by its Command and Prohibitions, is the first and only Rule and measure thereof.* Whence it follows . . . that whatsoever God can be supposed to do or will will be *for that Reason* Good or Just, because he wills it.

Locke grew up in this Calvinist and voluntaristic milieu, and his early writings are dominated by the double theme that both the obligation and content of natural law are derived from God's will. The morality of things is not an intrinsic property, but their conformity or disconformity to a law that makes known the law-maker's will. Conscience is the judgment of our actions relative to a moral law. [106] In the latter half of the 1670s, while in France, Locke began to integrate his natural law voluntarism with the revival of Greek hedonism.

Hedonic moral philosophy was introduced into the seventeenth century along with the revival of the Greek atomism of Epicurus, Democritus, and Lucretius. Atomism served as a useful hypothesis for the experimental sciences, but it threatened to lead to atheism. Hobbes, for example, argued that once God had created the universe of matter in motion he had left it alone to run by its own efficient causes. Gassendi, Charleton, Glanvill and Boyle all argued that God was not only necessary to set matter in motion but also, because there were no causes in nature, to keep it in motion. Thus, voluntarism could absorb the atomistic hypothesis and retain God's providence. A parallel synthesis of Epicurus' hedonic moral philosophy was achieved by Gassendi and Charleton. Accepting the notion of pleasures and pains as the springs of human action, they added three Christian elements to Epicurus' theory: a providential God, the immortality of the soul, and heaven and hell as the reward and punishment for good and evil behaviour. 'Thus he [Locke]', Baker writes, 'not only crowns the anti-authoritarian protest with which Bacon had opened the century, but also brings to a full cadence that

---

[106] This interpretation has been put past doubt by Francis Oakley and Elliot W. Urdang, 'Locke, natural law and God', *Natural Law Forum*, 11 (1966), 92–109. I disagree with some details but not with their overall argument. My major difference is that Oakley and Urdang do not treat the syncretism of natural law with the revived hedonism that is at the heart of Locke's ethical theory after 1676. See also von Leyden, p. 43; and Philip Abrams, introduction, *John Locke, Two Tracts on Government* (Cambridge, Cambridge University Press, 1967), pp. 69–74.

incisive attack with which William of Ockham had initiated the revolt against scholasticism.'[107]

Locke, building on Gassendi, brings these two traditions together in the following way.[108] First, from hedonism, he defines natural 'good and evil' as 'nothing but Pleasure or Pain, or that which procures pleasure or pain to us'.[109] Secondly, although man has no innate disposition to moral conduct, he does have empirically verifiable motives – 'attractions' and 'repulsions' – to pleasures and from pains. This is then linked to voluntarism by a new concept: *moral good and evil*.[110]

*Morally Good and Evil* then, is only the Conformity or Disagreement of our voluntary Actions to some Law, whereby Good or Evil is drawn on us, from the Will and Power of the Law-maker; which Good and Evil, Pleasure or Pain, attending our observance, or breach of the law, by the Decree of the Law-maker, is that we call *Reward* and *Punishment*.

A voluntary act is *moral* relative to a law that is the will of the law-maker, as in voluntarism. It is good or evil because obeying or disobeying the law brings on reward or punishment; that is, pleasure or pain and, by definition, good or evil. The moral goodness of

[107] Baker, p. 186. The great texts of the synthesis of voluntarism and Epicurean hedonism are Pierre Gassendi, *De vita et Moribus Epicuri* (1647), *Philosophiae Epicuri Syntagma*, 1649; F. Bernier, *Abrégé* (1678) and *The Discourses of Happiness, Virtue, and Liberty collected from the Learned Gassendi* (1699); Thomas Hobbes, *Leviathan* (1651); Walter Charleton, 'apology', *Epicurus's Morals* (1656), and *The Darknes of Atheism Dispelled by the Light of Nature* (1652). See Charles T. Harrison, 'The ancient atomists and the English literature of the 17th century', *Harvard Studies in Classical Philology*, 45 (1934), 1–74; Thomas Mayo, *Epicurus in England* (Dallas, 1934); Kargon, pp. 63–93; Frederick Vaughan, *The Tradition of Political Hedonism from Hobbes to J. S. Mill* (New York, Fordham University Press, 1982).

[108] I am greatly indebted to Driscoll's study of the influence of Gassendi on Locke's hedonism.

[109] *Essay* 2.28.5. Compare 2.20.2, 2.21.42. Pleasure and pain are first discussed in this way in July 1676: 'Pleasure and pain', MS Locke f. 1, pp. 325–47, in von Leyden, pp. 263–72. Compare *Essay* 2.7, 2.8.13, 4.3.6. Note that pleasures and pains are mental states for Locke. Compare letter to Molyneux, *Correspondence*, vol. 4 (1655).

[110] *Essay* 2.28.5. This synthesis is first introduced in a manuscript, *c.* 1687, that was intended as chapter 21 of the first edition of the *Essay*: 'Of Ethick in General', MS Locke c. 28, fols. 146r–152r. It is printed in King, vol. 2, pp. 122–33. However, an important section is omitted, which is reprinted in von Leyden, p. 72. Earlier attempts to combine voluntarism with Gassendian hedonism are made in the hedonic manuscripts of the late 1670s to early 1690s: 'Pleasure and Pain' (1676); 'Happynesse' (September 1676), MS Locke f. 1, fols. 445–7, in Driscoll, pp. 101–2; 'Happynesse' (October 1678), MS Locke f. 3, pp. 304–5, in King, vol. 1, p. 216; 'Thus I think' (1685–9?), MS Locke c. 28, fols. 143–5, in King, vol. 2, pp. 120–2; 'Ethica' (1692), MS Locke c. 42, p. 224 and 'Morality', MS Locke c. 28, fols. 139–40, both in T. Sargentich, 'Locke and ethical theory', *Locke Newsletter*, 5 (1974), 24–31.

a voluntary action is its 'rectitude' and moral evil its 'pravity' or
'obliquity'.[111] Moral good and evil are like natural good and evil in
virtue of their relation to pleasure and pain. They are unlike them, or
a special case, in virtue of referring only to voluntary acts and
pleasure and pain in the form of rewards and punishments attached
to a law.

Let me call such an ensemble of law-maker, laws, punishments,
and rewards and the schedule of morally good and evil acts a juridical
apparatus.[112] There are three types of this apparatus. The first comprises God, divine or natural law, the reward of heaven and the
punishment of hell, and the schedule of sins and duties. Conscience,
or judgment, compares an action to divine law to determine if it is a
sin or duty.[113] This providential apparatus is one of the great governing mechanisms of the early modern European church and state. The
practice associated with it is attrition: the fear of divine punishment
(hell) and the hope of divine reward (heaven) are necessary to
motivate people to act in accordance with the moral and legal systems. Every theorist, with the important exceptions of Richard
Overton and Pierre Bayle, held that belief in providentialism must
underlie any stable social order.[114] It was, of course, deeply intwined
in a multiplicity of practices in early modern Europe and partially
enforced in this world by the penitential and disciplinary powers of
the churches. This is why, according to Locke, atheists cannot be
tolerated. They have no motive to obey the law or keep their promises if they calculate that they can avoid secular punishment; only
fear of an omniscient, punishing God will govern their conduct in
these circumstances.[115] Conversely, and this is Locke's toleration,

[111] *Essay* 2.28.6, 15–16; 1.3.8. This distinction between right – the relation of an action
to a law – and good – the relation of an action to pleasure and pain – is brought out
clearly in 'Voluntas' (1693), MS Locke c. 28 fol. 114, in von Leyden, pp. 72–3 and
Colman, pp. 48–9. I am indebted to the fine work of von Leyden and Colman even
though my interpretation differs in some respects. Von Leyden argues that Locke
fails to reconcile hedonism and voluntarism, and Colman argues that Locke is not
a voluntarist with respect to the content of natural law.
[112] I include within the term 'apparatus' discursive and non-discursive (techniques,
institutions, etc.) elements.
[113] *Essay* 2.28.7–8.
[114] Richard Overton, *Mans Mortallitie* (Amsterdam, 1643). Pierre Bayle argued against
Antoine Arnauld's providential argument that fear of divine punishment is a
necessary condition of social order and began to explore the radical possibility of a
society of atheists, thus contesting the whole providential apparatus of
Christianity. Pierre Bayle, *Pensées diverses sur la comete* (1682). See Rex, pp. 52–67;
and for providentialism see D. P. Walker, *The Decline of Hell* (London, RKP, 1964).
I am indebted here to many discussions with David Wootton.
[115] *A Letter Concerning Toleration*, pp. 47, 51. See Tully, introduction, *A Letter Concerning
Toleration*, p. 8.

belief in *any* providential God will do (hence the scandal associated with the publication of the first *Letter Concerning Toleration*.[116]

Although Locke always held that providentialism was a necessary condition of social order, he also realized that it was the major cause of social disorder.[117] Two false beliefs had been introduced into Christianity by the various priests: that there is only one right way to worship God, and that it is a Christian duty to take up arms to protect and spread the true faith. Since this duty was enforced by teaching the providential threat of eternal damnation for non-compliance, the pastorate of each faith were powerfully motivated to take up arms. The priests inculcated these beliefs to gain power, and the overall consequence had been one hundred years of European wars. This is a fairly common analysis of the age of religious wars. Locke's solution in the *Letter Concerning Toleration* is to correct the two 'false' beliefs: God tolerates many ways of worship, and faith is to be spread by persuasion, not arms. Now, one faces divine punishment for using coercion in matters of faith. This would have removed the cause of religious war and legalized dissent while preserving providentialism as an instrument of social control. However, it would also have dis-established the Anglican Church and delegitimated the penal practices of all churches, and so it was decisively rejected.[118]

The second juridical apparatus involves the state: the sovereign or law-maker, the laws, the rewards and punishments of the penal system, and the codes of legal and illegal acts.[119] This is the foundation of political theory and practice in the early modern period. The gradual juridicalization of society against feudal and city particularism and trial by battle includes the military and penal institutions that developed around this apparatus, and the great legal schools of Thomism, voluntarism, and humanism that constructed juridical discourses to administer and justify it, as well as to legitimate resistance to its absolutist variant. By the mid seventeenth century the hegemonic sovereign of this apparatus was no longer the feudal lord, the Empire, the free city, estate, or Catholic Church, but the consolidating state.[120] Every political writer from the University of Bologna in the twelfth century to Locke, and even

---

[116] See the establishment attack on the *Letter* by Thomas Long, *The Letter for Toleration decipher'd and the Absurdity of an Absolute Toleration Demonstrated* (1689).
[117] John Locke, *Two Tracts*, pp. 158–61.
[118] See Jonas Proast (1689). See the tell-tale argument in Joseph Glanvill, *The Zealous and Impartial Protestant*, p. 3.    [119] *Essay* 2.28.7,9.
[120] J. H. Shennan, *The Origins of the Modern European State: 1450–1725* (London, Hutchinson, 1974).

to Hegel, held, correctly, that this apparatus of legal relations *constituted* political society; that it was the 'constitution' of political society. (We still call our fundamental laws our 'constitution', even though other relations are more fundamental now, and our moral and political theories are still trapped in these juridical discourses.) The state juridical apparatus is the model for this concept of governance: power is exercised by a sovereign body through the law and by means of punishments and rewards in order to bring about a certain kind of conduct.[121]

The third, and for Locke the most effective governor, is what I will call the 'humanist' juridical apparatus. Every society, culture, group, or party has its intersubjective opinions about appropriate and inappropriate belief and action. These are promulgated by the community through what he calls the laws of 'reputation', 'fashion', or 'opinion'. Judged by their conformity to or disagreement with the laws of reputation, actions are called virtues or vices. The rewards and punishments attached to these laws and enforced by the community are praise and blame, acclaim and opprobrium, honour and dishonour, and so on.[122]

Thus the measure of what is everywhere called and esteemed *Vertue* and *Vice* is this approbation or dislike, praise or blame, which by a secret and tacit consent establishes itself in the several Societies, Tribes and Clubs of men in the world; whereby several actions come to find Credit or Disgrace among them, according to the Judgment, Maxims or Fashions of that place.

I call this juridical apparatus 'humanist' because what Locke has done here is to translate humanism, its virtues and vices and motives of honour, praise, glory and reputation, into his juridical framework. Humanism is not – as many argued then and still do now – an alternative form of political theory and practice.[123] It is one type of juridical governance. As he states in his correspondence, and as we

---

[121] See, Tully, 'The pen', pp. 498–502, and introduction to *A Letter Concerning Toleration*, pp. 11–16.   [122] *Essay* 2.28.7, 10–13.

[123] A contemporary statement of the view that civic humanism or classical republicanism is different in kind from juridical government is presented by John Pocock, 'Virtues, rights, and manners: a model for historians of political thought', in J. G. A. Pocock, *Virtue, Commerce, and History* (Cambridge, Cambridge University Press, 1985), pp. 37–50. This difference is based primarily on distinctive features of the *languages* of republican and juridical political thought: of virtues and vices and of rights and obligations respectively. As important as this difference unquestionably is, however, in *practice*, and even in some features of its language, early modern republicanism is a strategy of juridical governance of conduct, not an alternative to it, as Vico stresses in his *New Science* (1725). See Jeffrey Barnouw, 'The critique of classical republicanism and the understanding of modern forms of polity in Vico's *New Science*', *Clio*, 9, 3 (1980).

see below, all politico-ethical regimes fall within these three great ensembles of knowledge and techniques.[124]

The humanist juridical apparatus is the most effective *de facto* governor of belief and action. People do not seriously reflect on God's punishment and, if they do, they dream of making reconciliations concerning present sins. With respect to the law of the Commonwealth 'they frequently flatter themselves with the hopes of Impunity'. But no one can escape the punishment of the censure and dislike of the company he keeps. Nor is there one person in ten thousand strong enough to bear up under the constant ill opinion of his friends. 'This is a burthen too heavy for human sufferance: And he must be made up of irreconciliable Contradictions who can take Pleasure in company, and yet be insensible of Contempt and Disgrace from his Companions.'[125]

Locke first mentions these three laws in a manuscript written in 1678.[126] It is clear by the context that he is beginning to draw into his juridical framework the powerful analysis of belief and behaviour in the terms of interests and reputation carried out in France, especially the analysis by Pierre Nicole.[127] From as early as his famous 'Diana' letter of 1659 Locke was deeply involved in the rich English analysis of the determinants of belief and action.[128] This tradition, which as Neil Wood has shown, is Baconian in inspiration, took interest, party, custom, and education as the determinants of conduct, as we have seen.[129] In his first period of political exile, 1675–9, Locke began the process of standing back from these two modes of analysis and working them into his deeper tripartite juridical apparatus. Here is a classic statement on reputation from this period:[130]

The principal spring from which the actions of men take their rise, the rule they conduct them by, and the end to which they direct them, seems to be credit and reputation, and that which at any rate they avoid, is in the greatest part shame and disgrace... this puts men upon school divinity in one country,

---

[124] *Correspondence*, Letter of James Tyrrell, vol. 4, letter 1309, pp. 110–13.

[125] *Essay* 2.28.12.

[126] 'Adversaria', MS Locke f. 247–8, in Aaron and Gibb, p. 93. 'Law' (1678), MS Locke, f. 3, pp. 111–12. See also *Draft A*, 25 and *Draft B*, 158. The tripartite classification is crystal clear in 'Of Ethick in General' (1687). Compare von Leyden, pp. 67–8.

[127] For the French analysis of interests and reputation see Nannerl Keohane, *Philosophy and the State in France* (Princeton, Princeton University Press, 1980), pp., 262–317.

[128] *Correspondence*, vol. 1, letter to Tom (1659), 81. Compare *Draft A*, 24–6; *Draft B*, 157–62; 'Of Study', in King, vol. 2, p. 188.    [129] Wood, pp. 94–107.

[130] 'Credit, Disgrace', MS Locke f. 3, pp. 381–2, December 1678, in King, vol. 1, p. 203. The passage is a paraphrase of Pascal, *Pensées* (1670), 821 (Lafuma numbers).

and physics and mathematics in another; this makes merchants in one country and soldiers in another . . . Religions are upheld by this and factions maintained, and the shame of being disesteemed by those with whom one hath lived, and to whom one would recommend oneself, is the great source and director of most of the actions of men . . . He therefore that would govern the world well, had need consider rather what fashions he makes, than what laws; and to bring any thing into use he need only give it reputation.

This explanation of virtue and vice was immediately attacked by James Lowde, and later by the third Earl of Shaftesbury and many others, as moral relativism.[131] This, however, was Locke's point. The humanist juridical apparatus provided an explanation of the cultural diversity of moral practices which Europe's global expansion had uncovered, refuting the old consensus justification of natural law.[132] Secondly, it explained, along with providentialism, the division of Europe into warring factions, and so the sceptical crisis. The only moral principle that is in fact culturally invariant is preservation of the community, and this is all that is required as an empirical foundation for the new natural law theory centered on preservation.[133] Thirdly, it provided a means of relativizing both humanist and Aristotelian ethics.[134] I have been unable to find a parallel to this remarkable conceptual innovation in the seventeenth century. Although this strategy explains and accepts culturally relative moralities, it does not lead to a complete moral relativism. Divine law remains as the true standard of morality, as Locke emphasized in the second edition of the *Essay* in response to Lowde.

The problem of how one comes to know divine law by the use of reason still remains, as Locke's critics point out. I want to mention one solution that Locke rejects, in order to explicate one further feature of the providential apparatus. To bring natural law philosophy in line with the new voluntaristic concept of reason and the experimental sciences, Cumberland argued that God had attached

---

[131] James Lowde, *A Discourse Concerning the Nature of Man* (1694). In the preface Lowde attacked *Essay* 2.28.11. Locke replied in the 2nd edition, 2.28.11 note. Shaftesbury linked Locke's voluntarism and his relativism: 'Thus virtue, according to Mr Locke, has no other measure, law, or rule, than fashion and custom; morality, justice, equity, depend only on law and will, and God indeed is a perfectly free agent in this sense; that, free to will anything, that is however ill: for if He wills it, it will be made good; virtue may be vice, and vice virtue in its turn, if he pleases. And thus neither right nor wrong, virtue nor vice, are anything in themselves; nor is there any trace or idea naturally imprinted on human minds. Experience and our catechism teach us all!' Third Earl of Shaftesbury, *The Life, Unpublished Letters and Regimen of A. A. Cooper . . .*, ed. B. Rand (New York, Macmillan, 1900), pp. 403–4.

[132] *Essay* 1.3.10. Locke abandoned universal consent as the basis of morality as early as the *Essays on the Law of Nature*, pp. 165–75.

[133] See p. 60 below.      [134] 'Of Ethick in General', pp. 124–6.

to natural law natural punishments and rewards in this world. The hangover that follows from overdrinking, for example, is a punishment God annexed to overdrinking because it is a sin. It follows that one can work back from empirical observations of the pleasures and pains that result from human actions to hypotheses of what natural laws must be. Hobbes had moved in this direction, as had Samuel Parker and Joseph Glanvill. [135] Henry Lee puts this theory forward in a self-revelatory way, citing Cumberland's proof that there are 'natural advantages' annexed to morally good acts: 'health, strength, beauty, long-life, wisdom, memory, honour, riches, power, ease of mind and inward pleasure'. [136]

James Tyrrell attempted to draw Locke into this (latitudinarian) movement, but he rejected it for two reasons. [137] First, it assimilated a moral law to a descriptive law of natural phenomena and thus to what is not, properly speaking, a law but merely a regularity. [138] Here Locke is following Boyle's *A Free Inquiry into the Vulgarly Received Notion of Nature*. [139] Such an assimilation leads, as Locke was well aware, to a kind of deistic necessitarianism, and elides the necessary features of a law: that it applies to voluntary actions and is enforced by the free will of the law-maker. Without this, there is no substantive distinction between natural and moral good, as Locke stresses in 'Of Ethick in General'. The second reason for rejecting it is that it could be and was used by the latitudinarians to justify the use of coercion against dissenters. [140]

With these three apparatus (Christian or providential, sovereign, and humanist) in hand, we can turn to the explanation of conduct. Locke argues that the fact of both global and historical moral relativity refutes the theory that there are either innate practical principles or innate dispositions to them. The defining feature of a practical as opposed to a speculative principle is that it affects our activity. This is not because we are disposed to act in accordance with it or because we incline towards good and away from evil action. Rather, what guides action is our basic motivation set: 'a desire of

[134] 'Of Ethick in General', pp. 124–6.
[135] Samuel Parker, *A Demonstration of the Divine Authority of the Law of Nature and of the Christian Religion* (1681); Hobbes, *Leviathan*, 2.31, pp. 406–7.
[136] Lee, *Anti-Scepticism*, p. 12. Of course, to disagree with Hobbes, these are not the only rewards.
[137] James Tyrrell, *A Brief Disquisition of the Law of Nature, according to . . . Dr. Cumberland's . . . Latin treatise* (1692). In the preface Tyrrell attempts to align Cumberland and Locke. [138] *Essay* 2.28.6. Compare 'Of Ethick in General', p. 128.
[139] Boyle, *Works*, vol. 4, p. 367. Compare *Christian Virtuoso*, 5, p. 46.
[140] This is brought out most infamously in Samuel Parker, *A Discourse of Ecclesiastical Politie* (1670). See Locke's Letter to Tyrrell, *Correspondence*, vol. 4, letter 1309, pp. 110–13.

Happiness, and an aversion to misery . . . do constantly . . . operate
and influence all our actions, without ceasing'. These are 'the constant Spring and motives of all our Actions', but they are 'inclinations of the appetite to good, not impressions of truth on the
understanding'.[141] Therefore, for a practical principle to influence
action it must be related to man's empirically verifiable motivations.
This is done by making a practical principle a law within one of the
three juridical apparatus. This is what Locke means when he says
that every practical principle requires a reason which justifies it.[142]
This justification appeals to a reason or ground from which the practical principle can be deduced and which is its foundation. Thus,
there are three foundations of, for example, the principle that men
should keep their compacts, corresponding to the three juridical
apparatus. Locke's statement is thus worth quoting in full because it
brings voluntarism, hedonism, and the three ethical systems
together into a comprehensive penalism:[143]

That Men should keep their Compacts, is certainly a great and undeniable
Rule in Morality. But yet, if a Christian, who has the view of Happiness and
Misery in another Life, be asked why a Man must keep his Word, he will *give*
this as a *Reason*: Because God who has the Power of eternal Life and Death,
requires it of us. But if an *Hobbist* be asked why; he will answer: Because the
Publick requires it, and the *Leviathan* will punish you, if you do not. And if
one of the old *Heathen* Philosophers had been asked, he would have
answer'd: Because it was dishonest, below the Dignity of a Man, and
opposite to Vertue, the highest Perfection of human Nature, to do
otherwise.

Of course the Christian apparatus is the 'true ground of morality'
because the Law-maker is God, the author of truth, and the rewards
and punishments, heaven and hell, are the greatest pleasures and
pains.[144]

Given this, what governs human action? As in the case of assent,
Locke's first answer is a deterministic one. An individual's judgment

---

[141] *Essay* 1.3.3.    [142] *Essay* 1.3.4.    [143] *Essay* 1.3.5.
[144] *Essay* 1.3.6 (lines 11–12 added in 2nd edition in response to Lowde's charge of
relativism). Burnet doubts the efficacy of the juridical apparatus: 'Do we not see
men every day, in spite of laws external or internal, divine or human, pursue their
lusts, passions and vicious inclinations? Though they have not only the terrors of
another life to keep them in awe and order, but see before their eyes God's gibbets,
whips, racks and torturing engines'. Locke replies: 'What! Whilst they have the
terrors of those things as unavoidable for that action before their eyes'.
Porter, p. 43.

of the greater good in view determines the will. This appears in the first edition of the *Essay* and in a number of the manuscripts.[145] It is conformable with his penalism but, like the first account of probabilities determining assent, conduct is necessarily governed by whatever greater good is ready to hand. Locke asked William Molyneux to solicit comments on the first edition and William King replied, pointing out the determinism of this argument.[146] Locke then reworked the argument, in continual correspondence with Molyneux, and published a new and definitive account in the second edition. The materials for the new account were already available in manuscripts of the 1670s, so he probably published the first chapter 21 without much thought and from an old manuscript. The new account, like the account of assent, is heavily indebted to Gassendi, just as the first is, it seems, to Hobbes.[147]

Locke argues that his first view cannot be true, because if it were everyone who has considered Christianity would be an unfailing Christian in practice. This is so since they would be aware that heaven and hell outweigh all other good and evil, and so they would be motivated to live a Christian life to gain infinite pleasure and avoid infinite pain. Yet it obviously is true that everyone who has considered Christianity is not a practising Christian, therefore the greater good in view does not determine the will.[148]

In this self-criticism, precipitated by King, Locke argues that the criticism holds even if heaven, hell, and the immortality of the soul are only probable, not certain. All voluntarists hold this view, because heaven and hell are contingent features of the universe. Locke opens the *Essay* by equating faith with opinion, not knowledge, and re-emphasizes this in the response to Stillingfleet's intellectualist assault on the *Essay*.[149] Here he employs a variant of

---

[145] *Essay* 2.21.29, 1st edition. The sections of the 1st edition of 2.21 that were omitted by Locke in the later editions are reprinted by Nidditch in the *Essay*, pp. 248–73.

[146] Locke to Molyneux, 20 September 1692, *Correspondence*, vol. 4, letter 1538; Molyneux to Locke, 15 October 1692, vol. 4, letter 1544 (contains King's comments); Locke to Molyneux, 15 July 1693, vol. 4, letter 1643 (contains new chapter outlines for 2nd edition of 2.21). See Molyneux's own criticisms, letter 1579.

[147] For Locke's apparent debt to Hobbes in his first account see S. Lamprecht, *The Moral and Political Philosophy of John Locke* (New York, Columbia University Press, 1918), pp. 89, 98. For his debt to Gassendi in the second account see Bonno, pp. 241–2; and Driscoll, p. 108.

[148] *Essay* 2.21.31, 38.

[149] *Essay* 1.1.3. Compare 4.18; 'Faith and Reason', August–September 1676, MS Locke f. 1, pp. 412–32, in von Leyden, pp. 272–81; and Biddle, pp. 421–2.

Pascal's wager, a decision-theoretic form of probable reasoning that had actually developed in England prior to the *Pensées*.[150] Locke's source however seems to be the *Pensées*.[151] This argument contains two types of probable reasoning: (1) assessing the grounds of probability for the belief that Revelation is the word of God and, therefore, that heaven and hell exist and the soul is immortal (the kind of reasoning we have seen in the section on assent), and (2) calculating the relative weights of goods; that is, a probability calculus of pleasures and pains (the form of probable reasoning most closely connected to the juridical apparatus since it is a matter of weighing the relative pleasures and pains of the three systems of punishments and rewards). Once Locke had mastered the concept of probability in 1676, he realized that a demonstrable ethics was no longer necessary: probability and opinion are sufficient for all our concernments.[152]

How is it, then, that people can have the greater good in view yet not be moved by it, if pleasure and pain, happiness and misery, are the constant springs of human action? The answer is that the greater good is absent and "'tis against the nature of things, that what is absent should operate, where it is not'.[153] A residual disposition or occult force acting at a distance was lurking in the first theory and is now removed in the second edition. What determines the will, therefore, must be something present, and this is *uneasiness*. This now becomes the immediate determinant that always governs behaviour. It is first introduced in 2.20.6 of the second edition, contradicting the old view three passages earlier. Locke had immense difficulty defining the concept and continued to refine it throughout his manuscripts and correspondence. Pierre Coste, who translated the *Essay* into French, warned the reader that there were no French equivalents and used 'inquietude'. Again, there is an earlier manu-

---

[150] For example, in Chillingworth, *The Religion of Protestants* (1633), in *Works* (1844), pp. 203–4. See van Leeuwen, p. 30.
[151] The first appearance of the wager is in his journal, 29 July 1676 (reprinted in Aaron and Gibb, pp. 81–2). Locke then used it in several places in the *Essay*. For Locke's relation to Pascal see John Barker, *Strange Contrarieties: Pascal in England during the Age of Reason* (Montreal, McGill-Queen's University Press, 1975), pp. 36–7, 48–9, 50–6.
[152] The point of Locke's journal entry on the wager is that a demonstrable ethics is unnecessary to morality. Compare 'Faith and Reason' (1676); Locke's reply to Tyrrell's request for a demonstrable ethic, *Correspondence*, vol. 4, letter 1309; and *Essay* 1.1.5, 2.21.70 (part 1, n. 60). Pascal's wager is at *Pensées* 418 (Lafuma numbers). For a modern reconstruction see Hacking, pp. 63–72.
[153] *Essay* 2.21.37.

script on uneasiness and, secondly, the possibility of a connection with Gassendi.[154]

Uneasiness is any present mental or physical *pain* to which is always joined a desire equal to the pain.[155] Since desire is always uneasiness for some absent good, in reference to any pain felt, the absent good is the ease of pain. This simple mechanism can explain the attraction of an absent positive good as well, without invoking any occult forces. An absent positive good (heaven, honour, etc.) does not in itself cause desire equal to its greatness of pleasure because it cannot, in itself and at a distance, cause 'pain for it', and so, instead, uneasiness, equal to its greatness. A present pain, and so an uneasiness, must be 'raised' for an absent positive good before a person can be moved towards it. 'And therefore', Locke concludes, 'absent good may be looked on and considered without desire' unless and until an uneasiness has been raised for it.[156] 'I am forced to conclude, that *good*, the greater good, though apprehended and acknowledged to be so, does not determine the will, until our desire, raised proportionably to it, makes us uneasy in the want of it.'

Since it is this micro-mechanism of pain that determines the will, it is wrong to call Locke a voluntaristic hedonist, or to suggest that he makes pleasure the motive force of action. The term 'penalism' captures both the penal features of the theory and the centrality of 'ease of pain' as the basic human drive. Even the infinite pleasures and pain of heaven and hell can be contemplated without desire or aversion until a person has cultivated an uneasiness for heaven and made it part of his or her happiness.[157] Then, a person will be moved not directly by pleasure but by a present pain or uneasiness he or she has acquired for it. This is because all present pain makes a necessary part of our misery whereas absent good does not make a necessary part of our present happiness.[158] 'Though, as to pain, that they are always concerned for; they can feel no *uneasiness* without being moved. And therefore being *uneasie* in the want to whatever is judged necessary to their Happiness, as soon as any good appears to mark a part of their portion of happiness, they begin to desire it.'

This little penal mechanism is partly implanted in the mind by God. The pain and uneasiness annexed to hunger is set in place by

[154] For 'uneasiness', see 'Will, pleasure, pain' (July 1676), MS Locke f. 1, pp. 317–19, in Aaron and Gibb, p. 80; 'Pleasure and Pain' (August 1676), in von Leyden, pp. 263–72, pp. 269–70; *Correspondence*, vol. 5 (1798) (a clarification intended for the 4th edition). For Gassendi, see Driscoll, p. 101.
[155] *Essay* 2.21.31.　[156] *Essay* 2.21.35.　[157] *Essay* 2.21.36–8.　[158] *Essay* 2.21.43.

God to motivate humans to seek preservation. The pain of sexual lust is implanted by God to drive men to marriage and reproduction:[159] '*it is better to marry than to burn*, says St. *Paul*; where we may see, what it is that chiefly drives men into the enjoyments of a conjugal life. A little burning felt pushes us more powerfully, than greater pleasures in prospect draw or allure.' However, the vast majority of our uneasinesses are acquired, such as the uneasiness for 'Honour, power or Riches', and produced by custom and education.[160] The concept of uneasiness now becomes the instrument to link the will to the juridical apparatus and so to explain and reform conduct.

Before Locke turns to this he adds one final feature. Uneasiness solves the problem of the absent good but not the problem of determinism, for now it determines the will. Locke thus introduces a power of the will to suspend the solicitations of present unease and to examine which course of action will lead to the greatest pleasure. The power is the freedom of the will and the foundation of liberty.[161] 'For during this suspension of any desire, before the will be determined to action, and the action (which follows that determination) done, we have the opportunity to examine, view and judge, of the good or evil of what we are going to do.' Once the judgment is made, and an uneasiness aligned with its object, the will is determined. There is a direct parallel with this Gassendian account of behaviour and the earlier account of belief. With respect to assent we have the power to suspend our acquired and customary determinants of judgment and to examine the grounds of probability. Here, we have the power to suspend our acquired and customary determinants of the will and to judge our course of action in accordance with grounds or measures of pleasure and pain, good or evil. Then, behaviour follows. As Locke states, God himself is determined by what is best, and it is therefore no abridgment of our freedom to say that we are determined by what we judge to be the best. Freedom consists in suspension and examination.[162] This new account provoked a response by Locke's close friend the Dutch Arminian, Phillip van Limborch. The correspondence that followed is the clearest expression of two views of intellectual liberty in the late seventeenth century.[163]

---

[159] *Essay* 2.21.34.      [160] *Essay* 2.21.45.      [161] *Essay* 2.21.47.

[162] *Essay* 2.21.48–52. For the parallel between suspending assent and the will compare pp. 31–2 above and Passmore. For the similarity with Gassendi see Bonno, pp. 241–2, and Driscoll, pp. 108–9. For the introduction of suspension and examination with respect to the will, see 'Will, pleasure, pain' (1676).

[163] *Correspondence*, vol. 7, pp. 268–70, De Beer introduces the Limborch-Locke controversy, which runs from 2881 to 3200. For a summary of the debate over the indifferency of the will from Descartes to Anthony Collins, see A. O. O'Higgins, introduction, *Determinism and Freewill* (The Hague, Martinus Nijhoff, 1977).

Limborch argued that after a practical judgment is made the will remains 'indifferent'; free to act or not to act in accordance with it. This autonomy of the will, which follows Descartes, is more voluntaristic than in Locke.[164] Locke had held this view in 1660 when he justified imposition of religious uniformity in England. If practical judgment, and hence conscience, is separate from the will, then dissenters can be forced to conform to religious practice without compromising their religious beliefs, since conformity requires only an act of the will. They can be said to enjoy freedom of conscience or 'inner' belief. What the dissenters wanted was freedom of religious practice, not just inner faith, and they broke with the long-standing Protestant separation of judgment and will. They argued that practical judgment is non-contingently linked to and determines the will, so that freedom of conscience entails freedom of practice. To impose uniformity on dissenters is to force them to compromise their beliefs and so to commit the sin of hypocrisy. Therefore, they have a right and a motive to resist imposition. When Locke moved to the defence of dissent in 1667 he put forward this view to justify toleration, as did John Owen, the Master of Christ Church and indefatigable defender of dissent. Therefore, in England the theory that the judgment determines the will was associated with the revolutionary struggle for toleration, and the indifferency theory with latitude and uniformity.[165] What Limborch, and presumably Descartes, wanted was the opposite: a theory that would justify intellectual freedom for minorities without entailing any disorderly consequences in the realm of practice. This kind of objection had been advanced earlier by King and Molyneux. Locke added yet another section to chapter 21 in the fifth edition in which he explicitly rejected the indifferency theory of the will.[166]

The moral judgment involved in examination is an exercise in probable reasoning; of weighing the relative pleasures and pains of possible actions: 'Judging is, as it were, balancing an account, and determining on which side the odds lies [sic].'[167] The judgment of present pleasures and pains cannot be mistaken: 'Things in their present enjoyment are what they seem; the apparent and real good are, in this case, always the same.' If the pains of honest industry and

---

[164] This is the sixth difficulty in the sixth set of objections urged against Descartes's *Meditations on First Philosophy*. Note how Norris, following Malebranche, takes the indifferency line against Locke: pp. 16–17. For attacks on Descartes's voluntarism, see Cudworth, pp. 27–9 and Lowde, pp. 59–68.

[165] See Tully, introduction to *A Letter Concerning Toleration*, pp. 5–7.

[166] *Essay* 2.21.71, 283.16–284.21.

[167] *Essay* 2.21.67. Compare 2.21.47, 52, 53.

of starving with hunger and cold are set before us, 'no body would be in doubt which to chuse'.[168] Misjudgment arises because things are called good or bad in a double sense: with respect to the pleasure or pain of the action and with respect to the pleasure or pain *consequent* to the action. We cannot help but be concerned with and desirous of these future pleasures and pains, and so they make part of our happiness.[169] However, we misjudge the weight of future or consequential pleasures and pains relative to the present ones. Future goods are at a disadvantage, and so their relative pleasure misjudged, because they are absent or unfamiliar. Hence, even when one suspends present uneasiness, the closer and more familiar causes us to misjudge; to employ wrong measures of good and evil, analogous to wrong measures of probability:[170]

> because the abstinence from a present pleasure, that offers itself, is a Pain, nay, oftentimes a very great one, the desire being inflamed by a near and tempting object; 'tis no wonder that that operates after the same manner Pain does, and lessens in our Thoughts, what is Future; and forces us, as it were, blindfold into its embraces.

It is not only that people misjudge absent good but, more importantly, that they make their judgments relative to a subjective and inconstant standard. Their moral standard is their background, acquired uneasiness for some things and against others which Locke calls mental 'relish'.[171] This is another concept that dates from 1678 and denotes those acquired uneasinesses that are fairly stable or habitual, as opposed to violent or contingent uneasinesses.[172] Because these are subjective and various, people pursue different life plans and place happiness in different things. Therefore, moral judgment is subjective and relative: 'The mind has a different relish, as well as the Palate; and you will as fruitlessly endeavour to delight all men with Riches and Glory, (which yet some men place their Happiness in,) as you would to satisfy all men's hunger with cheese and lobster.' To different men these are different things relative to their mental relish. Happiness and misery, good and evil are a matter of mental taste.[173]

People choose correctly here because we all seek happiness and what counts as pleasure is relative to our background relish. What saves Locke from relativism is the nature of heaven and hell. These pleasures and pains infinitely outweigh all others, and this for every

---

[168] *Essay* 2.21.58.    [169] *Essay* 2.21.61.    [170] *Essay* 2.21.64.
[171] *Essay* 2.21.57.    [172] 'Happynesse' (1678), in King, vol. 1, p. 216.    [173] *Essay* 2.21.55.

palate:[174] '[Heaven] being intended for a state of Happiness, it must certainly be agreeable to every one's wish and desire: Could we suppose their relishes as different there as they are here, yet the Manna in Heaven will suit every one's Palate.' Locke offers two proofs of this; one from Revelation, which appears to be a paraphrase of Gassendi, and the second an empirical argument from the fact that we are never satisfied with earthly pleasures to the possibility of some future happiness that satisfies all desire.[175]

Relish is the acquired mental habit in virtue of which specific ways of thinking and acting are pleasant to the agent. There is, in turn, a fairly settled range of uneasiness for these ways of thinking and acting. Relish is the mechanism that brings absent goods within one's view of happiness, renders them desirable, and thus disposes the agent to them.[176] When people are governed by this standard in thought and action, they are acting in accordance with their overall desire for happiness. This utilitarian and hedonic search for happiness is how they ought to act; 'the inclination, and tendency of their nature to happiness is an obligation, and motive to them'.[177] Moral error is not so much misjudging relative to one's habitual relish but acquiring a relish that does not lead to the greatest or true happiness. Since the relish is acquired, it is malleable and so capable of reform. Relish is in fact the disposition to judge and act in specific ways, acquired by custom and education and exposed in Locke's attack on the various dispositional theories.[178] 'Fashion and common Opinion having settled wrong Notions, and education and custom ill Habits, the just values of things are misplaced, and the palates of men corrupted.' It is possible to reform corrupt palates and implant new habits to govern conduct. 'Pains should be taken to rectify these [habits]; and contrary habits change our pleasures, and give a relish to that, which is necessary, or conducive to our Happiness.'

Locke now lays out his reform project. Man has the power to change the pleasantness or unpleasantness that accompanies physical and mental action. The relish of the mind is malleable like that of the body.[179] Actions are pleasing or displeasing with respect to the performance of them and with respect to the rewards and punishments annexed to them. The first step is to suspend *de facto* desires and to

[174] *Essay* 2.21.65.
[175] 'Happynesse', in King, vol. 1, p. 216 (*Ps.* 16:11). This appears in 2.21.29 of the 1st edition and 2.21.41 of the 2nd. For the parallel with Gassendi, see Driscoll, p. 100. See 'Pleasure and Pain', in von Leyden, p. 269, and 'Happynesse' (26 September 1676), MS Locke f. 1, fols. 445–7, in Driscoll, pp. 101–2 for unease of earthly happiness. [176] *Essay* 2.21.55, 57. [177] *Essay* 2.21.52. [178] *Essay* 2.21.69. [179] *Essay* 2.21.69.

examine the consequences of actions using the probabilistic reasoning of weighing future pleasures and pains. This kind of probabilistic reasoning is best exemplified in Pascal's wager, and Locke now introduces it in his most polished presentation. He concludes:[180]

The Rewards and Punishments of another life, which the Almighty has established, as the enforcements of his Law, are of weight enough to determine the Choice, against whatever Pleasure or Pain this life can shew, when the Eternal state is considered but in its bare possibility.

Heaven and hell are thus the 'true foundations' of morality because they outweigh all other pleasures and pains. The second step in an examination is 'due consideration' of the pleasures and pains reason has discovered.[181] By this, Locke means that the person should reflect repeatedly and silently on the end until it has become fixed in his mind. In *Some Thoughts Concerning Education*, which is the application of this theory to the education of gentlemen, he explains this step in the formation of a young pupil. To imprint on the mind a true notion of God and instill love and reverence, it is necessary to tell the pupil that God hears, sees, and governs all and rewards those who obey. No questions are permitted, and the pupil is to consider this in silent and simple prayer morning, noon, and night.[182]

These two steps are insufficient in themselves to break an old relish or to create a new one for the virtues that have these rewards. If they were sufficient his original theory would have been true. Reason 'recommends' and consideration gives a certain pleasant colour to the action. This is true for Pascal as well and they both introduce into their theories at this point the modified Aristotelian step that one becomes virtuous and finds pleasure in doing virtuous acts by practising the virtues. For Locke, as for Pascal, this process is analysed mechanistically, not teleologically, as with Aristotle. The third step, what Pascal calls *la machine*, is called by Locke 'use and practice'.[183]

By the continual repetition of an activity it gradually becomes both habitual and pleasurable. As with 'Bread and Tobacco' so with 'vertue too'. Summing up, Locke writes: 'reason and consideration at first recommends, and begins their trial, and use finds, or custom

---

[180] *Essay* 2.21.70. Compare 1.3.13, 2.21.60.     [181] *Essay* 2.21.45, 69.

[182] *The Educational Writings of John Locke*, ed. James Axtell (Cambridge, Cambridge University Press, 1968), 136, pp. 241–2. The force of constantly repeating ideas until they are imprinted on the mind is explored in the *Essay* (2.10.6).

[183] *Essay* 2.21.69. Compare the final section of 'Happynesse' (1678), on acquiring virtue by 'use and practice' in King, vol. 1, p. 220. In Locke, use and practice immediately precede the wager argument (2.21.69–70), whereas in Pascal they follow it (419, compare 125, 126).

makes them pleasant'. Therefore, it is continual repetition that makes activities pleasant. 'But the pleasure of the action itself is best acquired, or increased, by use and practice.' 'Repetition', as he explains, 'wears us into a liking, of what possibly, in the first essay, displeased us.' The key, then, to governing conduct is the formation of mental and physical habits, the acquisition of which will, in turn, recommend things to us that reason is impotent to do. 'Habits have powerful charms, and put so strong attractions of easiness and pleasure into what we accustom our selves to, that we cannot forebear to do, or at least be easy in the omission of actions, which habitual practice has suited, and thereby recommends to us.'

To summarize, the problems of war, ungovernability, and the legitimation crisis gave rise to the question of what factors govern thought and action. One powerful answer was 'interest'; a concept that took on its modern form in this period, especially in France. Locke rejected this because what a person takes to be his or her interest is constituted by a more fundamental factor: custom and education. This is the Baconian answer. Locke took this two steps further. First, custom and education do not govern conduct, but rather the habits formed by them. Habit is understood not as it had been previously, against a background of teleological nature and human nature, but against the view of man as a malleable blank tablet, indifferent to manipulation. Reason and interest were power- less against mental and physical habits. [184] Locke's life-long analyses are brought together in this final form for the first time in chapter 33 of book 2, added to the fourth edition of the *Essay*. He opens by rejecting the argument that 'self-love' or interest explains belief and action (probably thinking of Pierre Nicole). [185] Secondly, he says that 'education' and 'custom', and to some extent 'interest', describe a process but do not explain it. The correct answer is that custom, in the sense of repetition, establishes habits of thinking (assent), of willing, and of bodily movement that govern conduct. [186]

Custom settles habits of thinking in the understanding, as well as determin- ing in the will, and of motions in the Body; all of which seems to be but trains of motion in the animal spirits, which once set a going continue on in the same steps they have been used to, which by often treading are worn into a smooth path, and the motion in it becomes easy and as it were Natural.

[184] *Education*, 110, p. 215.
[185] *Essay* 2.33.2. In 1677 Locke had translated three essays by Pierre Nicole: *On the Existence of a God, On the Weakness of Man, On the Way of Preserving Peace*. See John Locke, *Discourses translated from Nicole's Essays* (1828). The second of these articles is one of many examples of analysis in the terms of self-interest or *amour-propre*.
[186] *Essay* 2.33.6.

Once these habits are formed, reason is powerless.[187] The only way
to break them is, as we have seen, to set up counter-practices that
make probabilistic reasoning and virtuous action habitual.

Locke then analysed the processes of custom and education into
the practice of training by continuous repetition and due consideration. This is how principles and dispositions that are said to be
innate come to be implanted habits. His deepest insight, however,
was his discovery that this process of habit formation is governed by
the three juridical apparatus, especially the humanist one. As we
have seen, a human being, in virtue of his or her sociability, takes
pleasure in company and in the approval of peers. The means to this
pleasure, and to avoid the pain of disrepute, is to think and act in
what are taken to be virtuous and praiseworthy ways. Habits are
gradually formed and so the customs of various societies reproduced. Thus, the humanist juridical apparatus is, by 'tacit
consent', invested in and constitutive of our most basic social practices. The appeal to praise and blame, good- and ill-repute, is used
explicitly to govern in the educational systems. The appeal to love of
reputation is the means of drawing the student into ways of thinking
and acting that gradually become habitual. Once these habits are
settled we cannot bear the reproach with which we are punished for
our unconventional opinions. By this means, authorities secure
their domination, pass off their legitimating beliefs as sacred and
innate and so precipitate a century of wars.[188] The most absurd
beliefs and practices can become the object of reverence in this way,
says Locke, coming close to Nietzsche:[189] 'In history he shall see the
rise of opinions, and find from what slight, and sometimes shameful
occasions, some of them have taken their rise, which yet afterwards
have had great authority, and passed almost for sacred in the world,
and borne down all before them.'

## THREE PRACTICES OF GOVERNING

I want to turn now to Locke's account of how these three apparatus
had been used to govern conduct, and, secondly, how they could be
and were being used to govern the reform of conduct and to
establish a new mode of domination and subjection.

The operation of the providential apparatus, the first practice of
governing, is explained in the *Reasonableness of Christianity* (1695). It

[187] *Essay* 2.33.13.
[188] *Essay* 1.3.22–7.
[189] 'Of Study', in King, vol. 1, pp. 202–3.

builds upon two early manuscripts: 'Of Ethick in General' (1687), intended as a chapter of the *Essay*, and the earlier 'Faith and Reason' (1676). Locke published the *Reasonableness* in response to *Christianity not Mysterious* by the radical deist John Toland.[190] Toland argued that Scripture, not popes, councils, or tradition, must be the guide in ethics. Given this, there are two positions, the first being that reason is 'the instrument, but not the rule of our belief'. On this view, which he rejected, the mysteries of the Gospel are taken to be either contrary to reason or above reason, yet are nonetheless accepted on faith. In both of these cases, 'the several doctrines of the new Testament belong no further to the enquiries of reason than to prove 'em divinely reveal'd, and they are properly mysteries still'. He rejected this view. Reason must be the *rule* and not merely the *instrument* of belief; or, as he put it, 'reason is the only foundation of all certitude'.[191]

The instrumental view Toland rejects here is Locke's view in chapter 18 of book 4 of the *Essay*, worked out in 1676 and similar to Boyle's argument. Faith is opinion or 'belief', not knowledge, yet it has the highest degree of assurance.[192] Nothing in faith can contradict intuitive or demonstrably certain knowledge, but the number of these truths is very slight in any case. If faith appears to contradict belief, on the other hand, then we must accept faith.[193] The reason for this is that faith has a higher degree of assurance, because 'whatever GOD hath revealed, is certainly true; no doubt can be made of it'. Therefore, 'an evident *Revelation* ought to determine our assent even against Probability' because Revelation is 'another principle of Truth, and Ground of assent'. The role of reason in ethics is instrumental: to judge in accordance with the grounds of probability (witnesses, miracles, etc.) if Scripture is divine Revelation or not (and to interpret): 'it still belongs to *Reason*, to judge of the Truth of its being a Revelation, and of the significance of the words, wherein it is delivered'.[194] This classic voluntarist account of reason in ethics undercuts the old authorities and enthusiasm. It also undercuts the use of reason to judge the content of Scripture, in opposition to Toland and the radical deists.

---

[190] For Toland and Locke, see Biddle, pp. 417–22; M. Jacob (1976), pp. 201–51, and *The Radical Enlightenment* (London, George Allen and Unwin, 1981).
[191] John Toland, *Christianity not Mysterious* (1696), pp. 5–6.
[192] 'Faith and Reason' (1676), in von Leyden, pp. 272–84. Robert Boyle, *A Discourse of Things above Reason*, in *The Works of Sir Robert Boyle*, ed. T. Birch (1772), D. McKie, 6 vols. (Hildesheim, Olms, 1965–6), vol. 4.
[193] *Essay* 4.18.5, 9, 11.   [194] *Essay* 4.18.10, 9, 8.

Toland's work was taken to be an extension of Locke's work by Bishop Stillingfleet.[195] Locke wrote the *Reasonableness* to distance himself from Toland and, in the final triumph of his voluntarism, to show that reason, in the sense of demonstration, could not provide an independent foundation for morality. He argued that the rationalists have the argument upside down: reason cannot be an independent rule for judging Christian ethics, because Scripture is the foundation of our moral reasoning, and this because Scripture has spread and become habitual for thought and action by the historical operation of the providential juridical apparatus.

The use of reason prior to Christianity failed to produce an ethical system. All the pagan philosophers could do was teach how to use their moral vocabularies, virtues, and vices, and to back this up with praise and blame. The diversity of moral codes shows that there has been no rational consensus except on the rule of preservation. These rational systems are useless because they are too complex for the majority to check. The pagan philosophers only discovered those moral principles that coincide with conveniency. Even if they had discovered all the moral principles, these would not constitute a morality because they lack the 'force of law', 'obligation', and sufficient motivation. They would be obeyed only when it was convenient; when praise and blame and one's relish were in conformity with them. For these to be a 'true' morality, the laws must be made for all of us, not by us, by a law-maker who has 'punishing power'.[196]

Therefore, Revelation is a necessary condition of morality. Christianity as revealed by Jesus is the true morality. First, it revealed a law-maker, his laws and duties, and his punishments and rewards applicable to and understandable by all. This is 'the true ground of morality'.[197] Clearly, it provides the strong motivation that the pagans with their rewards of praise for virtue could not. With Christ's Revelation of heaven and hell 'interest is come about to her [virtue] and virtue is visibly the most enticing purchase and by much the best bargain'.[198] The obligation that only the providential apparatus can provide seems to point in two directions. Sometimes Locke says we have an obligation to obey God because his rewards and punishments bring true happiness and misery. At other times,

---

[195] Edward Stillingfleet, *A Discourse in the Vindication of the Doctrine of the Trinity* (1697), p. 273.
[196] *Reasonableness of Christianity*, in *The Works of John Locke* (Germany, Scientia Verlag Aalen, 1963 (1823)), vol. 7, pp. 88–90, 93; 'Of Ethick in General', in King, vol. 2, pp. 124–5, 130–1.   [197] *Reasonableness*, pp. 87, 90, 92.   [198] *Reasonableness*, p. 94.

the obligation is founded on the law being the will of the omnipotent creator.[199] However, when Locke argues this way, he standardly adds, as a traditional voluntarist would not, reference to God's rewards and punishments. Thus, the theory of obligation as well is neither pure voluntarism nor pure hedonism but what I have called penalism.

Locke now turns from the pagan philosophers to the rationalist tradition in Christendom. Christian philosophers have come closer to demonstrating ethics than the pre-Christians, but this is not because, as they assume, they have an independent rule of reason to test moral principles. It is rather because their first principles are derived from Revelation. We grow up with the Gospel from the cradle. It seems 'natural' to us and we take it for 'unquestionable truths'. Rationalists think they have discovered the foundations of morality, but they only 'confirm' Revelation. We would be lost without it. Revelation is the foundation of reason, of what we take to be 'self-evident':[200]

A great many things which we have been bred up in the belief of, from our cradles, (and are notions grown familiar, and, as it were, natural to us, under the Gospel) we take for unquestionable obvious truths and easily demonstrable; without considering how long we might have been in doubt or ignorance of them, had Revelation been silent. And many are beholden to Revelation, who do not acknowledge it. It is no diminishing to Revelation, that reason gives its suffrage too to the truths Revelation has discovered. But it is our mistake to think that because reason confirms them to us, we had the first certain knowledge of them from thence; and in that clear evidence we now possess them. The contrary is manifest . . .

Thus, God spreads Christianity by the same mode of governance as other opinions are spread. Jesus revealed the providential apparatus, and it slowly spread and sank in as people considered its force.[201] Even Islam is an offshoot of this historical process.[202] It became part of European education, thus enforcing it with the humanist apparatus, and so gradually thinking and acting in accordance with the Gospel has become 'second nature', the foundation of our rationality.[203] What the Enlightenment, prefigured in Toland, called reasonable is just acquired dispositions to think and act in

---

[199] *Essay* 1.3.5–6; 'Voluntas', 1693, in von Leyden, p. 72; 'Of Ethick in General', p. 130; *Reasonableness*, pp. 89–90.

[200] *Reasonableness*, pp. 88, 90–1. Compare 'Faith and Reason', in von Leyden, pp. 275–80.

[201] *Reasonableness*, pp. 93–4, 92, 86.   [202] *Reasonableness*, p. 86.

[203] Compare *Essay* 1.3.22, 1.4.9: 'if the Fear of absolute and irresistible Power set it [the idea of God] on upon the Mind, the *Idea* is likely to sink the deeper, and spread the farther'.

accordance with Scripture. Hence the title: the *Reasonableness of Christianity*. The rationalist, whether the Thomist-scholastic or the new deist, is inside the language-game: he or she takes for granted the principles and ways of acting that the voluntarist explains as having been laid down by the normal operation of the juridical apparatus. For Locke, then, the providential juridical apparatus governs conduct, laying down its own causal and rational grounds of obedience as it proceeds.[204]

When Locke writes in the *Reasonableness* that the self-evident principles on which Christian philosophers base their demonstrations come from Scripture, he is thinking, I believe, of the non-trivial, demonstrable principles advanced in the *Essay*. The sample of demonstrably certain, non-analytic knowledge he presents is precisely the providential apparatus:[205] 'He also that hath the idea of an intelligent, but frail and weak Being, made by and depending on another, who is eternal, omnipotent, perfectly wise and good, will as certainly know that man is to honour, fear and obey God, as that the Sun shines when he sees it.' This is repeated to illustrate his non-syllogistic form of demonstration and then it is put forward as the foundation of demonstrable ethics.[206] Although the existence of an omnipotent, creating God can be demonstrated by reason, experience, and reflection alone, his providence and laws cannot, according to Locke and voluntarists generally.[207] Nor can Christian ethics be deduced from scholastic maxims: "'Tis from Revelation we have received it [Christianity], and without Revelation these *Maxims* had never been able to help us to it.'[208] But, once we see that the Christian rationalist is starting from revealed providentialism, it is possible to draw some conclusions about natural law. Specifically, it is possible to deduce the principle that mankind ought to be preserved from the providential premises; this can be confirmed by Revelation and by observation of early culture. A basic set of rights and obligations can then be derived from this one law within its juridical framework, as Locke shows in the *Two Treatises of Government* and as I have argued elsewhere, thus justifying and giving a normative structure to the seventeenth-century politics of preservation.[209]

---

[204] *Reasonableness*, pp. 87–92.    [205] *Essay*, 4.13.3.
[206] *Essay* 4.17.4, 4.3.18.    [207] *Essay* 4.10.    [208] *Essay* 4.7.2.
[209] The basic premise that mankind ought to be preserved is deduced from the providential apparatus by Locke first in 1681, 'Preservation' (August 1681), MS Locke f. 5, pp. 88–91, in King, vol. 1, pp. 228–30. This is worked out in the *Two Treatises of Government*, book 2, section 6. See James Tully, *A Discourse on Property* (Cambridge, Cambridge University Press, 1980). Preservation is said to enjoy universal consent in 'Of Ethick in General' (p. 125), and to be the fundamental moral principle in *Education* (116) and the *Two Treatises* (2.135).

Nietzsche is thought to be the first to suggest that some of the processes of rationalization in thought and action that we call modernity,
which are now habitual, are the continuation of Christianity by other
means.[210] This hypothesis has been supported by the work of
Michael Foster, Francis Oakley, Robert Hooykaas, and a new
generation of historians of science and politics.[211] They specify,
however, that it is a particular type of Christianity which lies at the
seventeenth-century foundations of modern science and politics,
voluntarism, and that voluntarism is the theological expression of
the creative God of Revelation. What this study seems to suggest is
that Locke and some of his contemporaries were aware that this process was taking place.

Once the foundational nature of Scripture is understood, it is
unnecessary and irrelevant to demonstrate ethics, because the Gospel
provides a 'perfect body of ethics': 'reason may be excused from that
enquiry, since she may find man's duty clearer and easier in Revelation
than in herself'.[212] How do we know Scripture is true? As we have
seen, the assessment of the evidence for Scripture being a divine
Revelation in accordance with the new grounds of probability shows
that it is probably a divine Revelation, and thus rational to believe.
This probability is in turn sufficient, given the overwhelming
pleasures and pains of heaven and hell, to provide reason and
motivation to become Christians. But, first, how does one know that
what God says is true, since we have no independent criterion?
Locke says we know solely in virtue of its being the word of God.[213]
When Thomas Burnet responded to the *Essay* by claiming Locke was
a voluntarist, as the third Earl of Shaftesbury was to do more famously,
and challenging Locke to make it explicit, he put this question of
truth to him.[214] Locke replied in a brief appendix to his first response
to Bishop Stillingfleet. This response is standardly taken to be a case
of Locke dodging the question.[215] But he clearly answers the question and, in so doing, admits his voluntarism. He says that God does
not lie, because lying is a weakness. Thus, truth follows from

[210] F. Nietzsche, 'What is the meaning of ascetic ideals?', in *On the Genealogy of Morals*,
section 27, p. 160.
[211] See above, nn. 93, 95 and Merchant, pp. 192–235.
[212] Locke to Molyneux, 5 April 1696, *Correspondence*, vol. 5, 2059. Compare letter to
Molyneux, vol. 4, 1309.
[213] *Reasonableness*, p. 92, *Essay* 4.18.10.
[214] Thomas Burnet, *Remarks Upon An Essay Concerning Humane Understanding* (1697). For
the third Earl of Shaftesbury see n. 131 above.
[215] See Oakley (1966), p. 106.

omnipotence. Any law of the almighty is for that very reason true.[216]

This voluntarist thesis that truth *is* the word of the most powerful is driven home in the late work *A Discourse of Miracles* (1702). The problem here is how to know that the miracles, that are evidence for the belief that Scripture is the word of God, are God's work. The criterion for an extraordinary event being a miracle from God is 'the carrying with [an extraordinary event] the marks of a greater power than appears in opposition to it'.[217] Therefore, God's omnipotence is the ultimate ground of both the truth of and assent to Christianity:[218]

His power being known to have no equal, always will, and always may be, safely depended on, to show its superiority in indicating his authority, and maintaining every truth that he hath revealed. So that the marks of a superior power accompanying it, always have, and always will be, visible and sure guide to divine Revelation; by which men may conduct themselves in their examining of revealed religions, and be satisfied which they ought to receive as coming from God.

This voluntarism runs through the other two juridical apparatus: the sovereign civil power decrees and enforces what is and is not a crime; the community wills and enforces virtue and vice.[219]

The second practice of governing is the use of the humanist apparatus in the education of elites. This is laid out in *Some Thoughts Concerning Education* and *On the Conduct of the Understanding*. The aim is to inculcate habits of probabilistic reasoning and virtuous behaviour; habits that will replace the 'old custom'. The programme is based on the new view of human nature: the gentleman's son is considered 'only as white paper, or wax, to be moulded and fashioned as one pleases'.[220] The governor's objective is 'to fashion the carriage, and form the mind; [to] settle in his pupil good habits, and the principles of virtue and wisdom'.[221] The key to good habits is not the memorization of rules, as it had been, but practice, because 'As in

---

[216] *An Answer to Remarks Upon an Essay Concerning Humane Understanding*, in *Works*, vol. 4, pp. 186–9: 'Whether an infinitely powerful and wise Being be veracious or no; unless falsehood be in such reputation ... that ... lying [is] to be no mark of weakness and folly' (p. 187); 'Whoever sincerely acknowledges any law to be the law of God, cannot fail to acknowledge also, that it hath all the reason and ground that a just and wise law can or ought to have' (p. 188).

[217] *A Discourse of Miracles*, in *Works*, vol. 9, pp. 256–65, p. 259.

[218] *A Discourse of Miracles*, in *Essay* 4.19.15, 4.16.13; *Reasonableness*, pp. 86–7.

[219] 'Of Ethic in General', pp. 130–2. This is one of the major themes of the *Essay*: 2.28.14, 2.32.11, 17, 3.5, 3.9.8–11, 3.10, 3.11.25. The doctrine is summarized at 4.4.10. See Tully, *Discourse*, pp. 8–27.

[220] *Education*, 216, p. 325.     [221] *Education*, 94, p. 198.

the body, so in the mind; practice makes it what it is', and 'most even of those excellencies, which are looked on as natural endowments, will be found, when examined into more narrowly, to be the product of exercise, and to be raised to that pitch only by repeated actions'.[222] By 'practice' he means the continual repetition of mental and physical behaviour until it becomes habitual and pleasurable.

This assault on the Renaissance techniques of memorizing rules, and its replacement with education as habit formation by repetition and drill, by 'exercises', is part of a much broader dispersion of techniques of discipline by drill throughout Europe from roughly the time of the revolutionary reform of training in the Dutch army in the 1590s.[223] The second transformation marked by Locke's practice theory of education is the replacement of corporal punishments by praise and blame as the major techniques of habit formation and reformation.[224] Of course, he still advocates the use of the whip, but not as often as before. The rewards and punishments are esteem and disgrace. Once love of credit and apprehension of disgrace are instilled, these can be manipulated to train the child.[225] The very first step is thus to cultivate a love of reputation in the pupil; this then provides the basis for subtle, detailed, and closely supervised governing of drill and repetition.[226]

As we have seen, the first idea to be imprinted on the mind is the providential apparatus, the foundation of virtue.[227] Then, Christian virtues, with a strong stress on the mercantile and neo-stoic virtues of discipline and industry, are impressed by constant repetition and praise and blame.[228] Mental habits are formed in the same manner. Just as in the training of animals, the mind can be made 'obedient to discipline' and 'pliant to reason' and so 'habits woven into the very

---

[222] John Locke, *Of the Conduct of the Understanding*, in *Works*, vol. 3, 4, p. 214. Locke wrote this as an addition to the fourth edition of the *Essay*, but it was not published until 1706. For the role of practice forming mental and physical habits, compare 28, pp. 255–7, and *Education*, dedication, 2, 10, 17, 32, 41, 42, 64, 66, 70, 94, 105, 185.

[223] In addition to Foucault, 1976, pp. 135–95, see the important article and review of the literature on this issue from Weber onwards by Murray Field, *The Structure of Violence* (Beverly Hills, Sage Publications, 1977), pp. 169–204.

[224] See Margaret J. M. Ezell, 'John Locke's images of childhood: early eighteenth century response to *Some Thoughts Concerning Education*', *Eighteenth Century Studies*, 17, 2 (Winter 1983–4), 139–56, 152–3.

[225] *Education*, 56, pp. 52–3: '*Esteem* and *Disgrace* are, of all others, the most powerful Incentives to the Mind, when once it is brought to relish them. If you can once get into Children a Love of Credit, and an Apprehension of Shame and Disgrace, you have put into them the true Principle, which will constantly work, and incline them to the right.' Compare 57, p. 153.  [226] *Education*, 61, pp. 155–6.

[227] *Education*, 136, pp. 241–2. Compare 61, p. 156.

[228] *Education*, 33, 38, 42, 45, 64, 70, 103–5, 110, 185.

principles of his nature'.[229] Natural philosophy is taught by studying
the various 'hypotheses', which are probable, not certain. Since the
sciences only treat of body, the other half of nature, spirit, should be
taught by inculcating the Bible, preferably in the form of an
epitome. This should precede and provide the foundation for
natural philosophy.[230] Theology in the juridical sense is the basis for
all other areas of knowledge as well.[231] The fundamental principle of
politics and morality is the preservation of mankind. The best training for applying this principle in politics is the practice of caring for
animals.[232]

In the *Conduct* Locke lays out the central mental habits. He says
that a person's ability to reason varies in accordance with his
occupational practices, with, of course, the labourer on the bottom
and the person with this new education on top.[233] The habit of
reasoning with probabilities is to be learned early by use and exercise
in mathematics and bookkeeping and by studying Chillingworth's
sermons.[234] The two primary habits of suspension and examination
are taught in order to break old prejudices. Locke suggests developing an 'indifferency' to assent, like the sceptic, then a passion to
close with the truth after examination. Since 'tyranny' of passion is
the greatest problem, only counter-passions, formed by detailed
training, can guard against or cure it.[235]

Although not everyone has the time and leisure for this, everyone
can learn their calling and the rudiments of the after-life by exercises
on Sunday. The basics of theology, God, duty and the possibility of a
future life can be absorbed by everyone. As Locke stresses in the
*Reasonableness*, Christianity is a simple ethic for the poor who labour;
an ethic of discipline, industry, honesty, and sobriety. All that is
required is the Gospels, training on Sundays, and practice, as the
Huguenot peasants have proven in adverse conditions in France.[236]
The simplified and austere neo-stoical Christianity renders casuistical
authorities unnecessary. The final step in this direction, which
played such an enormous role in the eighteenth century, is the argument that there is not one right answer in any moral situation, and

[229] *Education*, 34, p. 138; 42, p. 146.
[230] *Education*, 190–4.
[231] *Conduct*, 4, p. 214.
[232] *Education*, 116, pp. 225–7.
[233] *Conduct*, 3, pp. 208–13.
[234] *Conduct*, 6–7, pp. 222–5; *Education*, 188, 210–11, pp. 296, 319–21.
[235] *Conduct*, 11–12, pp. 230–3; 45, pp. 284–8.
[236] *Conduct*, 9, pp. 225–7; *Reasonableness*, p. 98.

that therefore God rewards effort and sincerity, not sophistication.[237] One's conduct depends solely on one's tutor, as Pamela observed, or, as Locke calls him, one's 'governor'.

The humanist technique is thus used to educate by habituation and to implant the providential apparatus. To borrow a phrase from Thomas Kuhn, it is a 'disciplinary matrix' which, through love of reputation, reproduces itself, governing even the new elites it trains and legitimates. In the eighteenth century this practice of education, premised on the pupil as malleable raw material, gradually became more popular than either the Augustinian model of the pupil as fallen or the model of the pupil as innately good.[238] In addition to the schools and dissenting academics, it was carried forward in the crazy-quilt of practices set up in the late seventeenth century to moralize and discipline all segments of the population, not only the gentry, by organizations such as the Society for Promoting Christian Knowledge.[239]

The third practice of governing is the legal apparatus of the early modern state. I want to look at this in the case of Locke's report, to the Board of Trade in 1697, on reform of the poor law system. The problem the Board faced was 'the multiplying of the poor' and, consequently, 'the increase of the tax for their maintenance'.[240] Gregory King had just submitted his famous report showing that the majority of the population was dependent to some extent on parish poor relief. In addition, others published calculations of the increase in poor rates since 1660. Since the Restoration, over seventy proposals had been put forward to correct the system of houses of correction and work. This system had been used since the 1550s not only, as earlier, to support the surplus population but to 'correct' and 'reform' it in 'virtue' and 'industry'. Indeed, many of the early houses of correction and work were disbanded monasteries in which monastic

---

[237] See Letters to Denis Grenville, *Correspondence*, vol. 1, 328, 374, 426; *Essay* 2.21.47, 3.10.12. The argument that sincerity, not true knowledge, is the key Christian virtue is one of the main arguments of *A Letter Concerning Toleration*. It is first introduced by Locke to justify toleration in *An Essay Concerning Toleration* (1667). It leads to Bayle's famous paradox in the *Pensées diverses*. For the role of sincerity in the eighteenth century, see Leon Guilhamet, *The Sincere Ideal* (Montreal, McGill-Queen's University Press, 1974). [238] Ezell, pp. 140–2.
[239] See Hundert (part 1, n. 9); Dudley Bahlman, *The Moral Revolution of 1688* (New Haven, Yale University Press, 1957); Leo Radzinowicz, *A History of English Criminal Law and its Administration from 1750* (2 vols., New York, Macmillan, 1956), vol. 2, pp. 1–29; M. G. Jones, *The Charity School Movements* (London, Archon, 1964 (1938)).
[240] John Locke, *A Report of the Board of Trade to the Lords Justices Respecting the Relief and Employment of the Poor* (1697), in H. R. Fox Bourne, *The Life of John Locke* (2 vols., London, 1876), vol. 2, pp. 377–91, 377–8.

discipline continued. The system fell into disrepair during the Civil War and early Restoration. By the time Locke wrote there were roughly 200 workhouses spread throughout the country.[241] Here is his solution.

The cause of the problem is not 'scarcity of provisions nor want of employment' but rather 'nothing else but the relaxation of discipline and the corruption of manners'. This is so because virtue is always joined to industry and vice to idleness. He then lays out a vast scheme to use the disciplining practices of the law, the Royal navy, the houses of correction and work, the compulsory apprenticeship system, deportation, and control of travel by passes and badges to make the poor docile with respect to the law and useful in employment.

There are three classes of people on relief: those who can do nothing towards their own support; those who can do something but not all; and those who could be self-maintaining yet have either large families or claim they cannot find work and engage in begging. The first remedy for the last sort of 'begging drones' who live upon others' labour is the strict enforcement of the Elizabethan poor laws. These provide for parish houses of correction, punishment of vagabonds, compelling the able-bodied to work, apprenticing children, providing for the impotent paupers, and enforcing poor rates by parish overseers, guardians, and justices of the peace. In addition, a new law is required. All able-bodied men over fourteen and under fifty caught begging outside their parish in the maritime counties without passes are to be seized and taken to the nearest seaport. They are to be kept at 'hard labour' until one of his majesty's ships arrives and then placed in three years' service 'under strict discipline', at soldier's pay (minus subsistence cost) and punished with death for desertion. If the beggar is maimed or over fifty, he is to be sent to the closest house of correction for three years of hard labour.[242]

To upgrade the houses of correction the master should receive his pay from what the 'inmates' produce. The local justice of the peace is to inspect them and if any are 'not at all mended by the discipline of the place', is to order longer and more severe discipline. Nobody is to be dismissed without 'manifest proof of amendment, the end for

---

[241] For a survey of the major proposals, see F. M. Eden, *The State of the Poor* (3 vols., London, 1797). Also, Dorothy Marshall, *The English Poor in the Eighteenth Century* (London, Routledge & Kegan Paul, 1926); E. M. Leonard, *The Early History of English Poor Relief* (Cambridge, Cambridge University Press, 1900).

[242] *Report*, p. 378. All following quotations from the *Report* unless otherwise noted.

which he was sent'. If a beggar has a forged travel pass, he shall lose his ear the first time and 'be transported to the plantations, as in the case of felony' for a second offence. This means in effect, as Locke points out in the *Two Treatises*, that he has the status of a slave.[243]

If a female over fourteen is found begging outside her parish, she is to be returned and the officer rewarded out of her poor relief. If she is caught a second time, or is more than five miles from her parish the first time, she is to be taken to the closest house of correction for three months' hard work and 'due correction'. Boys and girls under fourteen caught begging out of their parish are to be sent to the workhouse, 'soundly whipped', and worked until evening. A second offence, or being more than five miles out of their parish, is to be met with six weeks of hard labour in the workhouse.

The local parishioners are compelled to employ those who claim they cannot find work and to give them a small wage. If these men refuse to work, they are to be placed aboard one of his majesty's ships for three years, their wages going to the parish.

For women with children and the elderly, 'being decayed from their full strength', part-time work is to be organized in woollen and other manufacture. This 'shows us what is the true and proper relief of the poor'. It consists in 'finding work for them and taking care they do not live like drones upon the labour of others'.

The main targets of this proposal are the children of the labouring poor, who are a 'burden to the parish' and are 'maintained in idleness'. Children of three to fourteen are to be sent to working schools in each parish, thus freeing the mother for labour. The children will be better provided for than at home, 'and from infancy be inured to work, which is no small consequence to the making of them sober and industrious all their lives after'. Diet will consist in a 'belly full of bread daily' and, 'if it be thought needful, a little warm water-gruel in winter'. These schools will thus reduce the parish-relief and, with proper management, aim for maintaining themselves out of the products of child labour. Locke's friend Thomas Firmin was experimenting with making his workhouses profitable throughout this period. Children will come to work because, echoing the *Essay*, the alternative is starvation.[244] Various kinds of manufacturing appropriate to local needs are to be instituted. Another advantage is that the children 'may be obliged to come constantly to church every Sunday . . . whereby they may be brought to some sense of religion'. At the age of fourteen, the disciplined and industrious young men

[243] *Two Treatises*, 2.23.     [244] *Essay* 2.21.58.

and women are to be placed in compulsory apprenticeship with local manufacturers and landlords until the age of twenty-three. Locke then outlines an elaborate system of managers, guardians, overseers, beadles, and justices of the peace which, by a series of interlocking monetary and legal rewards and punishments, makes it in the interest of each to enforce the whole process of reform and habituation.

Locke's proposal is similar to about 100 others written between 1660 and 1760. In addition, Locke wrote notes on a system of work, relief, and correction for colonial settlement.[245] His reform proposal was not instituted nationally, but it was applied almost immediately in Bristol and it continued to influence projects to reform the poor throughout the eighteenth century. Indeed, it continued to be praised until the time of the Webbs. The importance of the document is that it displays the objectives of the new mode of governing: to deconstruct old customary ways of life and to produce new ones. The aim is to use the law, the navy, corporal punishment, the threats of divine punishment, economic incentives, and the activity of repetitious labour, from age three onwards, to fabricate an individual who is habituated to docility and to useful labour. It should not be forgotten that the overseers and guardians were drawn into this system as well. Further, the governing of each individual is integrated into the collective welfare-warfare policy of increasing the strength of the mercantile state by means of passes, badges, apprenticeship, the use of the navy and the type of work done in each workhouse. It is out of these houses and their experimentation in moulding human behaviour that many of the early factories, reformatories, and public schools developed.[246]

Locke's proposal was republished in 1790 with a preface that captures the spirit of this juridical practice of governance:[247]

the object of republishing [Locke's report] is to explain, and, if possible, procure strength and permanency for a system of parochial occonomy, congenial to the sentiments of Mr. Locke, who appears from the whole tenor of

---

[245] See Ernesto De Marchi, 'Locke's *Atlantis*', *Political Studies*, 3, 2 (June 1955), 164–5. Part of the journal entries is reprinted in Charles Bastide, *John Locke, ses théories politiques et leur influence en Angleterre* (Geneva, 1970 (1906)), Appendice 1, 'Les projets de réforme sociale de Locke', pp. 377–9.
[246] Austin van der Slice, 'Elizabethan houses of correction', *Journal of the American Institute of Criminal Law and Criminology*, 27 (May–June 1936–March–April 1937), 45–67; E. Furniss, *The Position of the Labourer in a System of Nationalism* (New York, A. M. Kelley, 1965 (1920)); Rusche and Kirchheimer, pp. 24–52; Sidney Pollard, *The Genesis of Scientific Management* (Cambridge, Mass., Harvard University Press, 1965), pp. 163–97; Sidney and Beatrice Webb, *English Local Government: English Poor Law History*, pt 1, *The Old Poor Law* (London, Longmans, Green & Co., 1927), pp. 102–20.    [247] John Locke, *Report* (London, 1790), preface, p. viii.

his reasoning in that memorial, to be convinced that rewards and punishments, and the mixing habits of industry with principles of religious duties, were the best and surest means of effecting that reformation in the manners of the people, which in those days was judged essential to the strength and safety of the nation; and which in our time, from the great increase of profligacy and dissoluteness of the lower order of people, is become a more pressing object of national concern.

The work of Michael Ignatieff and Michel Foucault has thrown light on the dispersion of these techniques of governing in eighteenth-century England and France.[248] Foucault argued that the social science disciplines that explain and are employed to administer and reform the behaviour of individuals and of populations of modern states have their roots in the diverse reform projects of the early modern period. He distinguished this disciplinarian power and knowledge from juridical power and knowledge because the former refers behaviour to a norm or statistical regularity, and adjusts it relative to criteria of normality and abnormality. In contrast, the juridical refers to the law and criteria of legality and illegality and is primarily repressive. However, it should by now be clear that the techniques of reform and behavioural fashioning of the disciplines developed partly out of a long tradition of using the law to reform, and not simply to repress. Secondly, if we ask in what conceptual framework the concept of a law of human behaviour as a statistical regularity emerged, the answer is the juridical combination of a voluntaristic theory of observed regularities in nature and the probability theory that we see with Boyle and Pascal. And we should not be surprised to see systematic attempts to explain, predict, and administer people in accordance with these two forms of knowledge, and with the techniques of the juridical apparatus, by political economists such as John Graunt, William Petty, Charles Davenant, John Cary, and Pieter de la Court.[249]

'True politics', Locke states, summarizing the juridical mode of domination, 'I look on as a part of moral philosophy, which is nothing but the art of conducting men right in society and supporting a

[248] M. Ignatieff, *A Just Measure of Pain: The Penitentiary in the Industrial Revolution 1750–1850* (New York, Pantheon, 1978). For the use of Locke's providential and humanist governors in eighteenth-century education see Jones, especially p. 5.

[249] John Graunt, *Natural and Political Observations ... made upon the Bills of Morality* (1662); William Petty, *Political Arithmetick, or a discourse concerning the extent and value of land, peoples, buildings...* (1690), Charles Davenant, *An Essay on the Probable Methods of Making a People Gainers in the Balance of Trade* (1699); John Cary, *An Essay Towards Regulating the Trade and Employing the Poor of this Kingdom* (1717); Pieter de la Court, *Considérations sur L'Etat, ou la Balance Politique* (1662). See Michael Hunter, *Science and Society in Restoration England* (Cambridge, Cambridge University Press, 1981), pp. 118–34.

community amongst its neighbours.'[250] Section 116 of *Education* illustrates one further aspect of this new politics of reform. As we have seen, the practice of toleration was intended, *inter alia*, to undercut the religious motive for warfare. In section 116 Locke moves against the second great early modern war motive – the Renaissance humanists' glorification of warfare and the identification of military achievements with heroic virtue. This motivation is the product of two habit-forming practices: teaching children delight in inflicting pain and, secondly, the central position of the history of battles and martial virtue in the humanists' curriculum. 'By these steps unnatural cruelty is planted in us.' These are to be replaced by practices that instill habits of care and compassion and an overall concern with preservation. In section 71 he stresses that the population must still be trained to fight wars, but now in a more disciplined, controlled manner – where war is a rational instrument of the policy of preserving the state in a condition of international rivalry, not an arena where virtuous acts are performed and glory achieved. Thus, the new model of governance involves, and is perhaps best exemplified in, the incremental bureaucratization of violence in this period and the integration of warfare into the rationalizing state.[251]

## THE PENALIZED SELF

I want to ask, finally, what kind of self is produced by subjection to a way of governing action that aims at forming habitual mental and physical conduct. The answer is provided by Locke himself, who added an important chapter on personal identity to the second edition of the *Essay*.

Locke located the identity of the person or self solely in consciousness, and not in substance, thus making his most radical departure from his predecessors. The self or person is constituted by consciousness alone, and this is consciousness of sensations and perceptions. The '*Self*', he writes, 'is that conscious thinking thing ... which is sensible, or conscious of Pleasure and Pain, capable of Happiness or misery, and so is concern'd for its *self*, as far as the consciousness extends.'[252] Although the 'person' or self is conscious of all sensations of pleasure and pain, it is constituted by consciousness

---

[250] Draft letter to the Countess of Peterborough (1697), MS Locke c. 24, fols. 196–7, in *Education*, pp. 395–6.
[251] See William H. McNeill, *The Pursuit of Power* (Chicago, University of Chicago Press, 1981), pp. 117–85.    [252] *Essay* 2.27.17.

of voluntary actions; that is, those actions the self is conscious of having performed. Secondly, the concern for self that is part of consciousness is primarily concern for rewards and punishments, pleasures and pains, attached to voluntary actions. Therefore, he concludes, 'self' only belongs to voluntary agents capable of a law: it 'is a Forensick Term appropriating Actions and their Merit; and so belongs only to intelligent agents capable of a Law, and Happiness and Misery'. This subjectivity is founded in the constitutive 'concern' or uneasiness of self for happiness.[253] 'All which is founded in a concern for Happiness, the unavoidable concomitant of consciousness, that which is conscious of Pleasure and Pain, desiring that that Self, that is conscious, should be happy.'

Thus, the penalized self is for Locke the ontological self. As he says, 'In this *Personal Identity* is founded all the Right and Justice of Reward and Punishment; Happiness and Misery, being that, for which every one is concerned for *himself*.' On judgment day everyone 'shall receive his doom', on the basis of this self that is the consciousness of having performed voluntary actions for which he can be held accountable.[254] Therefore, the self which is concerned about, and thinks and acts with continual reference to the juridical apparatus, is the ontological self: 'And to receive Pleasure or Pain, i.e. Reward or Punishment, on account of any such Action, is all one, as to be made happy or miserable in its first being.'[255]

The self whose thought and action is always guided by a concern to be rewarded by the juridical apparatus and to avoid its punishment is the kind of self God created. Locke could assume that this penalized self was constituted prior to the juridical apparatus that governs and subjects it. We should ask, rather, if this self, so familiar to us in its relative regularity and law-abidingness, is not a product of centuries of subjection to juridical governance. Is it not a form of subjectivity that continues to be imposed on us in virtue of the juridical mode of governance being invested in our social practices? This is a regime that not only subjects us in our everyday practices but also governs even modern states, as Hobbes dreamed, like a 'mortal God'. For what is said to be the fundamental governor of the conduct of the modern world but the apparatus of deterrence, with its threat of nuclear annihilation for misconduct?[256]

---

[253] *Essay* 2.27.26. Compare 2.27.9, 14, 25.
[254] *Essay* 2.27.18.    [255] *Essay* 2.27.26.
[256] I would like to thank John Dunn, Guy Laforest, Edmund Leites, David Norton, Quentin Skinner, and Charles Taylor for their helpful comments, and Vivian Pelkonen for typing several drafts. I am pleased to acknowledge the assistance of the Social Sciences Research Subcommittee of McGill University.

# 2

◁ ══════════════════════════════════════ ▷

# Laxity and liberty in seventeenth-century English political thought

MARGARET SAMPSON

These Cases of Conscience have spoyled the World[1]

by these doctrines a man is taught how to be an honest thief, . . . and by these we may not only deceive our brother, but the law; and not the laws only, but God also.[2]

Since their first appearance in English in the seventeenth century, the words 'casuist' and 'casuistry' have generally carried the pejorative connotation, namely 'Subtility of wit with a chiverell conscience'; the 'subtill distinctions of the most learned', exploited in such a way as to make 'foule sinnes to passe along as no sinnes'.[3] That only 'the Want of Conscience, makes the Case of Conscience' became something of a commonplace; 'Men usually set themselves to justifie what they do and love to do', exploiting their reason in order to 'argue and dispute in defence of those lusts which they are loath to part with'.[4] So too in seventeenth-century French usage 'casuiste' and 'casuistique' came to imply sophistry in the service of sin, 'des excuses à la mauvaise cupidité', 'raffiner' sins out of existence, the 'art of cavilling with God', in Pierre Bayle's *Dictionnaire historique et critique* of 1696.[5] 'Pleaders in the court of conscience find out more distinctions and subtleties than the pleaders in the civil law-courts',

Quotations from French works are given in their contemporary English translations where possible.

[1] [Thomas Pittis,] *A Private Conference, Between a Rich Alderman and a Poor Country Vicar, made Publick* (London, 1670), p. 21.
[2] Jeremy Taylor, *Dissuasive from Popery* (London, 1664), in *The Whole Works* (London, 1849), vol. VI, p. 274.
[3] R[ichard] B[ernard,] *The Isle of Man*, seventh edition (London, 1630), pp. 27, 105: 'opinions how a friend to sinne'.
[4] Samuel Shaw, *The True Christian's test* (London, 1682), p. 321. Edward Reynolds, *The Lords Property in his Redeemed People* (London, 1660), p. 12.
[5] Antoine Godeau, *Cours Complet de Morale* (Lyon, 1756), vol. I, p. 4; [Godefroi Hermant,] *Apologie pour Monsieur Arnauld* (n. p., 1644), p. 180; Pierre Bayle, *A General Dictionary, Historical and Critical* (London, 1738), vol. VII, p. 196.

72

Bayle complained; morality ought instead to be the simple product of 'good sense, and . . . the light which the reading of the gospel darts into the mind'.

Bayle's definition occurred as a footnote to his entry on St Ignatius Loyola referring to 'the horrid depravity' characteristic of Jesuit casuistry. His authority, unsurprisingly, was Blaise Pascal's pseudonymous *Lettres provinciales* of 1656–7, which had 'set upon the Jesuites Moralls as giving scope to Liberty' as a somewhat desperate last resort by the French Jansenists in their struggle to defend an Augustinian doctrine of grace against the 'Molinism' or pelagianism of the Counter-Reformation church, associated with the Jesuits in particular.[6] In the face of ecclesiastical censure, Pascal's fun at the expense of 'la théologie morale des Jésuites et Nouveaux casuistes' was intended by his mentor, Antoine Arnauld, to snatch victory from the jaws of defeat by taking the controversy out of the arcane realms of soteriological debate at the Sorbonne and into the salons of polite society.[7] Pascal entertained his sophisticated audience by adopting the naive stance of the amateur towards the science of casuistry: 'without troubling himself with opposing Casuist to Casuist, he confounds them pel-mel. . . undertaking to render them all alike odious and despicable' by creating the impression that excuses had been found for almost every sin against divine and civil law.[8] The immediate literary success enjoyed by the *Provinciales*, which were taken by Perrault as evidence for the superiority of modern over ancient prose, was followed up by the Jansenists in a much less entertaining publication, *La Morale pratique des Jésuites*, of 1669 (translated into English a year later), which succeeded in obtaining papal condemnation of sixty-five laxist propositions, duly reported in England as *A Decree Made at Rome, 2 March 1679, Condemning Some Opinions of the Jesuits and other Casuists*.[9] By the end of the century, a

---

[6] [Blaise Pascal,] *Les Provinciales, ou Les Lettres écrites par Louis de Montalte à un provincial de ses amis et aux R. R. P. P. Jésuites* (Paris, 1656–7); [Jacques Nouet, Francois Annat,] *An Answer to the Provinciall Letters* (Paris, 1659) (translation by Martin Green of the French original of 1657). For an introduction to the Jansenist context of the work, see Walter Rex, *Pascal's Provincial Letters* (London, 1977), Jan Miel, *Pascal and Theology* (Baltimore, 1969), pp. 111–47, and Alexander Sedgwick, *Jansenism in Seventeenth-century France* (Charlottesville, 1977), chapter 3. For a hostile view, see the Abbé Maynard's *Les Provinciales et leur Réfutation* (Paris, 1851).

[7] [Antoine Arnauld,] *La théologie morale des Jésuites et nouveaux Casuistes* (Paris, 1643).

[8] [John Evelyn, translator,] τὸ μυστήριον τῆς 'Ανομίας. *Another Part of the Mystery of Jesuitism* (London, 1664), p. 171.

[9] Charles Perrault, *Paralelle des Anciens et des Modernes en ce qui regarde Eloquence*, second edition (Paris, 1694), vol. II, p. 122. The decree of Innocent XI condemning 'Laxismus' was republished by the Belgian Jansenists with ascriptions to Jesuit sources. See [Gilles Estrix,] *Refutatio Accusatoris Anonymi Damnatus ab Innocentio XI* (Moguntiae, 1679).

Jesuit critic of Pascal could acknowledge the 'terrible wound' which his 'extreamly well writ' *Provinciales* had dealt the reputation both of casuistry and of the Society of Jesus: 'never was there a diversion made to better purpose, nor with greater effect than this'.[10] Even today, Escobar, a Spanish Jesuit compiler of cases of conscience and butt of much of Pascal's humour, remains a synonym for 'equivocator' or 'prevaricator' in contemporary French dictionaries.[11]

Clearly, the French and English etymologies are not unrelated. In 1680, for example, the translator into English of a number of French Jansenist documents under the title *A Truth known to very Few: viz that the Jesuites are down-right compleat Atheists* included a definition of 'Casuistical doctrine' as that which 'makes sin to be no sin'. The Jansenists could not 'endure the name of Casuists', according to the Jesuit Jacques Nouet in his 1657 reply to Pascal, which was published in English in 1659. Only six months after Pascal had penned the eighteenth and last of his *Provinciales* in 1657, George Thomason had received the first English translation (according to Anthony à Wood, by John Davies of Kidwelly), revealingly subtitled *The Mysterie of Jesuitisme*, 'that they might the better please those ears, which itch to hear something against the Jesuites'.[12] A second edition 'with large additionalls' followed in the next year. In 1659 the editor (perhaps Henry Hammond) of *The Journall of all Proceedings Between the Jansenists and the Jesuits from the first coming abroad of the Provincial Letters* drew a sharp contrast between the legitimate study of 'Moral Divinity', concerned with the 'main conduct of Christian life', and the Jesuits' 'whole Libraries of Casuists', which 'openly and avowedly ... maintain Principles directly contrary to the Laws both of God and Man'.[13] In the same year both Richard Baxter and Samuel Clarke, themselves expert in 'Practical Divinity', recommended the Jansenians' 'book lately taught to speake English, called the *Mysterie of Jesuitisme*' as evidence for the corruption

[10] [Gabriel Daniel,] *Discourses of Cleander and Eudoxus on the Provincial Letters* (Cullen, 1694) (French original the same year), pp. 13, 9, 34.
[11] James Brodrick, *The Economic Morals of the Jesuits* (London, 1934), pp. 106–7; Antonius de Escobar, *Liber Theologiae Moralis, Viginti quatuor societatis Jesu* (Lugduni, 1659), sig. a8 r: 'If I often seem to adhere to more lax opinions it is not in order to define what I think but to explain what the Doctors could without an attack of conscience, set out for the purpose of allaying the fears of penitents.'
[12] [Nouet, Annat,] p. 59 and translator's preface, sig. A3 r. For a bibliographical guide to the controversy as it was followed in England, see Ruth Clark, *Strangers and Sojourners at Port-Royal* (Cambridge, 1932), pp. 101–13 and 278–83.
[13] P. Jansen, *De Blaise Pascal à Henry Hammond: Les Provinciales en Angleterre* (Paris, 1954), although Clark, p. 105 suggests that 'H.H.' may be the initials of Henry Holden.

emanating from the 'dunghills' of Roman casuistry.[14] A decade later the leading puritan divine John Owen claimed that there were 'very few... amongst us... who have not taken notice of the discourses and reports concerning Jansenisme from the neighbour Kingdom of France', taking comfort from the evidence therein not only of disunity within Roman Catholicism but also of the persistence within that church of an Augustinian 'system of Doctrines concerning the Grace of God, and the wills of men... agreeable unto the Scripture'. English Protestants learned also from Jansenist sources to interpret the casuistry of the Jesuits as part of a conspiracy to 'Increase... their own Interest in the Consciences, and over the outward concerns of men' for the 'promotion of their own Secular Interest and advantages'.[15] By contrast, Protestant 'Practical Treatises' were thought to 'press to the Duties of Holiness', 'which made Austin to say ... the more the better, so long as they are helps to Godlinesse'.[16]

By 1676, David Clarkson believed that English translations of Jansenist propaganda had become altogether too influential, deploring the consequence that 'the Society only [is] ... noted as the sinck, when the corruption is apparent everywhere'. His researches in Roman casuistry were designed to establish that 'the expedients they have to justifie all sin in the World and make it no sin' were not peculiar to the Jesuits but 'common and generally followed' and hence part of a much wider and more sinister conspiracy 'drawing the world into the bosom of the Popes Church and intangling it there by all the charms of such a Religion as dissolute persons would make for themselves'. Casuistry for Clarkson was a 'deadly Venome' conveyed to 'all sorts among them' by the practice of forced auricular confession.[17] The conspiracy theory had thus – as the Jesuit Gabriel Daniel noted with some satisfaction – succeeded even beyond the expectations of its Jansenist contrivers.[18]

The polemical victory of the Jansenists in rendering Jesuit casuistry

---

[14] Richard Baxter, *A Key for Catholicks, To open the Jugling of the Jesuits* (London, 1659), p. 58. Samuel Clarke, *Medulla Theologiae: or The Marrow of Divinity Contained in sundry Questions and Cases of Conscience* (London, 1659), 'To the Christian Reader'. See John Barker, *Strange Contrarieties: Pascal in England during the Age of Reason* (Montreal, 1975), pp. 14–15.

[15] John Owen, preface to Theophilus Gale, *The True Idea of Jansenisme, Both Historick and Dogmatick* (London, 1669).

[16] John Bartlet, *The Practical Christian* (London, 1670), sig. A5 r.

[17] [David Clarkson,] *The Practical Divinity of the papists. Discovered to be Destructive of Christianity and Mens Souls* (London, 1676), 'Advertisement to the Reader', and p. 413. See in particular chapter IX: 'What Crimes are no sins in their account'.     [18] Daniel, p. 13.

for ever more synonymous with moral laxity in the public mind
owed more than a little to the ineptitude of the earliest Jesuit defences
of their casuistry.[19] Pirot's *Apology* for even the most outlandish doctrines attributed to the Society seemed only to prove Pascal's case
for him, occasioning many 'grave and authentic censures' which
were duly reported in England.[20] The publication of pseudonymous
works allegedly by non-Jesuits and defending the same doctrines was
a ruse which was quickly discovered, again with unfortunate consequences for the Jesuits.[21] It was apparent to Daniel that what was
required was not so much a defence of individual doctrines divorced
from their casuistical context as an explanation of that context
addressed to the same lay audience so successfully tapped by Pascal.
Casuistry, Daniel laboured to establish, was intended not for the
spiritual improvement of the laity but for the pastoral use of the
clergy; the criteria by which it should be judged were not those
appropriate to exhortatory or devotional literature but rather those
of jurisprudence. This contrast between the rhetorical and the juristic
contexts was unwittingly revealed by Clarkson in the course of his
diatribe against casuistry: 'Covetousness is one of these capital
crimes, which in general they heavily ... inveigh against, as most
pernicious: yet when they come to direct conscience, and give particular rules for practice; it is shrunk into a harmless venial.'[22] Like
the civil law, Daniel explained, casuistry was concerned not to
recommend standards of conduct but to judge particular instances
of conduct after the event: 'the question here, is, not what is most
perfect; but only what is lawful; nor that which is counsell'd but that
which is forbidden'. Just as in civil law circumstances could alter the
nature of a crime, so in casuistry they could determine whether a sin
be considered mortal or venial. In neither instance did the recognition of extenuating circumstances create incentives to wrongdoing, for 'cases' were only to be consulted *post facto*, when

[19] See A. Degert, 'Réaction des *Provinciales* sur la théologie morale en France', *Bulletin
de Littérature Ecclésiastique* (1913), 400–20.

[20] [Georges Pirot,] *Apologie pour les Casuistes. Contre les Calomnies des Jansenistes* (Cologne,
1658), condemned by Papal decree of 21 August 1659. Before that there had been
published *Le Sentiment des Jésuites sur le Livre de l'Apologie*, which argued that Pirot's
opinions were not those of all Jesuits, nor were they held only by Jesuits. The
Jesuits came to recognize that Pirot's *Apologie*, which was published without the
permission of his Provincial, was 'imprudement' to say the least. See *Apologie pour la
doctrine des Jésuites* (Liège, 1703).

[21] *La Morale de Jésuites Justement condamnée dans le Livre du P. Moya Jésuite, Sous le Nom
d'Amadeus Guimenius. Par la Bulle de ... Innocent XI* (n.p., 1681). *A Truth known to very
Few: viz that the Jesuites are down-right compleat Atheists* (London, 1680), translated the
Sorbonne's censures of Pirot and Moya as evidence for 'the prodicious Itching that
the false Divines of these Times have written upon Morals and Morality ... who far
from checking their sins by timely reproofs, cherish and nurse up the same'
(pp. 1–3).    [22] Clarkson, p. 274.

apportioning punishment or penance. Far more dangerous and socially disruptive was Pascal's wilful misrepresentation of casuistry which, 'by casting it in a vulgar Language among the people', in a sense made a reality of his charge against the Jesuits, namely that of promoting laxity amongst the laity by providing it with excuses for sin, good against both God's law and the magistrate's. 'To publish such questions in a vulgar language, to make them the subject of mirth... and expose them even to the eyes of Women' gave them a currency which they would not otherwise have enjoyed, turning them into a species of rhetoric rather than of jurisprudence.[23]

The leader of French Jansenism, the Abbé Saint-Cyran, had accused the Jesuits of blaspheming against God's law by likening it to mere human law, but the parallel between casuistry and legal reasoning was one which was becoming more pronounced in the Counter-Reformation church, especially after the Council of Trent had reconstructed the role of the priest in the confessional by analogy to 'a secular criminal jurisdiction of a Roman law type'.[24] Paulo Sarpi noted that the Council of Trent obliged the penitent 'in Confession, ... to expiate the circumstances, which alter the nature of the sin, because otherwise, one cannot judge of the weight of the Excesses, and impose a condign Punishment'.[25] The novel emphasis in the Counter-Reformation church on the confessional as a potent means of reaching out to and converting the laity had inspired the Society of Jesus to produce not only the magnificent volumes of moral theology associated with such neo-scholastics as Suarez, Bellarmine, Lugo, and Lessius: 'un nombre innombrable de Commentaries sur la somme de Saint Thomas où par une curiosité effrenée, on a multiplié les questions jusques à l'infini',[26] but also more modest

---

[23] Daniel, pp. 353–4; Nouet, p. 45.

[24] Jean Duvergier de Hauranne, Abbé de Saint-Cyran, *Tome Second de la Somme des Fautes et Faussetez capitales Contenue en la somme Théologique du père F. Garasse* (Paris, 1626), p. 119. John Bossy, 'The social history of confession in the age of the Reformation', *Transactions of the Royal Historical Society*, 5th series, no. 25 (March 1975), 23. See also Daniel, p. 118, and *The Catechism for the Curats, Compos'd by the Decree of the Council of Trent* (London, 1687), p. 265.

[25] *The History of the Council of Trent* (translated into English by N. Brent) (London, 1676), p. 327. See too Theophile Brachet, *Le Pacifique Véritable Sur le débat de l'usage légitime du Sacrement de Pénitence* (Paris, 1644), and Daniel, pp. 118–19.

[26] Godeau, vol. I, pp. 2–3. Etienne Bauny, who produced a Latin *Theologia Moralis* (Paris, 1640), also published in Paris the controversial *Somme des Pechez qui se commettent en tous estats de leurs conditions et qualitez et en quelles occurrences ils sont Mortels, ou Veniels*, which had reached a sixth edition by 1641. Valère Regnault published a number of confessor's manuals: *Compendiaria Praxis difficiliorum casuum conscientiae* (Coloniae Agrippinae, 1622), *De prudentia et caeteris in Confessario requisitis* (Brixiae, 1611), *Praxis Fori Poenitialis* (Coloniae Agrippinae, 1622), and in 1623 published a translation in Lyons, *La practique Succincte et Racourcie des Plus Difficiles case de conscience, qui se présentent soutenfois en l'administration du S. Sacrement de Penitence*.

compilations, such as those of Escobar in Spain and of Bauny and Regnault in France, which culled cases from a number of such authoritative sources and made them accessible in single-volume form, often in the vernacular, to the local priest. 'By taking the authority from all casuists', the Jansenists could thus be charged with placing the parish priest in the same position as those 'Lawyers who have the Institutes, the Code and the Digests almost by heart, and yet are not able to advise, or counsel aright one of their farmers in a suit against his neighbour'. Where the noted reformer of the confessional, St Charles Borromeo, had recommended the prudence of Jesuit casuists to confessors, the Jansenists seemed to offer 'no means to clear up doubts in Morality' other than awaiting '*particular revelation on high* in every particular', leaving the parish priest 'wholly guidelesse in the many doubts which daily arise'. Daniel claimed to know personally of rigorist priests who 'declaim and thunder out abroad against the Jesuits Morals, and yet in their closets, Cardinal Lugo, Lessius, Sanchez, Layman and Azor are the advocates they consult'.[27]

The analogy between casuistical and legal reasoning allowed the Jesuits to defend the existence of reasonable doubt in moral matters, as did the Aristotelian distinction – which Nouet claimed that 'Everyone knows' – between mathematical certainty and practical or probabilistic reasoning.[28] Against St Paul's 'all that is not of faith is sin', Daniel maintained that we might act with a doubt in situations in which more than one judgment was probable and 'yet not offend God'. By probable he meant 'an opinion backed and supported by considerable authority or by some important reason', agreeing with Sanchez that 'the authority of one grave doctor may make an opinion probable'. 'Probabilism' he defined in opposition to tutiorism as the casuistical concession 'That one is not oblig'd to follow the more safe opinion, and, that it is lawfull to follow the less probable and less safe, and quit the more safe and more probable opinion.'[29] In Nouet's words, if in a particular case there existed more than one 'probable opinion', that is, if authoritative divines

---

[27] Daniel, pp. 145, 120; Nouet, p. 503.     [28] Nouet, p. 292.

[29] Daniel, pp. 127, 108, 104, 134. See Massimo Petrocchi, *Il problema del lassismo nel secolo XVII* (Rome, 1953), p. 22. See also Thomas Deman, 'Probabilisme', in *Dictionnaire de théologie catholique*, vol. XIII (Paris, 1936); R. P. Richard, *Le Probabilisme Morale et La Philosophie* (Paris, 1922), and articles by P. Mandonnet in *Revue Thomiste*, vol. X (1902), 5–21, 315–35. For a non-technical introduction to the meaning of probabilism in moral theology, contrasted with its modern quantitative meaning, see Ian Hacking, *The Emergence of Probability* (Cambridge, 1975), pp. 22–5.

disagreed, then it is 'lawfull for anyone to pick and chuse ... that which squares best with himself'. The less probable and less safe of two opinions could be followed, provided only that it was a truly probable opinion.[30]

This was a doctrine 'much older than the Jesuits' and 'taught... in all the schools of Christendom', particularly by the Dominicans, before the Jansenists, 'so seeming zealous for strict, in opposition to loose moralls', managed to associate it in the public mind with Jesuit laxity. Although 'It looks well to say that one is oblig'd always to follow the more safe opinion', Daniel claimed that as a matter of confessional practice this would be 'to condemn or damn all the world', citing as an instance the popularity of the triple contract as a means of avoiding the sin of usury, which was based on a probable but less safe opinion.[31] In his Eighth Letter Pascal had indeed lampooned both Bauny's suggested method of committing usury without appearing to do so and Escobar's 'Contract Mohatra', extracted from the writings of Lessius, Suarez, and Sanchez, whereby 'one buys goods dear and for credit and simultaneously sells them to the same person cheap and for cash'.[32] Jesuit laxity here probably represented a necessary accommodation to social reality, for the case of usury was one in 'which established doctrine and general practice clashed head on', and had Jansenist standards 'ever been successfully imposed, they would have effected a revolution in economic life'.[33]

'To condemn or damn all the world' was in any case what the Jansenists, with their Augustinian notion of an elect, were more than prepared to do. Arnauld, for example, believed that the 'common sort of people ... live in such a manner, that they are not worthy to communicate', complaining that they were yet urged by the Jesuits to do so daily.[34] His attack on the practice, *De la Fréquente Communion*, published in 1643 at the suggestion of Saint-Cyran, contained the

[30] Nouet, p. 21 cited Suarez on the four conditions which must be met before an opinion could be judged probable: 'that it doth not strike at those Truths, which are universally received in the Church, ... that it doth not wound common sense, ... that it be grounded on reason and maintained by some irreproachable Authority, ... that if it hath not the generall vote of the Doctours, at least it be not generally condemned'. [31] Daniel, pp. 53, 368, 143–50. [32] Pascal, pp. 165–7.
[33] Robin Briggs, 'The Catholic Puritans: Jansenists and Rigorists in France', in Donald Pennington and Keith Thomas (eds.), *Puritans and Revolutionaries* (Oxford, 1978), pp. 351–2. See also René Taveneaux, *Jansénisme et prêt à intérêt* (Paris, 1977), and his 'Jansénisme et vie sociale en France au XVIIe siècle', *Revue d'histoire de l'église de France*, 54 (1968), 27–40.
[34] *The Moral Practice of the Jesuites ... By the Doctors of the Sorbonne* (London, 1670) (French original, 1669), p. 153.

beginnings of the Jansenist campaign against a modern casuistry
'plus faciles, et plus accommodantes aux vices' in comparison with
the rigour of the Scriptures and Church Fathers, a campaign which
was taken up in his *Théologie morale des Jésuites* of the same year.[35] The
Counter-Reformation church required that the Sacrament of
Penance – consisting of Contrition, Confession, Satisfaction and
Absolution – precede the Eucharist in order to restore the penitent
to the necessary state of justice from which he had fallen on account
of mortal sin.[36] Arnauld claimed that 'complaisant Directors' would
find no difficulty in offering absolution when guided by the rules of
the new laxist casuistry. By thus 'pretend[ing] condescension to
mens weaknesses and infirmities, and never imploy[ing] the knife
and the Lance in the cure of their wounds' the Jesuits were able to
woo penitents and their fees away from more severe spiritual
directors.[37] The Jesuits defended frequent communion on the
grounds that the Sacraments were themselves 'les médecins', which
could 'weaken mens vices': 'encore que vous foyez malade,
approchez vous ...', counselled the Jesuit who had inspired
Arnauld's initial attack.[38] The Jansenists took particular delight in
translating from the volume with which the Flemish Jesuits had com-
memorated their first centenary, *Imago Primi Saeculi Societatis Jesu A
Provincia Flandro-Belgica*, in 1640, both the year of the posthumous
publication of Jansen's *Augustinus* and the year 'when the pernicious
Morals of the Jesuites were attaqued with such zeal and success in
France'. Here the Jesuits had offered a hostage to their fortunes in
both England and France when they complimented themselves on
the fact that 'When the Society was first established people
communicated but once a year', but now 'Crimes are ... expiated
with much more alacrity and ardour than they were heretofore
committed'; 'Nothing is more ordinary now than monthly, yea then
weekly confession and many are no sooner stained with sin but they
cleanse themselves by confessing their faults.'[39]

Arnauld argued that Jesuit anxiety to avoid popular 'distaste of the
Sacraments' and the making of repentance 'an intollerable yoke' served

---

[35] Hermant, p. 170.    [36] Brachet, pp. 3–5.
[37] Arnauld, *De la Fréquente Communion*, 7th edition (Paris, 1683) (1st edition, 1643),
    pp. 495, 554, Hermant, p. 171, Arnauld, *Moral Practice*, p. 144.
[38] Arnauld, *De la Fréquente Communion*, pp. 132–3. François Rénard, *Remarques
    judicieuses sur le livre intitulé De la Fréquente Communion* (Paris, 1644), included Pierre
    de Sesmaison's answer to the query of the princess Anne de Rohan: *Question s'il est
    meilleur de communier souvent, que rarement?*, rejecting the contrary opinion of Saint-
    Cyran, p. 84.    [39] Arnauld, *Moral Practice*, pp. 131–3. See also Hermant, p. 142.

not to reform manners and morals but rather the reverse: 'to perswade men that there is nothing easier than for the most hardned sinners to re-enter into *Grace*'. Jesuit casuists and confessors were thus prepared 'to sell the blood of Jesus Christ cheap' for the material gain of their Society.[40] The Jesuit Petau responded that the church embraced both innocents and sinners and that the Sacraments were intended for all. 'La plus grande perfection n'est point de commandement' as it had been in the early church, but was now a counsel of perfection. The church, like a kind mother, approved 'Un relaschement' of rigour.[41] Jesuit defenders pointed out that other divines, ancient and modern, held that the church allowed a diversity of opinions in order that the penitent might chose the less severe and more benign and the way of Jesus Christ remain sweet.[42] This recognition that a relaxation of morality had occurred within the history of the church, and that a double standard of morality was the consequence, could of course be met by the rigorist with biblicism: St Paul's command that we are obliged to seek perfection.

Since Scripture provided 'une loi decisive, simple, certaine et immeuble' the rigorist bishop Antoine Godeau, who enjoyed a considerable reputation in England, held that casuistry was, strictly speaking, unnecessary. Conscience could be examined in the confessional by the priest, using both tables of the Decalogue and nothing more.[43] His vernacular *Cours Complet de Morale, à l'usage des Curés* might well be thought, however, to give the lie to his argument here. Against the new casuists and against neo-scholasticism in general, Godeau held that there existed a sharp distinction between human or natural prudence on the one hand and Christian prudence, the realm of Grace, on the other. Doubt and reasoned debate were appropriate to the natural realm, for example, in the studies of jurisprudence and science, but to subject the mysteries of Grace to 'that ardour of questioning and disputing everything' could result only in a dangerous scepticism 'as their theology became stuffed with an heap of innumerable opinions, by which all things though never so

---

[40] Arnauld, *Moral Practice*, pp. 152, 142, 159, and Nouet, pp. 41–2.

[41] Denys Petau, *De la Pénitence Publique et de la Préparation à la Communion*, 3rd edition (Paris, 1645).

[42] *Response aux Lettres que les Jansenistes publient contre les Jesuites* (n.p., n.d.), citing Duval from the Sorbonne.

[43] Godeau, vol. I, pp. 82, 8, vol. III, p. 314. The frontispiece to the 1679 edition of the *Mysterie of Jesuitism* showed Moses delivering the Law of the Ten Commandments (reproduced in Barker, p. 22). For Godeau's English reputation see Basil Kennett (translator), *Pastoral Instructions and Meditations . . . Recommended to the Clergy of his Diocese By Antony Godeau, Bishop of Grasse and Vence* (London, 1700).

contrary are made probable'.[44] Nouet was quite right to accuse the
Jansenists and their rigorist sympathizers of believing that 'you have
found the evidence of the truth and falsehood of all things'.[45] With
intentional naivety, Godeau claimed that 'La regle des actions des
Chrétiennes' was unchangeably to be found 'dans l'Evangile et dans
les Saints Pères'. That rule could be summarized as the law of charity
or love, which 'comprends tous les vertus': 'la charité est le premier
principe de la Morale Chrétienne'.[46] Gale, the English historian of
Jansenism, noted approvingly that their doctrine made Virtue 'to
consist, radically and principally in Love to God' on the grounds that
'mans chiefest good and virtue consists in adhering to God: which is
done by *love*', which seemed 'very exotick to the Sectators of Aristotles
Morals', such neo-scholastics as Suarez and Vasquez.[47]

This emphasis on the primacy of love in moral theology was
thought by the Jesuits both to smack of 'the spirit of Luther, who
teacheth that all Morall Vertues and all the good works we do before
we have Charity are sins' and to represent a misunderstanding of
casuistry, which by definition specified the minimal obligations of
justice, leaving the task of inspiration to love or charity to
devotional literature.[48] Most scandalous to the French rigorists and
to their English sympathizers were the casuists' attempts to determine the precise degree of love of God and contrition for sin
required to restore a penitent to the necessary state of justice before
Communion.[49] English readers were told that the Jesuits believed
that, except on the death bed, 'The affirmative Command of the
Love of God and of the Neighbour is not special, but general and
men satisfye thereto in fulfilling the other precepts.' Clarkson maintained that according to Roman casuistry: 'No precept requires any
special act of love to our Brethren . . . 'Tis enough that we do nothing

[44] Godeau, vol. I, pp. 85–97; Jurisprudence recognizes doubt and natural science
changes in opinion as in the cases of Galileo and Copernicus (on the relationship
between probabilism and science see Benjamin Nelson, 'The early modern revolution in science and philosophy . . . probabilism', in R. S. Cohen and M.
Wartofgsky, *Proceedings of the Boston Colloquium for the Philosophy of Science, 1964/6*
(Dordrecht, 1967), pp. 270–1, 5–6, and his ' "Probabilists", "antiprobabilists" and
the quest for certitude in the sixteenth and seventeenth centuries', *Actes du Dixième
Congrès Internationale d'histoire des Sciences, 1962* (Paris, 1964), vol. I, pp. 269–73). On
scepticism see Godeau, p. 6, 'ces nouveaux Casuistes . . . ont presque réduit la
science des moeurs au Pyrrhonisme, où il n'y a rien de certain, mais où tout dépend
du caprice . . . des auteurs'. See also Gale, p. 156: 'Hence their theology became
stuffed with an heap of innumerable opinions, by which all things though never so
contrary, are made probable: whence a general . . . Scepticisme.'
[45] Nouet, p. 292.      [46] Godeau, vol. I, p. 101 and vol. I, bk. 2.
[47] Gale, pp. 141–2.      [48] Nouet, p. 173.
[49] [Godeau,] *Contre La Mauvaise Morale du Temps aux Evesques de l'Eglise* (n.p., n.d.),
p. 6.

against them.'[50] Rigorists argued that by dealing exclusively with obligations of justice, modern casuists deliberately accommodated themselves to the laxist spirit of the age:

Men believe nowadays that they do very well to hold themselves precisely to that which they cannot omit without injustice; and they ordinarily trouble themselves little about charity, provided they can perswade themselves that they do what they ought of Justice.

So that to tell them that an action is in some sort against Charity, and not against Justice, is to give them Liberty to commit it.[51]

As Briggs has shown, the French Jansenists had constantly to defend themselves against the charge of crypto-Protestantism and, indeed, Arnauld felt obliged to attack the 'impiety' of Calvin's moral theology.[52] It was, nevertheless, Calvin who had thought that while the precepts of justice were to be found both in heathen natural law and the Old Testament, those of love or charity were given by the Grace of God to his church alone in the New Testament.[53] The English Calvinist William Dell blamed St Thomas for having imported Aristotle into an Augustinian church, thus 'reviving free-will, and teaching morall vertues and natural philosophy'.[54] Emphasis on love, after faith, could result in a spectacular degree of rigorism, 'For all love either terminates on God, and so 'tis Charity, or on the creature, and so 'tis concupiscence', often affirmed in order to deny the ability of natural man to fulfil God's law without Grace. In Bayne's explanation in 1635, all sins were deserving of death because '*the least sinne is contrary to charity*'.[55]

By contrast, probabilism, 'called an Invention of the Jesuits to palliate crimes and give scope to libertines', summed up all that was found inappropriate in the application of reason and justice to Christian morality by French and English puritans. Jesuit laxity and

---

[50] *Truth known to very Few*, pp. 7, 68.
[51] [Nicolas Perrault,] *The Jesuits Morals*, tr. Israel Tonge (London, 1670) (French original, 1667), p. 308.
[52] Briggs, pp. 334–5. [Arnauld,] *L'Impiété de la morale des Calvinistes* (Paris, 1675). In particular, the Jansenist critics of casuistry were accused of reiterating the Calvinist Pierre Dumoulin's *Catalogue ou dénombrement des traditions Romaines*, an addendum to his *Des Traditions et de la Perfection et suffisance de l'Escriture Saincte* (Geneva, 1632), which was translated into English in the same year.
[53] G. R. Potter and M. Greengrass (eds.), *John Calvin: Documents of Modern History* (London, 1983), pp. 19, 24.
[54] William Dell, *The Testimony of Martin Luther... touching Universities, Humane Learning, or Philosophy*, in his *Several Sermons and Discourses* (London, 1652), p. 19, which concluded, citing Augustine, that (p. 30): 'humane learning hath its place and use among humane things, but hath no place, nor use in Christ's Kingdome'.
[55] Gale, p. 110. Paul Bayne, *A Helpe to true Happinesse*, 3rd edition (London, 1635), pp. 21, 29: 'every breach of Gods law is sinne ... deserving death'.

probabilism were thought to be the direct result both of the Thomist confusion of the realms of Grace and nature and of the neo-Thomist elevation of the natural law of justice at the expense of that 'which they terme supernatural', the law of love. Furthermore, as Daniel recognized, probabilism was central to the entire Jansenist conspiracy theory of Jesuit casuistry. In Nicole's preface to the *Provincial Letters*, 'This corruption indeed is the source of all the rest':

The Main design of their Morality we find to be this; *viz* to draw all the world to themselves by accommodation and compliance. To this end are their maximes levelled to the severall humours of men. And because these contrary inclinations oblige them to have contrary opinions, they have been forced to change the true rule of manners, and foyst in another. . . a Monster called the DOCTRINE OF PROBABILITY.[56]

In the last years of the Interregnum, translations of Jansenist works in England and direct contact with the Jansenists in France by royalist exiles ensured that divines of all theological and political persuasions were made well aware of 'that new invented engine of the doctrine of probability' which, by 'allowing to anyone a leave of choosing that which is confessedly the less reasonable', enabled the Jesuits to 'entertain all interests and comply with all persuasions'. In Clarkson's summary, 'He is excused from sin, who ventures on it upon some probable reason.'[57]

By the time of the Popish Plot in England and the third edition of the English *Provincial Letters*, now simply entitled the *Mysterie of Jesuitisme*, the 'Theological Bawd commonly called Probability' was sufficiently well known amongst the public at large in England, if in a garbled version, to form an element in Whig political propaganda:

If a thing seems to me probable, if I do it, it's no Sin in me, and if I have the opinion of one or two Priests, of whom I have a good opinion for their abilities, which tell me that I may do it, then it's probable to me, and I may do it without Sin; therefore if it seems to me probable that it will be for the propagating of the Roman Catholic Faith, if such an heretical or schismatical

[56] Nouet, preface. Gale, p. 142.
[57] Jeremy Taylor, quoted in H. R. McAdoo, *The Structure of Caroline Moral Theology* (London, 1949), p. 84. See too Robert South's reference to 'a generation of men, who have framed their casuisticall divinity to a perfect compliance with all the corrupt affections of a man's nature by that new invented engine of the doctrine of probability', ibid., p. 89. For Taylor's admission of Jansenist influence on his treatment of 'this academicall or rather sceptic theology', Jesuit probabilism, see his remark: 'I refer the reader to the books and letters written by their parties at Port-Royal, and to their own weak answers and vindications', quoted in Thomas Wood, *English Casuistical Divinity during the seventeenth century* (London, 1952), p. 60. On direct contact with the Jansenists see Clark, pp. 52–7 and her chapter X, 'The better kind of papists'. [David Clarkson,] *The practical Divinity of the Papists Discovered to be Destructive of Christianity and Men's Souls* (London, 1676), pp. 376–7.

Prince were killed, if a Priest tell me I may do it, then it's to me probable, and I may do it without sin.[58]

Israel Tonge was himself the translator of the Jansenist *Jesuit's Morals* in 1671, which he believed the Jesuits had conspired against with the result that 'the third part was never printed and few of the two first sold, to the great losse of the undertaker'.[59] Titus Oates flattered his patron with the information that the Jesuits had planned to assassinate him for his efforts and in 1679 Tonge gained his revenge by publishing all his previously unsaleable translations of Jesuit material: *Jesuitical Aphorisms, . . . The New Design of the Papists Detected; . . . An Account of the Romish Doctrine in Case of Conspiracy and Rebellion.*[60]

Nevertheless, when, after the Glorious Revolution, the Whig divine Thomas Long sought to justify obedience to the changed government by 'resolving certain queries', he recognized that prob-abilistic reasoning would be the most persuasive form in which to address the consciences of his doubting audience. 'To turn the scales and warrant our resolution in a case so doubtful', he likened the case of conscience to a criminal case in which only 'probable circumstances' could be alleged against the accused. Although aware that 'Divines, when they treat of Law-matters, and moot-cases . . . are guilty of many Blunders', he nevertheless appealed to the legal principle that: 'when the case is dubious, we should choose the part which infers the least danger, in case we should err, as Aristotle says . . . "It is much better to Absolve the Guilty then to condemn the Innocent." '[61]

It was only in the second half of the seventeenth century that the doctrine of reasonable doubt became firmly established as a rule of evidence in English law.[62] In 1632 Andrew Delamore had referred to

[58] *The Jesuites' Reasons Unreasonable* (London, 1662), p. 5; [Etienne Pasquier,] *The Jesuits Catechism* (London, 1679) (dedicated to Shaftesbury and running into three editions by 1685), p. 46.
[59] Israel Tonge, *Journall of the Plot* (London, 1678), in D. C. Greene, (ed.), *Diaries of the Popish Plot* (New York, 1977), p. 3.
[60] Titus Oates, *A True Narrative of the Horrid Plot and Conspiracy of the Popish Party* (London, 1679), p. 19. See also John Kenyon, *The Popish Plot* (London, 1972), pp. 242–3. John Miller, *Popery and Politics in England, 1660–1688* (Cambridge, 1973), p. 156.
[61] Thomas Long, *A resolution of Certain Queries concerning Submission to the Present Government* (London, 1688), pp. 56, 48, and his *Historian unmask'd* (London, 1688), p. 12. On this controversy see Mark Goldie, 'The revolution of 1689 and the structure of political argument: an essay and an annotated bibliography of pamphlets on the allegiance controversy', in *Bulletin of Research in the Humanities* (Winter 1980), 473–563.
[62] See Theodore Waldman, 'Origins of the legal doctrine of reasonable doubt', *Journal of the History of Ideas*, XX (1959), 229–316, Henry G. van Leeuwen, *The Problem of Certainty in English Thought, 1630–90* (The Hague, 1963), and, most recently, Barbara Shapiro, *Probability and Certainty in Seventeenth-century England* (Princeton, 1983), pp. 179–83.

the 'equitable and approvable' rule of law: 'That in every doubtfull case, the Accused ought to have the advantage, and . . . That the accuser not proving the crime objected, the Partie charged ought to be acquitted.'[63] Sir Matthew Hale stated in his *Historia Placitorum Coronae*, compiled largely during the Interregnum, that 'the best rule *in dubiis* is rather to incline to acquittal than conviction', which may explain his own tutiorist refusal to sit on the prosecuting side under Cromwell, 'thinking it the safer course in so dubious a case'.[64] In 1660, when J. Phillips attempted to 'reduce' the complexity of English law to 'general Rules', he included: 'Benignior sensus in verbis dubiis est praeferendum', which he translated as 'In doubtful things, the most favourable construction is to be preferr'd.'[65] By 1705, Bernard Mandeville believed 'that mighty Saying, that it is better that 500 guilty People should escape, then one innocent Person should suffer' had become such a shibboleth that it made a mockery of the deterrent intent of the criminal law.[66]

In his defence of legal reasoning and of the common law as the accumulation of past practical or probabilistic wisdom against the theoretical strictures of Thomas Hobbes, Hale explained that 'since the Subject of Laws are Morall Actions, there cannot be expected that precise certaintie or Evidence thereof, as there is to be found in Mathematicks'. 'The great variety of Circumstances which Accompany moral Actions. . . Strangely diversify the application of the Generall Laws', with the result, Hale claimed, that:

> the decisions are more difficult and inevident, and the variety of Mens judgements give different Theorys and make different Conclusions touching them: And therefore to settle and determine these is required much Exercise of the reasoning Faculty, much Judgement and advertence which doth not so commonly fall under ordinary Capacities, this we may easily perceive in the Curious and Subtile Works of Many Writers of Morall Philosophy and the Schoolmen and Casuists of this and former Ages.

Although he made extensive use of Roman casuists himself, the moral uncertainty which he attributed to 'the Curious distinctions

---

[63] [Andrew Delamore,] *Antiduello* (London, 1632), p. 41.
[64] Sir Matthew Hale, *Historia Placitorum Coronae* [1676] (London, 1736), vol. I, p. 509, and Sollom Emlyn's preface, p. ii. On dating see D. E. C. Yale's *Introduction to Sir Matthew Hale's Prerogatives of the King*, Selden Society (London, 1976), pp. xxiv–xxv. See also Gilbert Burnet, *Life and Death of Sir Matthew Hale* (London, 1682), pp. 22–4, describing Hale's decision to remain on the Bench during the Commonwealth: 'to have Justice and Property kept up at all times. . . But he had greater Scruples concerning the proceedings against Felons . . . for in matters of Blood, he was always to chuse the safer side'.
[65] J. Phillips, *The Principles of Law Reduced to Practice* (London, 1660).
[66] Bernard Mandeville, *The Fable of the Bees*, 2nd edition enlarged (London, 1723) (1st edition, 1705), p. 309.

and definitions contained in the Writings of Casuists and Morall philosophers' only served in Hale's view to emphasize the necessity for 'a certaine and determinate Law' by which men could regulate their lives. That law was given its perfect expression in the Gospels, summarized by Christ in his two commands: that we love God and that we love our neighbours as ourselves. Love, or charity, represented in practice the aspiration that we do unto others as we would have done unto ourselves. Justice, by contrast, took the 'negative' or 'prohibitory' form: 'it is not just to do that to another which we would not that another should do to me', and was given adequate expression in the laws of the land.[67] This negative form of the golden rule had been used also by Roman casuists to illustrate the principle of equality in commutative justice, appearing, for example, on the title page of Molina's volume on the subject.[68]

When compared with the law of love or charity, that of justice implied a less exacting, more pragmatic morality, with the presumption always in favour of the possessor, as Bishop Sanderson explained, when applying 'Christian prudence' and 'that sovereign rule had been used also by Roman casuists to illustrate the principle socially disruptive:

if another rule given by the Casuists be well considered, which in matters of Commutative Justice concerning *meum et tuum* is of excellent use to free the conscience from being perplexed with unnecessary scruples on the one side, as that maxim formerly mentioned of *pars tutior* is useful to preserve it from too much liberty and looseness on the other side; and that is this: '*In rebus dubiis melior est conditio possidentis.*'[69]

The equally famous Protestant casuist, Richard Baxter, agreed with Sanderson on the dangers of scrupulosity in this case, tracing it to the lack of experience in 'merchandize' of most divines who wrote treatises on usury: 'it is a bad thing to corrupt religion and fill the world with causeless scruples by making that a sin which is no sin'.[70]

---

[67] *Reflections by the Lord Chief Justice Hale on Mr Hobbes, his Dialogue of the Law*, published by W. Holdsworth, 'Sir Matthew Hale on Hobbes: an unpublished MS', *Law Quarterly Review*, 37 (July 1921), 286, 290. *Some Chapters touching the Law of Nature*, BL Addnl MS 18, 235, ff. 61v, 71v, 72, 67v, 69, 68, 68v, 70.

[68] Bernard Dempsey, *Interest and Usury* (London, 1948), p. 135.

[69] *The Works of Robert Sanderson*, collected by William Jacobson (Oxford, 1854), vol. V, p. 131.

[70] Richard Baxter, *Chapters from a Christian Directory*, selected by J. Tawney (London, 1925), p. 131. Although in his treatment of the eighth commandment in his *Catechising of Families*, in *The Practical Works of Richard Baxter* (London, 1707), vol. IV, p. 125, he notes that 'The great difference of Mens Judgements about Usury, should make all the more Cautelous to venture on none that is truly doubtful', he nevertheless rejected the notion that 'all usury be against Justice or Charity to our neighbour' in his *Christian Directory*, pp. 124–5.

For John Blaxton, the author in 1634 of *The English Usurer*, the very
existence of debate and doubt on the subject had provided proof
that usury could not sit with a good conscience; 'because it cannot be
done in fayth, that is to say, in a sound perswasion out of the word of
God, that it is lawfull: and whatsoever is not of fayth is sinne'.[71]
Indeed, throughout the century it was the debate over usury more
than any other case of conscience which made rigorist divines sus-
picious of casuistry.

Granted that it was only man's lack of charity which had made
casuistry necessary in the first place, Baxter insisted that men had to
be taken by the practical divine as he found them, for to set unrealistic
standards of conduct was effectively to abandon all claim to jurisdiction over the laity and their economic activities. It was his largely
pessimistic and Augustinian account of human nature which persuaded Baxter too of the continued necessity of laws and lawyers for
'the diverting men from Sensuality and Idleness, the maintaining of
propriety and Justice, and consequently the Peace and Welfare of
the Kingdom'.[72] Sir John Davies made a similar point in his *Law
Reports* when defending the connection between the increase in commerce and litigiousness: 'Indeed if we all lived according to the Law
of Nature, we should need few Laws and fewer Lawyers. Do as thou
wouldst be done unto were a rule sufficient to rule us all, and every
man's conscience would supply the place of an advocate and a
judge.'[73] So, too, the political theorist John Locke had recognized
that 'The great Principle of Morality, *To do as one would be done to*, is
more commended than practised', arguing that the blindness to
natural law induced by self-interest was the reason for which men
had originally established legislatures and laws: 'for though the Law
of Nature be plain and intelligible to all rational Creatures; yet men
being biassed by their interest, as well as ignorant for want of study
of it, are not apt to allow of it as a Law binding to them in their
application of it to their particular cases'.[74]

In effect, Hale and Davies, along with many other defenders of the
common law during the Interregnum, had claimed that common
lawyers were the casuists of English society, treating of justice in its
application to particular cases, and hence that prudence could quite
literally become jurisprudence in its seventeenth-century sense of a
knowledge of the laws of England. It is perhaps not surprising, then,

---

[71] John Blaxton, *The English Usurer* (London, 1634), p. 22.
[72] *Additionall notes of the Life and death of Sir Matthew Hale* (London, 1682), pp. 26–7.
[73] *Les Reports des Cases et Matters en Ley* (London, 1674), 'Preface Dedicatory'.
[74] John Locke, *Two Treatises of Government*, edited by Peter Laslett, revised edition
(Cambridge, 1963), pp. 70, 549–52, 396.

that in 1688 some Englishmen should have turned to the probabilistic reasoning of 'Learned Men in the Law' rather than to that of Whig divines as 'the best Directors of my Conscience of this case'.[75]

At the end of the century George Dawson had argued that divines needed to learn the *Origo Legum* if they were 'to be able to declare when and where the Conscience offends, and when not'. For although he noted the contemporary view that: 'all Cases and Controversies, which may arise about *Meum* and *Tuum* . . . belong to the learned Lawyers and Reverend Judges, who are presumed to be best skilled in the Laws and Customs of the Land, as their proper study, and not to Divines' he agreed with Sanderson, who held earlier in the century that this wrongly excluded the divine from many areas which 'relate to Morality and Practice in point of Conscience'.[76]

Famously, however, John Locke, as neither a lawyer nor divine, urged during the Exclusion Crisis that the laity or the people should act as their own casuists, 'when they are perswaded in their Consciences, that their Laws, and with them their Estates, Liberties, and Lives are in danger and perhaps their religion too'. In order to help them 'resolve the conscience' in a revolutionary direction, however, he needed to overcome the argument of Sir Robert Filmer and of most other conservative political theorists of the Interregnum period, namely that without the government and the laws, men would subside into a state of moral anarchy, or licentiousness. Significantly he chose as his authority on the existence of a 'standing Rule to live by' even in a state of nature the episcopal defender of 'things indifferent' within the Elizabethan church against puritan criticisms. The 'judicious Hooker' had needed to establish the premise of natural law or natural sociability, 'the Foundation of that Obligation to mutual Love amongst Men, on which he Builds the Duties they owe one another, and from whence he derives the great Maxims of Justice and Charity',[77] in order to counter puritan biblicism with a *jus gentium*, a region of human prudence, mediating between God's law and merely civil law, in which the Crown and ecclesiastical authorities could legislate. His puritan critics at the turn of the century predictably accused him of elevating human reason at the expense of God's Grace.[78] This perennial quarrel be-

[75] Goldie, p. 487.
[76] George Dawson, *Origo Legum: or a Treatise of the Origin of Laws, and their Obliging Power* (London, 1694), preface.   [77] Locke, pp. 452, 324, 310.
[78] See Andrew Willet, *An Antilogie or counterplea to an Apologicall epistle* (London, 1603), and *A christian Letter of certaine English Protestants unto Mr R. Hooker requiring resolution in his Ecclesiasticall Pollicie* (London, 1599). On this debate see Nicholas Tyacke, 'Arminianism in England, in religion and politics, 1604 to 1640', Oxford D. Phil. thesis, 1968, p. 25.

tween nature and Grace, or between natural justice and supernatural charity, would of course continue throughout the century, lending seventeenth-century English political thought its peculiarly repetitious and circular quality. As the divine William Sclater explained the problem natural law posed Protestant theology:

Schoolemen thus rule; Morals have all their power of binding from the dictate of natural reason; and therefore ought to be observed, because reason so directs. Mee thinkes th'opinion blunts the edge of Augustine's argument against the Pelagians, in the question of possible keeping the law by the strength of nature.

[For] After this rule, moralities are all known naturally and there is in nature an inclination to their performance.

Against this association between free will and natural law, and in order that 'dissolute nature might bee restrayned in mee by lawes', Protestantism was driven to a voluntarist insistence that 'there be ... moralities some, that are such by institution and divine positive law', by God's command in Scripture rather than by their 'conformitie to right reason'.[79]

In 1625, the puritan divine Cornelius Burges had held in his *New Discovery of Personal Tithes* 'That every mans conscience may stand upon a firme ground, it must bee guided in everything by a *Sure Rule*', but that that 'certaine and infallible Rule' was provided not by natural law but only by Scripture or the laws of the land; writing under James I, it is clear that he envisaged no fundamental incompatibility between the two.[80] From a defender of the right to personal tithes, however, Burges would find himself first a member of Parliament's Westminster Assembly of Divines, there criticizing the diversion of ecclesiastical wealth to secular uses; then a purchaser of Bishops lands during the Interregnum who, in 'his just endeavours to possess what he hath paid for', published his *No Sacrilege nor Sinne to Aliene or Purchase the Lands of Bishops*, which criticized the contrary doctrines of 'Schoolmen, Summists and Casuists'; and, finally, with the Restoration land settlement and the publication of his *Case Concerning the Buying of Bishops Lands*, a casuist in his own cause, 'His ability in casuisticall Divinity' mocked by royalist divines such as the church historian Thomas Fuller:

I doubt not but that he can give sufficient reason for the same, both to himself and any other ... The rather because lately he read his learned Lectures

---

[79] William Sclater, *The Quaestion of Tythes Revised, Arguments for the Moralitie of Tything, enlarged and cleared* (London, 1623), pp. 172–4.
[80] Cornelius Burges, *A New Discovery of Personal Tithes* (London, 1625), p. 23.

... on the Criticisms of Conscience, no lesse carefully then curiously weighing satisfaction to *scruples*, and if there be any fault, so able a Confessor, knows how to get his absolution.[81]

Paradoxically, casuistry came to enjoy such a reputation amongst both clergy and laity at precisely the time that numerous 'cases' were published in English – the 'Protestant casuistry' which provided the context out of which major developments in political thought emerged.

The historian of *Ancient Law*, Henry Maine, believed that Pascal's *Letters* dealt such a blow to the prestige of casuistry in Europe that 'ethical science' from then on became the exclusive preserve of those Protestant natural law theorists who followed in the footsteps of Hugo Grotius. In order to accentuate his contrast between Counter-Reformation casuistry on the one hand and Grotian natural law on the other, Maine emphasized the derivation of the latter from Roman law.[82] But post-Tridentine casuistry was equally 'saturated' in the notions of Roman jurisprudence, and here it will be argued, 'if I may call a Lawyer a Divine',[83] that Grotius can as well be understood as himself a casuist, specifying the cases in which war might be permissible, Evangelical counsels to the contrary notwithstanding. The extraordinary reputation of 'That learned Grotius' in mid-seventeenth-century England both as a devotional author and as a natural law theorist was such that in 1658, Baxter thought it necessary to publish an attack on the Arminianism of the 'Grotian Religion' which in turn inspired the royalist divines Henry Hammond and Thomas Pierce to produce vindications of his reputation, clearing him 'from all appearance of Popery', which failed nevertheless to persuade such puritans as John Owen.[84] Baxter was

---

[81] *No Sacrilege nor Sinne* (London, 1659), pp. 8–9; *Case Concerning the Buying of Bishops Lands* (London, 1659), Epistle Dedicatory. Thomas Fuller, *The Church-History of Britain* (London, 1655), bk XI, p. 179. Earlier, Fuller had revealed the ambivalence of the church's attitude toward casuistry when describing the qualities of the faithful minister in his *Holy State* (Cambridge, 1642, p. 83) who never 'troubles his Auditory with such strange hideous cases of Conscience, that it is more hard to find the case then the resolution' but 'He doth not onely move the bread of life and tosse it up and down in generalities, but also breaks it into particular directions, drawing it down to cases of Conscience, that a man may be warranted in his particular actions, whether they be lawfull or not.'

[82] Henry Sumner Maine, *Ancient Law: Its Connection with the Early History of Society and its Relation to Modern Ideas* (London, 1861), pp. 352–3.

[83] Richard Baxter, *Aphorismes of Justification* (London, 1649), p. 5.

[84] On the reputation of Grotius, see the frontispiece to *The Illustrious Hugo Grotius, Of the Law of Warre and Peace*, translated by Clement Barksdale (London, 1654): 'See you not Learning in his Lookes? See it more Lively in his Bookes'; Baxter, *The Grotian Religion discovered* (London, 1658), p. 4, J. C., *The Faithfull Steward* (Cambridge, 1655), p. 3, William Dillingham (ed.), Nathanael Culverwell, *An*

prepared to acknowledge the extent to which he had learned from
Grotius in areas other than soteriology and practical divinity. The
exception in the case of the latter, 'the happiest part of my learning',
is not altogether surprising, for a comparison even between the table
of contents of the Erastian Clement Barksdale's 1654 translation *The
Law of War and Peace* and that added by the English translator to the
*Mysterie of Jesuitisme* would suggest that Grotius was engaged in
debating the same cases of conscience which so scandalized Baxter
in his *Key for Catholicks*. Grotius can be described not only as a casuist,
as he was by Hale, but also as a probabilist. For example, his rule for
the interpretation of Christ's 'Evangelical counsels' of perfection
was that:

Equity itself and common sense, teaches us to restraine words that are
general and favourably to explain those that are ambiguous, and even to
recede somewhat from the propriety and common Acceptation of the
words, in order to avoid that sense which may bring along with it the greatest
inconveniencies.

He shared the probabilist emphasis on doubt rather than mathematical certainty 'in moralls, [where] even the least circumstances
varie the matter', acknowledging that 'in many Controversies... on
either side probable arguments may shew themselves, whether
intrinsical to the matter or from authority'. While he allowed that in
matters of small moment either argument could be followed, in
matters of greater import, such as those involving the life of a man,
'the safe way is to be preferred'.[85]

Despite this degree of 'equiprobabilism' he did agree with 'almost
all, as well Lawyers as Divines, [who] do now teach, that a man may
be rightly slain by us in defense of our goods'. He recognized that
Christ's Evangelical law 'requireth more of us', but insisted that
human laws ought 'to be made by men with sense of humane
imbecillity' and that a relaxation of morality represented a necessary
accommodation to reality: 'No wonder if in this matter, as in many
other, Discipline became looser with the time, and by degrees the
Interpretation of the Evangelical Law began to be accommodated to
the manners of the Age.'[86] As had the probabilist casuists, he
recognized that 'there are several Ways of Living, some better than
others, and everyone may chuse which he pleases of all those sorts'.[87]

*Elegant and Learned Discourse of the Light of Nature* (London, 1652), p. 78, Thomas
Pierce, *The New Discoverer Discover'd* (London, 1659), and Henry Hammond, *A
Second Defence of the Learned Hugo Grotius* (London, 1655). See also Richard Tuck,
*Natural Rights Theories* (Cambridge, 1979), passim.   [85] Grotius, pp. 34, 423, 426.
[86] Ibid., p. 193.      [87] Ibid., p. 64.

And indeed his treatment of the right of self-defence is identical to that of the Jesuit defender of probabilist casuistry, Gabriel Daniel:

When it is ask'd, whether, on some occasions it be lawful to kill, or strike, it is always without prejudice to the Evangelical Counsel; where our Saviour bid us . . . *to turn our left cheek* . . . There is not a Casuist, who do's not agree, that this conduct, in a Christian, is infinitly to be prais'd . . . But . . . it would be extravagant . . . to regulat, by these Counsels of Perfection, the strict obligations of a Christian in this matter.[88]

Daniel's Jansenist critic Petit-Didier rejected his claim that all theologians permitted killing in self-defence, arguing instead the extreme rigorist position that 'il n'est jamais permis de tuer de son autorité privé'.[89] For Daniel, however, 'All kinds of law', divine as well as civil, allowed a man to return force with force within 'the bounds of a just and moderate defence'. The casuist's problem, like that of the lawyer, was simply the practical one of determining the just bounds of that defence.[90]

For Joseph Hall, one of James's Calvinist bishops and representatives at the Synod of Dort, in his *Resolutions and Decisions of Divers Practicall Cases of Conscience in Continuall Use amongst Men* of 1649, the case *'Whether and in what cases it may be lawful for a man to take away the life of another?'* was more difficult to resolve, for he believed that by 'our Municipall lawes' 'of old even a killing *se defendendo* was no lesse then felony of death'.[91] In fact this severity served a largely deterrent purpose within the English criminal law: William Sheppard claimed that the usual punishment in practice was forfeiture of estates and a pardon.[92] Indeed the law reformer and regicide John Cooke, writing in the same year as Hall, believed that the English law allowed too much leeway to the right of self-defence: 'in case of an assault, the Law makes every man a Magistrate to defend himselfe but to kill a man for a Boxe of the eare, or any man that I may save without manifest danger of my own life is death by all other Lawes in Christendome'.[93]

[88] Daniel, pp. 353–4.
[89] [Petit-Didier,] *Apologie des lettres provinciales* (Rouen, 1697), p. 210.
[90] Daniel, p. 354.
[91] Joseph Hall, *Resolutions and Decisions of Divers Practicall Cases of Conscience* (London, 1649), p. 106. Sir Edward Coke in the *Third Part of the Institutes*, chapter 101, 'of death of a man *se defendendo*', admitted that there was no general excuse of self-defence in English law: 'Upon such a verdict the Court giveth no express judgement, for he is also to be pardoned of course: but the law hath given a judgement, that he shall forfeit all his goods and chattels, debts and duties.'
[92] William Sheppard, *Englands Balme* (London, 1657), p. 196.
[93] John Cooke, *The Vindication of the Professors and Profession of the Law* (London, 1646), p. 20.

Hall nevertheless turned away from English law to 'divers Casuists' in order to resolve the question of whether one could kill a thief or assailant, even if flight were possible. In casuistical manner, he proceeded to 'direct the intention' since 'charity forbids that this slaughter should be first in my intention, which is primarily bent upon my owne safety and the vindication of my owne just propriety'. The duty of charity, however, did not override the natural right to use force in self-defence: 'the blood that follows is but the unwilling attendant of my defence'. Like Grotius, he drew from his casuistical sources the Vitorian lesson that 'Anyone, even a private person, can accept and wage a defensive war', concluding that 'if hereupon his death shall follow, however I should passe with men, God and my owne heart would acquit me'.[94]

This was, of course, a casuistical principle which would be frequently cited by political theorists arguing a right of resistance to established authority for the rest of the century, usually giving Grotius as authority, but sometimes Bishops Hall or Hammond. During that mid-century exercise in Protestant casuistry which J. M. Wallace has taught us to call the Engagement Controversy, the 'born casuist' Anthony Ascham had already in 1648 borrowed extensively from Grotius in arguing that the 'people' or the laity could act as their own casuists against the biblicism both of royalist defenders of divine right and Presbyterian defenders of a rigorist interpretation of the Solemn League and Covenant, both of whom described engaging to the new Commonwealth as sinful.[95] Historians of political thought have long been aware of the significance of Hugo Grotius as the secularizing intermediary between the Counter-Reformation revival of Thomist natural law and the 'Protestant individualist ethic'[96] of seventeenth-century English political thought. More recently it has been shown that the process involved collapsing the notion of justice into mere recognition of individual rights, sym-

---

[94] Hall, pp. 104–6. Franciscus De Victoria, *De Indis et De Jure Belli*, edited by Ernest Nys, in The Classics of International Law, edited by J. B. Scott (Washington, 1917), p. 167.

[95] J. M. Wallace, 'The Engagement Controversy, 1649–52: an annotated list of pamphlets', *Bulletin of the New York Public Library*, 68 (June 1964), 384–405; 'The cause too good', *Journal of the History of Ideas*, 24 (1963), 150–4, and his *Destiny his Choice: The Loyalism of Andrew Marvell* (Cambridge, 1968). Anthony Ascham, *A Discourse: Wherein is Examined, What is Particularly Lawful during the Confusions and Revolutions of Government* (London, 1648). On Ascham, see G. W. S. V. Rumble, introduction to his edition *Of the Confusions and Revolutions of Governments* (London, 1649; New York, 1975).

[96] Grotius, p. 13; J. H. M. Salmon, *The French Religious Wars in English Political Thought* (Oxford, 1959), p. 69.

bolized perhaps by the changing translations of Grotius' *De jure belli ac pacis libri tres* from Barksdale's *Law of War and Peace* in 1654 to William Evat's translation of 1682, *The most excellent Hugo Grotius, his three books treating of the rights of War and peace*.[97] Furthermore, Christ's Golden Rule that we love our neighbours as ourselves, the law of charity, was restricted in seventeenth-century political thought to the casuistical principle of mere commutative justice, 'Do not unto others', most famously by Thomas Hobbes. The principle is also commonly to be found in more ephemeral literature such as the *Remonstrance* of those imprisoned for debt: 'The Law of Nature requireth of us, not to do that to another man, which we will not have done to ourselves, to render to every man his owne, and to confirme and distinguish his inheritance, birthright, propriety and possession.'[98]

It was this 'swallowing up' of natural law or justice into mere recognition of individual rights which allowed Grotius to agree with the casuists Navarrus, Soto, and Sylvester that there was a right to kill for a blow on the cheek despite 'the Evangelicall Law [which] hath clearly made such a deed unlawfull'; 'For although death and a blow are unequall, yet he which prepares to do me an injury, thereby gives me a right, i.e. a certain morall faculty, against himself *in infinitum*.'[99]

But while historians of political thought have successfully established the transmission of the Roman legal notion of a right to repel force with force through the neo-scholastic moral theologians of the Counter-Reformation to Grotius and thence to the English revolutionaries of the seventeenth century, they have paid less attention to the altered contexts in which those ideas were expressed. The Arminian Hugo Grotius, for example, revealed almost Jansenist or puritan horror at the fact that Roman divines could admit this right:

it is strange, seeing the will of God appears so manifestly in the Gospel, that there are found Divines, and those Christian Divines, who do not only think slaughter to be rightly admitted, that a blow may be avoided; but also for a reparation of honour, as they say. Which seemeth very contrary to Reason and Religion.

[97] For an introduction to the literature see J. H. Tully, 'Current thinking about sixteenth- and seventeenth-century political thought', *Historical Journal*, 24 (1981), 479.

[98] Thomas Hobbes, *Leviathan*, edited by C. B. MacPherson (Harmondsworth, 1968), p. 318, and *Philosophical Rudiments*, in the *English Works*, edited by William Molesworth (London, 1841), vol. II, p. 62; *The Prisoners Remonstrance* (London, 1649), p. 6.   [99] Grotius, p. 186.

Here he effectively excludes divines from his own province of justice
and natural law, choosing to ignore the implications of the fact that
the casuistical sources from which he drew so much bore titles such
as *De Justitia et Jure*. With the Protestant and Jansenist critics of
casuistry he can envisage only an exhortatory and not a juristic role
for the divine, that of preaching up the Evangelical counsels of charity,
or love, which as he admitted were essentially irrelevant to the conduct of contemporary life.[100] This contrast between the rhetorical
and juristic roles is evident in his own exhortatory religious writings,
which tell us that the 'law of Christ forbids us to revenge any kind of
injury whatsoever, whether it be offered in word or deed'.[101] As Page
noted in 1655, when defending theories of natural rights: 'There are
many things in the Law of God, which are seemingly against Nature
. . . as is the loving of our enemies, the doing good to them that hate
us . . .'[102]

## CASUISTRY AND SEVENTEENTH-CENTURY POLITICAL THOUGHT

Here it is hoped to take Wallace's recognition that seventeenth-
century political thought represented that apparent contradiction
in terms, 'Protestant casuistry', one step further, to suggest that the
translation of casuistry from the privacy of the confessional and
largely indigestible Latin tomes to the public political arena and
vernacular treatises written by the laity for the laity had greater
ideological significance than has perhaps been recognized. In
becoming political thought, casuistry did at last justify Pascal's
charge against Jesuit casuistry of promoting laxity amongst the laity
by telling them of rights good against both God's law and the magistrate's. It did so, however, as the Jesuits had predicted, by popularizing
essentially juristic notions, and addressing them to the laity in
the vernacular.

Previously, the seventeenth-century controversy over laxity in
Europe has been used by social historians to provide sparring points
in their continuing debate over Weber's postulated relationship between the Protestant ethic and the development of capitalism. In
1933, H. M. Robertson argued from Jansenist sources that it was
Jesuitry and not Calvinism which relaxed 'the discipline of the Christian

[100] Ibid., pp. 185–9.
[101] Hugo Grotius, *True Religion Explained* (London, 1632), bk 2, p. 117.
[102] John Page, *Jus Fratrum* (London, 1658), pp. 3–4.

in his conduct of commercial affairs'.[103] Although the polemically
tainted nature of his Jansenist sources on Jesuit casuistry has since
been remarked on by the Jesuit James Brodrick, Robertson has
nevertheless been taken by Immanuel Wallerstein as authority for
the position that 'Catholic theology, too, has proved its capacity to
be adaptable to its social milieu' and that as a consequence, 'There is
little reason at the abstract level of ideas why one couldn't have written
a plausible book entitled "The Catholic Ethic and the Spirit of
Capitalism".'[104] As Gordon Marshall has pointed out, however, the
issue of the accommodation to social reality through casuistical laxity
is essentially irrelevant to Weber's original thesis, which postulated
not the relaxation of a traditional Catholic morality but the construction of a new and at least as rigorous an ethic. This 'Protestant
ethic' was bolstered not by the negative sanctions of ecclesiastical
discipline but by a positive 'psychological sanction':

Calvinists were encouraged to *prove* their election by identifying the fruits of
true faith in appropriate everyday conduct . . . namely, diligence in lawfull
callings, asceticism with respect to material satisfactions; and constructive
utilization of one's time.[105]

While I take Marshall's point that the controversy over laxist
morality can neither confirm nor deny the validity of Weber's 1905
thesis, here it will be suggested that the controversy can be used to
explore further the question originally posed by Weber in opposition to Marxist determinism, namely the relationship between
ideas, specifically those associated with the Reformation, and social
change.[106] For Jesuit laxity was thought by Robertson to provide
evidence not only against Weber but also for economic determination, demonstrating that 'the spirit of capitalism has arisen rather
from the material conditions of civilisation than from some religious
impulse' on the grounds that 'Jesuits were, as the most prominent
casuists and confessors, most in contact with the lay world . . .
Everything points to a secular cause of the rise of the spirit of

---

[103] H. M. Robertson, *Aspects of the Rise of Economic Individualism* (Cambridge, 1933),
p. 109.
[104] Immanuel Wallerstein, *The Modern World-System* (New York, 1974), pp. 152–3.
[105] Gordon Marshall, *In Search of the Spirit of Capitalism* (London, 1982), p. 75.
[106] For another attempt to relate casuistry to the Weber thesis, see Benjamin Nelson,
'Conscience and the making of early modern cultures: the Protestant ethic beyond
Max Weber', *Social Research*, vol. 36, no. 1 (1969), 5–21, and his 'Medieval canon
law of contracts, Renaissance "Spirit of Capitalism" and the Reformation
"conscience": a vote for Max Weber', in R. B. Palmer and R. Hamerton-Kelly
(eds.), *Philomathes* (The Hague, 1971).

capitalism.'[107] In the brief narrative which follows a more paradoxical story will emerge.

The first attempt to provide a distinctively Protestant casuistry in England was the work of a common lawyer and coincided with the Reformation. In 1532, the year in which he entered into controversy with Thomas More over the independence of the spiritual from temporal jurisdiction, Christopher Saint-German's *Dialogus de Fundamentis Legum et de Conscientiae* of 1523 was translated into English. The main burden of *Doctor and Student*, as his work became known, was the contrast between English case law and canonist compilations of cases such as the *Summa Rosella* and the *Summa Angelica*.[108] In essence, Saint-Germain argued the irrelevance of ecclesiastical casuistry to the English layman on the grounds that the common law adequately applied the moral rules of the Bible and the Church Fathers to specific cases of conscience: 'The theme is that a knowledge of English law and its grounds is essential for the good direction of conscience in this realm... It is in human law, duly constituted, that justice concerning the possession of lands and the ownership of chattels is made plain.'[109] By the turn of the century, its reputation had already become that of a law 'student's introduction to English law', providing one of the few accessible volumes on the subject but by no means remedying the deficiency Francis Bacon found in English theologians, namely that 'They draw not their directions down *ad casus conscientiae*; that a man may be warranted in his particular actions whether they be lawful or not.'[110] By 1642 Thomas Fuller used a metaphor which occurred also to such diverse Protestant casuists as William Ames, Jeremy Taylor, and Richard Baxter to complain that 'in Case-Divinity Protestants are defective'; 'For (save that a Smith or two of late have built them forges, and set up shop) we go down to our enemies to sharpen all our instruments, and are beholden to them for offensive and defensive weapons in Cases of Conscience.'[111]

---

[107] Robertson, pp. xvi, 109.
[108] *St German's Doctor and Student*, edited for the Selden Society by T. F. T. Plucknett and J. L. Barton (1974), introduction p. xx and p. 274.    [109] Ibid., pp. 3–5.
[110] Francis Bacon's complaint of 1589, cited in Camille Wells Slights, *The Casuistical Tradition in Shakespeare, Donne, Herbert and Milton* (Princeton, 1981). See too A. E. Malloch, 'John Donne and the casuists', *Studies in English Literature*, II (1962), 57–76.
[111] Fuller, *Holy State*, bk. 2, ch. X, p. 90; William Ames, *Conscience with the Power and Cases thereof* (n. p., 1639; translation of his *De Conscientia* of 1630), preface. For other examples see McAdoo, p. 7, Wood, p. 41 and John T. McNeill, 'Casuistry in the Puritan age', *Religion in Life*, XII (1943), pp. 78–82.

The major argument of divines in favour of developing a new and distinctively Protestant casuistry in England was originally that same proneness to despair at the heart of Calvinism and of Weber's thesis, what Annesley later called that 'oversense of . . . [their] unworthinesse'.[112] In 1600 William Perkins published his *Case of Conscience, the greatest that ever was. How a man may know whether he be the child of God or no: Resolved by the Word of God*, and his editor is surely correct to find 'the most unique feature of Puritan casuistry' at the turn of the century to be 'its preoccupation with the problem of assurance of election'.[113] The metaphor of the penitent as patient was common to Protestant and Roman divines, but where the Jesuits had envisaged a doctor equipped with medicines and the Jansenists more brutally with a knife and lance, English divines sought 'to instruct and comfort all afflicted consciences' in such a way that they might learn to cure themselves.[114] Much of this instruction came from the pulpit, where preachers as 'masters of the special art of applying apposite concepts and images drawn from the infallible Word to present exigencies of every kind' encouraged their audience to engage in an 'enthralling drama of self-examination'.[115] The often lamented shortage of such effective 'practical preachers' in early seventeenth-century England encouraged many to publish their 'method of healing the diseases of the conscience' in vernacular treatises designed to comfort rather than to judge and trouble further the 'Wounded Conscience', to supplement the 'refreshing of . . . fainting soules' for which certain puritan divines were renowned.[116]

Perkins was the puritan minister who obtained an unrivalled reputation as 'an excellent Chirurgeon . . . at joynting of a broken soul, and at stating of a doubtfull conscience'. Nevertheless, his *Whole Treatise of the Cases of Conscience* of 1606 carried on its title page

[112] Samuel Annesley, 'How may we be universally and exactly conscientious?', in *The Morning Exercise at Cripplegate, Several Cases of Conscience Practically Resolved* (London, 1661), p. '21', i.e. 26. Although advocating tutiorism in 'lesser matters', he wrote that 'this rule will not reach all cases' and that (p. 16) 'Too many deal with their doubts, as Cripples with their sores, which might easily be healed but they make them a begging argument'; 'Do what you possibly can to get rid of your scruples.'
[113] *William Perkins, 1558–1602, English Puritanist, His Pioneer works on casuistry*, edited with an introduction by Thomas F. Merrill (Nieuwkoop, 1966), p. xiv.
[114] H[enry] H[olland,] *The Works of the Reverend and Faithfull . . . Mr Richard Greenham, Minister and Preacher of the word of God* (London, 1599), 'Epistle Dedicatory'.
[115] William Haller, *Foxe's Book of Martyrs and the Elect Nation* (London, 1963), pp. 79, 104.
[116] John Downame, *The Christian's Warfare*, fourth edition (London, 1634), 'To the Christian Reader'.

the rigorist text, Romans 14:23, 'Whatsoever is not of Faith is sin.'[117] Thomas Fuller noted too of this preacher who could 'pronounce the word *Damne* with such an emphasis as left a dolefull Echo in his auditor's ears a good while after' the seventeenth-century objection to his Calvinism:

> that his Doctrine, referring all to an absolute decree, hamstrings all industry, and cuts off the sinews of mens endeavours towards salvation. For ascribing all to the wind of Gods spirit, (which bloweth where it listeth) he leaveth nothing to the oars of mans diligence, either to help or hinder to the attaining of happinesse, but rather opens a wide doore to licentious security.[118]

After the turn of the century there were found many within the English Church to agree with her Roman Catholic, often Jesuit, critics that Protestant theology when preached directly to the people, 'being simple and propense to evil', encouraged their licentious behaviour by teaching them antinomianism: 'For perswade a man once, that being in Christ, and so justified from all his sins, hee hath no more neede of repentance: and what a flood-gate is opened to all impiety, when there is no more conscience of sin.'[119]

Where Robert Sanderson had complained that 'Bellarmine ... pretends that we make the liberty of a Christian to consist in this, [not] to be bound in Conscience, to be subject to no Law', other Protestant divines came to agree with the great Jesuit that 'Christian Libertie; it is more necessary to be knowne then commended or urged.'[120] Alexander Chapman complained that preachers had concentrated unduly on educating the people in the doctrinal differences between the Roman Church and their own, even including elaborate theological definitions in their catechisms intended for

---

[117] In 1646, the Presbyterian Samuel Rutherford in his *Divine Right of Church Government and Excommunication* (London, 1646), pp. 109, 112, used this text to argue that 'Every moral action is to be warranted by the Word' and 'Whatever is beside the Word of God, in morals is contrary to it', as did Alexander Rosse, *The Picture of Conscience drawne to the Life, by the Pencell of Divine Truth* (London, 1646), p. 18: 'where there is but little faith, there will bee much doubting; want of love is the cause of so many errors; and want of obedience to spirituall Superiours is the cause of so many scruples'.   [118] Fuller, *Holy State*, p. 90.
[119] Henry Burton, *The Law and the Gospell reconciled* (London, 1631), p. 35. On this question see C. F. Allison, The Rise of Moralism: The Proclamation of the Gospel from Hooker to Baxter (London, 1966).
[120] *Bishop Sanderson's Lectures on Conscience and Human Law*, edited in an English translation by Christopher Wordsworth (London, 1877), p. 115; [Alexander Chapman], *Christian Liberty Described in a Sermon Preached in the Collegiate Church at Westminster* (London, 1606), sig. B4v, A2: 'The subject of this treaty, is that which all men challenge and fewe do well is Libertye', A3v: 'It is better to be there where nothing is lawfull, then where all thinges; where there is no liberty, then nothing but liberty.'

the most rudimentary understandings. In 1604, Jeremy Corderoy, while noting that anti-papal polemic provided the best avenue to promotion within the church, chose 'rather to speake of the necessitie of good works . . . then against error in doctrine', since 'now most men offende in lewdnesse of life, more then in error of doctrine'. In response to contemporary moral decay, he retreated from Protestant doctrinal emphasis, urging instead that it was 'altogether impossible . . . that a man be saved except he hath lived a good life'.[121] Previous neglect of the ministry's pastoral function in restraining 'ungodlinesse in conversation' had the consequence amongst the Protestant laity, Chapman believed, that 'that which once was vice is now with them no vice, that which once was vertu is now non'. Chapman pointed to the absurdity of the preachers' hope that one could, 'urge *liberty* upon the multitude and then suppose an exhortation will restrain excesse', incidentally revealing the low expectations divines held of the ecclesiastical courts as a means of reforming morality.[122]

Lewis Bayly complained that 'in the multitude of opinions, most men have almost lost the practice of true religion'. The 'carnall gospeller' learned from Lutheran justification by faith alone 'that good works are not necessary' and from Calvinist predestination 'That if he be predestinated to be saved, he cannot but be saved: if to be damned no means can do any good.' 'What is this', he asked, 'but to be an implicite Atheiste?'[123] Against Calvinist preoccupation with assurance of salvation Bayly held that 'Despaire is nothing so dangerous as presumption', taking up Bancroft's warning to James at the Hampton Court Conference in 1603 of the licentious implications of puritan doctrine: 'how many in these days neglect holinesse of Life, presuming on persisting in Grace upon Predestination: "If I shall be saved, I shall be saved."'[124] Bancroft's preferred solution was to suppress puritan preaching within the church and to impose greater ecclesiastical uniformity and jurisdiction over the laity.[125] But the godly 'puritan' members of the laity were themselves well aware of the ungodly uses to which their own doctrines could be put: 'let us brag of a naked and bare faith as long as we will'.[126] For

[121] Jeremy Corderoy, *A Short Dialogue, wherein is proved that no man can be saved without good workes* (Oxford, 1604), 'To the Reader'. [122] Chapman, sig. c.
[123] Lewis Bayly, *The Practice of Pietie. Directing a Christian how to walk that he may please God*, thirty-fourth edition (Edinburgh, 1642), pp. 135, 107, 120.
[124] Ibid., p. 121. On the discussion of Predestination at the Hampton Court Conference, see Thomas Fuller, *The Church History of Britain* (London, 1655), bk 9, p. 11.
[125] On Bancroft, see S. B. Babbage, *Puritanism and Richard Bancroft* (London, 1962), p. 94. [126] Phillip Stubbes, *A Motive to Good Workes* (London, 1593), p. 40.

example, that predestination offered a thief the defence 'that it was not in his free will or choyce to forbeare stealing' worried puritans throughout the century, as did the salvation of the thief on the Cross.[127]

Although both Luther and Calvin had criticized juristic Roman casuistry, urging that the power of the keys should consist instead of preaching which could exhort to repentance, it was largely in the context of this early seventeenth-century Protestant concern over the reformation of manners that casuistry began to acquire its unsavoury reputation in England. 'Now adayes there is no sinne so grosse, which is not blanched and smeered over wyth... counterfait excuses and glosses', Phillip Stubbes had complained in his jeremiad of 1593 against contemporary morality, which he believed lent substance to the Roman reproach that 'our Religion were nothing else but ... playne Atheisme and Libertinisme'. His response was one which would become characteristic of seventeenth-century puritanism: a voluntarist appeal firstly to the Bible, especially the moral law of the Old Testament, and then to the godly magistrate 'that by the sword of authority you might suppresse vice'.[128] An uncompromising biblicism began to replace that reconciliation between the Gospels and the natural law attempted by the puritan casuists Perkins and Ames in order to establish that 'This may consist with our Christian freedom, to be tyed to doe dutie because God hath commanded' and that 'the law doth remaine as a rule of walking to the people of God'.[129] Arthur Dent's *Plaine Man's Pathway to Heaven*, which 'medleth not at all with any controversies in the Church ... but onely entreth into a controversy with Sathan and Sin', was only one of a lively genre, consisting of popular works designed to instill a higher standard of morality in the English people: 'Walk with the few godly, in the Scriptures narrow path to heaven but crowd not with the godlesse multitude, in the broad way to hell.'[130]

Bayly took sabbath-observance as the test-case for *The Practice of Piety*: 'Take away the Sabbath, and let every man serve God when he listeth, and what will shortly become of religion?', for the Ten

---

[127] Slatius, *Fur Praedestinatus*, 1651 (Latin translation of his Dutch work published at Dort in 1642, often mistakenly attributed to William Sancroft), translated into English in 1658. On this work see Dewey D. Wallace, *Puritans and Predestination: Grace in English Protestant Theology, 1525–1695* (Chapel Hill, 1982), p. 122.

[128] Stubbes, p. 166, Epistle Dedicatory, a4v, A5v.

[129] Samuel Bolton, *The True Bounds of Christian Freedome* (London, 1645), 'To the Christian Reader'. On Perkins and Ames, see George Mosse, *The Holy Pretence* (Oxford, 1957).

[130] Arthur Dent, *The Plaine Man's Pathway to Heaven* (London, 1601), p. 118.

Commandments appeared to him the only bulwark against anti-nomianism: 'He who fails in one fails in all.'[131] Thomas Fuller later explained the extremity of puritan biblicism over the sabbath thus: 'For although liberty on the Lord's day may be so limited in the notion of learned men, as to make it lawfull, it is difficult (if not impossible) so to confine it in the actions of the lewd people, but that their liberty will degenerate into licentiousnesse.'[132] This suggests that puritan divines were driven to an exaggerated rigorism precisely because their 'casuistry' of the sabbath was public and rhetorical. Their writings were exhortatory rather than juristic, designed to motivate the laity up to a higher standard of conduct, and in this context prudent accommodations or concessions to reality could only have appeared to be socially dangerous incentives to sin. Puritan preachers were highly conscious of the fact that they possessed no sanctions with which to threaten the laity other than those provided by their own powers of persuasion. Characteristically, they threatened the laity with the punishments of God in this world and the next, as in the *Catalogue of the fearfull Judgements that have happened to wilfull infringers, and profane and irreligious Sabbath-breakers*, which was appended to the *Godly Rules and Directions for all Sincere Christian Professors, for the strict observation of the Lords Day*, concluding that 'such shall one day finde the judgement of God, heavier then the opinions of men'.[133]

Since the earliest days of the Reformation, puritans had learned to associate ecclesiastical claims to jurisdiction over the laity with popish tyranny, and had come to place their reliance on the godly magis-trate in order to bolster their rhetoric with the tools of coercion, enforcing both attendance at church to hear the ministry of the word and the practice of all the duties of the Ten Commandments. The preacher Robert Pricke in 1609 warned: 'Take away the Magistrate and the publicke ministerie of the word and all other means of mans salvation do utterly cease.'[134] In this context, puritan horror at the command by the Stuarts that their invitation to laxity on the sabbath, the *Declaration of Sports*, be read from the pulpits can well be understood.[135]

Christopher Dow argued that sabbatarianism was an innovation

---

[131] Bayly, pp. 216–30.  [132] Fuller, *Church History*, bk 9, p. 148.
[133] A. B., *The Sabbath truly sanctified* (London, 1645).
[134] Patrick Collinson, *The Religion of Protestants* (Oxford, 1982), p. 155.
[135] Ibid., p. 146: 'That was the ultimate scandal of the royal Book of Sports, endorsing with the highest authority Sunday recreations which the godly considered sacrilegious and unlawful.'

which arose out of the seventeenth-century publishing phenomenon of seemingly numberless puritan catechisms and conduct books vying with each other in the amount of moral instruction they could incorporate under the rubric of the Ten Commandments. [136] In seeking 'to strike an equall course betweene an overnice strictnesse and a profane license', 'the one letting loose, the other ensnaring mens consciences', the defenders of James's *Book of Sports*, turned, as had Richard Hooker when defending the Elizabethan Settlement against puritan biblicism, to a natural law 'imprinted in the heart of man in the creation with an indelible character never to be blotted out' and divided according to 'the ordinary and common distinction betweene the morall, ceremoniall and judiciall laws'. [137] Francis White, Bishop of Ely, cited Hooker and described it as but

*a frantick Paradox* to maintaine, that Christians are obliged to nothing, but such things only as are ... commanded, by some expresse written Law of God in holy Scripture: For many things ... when they are commanded by ... lawfull authority come within the compasse of God's generall Law [which] ... obligeth people to performe them. [138]

Gilbert Ironside went so far as to argue that 'that which cannot be deduced out of the principles of naturall reason ... without revelation', in Primrose's words, 'without any outward Usher', could be neither moral law nor perpetually obliging. [139] Where the puritan William Gouge had urged tutiorism: 'Now to one that is not perswade one way or other, I would propound this question, whether may be the safer, to sanctify it, or not to sanctify it?' the opponents of sabbatarianism offered probabilism: 'where in matters of doubt men are of divers judgements ... and divers opinions, that which inclineth most to humanitie and equitie is to be preferred'. [140] Ironside appealed to Gerson against St Paul to argue that 'perhaps it is not alwaies a sinne ... to goe against the feares and scruples of our minds', and sought to reassure his audience that opposition to biblicist sabbatarianism did not entail abandonment of the cause of reforming the morals of the laity. 'Conscience is not let loose, as is supposed, but only bound in another way', he claimed, namely

[136] *A Discourse of the Sabbath and the Lords Day* (London, 1636), p. 1.
[137] Ibid., pp. 3–4; Gilbert Ironside, *Seven Questions of the Sabbath Briefly Disputed, after the manner of the SCHOOLES* (London, 1637), p. 68; David Primrose, *A Treatise of the Sabbath and Lord's Day* (London, 1636), p. 4.
[138] Francis White, *An Examination and Confutation of a Lawlesse Pamphlet* (London, 1637), p. 76.    [139] Ironside, p. 51 and Primrose, p. 4.
[140] William Gouge, *The Sabbath's Sanctification* (London, 1641), p. 41; Thomas Scot, *Christs Politician, and Saloman's Puritan* (London, 1616), p. 18.

through the revitalization of ecclesiastical jurisdiction attempted by the Laudian Church.[141]

In seeking to restore to the church the wealth and prestige it had lost during the Reformation, the Laudian Church set itself in determined opposition to the laity of seventeenth-century England. Indeed, the struggle to establish social control through ecclesiastical jurisdiction may have been more central to Laud's concerns than were the theological niceties of Arminianism.[142] As Christopher Hill long ago argued, the conflict between laity and Laudian Church came into sharpest focus over the question of tithes. Where the Laudian Church campaigned to have impropriated tithes restored to the church (often exploiting 'supernatural' rhetoric such as Henry Spelman's to do so), the lay Feoffees for Impropriations purchased impropriated tithes in order that they might fund puritan ministers of their own selection, on the model of those godly town corporations which had created salaried lectureships for puritan ministers. In suppressing the Feoffees, Laud claimed that they infringed that ecclesiastical jurisdiction which he was in the process of restoring, with the support of the King.[143]

For some Laudians this implied resuming for the clergy the power of the keys. Sparrow, for example, claimed for the priesthood 'the power of remitting sins': 'Priests were made God's Viceregents here on earth, in his name to retaine and forgive sinnes, not *declaratively* onely, but judicially . . .'[144]

The Laudian Immanuel Bourne suggested too that the power of priestly absolution offered an alternative solution to the problem of Calvinist despair: that the afflicted should seek absolution from their priest in order to quieten their consciences.[145] As the Jesuists Warford and Lessius had claimed in their English apologies for Catholicism at the turn of the century, absolution offered the sinner unrivalled 'comfort and assurance', 'tranquillity and quietness'.[146]

---

[141] Ironside, Epistle Dedicatory and p. 94. See p. 56: 'unlesse men have their bounds set them, they easily turne their lawfulle, and warrantable liberty into unwarrantable licentiousnesse'.

[142] Kevin Sharpe, 'Archbishop Laud and the University of Oxford', in H. Lloyd-Jones, V. Pearl and N. Tyacke (eds.), *History and Imagination* (London, 1981), pp. 146–64.

[143] Christopher Hill, *Economic Problems of the Church* (Oxford, 1956), ch. XI.

[144] Anthony Sparrow, *A Sermon concerning Confession of Sinnes and the Power of Absolution* (London, 1637), pp. 16, 18.

[145] Immanuel Bourne, *The Anatomie of Conscience* (London, 1623), pp. 31–2.

[146] [William Warford,] *A Briefe manner of examination of Conscience for a Generall Confession* (1604), edited by D. M. Rogers in the series English Recusant Literature, vol. 251 (London, 1975), sig. S3v; [Leonardus Lessius,] *A Consultatione which Faith is to be beleved, which Religione is to be imbraced* (1619), edited by D. M. Rogers, English Recusant Literature, vol. 251 (London, 1975), sig. D3.

English puritans, however, could only think it a 'miserable comfort' 'to submit yourselfe to a superiour's blind command' because of their adherence to the Lutheran doctrine of Christian liberty: 'we infringe our Christian liberty, and become the servants of men, in submitting and binding our Consciences to the ordinances of man'.[147]

For, while puritans were themselves implicitly moving away from the central concerns of sixteenth-century Protestant doctrine towards a frank moralism, antipopery remained so central to their understanding of Protestantism that they could by no stretch of the imagination move in the direction of Roman Catholicism as the Arminians so overtly did in their retreat from Calvinism. Puritan political thought, as it had evolved under Elizabeth, identified the national magistrate with the Protestant cause.[148] The puritan dilemma in the seventeenth century was of course that their ecclesiology required the backing of a godly magistrate who, in the case of the Stuarts, was increasingly perceived as taking the church towards Roman Catholicism through the sponsorship of Arminian doctrines and divines.[149] Seventeenth-century English Protestant political theory, whether puritan or Arminian, characteristically consisted of little more than a running together of God's law and the magistrates', rhetorically threatening rebels against either with biblical sanctions.[150] It is not altogether surprising, then, that puritans were, as Morrill has noted, slow to produce resistance theories, as civil war with a king seemingly drifting ever closer to popery became inevitable.[151]

Henry Hammond in his *Of Resisting the Lawfull Magistrate Under Colour of Religion* of 1644, described the Parliamentarians as 'perfect Jesuits in their principles', arguing that non-resistance based on Romans 13 and the Divine Right of Kings 'hath alwayes beene counted a principall head of difference between the Protestants and the worst of Papists'.[152] English Protestants had been made very familiar with the 'King-Killing doctrines of the Jesuits' during the polemic against

[147] Rosse, p. 77.
[148] See, for example, W. D. J. Cargill Thompson, 'Sir Francis Knollys's campaign against *Jure Divino* theory of episcopacy', in his *Studies in the Reformation: Luther to Hooker* (London, 1980).
[149] Nicholas Tyacke, 'Puritanism, Arminianism and Counter-Revolution', in Conrad Russell (ed.), *The Origins of the English Civil War* (London, 1973).
[150] J. P. Kenyon, *The Stuart Constitution* (Cambridge, 1965), pp. 16–19. For criticism of this generalization, see Derek Hirst, 'The place of principle', in 'Revisionism revised', *Past and Present*, no. 92 (August 1981), 81.
[151] John Morrill, introduction to his *Reactions to the English Civil War, 1642–9* (London, 1982), pp. 5–6.
[152] Henry Hammond, *Of Resisting the Lawfull Magistrate Under colour of Religion* (Oxford, 1644), p. 34.

Rome encouraged by James I, and throughout the century, translations of French anti-Jesuit works drove the lesson home. For
example, André Rivet's *State Mysteries of the Jesuites*, translated by
Peter Gosselin in 1623, had pitted the doctrines of Suarez, Mariana,
Bellarmine, and others against St Paul's 'Let every person be subject
to the higher powers.'[153]

When 'at the last moment' driven by events Parliament's supporters
began to argue a right to resistance against the Crown, they could
thus not turn to Protestant political theory which, as it had
developed in the seventeenth century, virtually ruled out the right
to use force in self-defence – that right which Skinner has shown to
be central to the 'Calvinist theory of revolution':[154] 'se defendendo
. . . yet makes no rule of self-defence against a King neither. It is the
necessary office of Christian love for Christs sake to be killed.'[155]
When early English puritan casuists such as William Perkins and
William Ames had held that the seventh commandment prohibited
'all private men to kill or slay', they had admitted the exception of
'the case of a just and necessary defence' on the grounds that 'the
Gospel doth not abolish the Law of Nature' which 'sets downe and
prescribes the distinctions of possessions, and proprietie of lands
and goods' and permits a right to repel force with force 'for our just
defence and for the claims of our needfull due and right'.[156] Both distinguished their position from that of the Roman casuists only in so
far as the latter permitted the use of force in defence of honour as
well as life and estates.[157] The latter question became particularly
controversial in England under James I, when duelling became
fashionable as a result of 'some French and Italian pamphlets' popularizing 'tinsell honour and reputation' and found support from legal
antiquarians who held that the right to batle existed in English
law.[158] The availability of an alternative remedy for libel in the courts

[153] See also *The Legend of the Jesuites* (London, 1623).
[154] Quentin Skinner, *The Foundations of Modern Political Thought* (Cambridge, 1978), vol.
II, part III, and his summary article, 'The origins of the Calvinist theory of revolution', in Barbara C. Malament (ed.), *After the Reformation* (Manchester, 1980).
[155] Robert Wilkinson, *A Sermon preached . . . upon occasion of the late Rebellion and Riots*
(London, 1607), sig. E3v.
[156] William Perkins, *Whole Treatise of the Cases of Conscience* (Cambridge, 1606), pp. 499–
501 and his *Exposition of Christ's Sermon on the Mount*, in his *Works* (Cambridge, 1613),
vol. III, p. 47; Ames, *Conscience*, bk. 5, ch. xxxi: 'What is a just cause that a man
should bee killed?'
[157] Ames, *Conscience*, bk. II, p. 197; Perkins, *Whole Treatise*, p. 502. See Mervyn James,
'English politics and the concept of honour, 1485–1642', *Past and Present* Supplement 13 (1978), p. 13.
[158] *The Charge of Sir Francis Bacon Touching Duells* (London, 1614), p. 10; William
Dickinson, *The King's Right* (London, 1619), sig. E3; [John Selden], *The Duello or
single combat: From Antiquitie derived into this Kingdome of England* (London, 1610).

allowed the seventh commandment to be brought by Protestant opponents of duelling to the service of the magistrate's divine right: 'God set Kings above men that every man might not be the Judge and revenger of his own griefe.'[159] Howard argued that the right to repel force with force was 'wicked and contrary to Christianity' with its Evangelical law of charity.[160]

Unlike the casuistry of Ames and Perkins with their 'Killing is not alwaies murther', seventeenth-century catechisms and conduct books generally recognized no exceptions to the commandment that thou shalt not kill. By the middle of the century, as we have seen, Baxter was able to contrast Protestant unity on the subject with the divided opinions of the Roman casuists, of whom Clarkson would write that 'if the civil Laws did give as much liberty to murder, as their rules for conscience do, Desolation would soon be brought upon the face of the earth'.[161]

Baxter's own retreat from Protestant soteriology and shift towards moralism had awaited his direct experience of anti-nomianism in the Parliamentary army: 'Antinomian Teachers, who are magnified as the only Preachers of Free Grace, do assert and proclaim that there is no more required to the perfect irrevocable justification of the vilest Murderer or Whoremaster, but to beleeve that he is justified, or to be persuaded that God loveth him.'[162]

Unlike 'practicall truths', he argued in 1649, *Aphorisms of Justification* were often 'better written than preached, and read than heard', admitting that 'the Antinomian conceit, That God seeth not sin in his justified ones' 'hath given great advantage to the Papists against us in the Doctrine of Justificiation'.[163] He cited Anthony Burgess's *The True Doctrine of Justification Asserted and Vindicated, From the Errors of Papists, Arminians, Socinians, and more especially ANTINOMIANS*, of 1648, on the difference between presumption and assurance of salvation and the 'necessity of fulfilling the conditions of the Gospel themselves upon all that will be justified and saved: He doth not justifie by the shedding of his blood immediately, without somewhat of man intervening . . . there must be somewhat in our selves to

---

[159] Dickinson, sig. D3; George Webbe, *The Practice of Quietnes* (London, 1615), p. 172: 'true grace and credit standeth more in yeelding obedience unto God, then in foolish hazarding of life or limmes for a blast of vaine reputation'.
[160] Henry Howard, Earl of Northampton, *Duello Foiled*, in Thomas Hearne (ed.), *A Collection of Curious Discourses* (London, 1771), vol. II, p. 237.
[161] Clarkson, p. 337.
[162] Richard Baxter, *Aphorismes of Justification* (London, 1649), p. 330. See W. M. Lamont, 'Comment: the rise of Arminianism reconsidered', in *Past and Present*, no. 107 (May 1985), 129.   [163] Baxter, *Aphorismes*, pp. 207, 47.

prove that title, or else all men should have equal right.'[164] Justification, when considered 'in point of Morality', 'in Morall and Politicke respects', led him, as it had Henry Hammond, to a rigorist emphasis on love or charity at the expense of faith; 'I take . . . some degree of Love to be part of justifying Faith, and not properly a fruit of it, as it is commonly taken.'[165] When in 1673 he published his own *Christian Directory* of casuistry, however, he recognized that while earlier puritan moralism had counselled saintly courses, casuistry required realism if jurisdiction over the laity were not to be abandoned: 'No kingdom on earth is so holy and happy as to have all or most of the subjects such confirmed eminent Saints, as will be contented to be undone, and will love and honour those that undo them. Therefore Men must be taken as they are.'[166]

When divines engaged in political controversy, did their publications represent naturalistic casuistry or moralistic exhortation? This was in one sense the point at issue between royalist and Parliamentarian divines in the early years of the civil war. Henry Ferne complained in his 1643 publication, *Conscience Satisfied*, that whereas Parliament had originally claimed religion as 'the main Engine to draw them into Arms', when justifying their actions *post facto*, 'Religion is not insisted on, . . . but Nature is rather sought unto by them, for a ground of self preservation.' This turn to nature he described in *The Resolving of Conscience* as a casuistical evasion of duty, 'the cleere light of the Law of God and this Land meeting them in the face'.[167] In seeking to persuade their 'Conscientious Readers' to a higher standard of conduct, royalist divines relied on the same mode of rhetoric exploited by puritans earlier in the century, namely the use of biblical texts, in this case Romans 13, to threaten their audience with sanctions in the next world: 'a Conscience that concludes for resistance wants the perswasion of faith and the judgement of charitie . . . and cannot safely appeare at Gods tribunall'.[168] The natural lawyer Dudley Digges expressed relief that on the basis

[164] Ibid., pp. 113, 95; Henry Hammond, *A Practical Catechism* (Oxford, 1646). See Anthony Burgess, *The True Doctrine of Justification Asserted and Vindiccated, From the Errors of Papists, Arminians, Socinians, and more especially ANTINOMIANS* (London, 1648), p. 16: 'We must not confound justification with the manifestation and declaration of it in our hearts and consciences . . . The Antinomian goeth into one extremity and the Papist into another.'
[165] Baxter, *Aphorismes*, p. 266.   [166] Baxter, *Christian Directory*, p. 143.
[167] Henry Ferne, *Conscience Satisfied. That there is no warrant for the Armes now taken up by the Subjects* (Oxford, 1643), pp. 2–3, and his 'Epistle to the Conscientious Readers among the People'.
[168] Henry Ferne, *The Resolving of Conscience* (Cambridge, 1642), section vii.

of Romans 13 'God is to be reckoned of the King's side, who will
overbalance their greatest forces': 'You are exhorted not to rebell,
because you may be hang'd, but . . . you shall certainly be damn'd . . .
though you escape a shamefull death, yet you have forfeited eternall
life.'[169] What the Parliamentarians called their right to self-defence
in natural law was in fact 'onely right of nature, which is not a command but a permission onely' and 'though nature doth not forbid it,
yet the Gospell doth . . . Private revenge is unanswerably prohibited
by the Evangelical Law', which required that Christians be as prepared as the early martyrs to resign their lives, since 'Perfect charity
is the fulfilling of the Law.'[170] By 1644, the Presbyterian Samuel
Rutherford went so far as to cite Jesuit authors in support of an
account of government based on the natural right to 'self-defence by
opposing violence to unjust violence', a right which Digges denied
could ever prevail over God's command that 'thou shalt not kill'.[171]

HENRY PALMER, in his *Scripture and Reason Pleaded for Defensive Armes* of
1643, described the 'whole controversy about Subjects taking up
armes' thus: 'Bookes written against Bookes, and Conscience pre-
tended against Conscience. In this perplexed condition, What shall
the people doe? What shall they resolve?',[172] a plaintive note which
would frequently be echoed during the Interregnum and after. For,
as John Canne recognized in the 'king-killing' year of 1649, the doctrine of Christian liberty became frighteningly empty of prescriptive
content in a state of political liberty: 'A blind Papist, I confesse,
walks by some rule, when not knowing the thing to be lawfull, yet
receives it, in regard he believes the Church cannot erre. But what
hath a poore blind protestant to help himself in point of conscience?[173] Palmer had urged the perplexed to have recourse to
divines like himself who could distinguish Romans 13 from a simple
command, by locating it in Paul's historical context.[174] For the
royalist divine Henry Ferne, however, such an approach was casuistical,
evidence for the 'crookednesse of the doctrines of these times' in
conflict with 'the clear light of Divine Scripture and rectified
Reason, the onely rules of Conscience'.[175] Their controversy caused
the Parliamentarian Charles Herle to conclude that 'Divinity gives

---

[169] [Dudley Digges,] *The unlawfulnesse of Subjects taking up Armes against their Soveraigne, in what case soever* (n.p., 1643/4), pp. 49, 85.    [170] Ibid., pp. 122–3, 43.
[171] [Samuel Rutherford,] *Lex, Rex: The law and the Prince* (London, 1644), pp. 4, 5, 6, 17; Digges, p. 43: 'the people could not agree together to dispense with Gods precept, Thou shalt not kill'.
[172] Palmer, 'Epistle to the Reader'.    [173] *A Snare is Broken* (London, 1649), p. 13.
[174] Palmer, p. 21.
[175] Henry Ferne, *The Resolving of Conscience*, 'Epistle to the Reader'.

onely generall rules of obedience to all lawfull authority, tels us not where that authority is', which could be determined only by the law of the land, thought by Ferne 'not fit to satisfie Conscience'.[176]

With Parliament's military victory against the King, however, both the legal argument and that from the natural right of resistance were rendered no longer relevant to political debate. In the crisis of legitimacy which accompanied the establishment of the Commonwealth, the temptation to return to biblicism proved irresistible to many defenders of the Rump. The text, Romans 13, was admitted by Cromwell 'a Malignant one; the wicked and ungodly have abused it very frequently, but (thanks bee to God) it was to their Ruine; yet their abuse shall not hinder us from making a right use of it'.[177] As J. M. Wallace has argued, 'Political casuistry . . . was so committed to the language of St Paul in Romans xiii that it was easy to confuse the divine right of kings with the divine right of power', as did the puritan divine John Dury in his engagement pamphlets.[178] In response, *A Pack of Old Puritans* rejoiced in the title of 'puritan' as signifying scrupulosity, noting that 'had this Doctrine of Master Dury's for blinde obedience, and non-resistance of the present powers from Romans 13 . . . been preached at the beginning of These Troubles' the Parliamentary cause would have been lost at the outset. As it was, Dury's argument would only satisfy 'such as through fear or interest, desire to bribe, corrupt, and cozen their Consciences'.[179]

Clerical opponents of engagement to the new regime flattered themselves on their rigorism and unwillingness to accommodate to political reality, as for example in *A Brief Resolution of that Grand Case of Conscience*:

And if by this stating of the Case it follow that the lot of the faithfull Subjects must be very unhappy at this time, and that great disorder must necessarily continue . . . I answer, that this is of the lot of the most pious Men under the Gospel, *who have their good things here mixt with tribulations, and must content themselves in the solaces of a good conscience . . . and expect their full payment of joyes without hardships to be payd them in another world.*[180]

[176] [Charles Herle,] *An answer to Doctor Fernes Reply entitled Conscience Satisfied* (London, 1643), pp. 3, 17.

[177] *A Most learned, Conscientious, and Devout-Exercise. . . By Lieutenant-Generall Crumwell: As it was faithfully taken . . . by Aaron Guerdon* (London, 1649), p. 1.

[178] John Wallace, 'The cause too good', p. 153; J[ohn] D[ury], *A Case of Conscience resolved: concerning ministers medling with state-matters in their sermons* (London, 1649), and his *Considerations concerning the present Engagement, whether it may lawfully be entered into; yea or no?* (London, 1649).

[179] *A Pack of Old Puritans* (London, 1650), pp. 34, 19.

[180] *A briefe resolution of that grand case of conscience* (London, 1650), p. 6.

The political turncoat Marchamont Nedham complained that such clergy, 'having an influence upon the noblest part of man, the *Soul* and the *Conscience*, can easily fasten what impressions they please, and actuate the zeale of mankinde, to carry on any designe, to the miserable imbroyling of *States* and *Kingdomes*.'[181] Presbyterian divines, the 'new nest of Jesuits', by preaching rebellion from their pulpits were worse than the Jesuits themelves, who at least only incited rebellion through the confessional.[182] Against Presbyterian 'scrupulosity', the secular 'de-facto theorists of political obligation' urged the laity to consult their own self-interest, namely the individual's natural right of self-preservation, and demonstrated that obedience was necessary in order to defend one's person and, more especially, one's property.[183]

The Engagement Controversy had quickly revealed the inadequacies of Romans 13 as political theory, but biblicist appeals to the text against secularizing 'Jesuitical' natural rights theories continued throughout the political debates of the century: 'God forbid that Protestants should ever part with their sound doctrine.'[184] Notoriously, William Sherlock was able to justify in 'casuistical' fashion his change of allegiance to William and Mary, with his assertion of the Church of Engand doctrine of absolute non-resistance under James II in terms of Romans 13: 'I am sure St Paul, who most expressly teaches this doctrine of Non-resistance, joyns these two together, Obedience to the present Powers, and Non-resistance, and deducts them both from the same Principle, That all Power is of God.'[185]

The predominantly Erastian tone of seventeenth-century natural rights theories has long been recognized. In his *Machiavellian Moment*, for example, J. G. A. Pocock discerned a 'principal motive' behind the attempts to construct a 'natural politics' of Hobbes, Harrington, and Nedham as being 'to deny separate authority to the clergy'.[186] As Nedham wrote of clerical pretensions during the Interregnum, it

---

[181] *Mercurius Politicus*, no. 55 (19–26 June 1651), in the series The English Revolution III, Newsbooks 5 (Cornmarket Press, 1971), vol. 3, 69.       [182] Ibid., 71.

[183] See Quentin Skinner, 'Conquest and consent: Thomas Hobbes and the Engagement Controversy', in G. E. Aylmer (ed.), *The Interregnum: The Quest for Settlement* (London, 1972), and his 'Ideological context of Hobbes's political thought', *Historical Journal*, vol. IX, no. 3 (1966), 286–317.

[184] *Just Principles of Complying with the New Oath of Allegiance* (London, 1689), p. 20. See Goldie, p. 543.

[185] *The Case of the Allegiance due to Soveraign Powers, Stated and Resolved* (London, 1691), p. 37.

[186] J. G. A. Pocock, *The Machiavellian Moment* (Princeton, 1975), pp. 396–8. See too his 'Time, history and eschatology in the thought of Hobbes', in *Politics, Language and Time* (New York, 1971), pp. 148–201.

was 'high time to lay the ax to the foot of these acorns': 'They have taken a *new Form*, but labour to hold up the *old Grandeur.*' New presbyters lacked the 'outward power' of the old priests but more than compensated for this deficiency in the extent of the power which they claimed over the conscience of the laity.[187] Indeed, the Presbyterian Samuel Clark wrote of the ministers' power over conscience: 'I see no reason, why it may not properly be called Jurisdiction.'[188]

The Interregnum exercise in lay Protestant casuistry, which has come to be called the 'de facto theory of political obligation', represented, more than anything else, a denial by the laity of this claim to ecclesiastical jurisdiction over conscience. Thomas Hobbes, recognizably a casuist himself in the Engagement Controversy, freely criticized the 'the Black Coats... who in matters of their own profession, such as is the mending ... of men's consciences have made more holes than they have found'.[189] Perhaps as part of the reaction against the reductionism of C. B. Macpherson's *Political Theory of Possessive Individualism*, however, historians of political thought have been reluctant to give due recognition to the fact that Erastian political theorists denied the clergy the power of determining conscience or 'medling' not only in political but also in socio-economic 'cases'.

This can be illustrated in the case of the Presbyterian divine Christopher Love who, according to Nedham, forfeited his title to godly minister when he preached rebellion in the second civil war. Nedham waged a campaign in the pages of *Mercurius Politicus* calling for 'impartiall execution of Laws' in the case of love:

Let Ministers live as other men, as members of the Civill State, and let their privileges ... flow from the Civill Power. Let them be examples of obedience to it, and not pretend they must have *Scruples* satisfied before they submit ...

To own men upon pretence of a *Godly Interest*, that are enemies to the Civill, is the greatest State-heresie in the world.[190]

---

[187] Marchamont Nedham, *The Case of the Commonwealth of England Stated* (London, [May, 1650]), edited by P. Knachel for the Folger Shakespeare Library (University Press of Virginia, 1969), p. 72, and *Mercurius Politicus*, no. 58 (10–17 July 1651), pp. 117–18.

[188] Samuel Clark, *Ministers Dues and Peoples Duty* (London, 1661), p. 25: 'the highest compulsory power imaginable', and p. 21: 'For controversiall points of faith, or practise, (which we call Cases of Conscience) which people understand not so well themselves, their Ministers have likewise power to determine ... as among us Justices of Peace have at the Sessions.'

[189] Thomas Hobbes, *Of Libertie and Necessity* (London, 1654), sig. A6.

[190] *Mercurius Politicus*, no. 60 (24–31 July 1651), 151 and no. 63 (14–21 August 1651), 198.

Christopher Love was not only a political rebel but also the author of a broadsheet, *Scripture Rules to be Observed in Buying and Selling*, part of a large body of clerical literature characterized by its secular critics as clerical 'busibodiness'. As Baxter addressed the laity in his *Poor Husbandman's Advocate*: 'You take such preaching for presumptuous medling with your estates.'[191] Secular political theorists during the Interregnum typically made use of the biblical text 'My Kingdom is not of this world' to prove that Christ's laws 'symboliz'd not at all with those which relate to the *meum* and *tuum* of this world'; 'no Text can be brought to prove an Acre must be sold at such a price or a commodity at such a rate; the worth of things in proportion one to another is a humane arbitrary custom'.[192] Clerical polemicists against grainhoarding, enclosures, and usury found themselves victims of their own biblicism when rhetorically asked: 'What text he hath [then] to prove the letting of Land is lawful?'[193] At the same time, their secular opponents took unto themselves the role of casuists in the extensive area of human prudence which they claimed was left free between God's commands and his prohibitions. Sir Robert Filmer, for example, maintained against clerical rigorism that usury was a doubtful case which 'concerns no Article of Faith; but it is a point of Morality and case of conscience, and in that regard it admits of a disputation without Scandall'.[194] Members of the laity were encouraged by secular directors of conscience to act as their own casuists and to resist clerical pretensions both in the political and the socio-economic spheres throughout the Interregnum. By 1684 *The Case of Usury Further Debated* had the defender of usury cite in hackneyed fashion 'My Kingdom is not of this World' as authority for the position that Christ did 'care not to interpose in Secular Affairs (such as are the Proprieties of Men) but disclaimed having anything to do to be a Judge or Divider amongst Men', and his clerical opponent answer: 'Does God's Word nowhere interpose in Secular Affairs, but leave all to Man's determination?'[195]

John Locke has been the secular political theorist whom intellectual historians have been most concerned to rescue from Macpherson's description of him as a bourgeois ideologue. In John

[191] *The Poor Husbandman's Advocate to Rich, Racking Landlords* (1691), edited by F. J. Powicke as *The Reverend Richard Baxter's Last Treatise* (Manchester, 1926), p. 48.
[192] Anthony Ascham, *Of the Confusions and Revolutions of Governments* (London, 1649), p. 27; R[obert] F[ilmer,] *Quaestio Quodlibetica, or a Discourse, Whether it may bee lawfull to take Use for Money* (London, 1653), p. 131.
[193] R. [Filmer,] p. 81 and *Considerations Concerning Common Fields and Inclosures* (London, 1653), p. 38.   [194] R. F[ilmer,] preface.
[195] *The Case of Usury Further Debated* (London, 1684), p. 21.

Dunn's *Political Thought of John Locke*, this takes the form of emphasizing the depth of his Calvinist convictions and the extent to which they determine the character of his political and social thought. But just as historians have begun to recognize that the Calvinist theory of revolution derived from Roman neo-scholasticism, so it has come to be Locke's Thomist heritage that has been appealed to against Macpherson. In particular, the point has frequently been made that, so far from arguing that a natural right to private property precedes civil government, Locke was far more Thomist in his conviction that the merely civil distributions of private property collapsed in the face of another's extreme necessity.[196] In more detail James Tully has argued that Locke resembles the Jesuit Francisco Suarez in his denial of a natural and exclusive right to private property and his insistence that property relations are merely the creation of civil laws sustained by an obligation in natural law to keep contracts.[197] There is, however, at least as much justification for likening Locke to more laxist neo-scholastics, such as de Lugo and de Soto, who explicitly defended the legitimacy of existing rights of property against claims based on need by repudiating the canonist principle that *iure naturali omnia sunt communia*, arguing instead that private property was indeed natural; but that even before the establishment of government, another's extreme necessity rendered the duty of charity obligatory to the propertied without necessarily creating claim-rights of justice in the propertyless. In the laxist version, the world has always been privatized and the contrast between a state of nature and of civil government is reduced.[198]

As Ryan's recent account would suggest, Locke's treatment is ambiguous, perhaps admitting of either interpretation:

no Man could ever have a just power over the Life of another, by Right of property in possessions; since 'twould always be a Sin in any Man of Estate,

---

[196] See S. B. Drury, 'Locke and Nozick on property', *Political Studies* vol. XXX, no. 1, p. 34, and her 'Robert Nozick and the right to property', in Anthony Parel and Thomas Flanagan (eds.), *Theories of Property: Aristotle to the Present* (Calgary Institute for the Humanities, 1979), p. 372.

[197] James Tully, *A Discourse on Property: John Locke and his Adversaries* (Cambridge, 1980), and his 'The framework of natural rights in Locke's analysis of property: a contextual reconstruction,' in Parel and Flanagan, pp. 115–35.

[198] Cardinal Joannis de Lugo, *Disputationum de Justitia et Jure* (Lugduni, 1646), vol. I, section VII, 'De necessitate excusante ab furto', no. 144, p. 450: 'Concedimus denique, dominium earum rerum non solum iure positivo gentium, sed iure naturae'; Domingo de Soto, *De Iustitia et Iure* (Salamanca, 1556), bk 5, question 3, article 4, p. 427: if the doctrine permitting theft in time of necessity 'non est iustitiae, sed charitatis', then the present owner could be considered 'suarum dominus'.

to let his Brother perish for want of affording him relief out of his Plenty. As *Justice* gives every Man a Title to the product of his honest Industry, and the fair Acquisitions of his Ancestors descended to him; so *Charity* gives every Man a Title to so much out of another's Plenty, when he has no means to subsist otherwise.[199]

In illustrating the Vitorian or Grotian right to defend one's person and property, Locke did, however, point to the persistence of that natural right in civil society, no matter what were the laws of the land:

> Thus a *Thief*, ... I may kill, when he sets on me to rob me of my Horse or Coat.
> And 'tis such *Force* alone, that *puts* him that uses it *into a state of War*, and makes it lawful to resist him. A man with a Sword in his Hand demands my Purse in the High-way, when perhaps I have not 12d. in my Pocket; This Man I may lawfully kill.[200]

This makes a mockery of Locke's alleged preference for life over private property, reminding us of nothing so much as the seventeenth-century complaint against Jesuit laxity, that its casuistical concessions created 'rights' good against God's law and the magistrate's; in particular, the right to kill in defence of a crown or even an apple. The crucial difference is, of course, that Jesuit casuistry was not addressed to the laity, whereas Locke was writing in the vernacular, seeking to persuade 'the people' of their right to revolution. I have argued elsewhere that it was Interregnum lay casuists such as Hobbes and Ascham who needed to maintain that the right to self-preservation was natural, while that to private property was merely civil, if they were to urge obedience to the Commonwealth as the only means of protecting one's private property.[201]

What Locke had in common with those Interregnum political theorists was his denial of jurisdiction to the clergy. Nedham's argument for religious toleration and for the 'more refined and spirituall' 'Independent or Congregationall way' was part of his campaign to deny the clergy not only the power of 'persecuting and punishing of men for their opinions in Religion' but also any civil jurisdiction whatsoever.[202] This is surely true also of Locke's *Letter on Toleration* of 1689, which told churchmen 'striving for power and ambition' that: 'The business of true religion is something quite different. It is not

---

[199] Locke, pp. 205–6; Alan Ryan, *Property and Political Theory* (Oxford, 1984), pp. 34–6, 43–5.    [200] Locke, pp. 321, 451.

[201] In my University Of Sussex master's thesis: ' "A question which hath non-*plust* many": the right to private property and the Engagement Controversy, 1648–1652'.    [202] *Mercurius Politicus*, no. 60 (24–31 July 1651), p. 150.

made for outward pomp, nor for ecclesiastical dominion, let alone for force; but for regulating men's lives in accordance with virtue and piety.'[203] He urged upon ambitious clerics the example of Christ's meekness of spirit, since 'no man can be a Christian without charity,' and without the faith which worketh, not by force, but by love'.[204] Ministers should be restricted to Christ's Kingdom, the realm of Charity and Grace, their task the promotion of piety rather than social justice. Conversely, the civil magistrate should seek that to implement Christ's commands in this world but rather to create the civil laws which will secure 'the just possession of these things that belong to this life': 'the whole jurisdiction of the magistrate is concerned only with these civil goods'.[205]

This reminds us surely of Tawney's claim that by the reign of James II a 'new world' had emerged in England, one in which the 'claim of religion, at best a shadowy claim, to maintain rules of good conscience in economic affairs' had finally vanished.[206] Here it has been suggested that seventeenth-century political thought should be interpreted as contributing to this exclusion of the church from socio-economic life through its attempt to monopolize the science of casuistry, defined by Tawney as: 'the application of general principles to particular cases which is involved in any living system of jurisprudence, whether ecclesiastical or secular'.[207]

Grotius, Hobbes, Nedham, and Locke all claimed justice as the exclusive territory of the lay casuist (or natural rights theorist) and held that the function of the divine was to promote piety by preaching up the counsels of perfection to be found in the Gospel of Charity. Divines thus found themselves relegated to the niche which they had earlier carved for themselves. The English clergy contributed to their own loss of jurisdiction over the laity through their repudiation of casuistry and preference for preaching up an unrealistic and rigorist morality as the best means of combating lay licentiousness. Baxter, along with many Laudian divines, seems to have been aware of the dangers of this approach, but his position, as Lamont has shown, was an impossible one. His almost obsessional fear of popery led him to favour the subjection of the clergy to the jurisdiction of the godly magistrate. While he shared Hammond's concern to strengthen pastoral discipline, he could not follow him in urging

[203] John Locke, *Epistola de Tolerantia: A Letter on Toleration*, Latin text edited by Raymond Klibansky, English translation by J. W. Gough (Oxford, 1968), p. 60.   [204] Ibid.   [205] Ibid., pp. 63, 65, 67.
[206] R. H. Tawney, *Religion and the Rise of Capitalism* (Harmondsworth, 1938), pp. 23–4.
[207] Cited in David Mitchell, *The Jesuits: A History* (London, 1980), p. 129.

an independent ecclesiastical jurisdiction on the basis of the power of the keys.[208] He thus found himself unable to offer a strenuous response to the anticlericalism of such secular theorists as Harrington and Hobbes.

Antipopery, then, which had united the political nation under Elizabeth and divided it under Charles I, ultimately also secured the independence of the laity from clerical 'busibodiness' or jurisdiction, political and social. Andrew Marvell, in his *Growth of Popery and Arbitrary Government*, drew the lesson from the reputation of casuistry in seventeenth-century England that the Roman Catholic laity must themselves have been more moral than their casuists, who freed men 'from all duty to God or Man':

> their Governors of Conscience, have so well instructed them in all the arts of circumventing their neighbour and of colluding with Heaven, that were the scholars as apt as their teachers, there would have been long since an end of all either true Piety or common Honesty, and nothing left among them but authorised Hypocrisy, Licentiousnesse and Knavery.[209]

Perhaps, however, the greatest hypocrisy of all was to be found in those secular political theorists from Grotius onwards who shared the Protestant suspicion of Roman casuistry as offering incentives to sin against God's law and the magistrate's, but who at the same time translated from Roman casuistical sources those cases which told the laity of relevant rights good against divine and civil law. Seventeenth-century English natural rights theories should be seen less as popish relics than as further evidence of the 'triumph of the laity' in the English Reformation. As the puritan divine Cornelius Burges had predicted in 1625: 'This indeede is that many Professors would have: Liberty, Liberty: Let them be noted for bountifull; but not bound to be just.'[210]

---

[208] William M. Lamont, *Richard Baxter and the Millennium* (London, 1979). Compare Baxter's *The Difference Between the Power of Magistrates and Church-Pastors and the Roman Kingdom and Magistracy* (London, 1671), with Henry Hammond's *Of the Power of the Keyes: or, of binding and loosing* (London, 1647).
[209] Andrew Marvell, *An Account of the Growth of Popery and Arbitrary Government in England* (London, 1678), in A. Gorsart (ed.), *Complete Prose Works* (London, 1875), p. 253. [210] Burges, *A New Discovery of Personal Tithes*, p. 37.

# 3

◁ ═══════════════════════════════════════ ▷

# Casuistry and character

EDMUND LEITES

As it was understood in medieval and early modern Europe, the study of 'cases of conscience' – what is today called 'casuistry' – was the resolution by expert minds of difficult moral cases. This was a form of analysis which received massive support from the Roman Catholic Church from the thirteenth century onwards. Numerous casuistical manuals were produced, often designed to aid the priest faced with the challenge of guiding the individuals who came to him in confession.

The church also sought to judge institutional practices, including its own, and in these matters, too, it called for the aid of casuists. For centuries, important members of the faculties of many distinguished universities devoted themselves to the moral analysis of issues in all conceivable areas of contemporary life – from matters of finance to relations between parents and children, from the treatment of Indians in the New World to the degree of sinfulness in masturbation. The Protestant Reformation did not put a halt to the demand for church-sponsored casuistry. Sixteenth-century Lutheran Germany produced a large body of casuistical literature. During the first sixty years of the seventeenth century, English Protestants also wrote and read a great deal of the same sort of writing.

By the first decades of the eighteenth century, however, casuistical literature produced by the clergy was no longer an important force in the religious, intellectual, and moral life of Protestant England. McAdoo writes that from 1660 to 1700, it 'vanished off the [English] theological map' with 'incredible speed'.[1] No prominent theologian wrote casuistical treatises, and the great texts of the seventeenth-

---

[1] Henry Robert McAdoo, *The Structure of Caroline Moral Theology* (London: Longmans, Green, 1949), p. 66.

century casuists were rarely referred to by the spiritually important figures of the time. After so many centuries in which church-sponsored casuistry was a culturally dominant force in the West, it generally came to be seen as an unnecessary and even morally dangerous institution.

This change was at least in part a function of the rise to cultural power of the belief that from the point of view of spirituality and morality, nothing was more important for the individual than his possession of a truly moral will. To encourage the formation and maintenance of such a will, of 'character' in a laudatory sense, was therefore seen to be a chief task of both moral and religious instruction. The methods of casuistry, however, had never been meant to create or transform character. Moreover, they generally dealt with questions about what was forbidden or permitted, rather than about what it would be morally and spiritually *best* for the individual to do. Of course, texts and sermons which sought to inculcate character had always existed alongside the efforts of casuists and, in fact, there was many a casuist who was as notable for his efforts to transform hearts and minds as he was for his fine legal determinations. For many centuries, the production of casuistry had been seen as compatible with a concern for moral and spiritual formation. In late seventeenth-century England, however, casuistry was explicitly rejected out of a concern for character. In the following pages, I shall argue that it came to be rejected because of the rise to prominence of two ideas: the conviction that a chief property of a truly moral will was its rationality and the belief that no one, however proper his intentions, could claim rationality for his will if he was governed by external authority. The exercise of judgment was therefore seen to be an essential component of moral maturity.

In a letter to Samuel Bold (16 May 1699) John Locke wrote,

The first requisite to the profiting by books is not to judge of opinions by the authority of the writers. None have the right of dictating but God himself, and that because he is truth itself. All others have a right to be followed as far as I have, and no farther, i.e. as far as the evidence of what they say convinces, and of that my own understanding alone must be judge for me, and nothing else. If we made our own eyes our guides, admitted or rejected opinions only by the evidence of reason, we should neither embrace nor refuse any tenet, because we find it published by another, *what name or character so ever he was.*[2]

---

[2] John Locke, *Works*, 11th edition (London: W. Otridge and Son, 1812), vol. 10, p. 317.

Locke's determination to have his beliefs founded on his judgment was not meant simply to nourish a mental freedom isolated from will and conduct. The exercise of judgment assumed its full moral significance for him only when it was a component of the exercise of will. In the debates that took place within Cromwell's army in 1647 and 1648, some fifty years before Locke wrote his letter, soldiers of the Leveller faction already had relied on this idea to advance their political programme. Cromwell's son-in-law and chief aide, Henry Ireton, an opponent of the Levellers, had argued that Parliament should be elected by men who had a permanent interest in England because they owned land – a freehold – or were members of a chartered English corporation. Giving power to the unpropertied, who were easily attracted to policies that would be to their short-term interest, would ultimately destroy England's wealth. Because Parliament had to have a regard to the long-term welfare of the kingdom, its members had to come from, and be elected by, the propertied class.

In their defence of the extension of suffrage to include many who were neither propertied nor wealthy, the Levellers argued that Society had no right to deprive anyone of the use of his judgment because of his poverty. 'Every man born in England cannot, ought not, neither by the Law of God nor the Law of Nature, to be exempted from the choice of those who are to make laws for him to live under, and for him, for aught I know, to lose his life under.' 'God and nature hath given him' this right to suffrage.[3] The speaker, Thomas Rainborough, a leader of the Leveller party, made it clear that the right to choose one's legislators was more than the simple right to have some say over one's life. The vote gave one the opportunity to use one's reason in matters of public concern:

I do think that the main cause why Almighty God gave men reason, it was that they should make use of that reason, and that they should improve it for that end and purpose that God gave it them. And truly, I think that half a loaf is better than none if a man he go anhungry: [this gift of reason without other property may seem a small thing,] yet I think there is nothing else that God hath given a man that any [one] else can take from him. And therefore I say, that either it must be the law of God or the law of man that must prohibit the meanest man in the kingdom to have this benefit as well as the greatest.[4]

---

[3] A. S. P. Woodhouse, ed., *Puritanism and Liberty, Being the Army Debates (1647–9) from the Clarke Manuscripts with Supplementary Documents*, 2nd edition (London: Dent, 1950), p. 56. [4] Woodhouse, pp. 55–6.

The Levellers did, however, restrict suffrage. Maximillian Petty was willing to deny the vote to apprentices, servants, and those who took alms. The second *Agreement of the People* (1648), in which Leveller figures had a hand, excluded servants, alms-takers, and those who received wages from private employers. The third *Agreement*, written solely by Leveller theorists, also excluded servants and those receiving alms.[5] How can these restrictions be reconciled with the belief that suffrage had to be universal so that everyone could make use of their judgment?

The exclusions actually reveal the high degree to which the Levellers' call for the expansion of suffrage was founded on an idea of will. Petty excluded certain classes of men from the vote because they would not be free to carry their judgments out in action. '[All] inhabitants that have not lost their birthright should have an equal voice in elections',[6] but servants, apprentices, and alms-takers had forfeited their electoral rights by making themselves subject to the will of another. Women were also excluded, probably because their votes would ordinarily be determined by the judgments of their fathers or husbands. Why, then, should they have the vote?

The Levellers would have revealed a greater devotion to their esteem for the moral will if they had called for the abolition of the hierarchies which deprived so many of the freedom to make their own choices. Perhaps they believed, as many puritans did, that generally superiors had moral responsibility for those they ruled, and hence had to have moral power over them. They did not call for ways of protecting those in subordinate positions from electoral coercion, as did proponents of the secret ballot. Nonetheless, the Levellers did limit their commitment to hierarchy, in their call for the extension of suffrage – for example, in their attempt to give the vote to self-employed tenants of the aristocracy.

The belief that judging for oneself was a necessary element of a rational and moral will was clearly a weapon not only against the limitation of suffrage, but against casuistry itself. A short interchange held among Leveller officers in December 1648, illustrates this. The question set for debate was central to the political and spiritual life of England at the time: 'Whether the magistrate [that is, the ruler or ruling body of the Commonwealth] have, or ought to have, any compulsive and restrictive power in matters of religion?'[7]

---

[5] Woodhouse, pp. 83 and 357; G. E. Aylmer, ed., *The Levellers in the English Revolution* (Ithaca: Cornell University Press, 1975), p. 162.
[6] Woodhouse, p. 53.       [7] Woodhouse, p. 125.

One of the officers doubted the propriety of their discussing the question at all:

That [which], I suppose, is [necessary to be agreed upon, is]: whether it be proper or conducing to your ends, whether it be like to be of good resentment of the wisest, or [even the] generality, of the people, [or whether it will not be held] but a subjecting of them, that a business of this nature should be of your cognizance [at all], it being that which hath taken the best wits to determine, whether the magistrate hath power in matter of religion or no . . . it being a matter of that profound and deep disputation as men have made it, . . . I do not apprehend that it is a matter proper for you to take notice of, to intermeddle in . . .[8]

The matter is better left to the learned for a decision. He was answered by a fellow-officer who said,

Every poor man [that] does understand what he does, and is willing that the commonwealth should flourish, hath as real an hand here as the greatest divine, and [for] all [the] divinity [you] have had from reading, if you had as many degrees [as there are hours] of time since the creation, learning is but the tradition of men. He is [as] properly concerned as [any] one [man] of England, and therefore [is as likely] to know, whether you give him any power or no.[9]

The conditions for one's participation in public life are that one will the public good and use one's judgment in the choices one makes on its behalf. Participation in public life is a right, for without it, men are deprived of the freedom to exercise their moral will in matters of public concern. The Leveller will not concede to his opponent that the exercise of this right is likely to lead to foolish choices. Moral issues had to be simple enough to permit a plain person to judge as well as anyone. How could one think for oneself if the issues were so complex that they ordinarily had to be left to the judgment of the learned?

The conviction that a good man's conscience would be able to answer adequately any question it might face was sustained by the common (although not unopposed) puritan belief that the truly moral will achieve a union with God. The Cambridge Platonists, who were more central to puritan culture than is commonly recognized, said that we know God when we live his will, and we live his will when our own life is thoroughly imbued with the spirit of moral goodness. Benjamin Whichcote wrote that: '[i]n his *natural perfections* we cannot communicate with' God, 'because we are creatures. His natural perfections are such as these, infiniteness, eternity, omniscience,

---

[8] Woodhouse, p. 126.    [9] Woodhouse, p. 127.

omnipotence, omnipresence, his immensity, ubiquity, *etc.* In these no creature can partake with him, nor by these declare him. But in his *moral perfections* we may, and ought; and 'tis religion in us to imitate God in his moral perfections.'[10]

Within decades, the esteem for the self-governing moral will severely undermined the claims of English Protestant casuists in spite of the merit of the arguments which they put forth on their own behalf. A typical defence of casuistry's externality was offered by England's last great casuist, Jeremy Taylor. Like Aquinas, Taylor divided conscience into two parts: one part Taylor called, as the medievals did, *synteresis*, 'the general repository of moral principles or measures of good' in man. For these principles to have any practical relevance, however, they had to be applied to particular cases. There was therefore also a 'discursive or reasoning' part to conscience, which Taylor called 'practical judgment'. Although everyone knew the first principles of morality, no one was immune from making a poor application to a particular case. The individual conscience could find help, however. Reflection about how best to apply God's law to particular cases had a long and notable history. Experts had made distinctions, untangled and analysed cases, and attempted to give order to the great variety of judgments made over the many centuries of Christian interpretation of God's law. It was not enough, therefore, to do what one's uninstructed conscience directed. '[H]e that never enquires', Taylor wrote, 'sins for want of enquiry, and despises his soul because he takes no care that it be rightly informed.'[11] If one lacked the necessary learning and skill to judge well, one had to rely on the judgment of those with better judgment. By the time of Thomas Aquinas, the terms, organization, and analyses associated with the application of divine law had already achieved a complexity and difficulty not unlike that of the modern law of the state. The accumulated body of applications and reflections on applications was ordinarily only to be mastered after years of study. It was not surprising that the casuists thought of themselves as experts who were needed for the resolution of difficult moral questions.

The casuists' belief in the need for a strong historical consciousness in moral matters was often justified by simply saying that valuable distinctions and reflections had already been made. Underlying

---

[10] Benjamin Whichcote, *Works* (Aberdeen: Alexander Thomson, 1751), vol. 2, p. 385.
[11] Jeremy Taylor, *Ductor Dubitantium*, in *Works*, ed. Reginald Heber (London: Longmans, Green, 1883), vol. 9, pp. 14, 8 and 184.

the cognitive justifications, however, was a belief that Christians were living within a tradition and that it was the possession of a common tradition which enabled Christians to talk, to explain, and to justify themselves to one another. How could a Christian refuse to make use of the language and reflections of the casuists, even if only to disagree with them? How complex or profound could Christians' understanding of one another be, if they did not make use of this tradition in their own thought?

Taylor, however, did not think that it was possible for anyone to master the tradition in all of life's domains, just as no one today could reasonably be expected to master all of modern law. When one knows one cannot judge well, it is reasonable to be guided by the casuist. 'He that cannot choose for himself, hath chosen well enough if he can choose one that can choose for him; and when he hath, he may prudently rely upon such a person in all particulars, where he himself cannot judge, and the other can, or thinks he can, and cannot well know the contrary.'[12] Even the casuist had to seek qualified help when faced with a problem outside of his special knowledge. Taylor's own casuistical work, *Ductor Dubitantium*, was chiefly meant to aid those who had to advise others. '[I]t requires more wisdom and ability to take care of souls', he wrote, 'than those men who now-a-days run under the formidable burdens of the preacher's office can bring from the places of their education and first employment.'[13] For the casuists, the complexities of their tradition represented the flowering of moral intelligence in the service of God. For proponents of the new idea of will, however, the tradition was seen to be nothing more than a thorough unwillingness to recognize the necessity and value of independent judgment. They were not satisfied by the casuists' concession that no one should follow advice which is perceived to conflict with what one is certain is a clear moral obligation. This did give one's conscience some veto power, but it was no assertion of its primacy.

By the late seventeenth century, the belief in the primacy of the moral will had become a central feature, although not unopposed, of English middle-class life. Expressing his opposition to the tendency towards moral simplification, the puritan casuist Richard Baxter had written that there was a 'vulgar Religion, that would hear no more but, *Think well, speak well and do well*, or *Love God and your neighbour, and do as you would be done by*'. He that does this truly, Baxter agreed, would be saved. 'But', he added, 'there goeth more into the building

[12] Taylor, vol. 9, pp. 20 and 23.    [13] Taylor, vol. 9, p. 37.

of a house, than to say, *Lay the foundation, and raise the superstructure*:
Universals exist not but in individuals; and the whole consisteth of
all the *parts*.'[14] The particularities of individual moral cases demanded
careful attention, a care illustrated by the lengthy analyses he
offered in his own *Christian Directory*. However much puritanism
favoured learned authority, the demand for a self governed in all
details by truly moral will had to create an antagonism to casuistry's
externality and, therefore, a hostility to casuistry itself.

The sermon on double doubts by John Sharp, who rose to positions of ecclesiastical eminence under William and Mary, illustrates
this. What should one do, he asked, when faced with a situation
where there was reason to think that the same act was both required
and forbidden, both a duty and a sin? This was the 'double doubt',
moral case which Roman Catholic casuists had extensively analysed.
They had attempted to refine their thinking about the matter by
arguing that both the apparent degrees of sin and duty of the act in
question and the probable truth of one's judgments about these
things were relevant. It would be one thing if one were sure that an
act was a great duty and had only the mildest of suspicions that it
might be a very small sin. It would be quite another (and more
difficult) matter if one weakly suspected it was a major duty, but was
confident it was a trivial sin. Obviously rules for the resolution of
double doubts had to be complicated, given the possible combi-
nations of sin, duty, and probability.[15]

After stating some of the traditional rules for the resolution of
double doubts, Sharp asked himself, 'why do I mention them at all,
since to the generality of men, for whom this Discourse is intended,
they seem altogether impracticable? for how few are there who are
competent judges of these different degrees of probability or sinfulness in an action that we here talk of, and much less are capable of so
balancing these things one with another, as to be able from thence to
form a good judgment on the whole matter?'[16] He did not reply by
saying that one had to rely on the experts' application of the rules
when one could not judge well for oneself. One had to judge for oneself, applying the rules the best one could:

---

[14] Richard Baxter, *Chapters from A Christian Directory*, ed. Jeanette Tawney (London: Bell, 1925), p. 13.

[15] For recent treatments of seventeenth-century analyses of probability, see Ian Hacking, *The Emergence of Probability* (Cambridge: Cambridge University Press, 1975); Francesco Fagiani, *Nel Crepusculo della probabilità* (Naples: Bibliopolis, 1983); and Barbara Shapiro, *Probability and Certainty in Seventeenth Century England* (Princeton: Princeton University Press, 1983).

[16] John Sharp, *Theological Works* (Oxford: Oxford University Press, 1829), vol. 2, p. 92.

if rules are to be given at all for the determining men in doubtful cases, we must give these, because we can be given no other; these being the only principles that men have to govern their actions by in these cases . . . and though they may have false notions of the dangers and degrees of particular sins, and so may sometimes make false applications of these rules to their own case; yet it is enough for their justification . . . that they have reasoned as well as they can; since they are not bound to act in doubtful cases according to what is best and reasonable in itself; but it is abundantly sufficient that they do endeavour it.[17]

Even men who brought in morally irrelevant considerations such as personal advantage to help themselves decide should not be blamed if the narrow considerations deemed morally relevant by the casuistical tradition were too hard to apply.[18]

In a later sermon, Sharp denied the utility of casuistry altogether. It came into being, he said, because people wanted to go as far as they could in gratifying their appetites without actually transgressing divine law. They therefore had to face complicated questions about the precise limits of their liberty because this was not a developed part of God's teachings. 'The laws of our great Master are not like the civil municipal laws of kingdoms, which are . . . wonderful nice, and critical, and particular in setting bounds to the practices of men.' Loving one's neighbour is a duty, but we have no law of God which defines 'how far we may seek our own, when our right cannot be obtained without prejudice' to another. Prayer is required, but 'we have not any law of God which defines how often we are to pray'. God commands temperance in both feelings and action, but he does not define 'to what degree we may be angry; or how we are to govern ourselves as to the quantity or kinds of our meat and drink; . . . or how splendid we may be in our apparel and equipage'. All questions about limits, however, were unnecessary, Sharp said, if one's aim was to be thoroughly good. Uneducated as one may be 'in the dry rules' of casuistry, 'there is scarce any case to be put concerning an action, but it is very obvious, without an instructor, to find out which side of the case, if it be chosen, will most minister to the ends of virtue, and religion, and charity. Or, if it be not obvious, then it is very certain the man needs not much deliberate about it, but may choose either side indifferently.'[19]

By the early decades of the eighteenth century, the dismissal of casuistry was thorough. Joseph Butler wrote:

let any plain honest man, before he engages in any course of action, ask himself, Is this I am going about right, or is it wrong? Is it good, or is it evil? I do

[17] Sharp, vol. 2, pp. 92–3.    [18] Sharp, vol. 2, p. 95.
[19] Sharp, vol. 2, pp. 192 and 186–8.

not in the least doubt, but that this question would be answered agreeably to truth and virtue, by almost any fair man in almost any circumstance.[20]

If we are persons of character, he commented, '[i]n all common ordinary cases we see intuitively at first view what is our duty, what is the honest part. This is the ground of the observation, that the first thought is often the best.'[21] Having doubts about particular cases was ordinarily a sign of moral weakness:

That which is called considering what our duty is in a particular case, is very often nothing but endeavoring to explain it away. Thus those courses, which, if men would fairly attend to the dictates of their own consciences, they would see to be corruption, excess, oppression, uncharitableness; these are refined upon – things were so and so circumstantiated – great difficulties are raised about fixing bounds and degrees: and thus every moral obligation whatever may be evaded.[22]

Butler's easy dismissal of the need for casuistry was a sign of its unimportance in his time.

Butler's assessment of casuistry is found in a collection of sermons which were first delivered to the lawyers of Lincoln's Inn. While denouncing casuistical methods with regard to the laws of God, he does not question the need for both refinement and complexity in the law of the state. This is worthy of note, given the apparent similarities between casuistry and law. Both are forms of social regulation. Secular law, like casuistry, controls the details of daily life through the resolution of particular cases. The history of these cases was the core of an English legal tradition which, like casuistry, had well-established institutions for its interpretation. Law could therefore be a common source of terms, arguments, and premises which the English could use to explain and account for much of their conduct to one another. One must ask, therefore, how it was that the law of the state was so acceptable to Butler.

There is a good answer to this question, but it cannot be arrived at unless the considerations which prompted it are themselves criticized. They take no account of a profound difference between casuistry and the courts of the state. Casuists, who advised the faithful on what was forbidden or permitted under God's law, attempted to guide men's wills through their judgments. Through modification of beliefs about what conduct would be acceptable to God, they might ultimately affect behaviour. Casuistry was vulnerable to the

[20] Joseph Butler, *Fifteen Sermons Preached at the Rolls Chapel*, in *Works*, ed. J. H. Bernard (London: Macmillan, 1900), vol. 1, p. 53.
[21] Butler, vol. 1, p. 100.     [22] Butler, vol. 1, p. 100.

challenge of the newly popular idea of the rational will precisely because casuists tried to reach the will of the individual via the route of his judgment. The courts of English law worked – and continue to work – very differently. Jurists, unlike casuists, do not have to rely on a belief in laws they administer in order to modify people's will. They can apply sanctions to affect behaviour, sanctions which are meant to be effective whether or not those who are commanded believe in the wisdom of the laws themselves or in the appropriateness of a particular judgment.

There is no law, Hobbes and Locke said, unless there is a law-giver capable of punishing those who disobey him. This is just the power which the courts possessed and the casuists lacked. It was, of course, true that God could punish those who did not live according to divine law, but the casuist had no such means at his disposal. The authority of courts of law survived the rise in popularity of the moral will just because their capacity to inflict pain was so central to their power. Legal decisions could modify intentions without having to modify judgments about what was morally right or wrong. One could retain one's own views while directing one's will in the light of the penalties which the courts would be likely to impose for dis-obedience. The rising concern with the formation of character saw no enemy in a world ruled by courts, as long as they did not seek to command belief.

The rejection of casuistry by authorities of the English Church promoted the transfer of power to the state. Casuistry was correctly perceived to be a more potent enemy of the law of the state than character. The call to rely on one's own conscience can even be seen as a covert way of making the state more powerful by having people control *themselves* with values that suit the state's interests.[23] There is more to the import of the new concern with the moral will than the rise of the state, however. Some advocates of the moral and rational will made serious efforts to provide people with the mental means to think for themselves.

John Locke was notable for his interest in providing the means by which his fellow men and women, poor or rich, powerful or unim-portant, could judge for themselves.

In his *Essay Concerning Human Understanding*, Locke proposed a method of moral reasoning by which all persons, save idiots and the feeble-minded, could know the true principles of morality and the relation any action had to them. The casuists would have said that

---

[23] See James Tully, pp. 12–71 above.

God created a church and experts to help the individual know God's will. Locke, in his devotion to the moral self, denied this, saying that the Lord would not have left our fate in the hands of others. '*Morality* is the proper *Science, and business of Mankind in general*, who are both concerned, and fitted to search out' the ways of achieving 'their *summum bonum*'.[24] Literacy was not even required for the successful use of Locke's method. All that was needed was an analytic approach to the common meanings of words, meanings which even the least educated had at his disposal. The meaning of the commandment to honour one's father and mother, for example, lay wholly in the meanings of 'honour', 'father', 'mother', etc. and in the way these terms were related. (They were joined in such a way that children were ordered to honour their parents, rather than the other way around.) By analysis, Locke wrote, 'we shall get more true and clear knowledge' than we could ever get by relying on the decisions of moral authorities, 'thereby putting our minds into the disposal of others'.[25]

Locke was enough of an intellectual to believe that the analytic skills needed to know God's will could not be acquired without much effort and self-discipline. Although God formed his law out of ideas whose boundaries are clear, distinct, and steady, men persisted in thinking with ideas whose boundaries are 'confused and imperfect'. Ideas that were not determinate therefore had to be given up, to be replaced by those that were; men had to 'have *Ideas*, clear and distinct *Ideas*, for which they make signs stand'. Unless this was done, he wrote, 'especially' with 'moral Words', 'who can wonder' that men's 'Thoughts and Reasonings end in nothing but Obscurity and Mistake, without any clear Judgment or Knowledge?'[26]

Locke's method was spare, compared to the multiple techniques of casuistry and law, but its successful use obviously required a development of one's mental powers. He therefore asked himself how people who work long and hard hours, day-in and day-out, could learn to think in this analytic manner, 'when all their whole Time and Pains is laid out, to still the Croaking of their own Bellies, or the Cries of their Children'.[27] They would need leisure sufficient to permit the development and use of their mental powers. As twentieth-century university instructors and students are aware, these skills are notably absent even in many who have spent their whole youth in school. How could the oppressed and uneducated of

---

[24] John Locke, *An Essay concerning Humane Understanding* (London: Thomas Ballet, 1690), p. 327.    [25] Locke, *Essay*, pp. 160 and 325.
[26] Locke, *Essay*, pp. 252 and 254.    [27] Locke, *Essay*, p. 353.

Locke's own time have been expected to make use of his method successfully?

Locke nonetheless affirmed that even someone who has spent and continues to spend his life in ill-paid and exhausting labour could become competent in the use of his method. 'God has furnished Men with Faculties sufficient to direct them in the Way they should take' to secure their everlasting happiness, 'if they will but seriously employ them that Way when their ordinary Vocations allow them the Leisure. No Man is so wholly taken up with the Attendance of the Means of Living, as to have no spare Time at all to think of his Soul, and inform himself in Matters of Religion.'[28] Otherwise, the common person's fate would be determined by other people's ideas of good and bad. 'Shall a poor Country-man be eternally happy, for having the Chance to be born [a Roman Catholic] in *Italy*; or a Day-Labourer be unavoidably lost, because he had the ill luck to be born [a Protestant] in *England*:'[29]

Three revisions of the *Essay* appeared during Locke's lifetime, dated 1694, 1695, and 1700. An edition appearing after his death in 1704 incorporated still more revisions. In none of them does he give any sign of wavering from a belief in the universal utility of his method. He had doubts, however.

In an unpublished manuscript entitled 'Labour', written after the publication of his *Essay*, he wrote that all men should be provided with sufficient time to learn what they needed to know; the social and economic order should allow men 'six hours' for the mind and six 'for provisions for the body and the preservation of health'. In the same manuscript, Locke drew away from this equal allocation of leisure and labour, saying it might not preserve 'the distinction that ought to be in the ranks of men'.[30] He still called, however, for a social and economic order in which labourers would have the leisure to study:

Let the Gentleman and Scholar employ nine of the twelve [hours] on his mind in thought and reading and the other three in some honest labour. And the man of manual labour nine in work and three in knowledge. By which all man kind might be supplied with what the real necessities and conveniences of life demand in a greater plenty then they have now and be delivered from that horrid ignorance and brutality to which the bulk of them is now everywhere given up.[31]

He never published these reflections. They would have been taken either as utopian fantasy or as revolutionary. Locke did not wish to

[28] Locke, *Essay*, p. 354.   [29] Locke, *Essay*, p. 354.
[30] Quoted by John Dunn, *The Political Thought of John Locke* (Cambridge: Cambridge University Press, 1969), p. 231.   [31] Dunn, pp. 231–2.

be seen as utopian. Read as a practical proposal, however, they would have challenged, as the Levellers had, the hierarchical character of the social order. He had no desire to take such a radical stand publically.

In *The Reasonableness of Christianity, As Delivered in the Scriptures* (first published in 1695 and republished in a second edition in 1696), Locke openly opposed the assertions of the *Essay*, doubting his facile affirmation that labouring persons would always have sufficient leisure to learn to use his analytic method effectively. In this book, he turns to Scripture to answer the needs of moral autonomy. '[B]efore our Saviour's time', humanity lacked an 'unerring Rule', 'which might be the sure guide of those who had a desire to go right; And if they had a mind, need not mistake their Duty; But might be certain when they had performed, when failed in it. Such a *Law of Morality*, Jesus Christ hath given us in the New Testament.'[32]

The doubts he now openly expressed about the utility of his analytic method for the poor were matched by doubts about its general power. It was most unlikely, he wrote, that reason would ever lead anyone to discover all the truths of morality. Neither the philosophers of the ancient world nor those since the coming of Christ have done so through their unaided reason. Some parts of God's law lay 'too deep for our Natural Powers easily to reach, and make plain and visible to mankind, without some Light from above to direct them'.[33] This light was the New Testament. Locke was an intellectual if he was anything. He could allow himself, however, to advocate what Baxter had called 'vulgar Religion' out of his belief that people must judge for themselves. His commitment to that idea drove him to both his rationalism and scripturalism. Is it reasonable to see them as but means of extending the power of the state?

During much of the medieval era, the laws of the kingdom and the casuistry of the church were often in opposition. The decline of casuistry did not, however, mean that the law of the state could now command unopposed the many details of daily life that once were within the purview of the casuists and their laws. With the rise of interest in the moral will, non-legal concern over the conduct and character of daily life took on new modes of expression, modes which in the long run were as or more effective than casuistry ever was. Prose fiction, particularly in the form of the novel, came to play

[32] John Locke, *The Reasonableness of Christianity, As delivered in the Scriptures* (London: Awnsham and John Churchil, 1695), p. 272. I quote from the first edition of Locke's text. With regard to the passages quoted, there are no changes of substance in the second edition.    [33] Locke, *Christianity*, p. 276.

an important role in the social imagination of eighteenth- and nineteenth-century England, a role which often put it in opposition to forms of life authorized by the courts. Hidden in the new fiction's history, however, was a debt to the casuistry which it replaced. It is all the more strange that it emerged out of collections of letters of advice, such as those written by Defoe and Richardson, addressed to imaginary individuals faced with perplexing moral circumstances. The novel had its birth in casuistry, but character became its chief concern.

# 4

◁ ═══════════════════════════════════════ ▷

## Prescription and reality*

JEAN DELUMEAU

## THE SOCIOLOGY AND HISTORY OF MENTAL OUTLOOK

For a long time sociologists and historians were prevented by a kind of reticence from studying the religion of 'ordinary people' both in the past and in their own time, and it was not until 1931 that Gabriel Le Bras took a lead from Durkheim, Hubert, and Mauss, and became the first French historian to reverse this trend.[1] He encouraged his readers to consider Christianity from below, as it affected the anonymous mass of the people, rather than at the level of doctrine and those who formulated it, and this opened the way to a great variety of research in the sociology of religion while, at the same time, providing a new impetus for the historiography of religion, for it became clear that much more needed to be known about the faith, the practice of Christianity, and the morals of the billion Frenchmen who preceded us. Lucien Febvre was reaching similar methodological conclusions at approximately the same time. In 1932 he wrote,

> It is almost unbelievable that we know so little about the basic elements, the most important and widespread religious practices, and so many of the great pilgrimages themselves. All we have are brief mentions scattered among inaccessible articles and journals, and too often even those are there for non-historical reasons.[2]

These calls for a new intellectual approach have found a receptive audience, especially in recent years, and a mass of new research

---

* This is a translation (with minor modifications) by Ian Patterson of Jean Delumeau's inaugural lecture at the Collège de France (1975), 'Le Prescrit et le vécu', in Delumeau, Le Christianisme va-t-il mourir?' (Paris, Hachette, 1977).

[1] See particularly the Etudes de sociologie religieuse (2 vols., Paris, 1955–6).
[2] Lucien Febvre, 'La Dévotion en France au XVIIe siècle', in Au Coeur religieux du XVIe siècle (Paris, 1957), p. 332.

134

followed their pioneering work. Canon Fernand Boulard and his fellow workers have tried to quantify religious observances and relate them to time of year, to social status, and to geographical criteria.[3]

There are now quite regular investigations into the religious beliefs (or absence of them) of our contemporaries, as well as their ethics. At the same time there has been an explosion of recent historical work on such diverse topics as the number of communicants in Bruges in the fifteenth and sixteenth centuries,[4] the number of ordinations in Avignon in the sixteenth century, in Reims and Gap in the eighteenth,[5] and the decline of the Huguenot population in the diocese of La Rochelle between 1648 and 1724.[6] An extremely detailed examination has been conducted under the direction of the late Victor-Louis Tapié into Breton altar-pieces of the seventeenth and eighteenth centuries, in terms of the subjects depicted, the materials used, the techniques involved, and the place of worship itself.[7] Pastoral visits,[8] sets of ex votos,[9] and hundreds of accounts of miracles[10] have been indexed. The places of origin of the French refugees who arrived in Geneva in the sixteenth century have been identified,[11] as have the sites of the religious houses and convents in Provence during the *ancien régime*,[12] the activities of missionaries such as Father Maunoir in Brittany[13] and St Jean Eudes in Normandy,[14] and so forth.

[3] Fernand Boulard, *Premiers itinéraires en sociologie religieuse* (Paris, 1954).
[4] J. Toussaert, *Le Sentiment religieux en Flandre à la fin du Moyen Age* (Paris, 1963), pp. 122–95.
[5] M. Venard, 'Pour une sociologie du clergé au XVIe siècle. Recherche sur le recrutement sacerdotal dans la province d'Avignon', in *Annales E.S.C.*, XXIII (1968), 987–1016. D. Julia, 'Le Clergé paroissial dans le diocèse de Reims au XVIIIe siècle', in *Revue d'Histoire Moderne et Contemporaine*, XIII (1966), 195–217.
[6] L. Pérouas, *Le Diocèse de La Rochelle de 1648 à 1724* (Paris, 1964).
[7] V.-L. Tapié, J.-P. Le Flem, A. Pardailhé-Galabrun, *Retables baroques de Bretagne* (Paris, 1972).
[8] See D. Julia, 'La Réforme post-tridentine en France d'après les procès-verbaux de visites pastorales: ordres et résistances', in *La Società religiosa nell'età moderna* (Naples, 1973), pp. 311–433.
[9] Investigation in progress, under the direction of Michel Mollat.
[10] Stéphanie Peigné, *Les Miracles de sainte Anne d'Auray (1634–1647)* (Mémoire de maîtrise, mimeo, Paris I, 1972). Published in part in J. Delumeau, *Un Chemin d'histoire* (Paris, 1981).
[11] P.-F. Geisendorf, *Liste des habitants de Genève (1549–1560)*, 2 vols. (Geneva, 1957 and 1963).
[12] *Atlas historique de la France, I: Provence, Comtat, Orange, Nice et Monaco* (Paris, 1969), under the direction of E. Baratier, G. Duby and E. Hildesheimer.
[13] See J. Delumeau, *Le Catholicisme entre Luther et Voltaire* (1st edition, Paris, 1971), pp. 202–3: map taken from the *mémoire de maîtrise* of Mme Petitjeans (mimeo, Rennes, 1969).
[14] Bertelot du Chesnay, *Les Missions de saint Jean Eudes* (Paris, 1967), map vi.

As the quantity of research has grown, so the questions about the religious life of the past have become increasingly rigorous and exacting in both scope and detail. The rise of historical demography in the aftermath of Pierre Goubert's work sent historians to parish registers in search of evidence about the sexual behaviour of our forebears. Similar systematic use of legal archives has led to a greater understanding of crime. And Philippe Ariès,[15] François Lebrun,[16] and Michel Vovelle[17] have tried in their work to arrive at a detailed comprehension of attitudes to death in pre-industrial societies; in order to do so they have used medical works, religious exhortations, accounts of epidemics, and a variety of contemporary reports, especially wills, all of which have been subjected to scrutiny from a number of angles.

Taken together, these investigations – in which the French have provided the model for other countries – create the beginnings of a religious sociology of Western society at the time of the *ancien régime*, a laudable ambition despite the obvious time-lag between intentions and results.[18] No area in the religious field, in fact, can be excluded *a priori* from the restless curiosity of retrospective sociology, for the principal reason that religion and society are formed by their interaction. So the field of enquiry must include cults, ceremonies and disciplines, institutions and groups with religious motivations, clergy and laity, beliefs and doctrines, attitudes to life and to death, and all varieties of moral behaviour; and it is taken for granted that the Christians of the past must be studied in the context of their local village or their town, their social milieu and work, and the level of development and economic situation of their period. Two separate but related objectives can therefore be discerned as aims of the project of religious sociology: first, the establishment of typologies of Christians and Christianities synchronically, as for example around 1500 and around 1700; and second, diachronically, the tracing of continuities and changes between one model of Christianity and another over a period of time. Every researcher must

15  Philippe Ariès, *Essais sur l'histoire de la mort en Occident du Moyen Age à nos jours* (Paris, 1975), translated as *Western Attitudes towards Death* (Baltimore, 1974). *L'Homme devant la mort* (Paris, 1977), translated as *Images of Men and Death* (Cambridge, Mass., 1985).
16  F. Lebrun, *Les Hommes et la mort en Anjou aux XVIIe et XVIIIe siècles* (Paris and The Hague, 1971).
17  M. Vovelle, *Piété baroque et déchristianisation en Provence au XVIIIe siècle* (Paris, 1973); *Mourir autrefois* (Paris, 1974).
18  For a bibliography and account of recent work on religious sociology see particularly R. Mehl, *Traité de sociologie du protestantisme* (Neuchâtel, 1966), and H. Desroche, *Sociologies religieuses* (Paris, 1968).

therefore be both a sociologist of the past and a historian, and will therefore be aware that alterations in religious behaviour can only occur in the long term, the *longue durée* which Fernand Braudel, the master of so many of my generation of historians, stressed so productively.[19]

Georges Gurvitch said that sociology and social psychology far from being mutually exclusive, are like two intersecting circles, overlapping in one basic area;[20] there can be no doubt that the areas of research I have outlined above only achieve their full significance as part of a synchronic apprehension of a general outlook and the reconstruction of a particular people at a particular time, their thoughts and feelings, their outlook on the world, and their susceptibilities. Since the work of Marc Bloch, and Ariès, Duby and Mandrou, the history of mental outlook or *mentalités* has attained academic respectability, particularly in France. Building on the experience we already have, what needs to be done in our chosen field – Western Europe between 1500 and 1800 – is to cast some light on the reciprocal relations underlying the religious behaviour of a community which is regarded as significant in terms of its mental equipment, its conceptual matrix, its scale of values, and its expressive style. This involves attempting to reach an overall understanding of religious experience, and assessing the degree to which the model of Christianity at any given period and place was incorporated into ordinary understanding.

To start with, three connections need particularly to be emphasized. The first is the approach which sees history as firmly rooted in geography, a relationship which has long been central to the work of Braudel and Maurice Le Lannou, but which takes on a particular importance in the religious context. It has proved possible to follow the diffusion of both the Protestant[21] and Catholic Reformations, and later of religious apathy, along the routes of the major rivers and in concentric circles around towns.[22] There has been shown to be a connection between the establishment of schools (all of which were religious foundations before 1789) and the development of roads.[23]

[19] F. Braudel, *Ecrits sur l'histoire*, translated as *On History* (Chicago, 1980).
[20] G. Gurvitch, *La Vocation actuelle de la sociologie* (Paris, 1950), pp. 31–5.
[21] E. Le Roy Ladurie's contributions to Ph. Wolff (ed.), *Histoire du Languedoc* (Toulouse, 1967), p. 319; and *Documents de l'histoire du Languedoc* (Toulouse, 1969), pp. 214–15.
[22] See for example the notes of a Montfortan missionary of the nineteenth century in L. Perouas, *P. Fr. Hacquet, Mémoires des missions des Montfortains dans l'Ouest, 1740–1779* (Fontenay-le-comte, 1964). See also Vovelle, *Piété baroque*.
[23] D. Julia, 'L'Enseignement primaire dans le diocèse de Reims à la fin de l'Ancien Régime', in *Annales Historiques de la Révolution française*, 200 (1970), 233–86.

Dominique Julia has identified areas of 'religious low pressure', which provided few recruits for the priesthood, and 'clerical water-towers', areas which had a surplus of priests (such as the dioceses of Normandy, which sent their overflow to the Paris region, the Massif Central, which sent priests to Languedoc and Aquitaine, or the dioceses of Gap and Embrun, which sent priests to Basse-Provence or the comtat Venaissin).[24] Researchers have also become aware of frontiers of religious sensibility and regional temperaments.[25] Father Perouas has shown that in the diocese of La Rochelle, in the seventeenth and eighteenth centuries, Protestant resistance was at its strongest in the woodland region of the South and in the Ile de Ré, from which he deduced the following 'dimorphism': the woods and the Ile de Ré were both isolated areas, and this encouraged religious fervour whether it was Protestant or Catholic; but where the landscape was predominantly open fields and salt marshes both per-suasions were equally undemonstrative.[26] Michel Vovelle similarly contrasted the western and central areas of Basse-Provence in the eighteenth century, where considerable changes occurred, with the southern and eastern areas, which remained static.[27] This concept of regional and even national temperament (of which Montaigne shows an awareness when he compares the respective combativeness of French, German, Swiss, and Italian soldiers)[28] is a factor that should not be overlooked in the study of religious attitudes. The austerity of St Charles Borromeo did not have any serious effect on Italian Christianity. And the same year that Luther sprang to prominence, 1517, the secretary of an Italian cardinal noted in his travel diary, 'When I see divine worship as it is offered in Germany and the deep composure of the faithful. . . I am heartbroken at the lack of religion in my own country.'[29] One must not of course jump from these instances to over-hasty generalizations, or take a simplistically determinist view. Yet the evidence of reciprocal connections be-tween religious man and the town or countryside in which he lived becomes extremely important in the studying of a time when, to use Maurice Le Lannou's trenchant formulation, such a person was still normally an 'inhabitant' in the full sense of the word, i.e. somebody

[24] Julia, 'La Réforme post-tridentine', p. 345.
[25] See F. Boulard and J. Rèmy, *Pratique religieuse urbaine et régions culturelles* (Paris, 1968).
[26] L. Perouas, *Le Diocèse de La Rochelle. Etude de sociologie religieuse* (Paris, 1964).
[27] Vovelle, *Piété baroque.*      [28] Montaigne, *Essais*, II, chap. 11.
[29] Don Antonio de Beatis, *Voyage du cardinal d'Aragon . . . en 1517–1518*, ed. Havard de la Montagne (Paris, 1913), p. 75.

who had not been 'separated' from his environment, or 'delocalized'
by 'moving away from his territory'.[30]

The second connection is the increasing inter-relationship between history and anthropology, a far cry from the days of Van
Gennep, who thought he could set the two disciplines up against
each other. That was, however, only possible in the context of a sort
of event-centered history which would not satisfy us today, register-
ing as it does only surface movements on the ocean of the past. Van
Gennep was proposing an ethnological approach which united and
explained events, rather than a historical one which, as it seemed to
him, merely enumerated and juxtaposed them.[31] But that argument
has long been superseded. Indeed Lévi-Strauss, particularly in *Structural Anthropology*, illustrates the way the two approaches have con-
verged, commenting on Lucien Febvre's *The Problem of Unbelief in the
Sixteenth Century* that 'any good history book ... is saturated with
anthropology'.[32] There are at least two significant reasons for this
growing collaboration.

The first is methodological. Ever since Marc Bloch we have been
aware of the advantages of moving back from the present into the
past, and thus of the 'living facts' which were the object of Van
Gennep's studies. In this respect, therefore, historians need to take
account of the investigations of oral historians who go out with tape
recorders to collect Breton or Dauphinois folk-tales, or to ask old
people in the Cévennes or Quebec about their religious beliefs.[33]
The level of interest in this sort of evidence-gathering indicates that
historical research is no longer confined to studying the dominant
culture of the past, the culture that occupies the forefront of the
historical stage and is officially expressed in written form, in books,
and in art and religion. Research is now turning more and more
towards a second, primarily oral, tradition of European culture
which for a long time was overshadowed by the elites and
overlooked by historians, but which nonetheless stubbornly
continued its secret existence through the centuries.[34] Part of the
process of bringing this alternative culture to light has been the
reconstruction of religious life, and this has proved not always to

[30] M. Le Lannou, *Le Déménagement du territoire* (Paris, 1967); and *Leçon inaugurale au Collège de France* (Paris, 1970).
[31] See N. Belmont, *Arnold van Gennep, le créateur de l'ethnographie française* (Paris, 1974), especially pp. 132–40.
[32] C. Lévi-Strauss, *Structural Anthropology* (London, 1968).
[33] Here I am thinking mainly of the investigations carried out by P. Joutard in the Cévennes, and by the University of Sherbrook in the cantons of East Quebec.
[34] See M. de Certeau, *La Culture au pluriel* (Paris, 1974), pp. 55–91.

tally as it ought to have done with the pattern set by the authorities.
The reconstruction also necessarily involves the same historical
facts as those which attract anthropological attention in the present:
beliefs, rituals, things, a whole range of memories, and categories of
thought, all of which belong to an oral culture, profoundly different
from the culture of the written word in which the contemporary
historian himself lives. Hence the wide variety of documentation
used by historians, which has enabled them to rediscover a civilisation which was gradually suppressed as Western culture developed,
but which was never entirely destroyed. These sources include
'repressive' texts (accounts of legal proceedings), descriptions of
festivals, tales and legends, songs and Christmas carols, and rituals
involving processions or blessings, as well as any other objects or
images which, however reluctantly, communicate something of the
living reality of a culture which in the past was usually denied a voice.
In this way ethno-history comes into being. When skeletons were
discovered at Moissac with coins not only of Charles VII and
François I in their hands, but also those of Louis XV and XVI
(Charon's obolus?), the archaeological find could only be understood in the context of a European ethno-history of religious
attitudes, and via a systematic study of the physical survival of the
dead.[35]

Obviously the dominant culture must not be ignored, but it
should not be taken at its own valuation. Although it had full scope
for self-expression, it rarely attempted any self-analysis. We must
therefore look beyond the utterances themselves to rediscover the
unconscious motivation underlying them, the mental equipment
that naturally came to hand, the most familiar images, and the
degree of sensitivity manifested in everyday life.

This brings us to the third connection, the relationship between
history and the study of language, primarily verbal language[36] but
also the language of image and ritual. Cultures are revealed in a
vocabulary and a syntax, a particular iconography, and the form and
content of liturgy. An examination of religious attitudes among
those whose task it was to expound Christianity to their congre-
gations needs to consider the changing structures of theological

---

[35] A. Varagnac, *Civilisation traditionelle et genres de vie* (Paris, 1948), pp. 212–17. See also
J. Bordenave and M. Vialelle, *La Mentalité religieuse des paysans de l'Albigeois médiéval*
(Toulouse, 1973). This probably was not an obolus for Charon, but a ritual by
means of which the living were guaranteed a peaceful inheritance from the dead
man, now no longer interested by virtue of the coins. See N. Belmont, *Mythes et
croyances de l'ancienne France* (Paris, 1973), p. 64.
[36] See R. Robin, *Histoire et linguistique* (Paris, 1973).

language, the themes and verbal emphases of sermons and hymns, and the subject-matter and style of sacred art. This leads us, as Saussure intended it should, from the individual *parole* to the collective *langue*. History is not by any means required to adopt a linguistic model, or to see linguistics as the only way in which to understand group behaviour, but linguistics can teach us how to read, by looking at a text as a whole, by temporarily breaking down the written sequence, analysing its themes and contents and quantifying their occurrences, and defining conceptual fields. All these steps are attempts to bring out what Alphonse Dupront has called the 'surplus of meaning' normally hidden beneath the 'seeming transparency' of a document.[37] For example, a study of joy in the Renaissance (a thesis currently in preparation) cannot exclude a semantic approach as this reveals on the one hand that in profane texts the vocabulary of sadness is much more extensive than the vocabulary of pleasure in all its forms and that, on the other hand, interiorized joy – joy in the full sense of the word – is more in evidence in mystical discourse.[38]

Nevertheless, the larger the project, the more cautiously historians should proceed and draw their conclusions, for the process of understanding religious attitudes is full of pitfalls. It is very difficult to claim to have assessed faith on the basis of figures tabulating Sunday activities, vocations for the priesthood, religious communities, retables and so on. One can agree that quantitative research is an integral part of religious history and still believe that belief and charity are essentially unquantifiable attributes. At best, it is outward signs of faith and collective attitudes that are measured, and not states of soul.[39] Besides, there is only a limited significance in unanimous religious observance at a time when it was legally required. Voltaire took communion more often than Pascal. It must be more strongly emphasized that statistics do not provide an adequate basis for determining the epochs and phases of Christianity. Keith Thomas's important recent work, *Religion and the Decline of Magic*,[40] which recreates everyday religion in England during the Reformation, is a product of a qualitative historiography which convinces by the variety and convergence of the documentation assembled.

There is a further danger, that of deciding *a priori* that religion is

---

[37] A. Dupront, 'Sémantique historique et histoire', in *Cahiers de lexicologie* (Paris, 1969); 'L'Histoire après Freud', in *Revue de l'enseignement supérieur*, 'L'Histoire aujourd'hui', nos. 44–5; 'Langage et histoire', communication to the *XIIIth Moscow International Congress of Historical Sciences, 1970*, ed. Naouka (Moscow, 1973).

[38] Thesis by Mme Chirat-Decornod.

[39] See especially R. Mols, 'L'Emploi et valeur des statistiques en histoire religieuse', in *Nouvelle Revue de Théologie*, LXXXVI (1964), 388–410.    [40] (London, 1971).

nothing but a projection of either the social or the unconscious.[41] This sort of reduction, which claims to be the ultimate explanation, in fact surely starts from a non-scientific premise. However detailed a sociological investigation may be, and however deeply the collective unconscious may have been plumbed, there can be no guarantee that everything has been classified, or that the object being studied has been illuminated in all its aspects. The progress of knowledge, in some ways, is like a growing circle of light; as it gets larger, the circumference separating the known from the unknown is also extended, so that the area of light and the border of darkness surrounding it increase simultaneously.

I would also like to deal with a more specific difficulty encountered by those trying to comprehend the collective beliefs, practices, and devotions of the past. As the world of the masses and the elites becomes more and more interconnected, how much reliability can be placed on the terms 'popular religion' and 'popular culture', and where should one say one ends and the other begins? Any attempt to isolate a Western popular culture in the sixteenth, seventeenth and eighteenth centuries, as if we were in a laboratory (though such cultures did exist, and possessed their own coherence), is almost sure to fail. With the additional problem of entering into communication with the popular culture of the past when its principle expression was oral, the enterprise appears even less secure. So much of the spoken word is lost to memory that we come up against a silence as discouraging in its effects as if nothing had ever been said.

Yet some reply can be made to these important objections. To begin with, we possess documentary records which, in their condemnations of certain forms of collective conduct, actually provide us with knowledge of them and thus help to resuscitate a semi-clandestine religion. Synodal statutes, pastoral letters, accounts of missions, confession manuals, catechisms, sermons, books about superstitions and demonology, trials, edicts, even treatises on law and order, all constitute a literature which can be used to reveal a rural culture of magic which was regarded with suspicion by the authorities. For, although processes of mimesis naturally operated from the top of the social scale downwards, there was some com-

---

[41] Compare on the one hand M. Mauss, *Sociologie et anthropologie* (Paris, 1950), pp. 285–309 (partly translated as *Sociology and Psychology* (London, 1979), by Ben Brewster); and on the other, S. Freud, *Totem and Taboo* (1912) (English translation in Standard Edition, vol. XIII), in which religion is presented as the repression of aggressive instincts.

munication in the reverse direction as well. The rituals of the period, or the *Traité des superstitions* by J.-B. Thiers,[42] who was a priest in the Perche region during Louis XIV's reign, do indeed contain condemnations of an agrarian religion which was celebrated alongside the official liturgies, but which at the same time responded to the people's need for security by integrating (and thus making available to us today) the blessings, incantations, and exorcisms designed to protect men and livestock, houses and harvests, and marriages and births. In this way age-old magism was taken into the heart of the dominant culture, but sanctified and rendered harmless. Any attempt to define satisfactorily the respective areas occupied by the two cultures and to situate them in relation to each other must, as I have said, be doomed to failure. There is, however, still the possibility of identifying them in terms of the conflict which separates them. As far as religious outlook is concerned, this may best be achieved by looking at the dialectic between prescription and reality.

## A TITANIC EFFORT OF RELIGIOUS ACCULTURATION

It is important, in my view, to concentrate on what the past can tell us about one major problem, that of dechristianization. Two points become immediately obvious to anyone tackling this historical question. The first is that, with a very few exceptions, most notably the recent thesis by Michel Vovelle,[43] dechristianization is usually regarded as beginning with the French Revolution, which is taken in this context as a kind of ground-zero. The second is that, although there are a substantial number of works devoted to dechristianization in the modern world,[44] there is no general book on the process of Christianization that preceded it. The assumption has been that the Roman Empire became Christian at the same time as its emperors, and that the barbarian nations bought Christianity lock, stock, and barrel the moment their leaders were converted; and through the ages historiography has seen European religious experience in terms of an *a priori* which became part of international law, *Cuius regio, huius religio*. As a result, there is no entry under

---

[42] First published 1679 and frequently reprinted thereafter.
[43] Vovelle, *Piété baroque*.
[44] I shall content myself with only two references here: A. Latreille, 'La Déchristianisation en France à l'époque moderne', in *Cahiers d'histoire*, XIV, 1 (1969), 13–35; and H. Desroche's article 'Déchristianisation', in the *Encyclopaedia universalis* (includes a bibliography).

'Christianization' in any dictionary of theology or religious history, or even in the new *Encyclopaedia universalis*; we talk today about 'dechristianization' without having any clear idea of an earlier, and presumably contrasting, state of affairs.

Those who exercised authority in the medieval church were well aware that their contemporaries, particularly those in the country-side, mingled varying doses of the Gospel with age-old rites and beliefs. They believed for a long time that the important thing was to Christianize paganism and that, gradually, the wheat would be separated from the chaff. For several centuries, therefore, the church spoke two languages simultaneously, a rigorous one directed at a narrow elite, and a language of compromise which was addressed to the masses. Christianity thus accepted the idea of integrating rural paganism. Does not tripartite division of society into those who prayed, those who fought, and those who worked imply some degree of indulgence towards the two latter categories? As long as people did not rebel against the church they would be saved, despite their ignorance, thanks to their good will and the prayers of the clergy. For a long time the medieval church eschewed elitism and closed its eyes to a certain amount of 'folklorization' of Christianity which did not seem to them to be an obstacle to Grace.

This attitude, however, which some people today view as based on a Christian logic of the Incarnation, underwent a gradual change for two principal reasons. The establishment of the mendicant orders in the thirteenth century signified a will to preach, an ardent desire to raise the level of religious life, first in the towns and later in the country. Then the disasters of the fourteenth and fifteenth centuries (plagues, famines, wars, the Turkish advance, the Great Schism, and the disorganization of the church) provoked a ferment within Christianity itself and a reappearance of magic, which had never in fact disappeared but merely continued in semi-obscurity. The contrast between the zeal of one group and the different religious experiences of others provoked a crisis of conscience among those who professed to be the best Christians. The West, they believed, either remained or had again become largely 'pagan', a term which appears frequently in the writings and pronouncements of the Christian authorities in the Renaissance and long after, as they pass judgment on their contemporaries, most of whom happened to live in the country. The policy of assimilating ancient and enduring magism into the church was replaced by one of excluding it, and thenceforth an attempt was made to impose the religion of a few upon millions of people.

It is not part of the historian's job to side with the churchmen of the period, to declare their Christianity the true kind, and to condemn the religion they opposed as 'superstitious'.[45] Those are not historical judgments. Yet it is impossible to understand what happened in Western Europe in the early modern period without recognizing this new ambition on the part of the Christian elite and the model of religious life which they wanted the population as a whole to adopt. It is only from this standpoint that one of the most significant aspects of the Reformation can be properly understood: the severity with which the 'paganism' of the ordinary people was regarded, and the concomitant rejection of 'idolatry', sometimes leading to iconoclasm.

Was this new awareness of 'superstition' and 'idolatry' (again, not terms that I would necessarily choose myself) absent from Catholicism? Certainly not. The Council of Trent criticized the veneration of images and the attribution of magical qualities to numbers in religious worship, with particular reference to the mass and to candles (twenty-second session). The Council Fathers and, later, the hierarchy (even the non-Jansenists), the internal missionaries, and the new seminary-trained clergy, all used fundamentally the same language in their encounters with 'superstition' as did the Protestant pastors and theologians. They too were waging a war against an earthly religion which they regarded as incompatible with salvation in the after-life. Of course, the Catholics still retained the seven Sacraments and the worship of the saints; but the most zealous priests did their utmost– though they were not always successful– to change people's behaviour where they believed it to have been oriented towards magic.

Thus to the extent that that both Reformations were involved in a massive programme of conversion they shared the same language. People who must have been Christians of long standing were classified as 'baptized Jews' and were even compared with the infidels overseas. As late as 1680, according to François Lebrun, peasants in Anjou were regarded by their bishop as being as backward, in religious terms, as if they had lived all their lives 'in unknown savage countries'.[46] Similarly, seventeenth-century Jesuits gave the name 'Southern Indies' to the south of Italy, and declared in 1651 that a mission to the kingdom of Naples was 'scarcely inferior'

[45] I am drawing here on an unpublished paper presented to the annual congress of French Studies, in Ottawa in 1972, by Natalie Z. Davis; and on Philippe Ariès, *Religion populaire et réforme liturgique* (*Rites et Symboles*, no. 4) (Paris, 1975), pp. 84–98.
[46] Lebrun, *Les Hommes et la mort*, p. 411, n. 93.

to a mission to the Indies. 'For, leaving aside the hope one may have of shedding one's blood for the faith out there, here in Italy the task is no less troublesome, and the work [of preaching the Gospel] is perhaps even greater.'[47] Indeed in Eboli some people believed there were a hundred gods, and some a thousand. So the missionaries set about their work of conversion, and believed themselves successful. Yet when Carlo Levi was in forced exile in Lucania in 1935–6, deep among the mountains, he had the feeling, confirmed by what the people there confided to him, that Christ stopped at Eboli (whence the title of his book).[48]

I shall return in a moment to the limits of this great endeavour, but first I want to emphasize the scale of it, both in area and depth. The comparison between India and Italy was not a coincidental one: missionaries were in both cases trying to prise the population away from 'paganism'. If, therefore, we can transcend the usual compartmentalization, we shall be better able to understand the famous argument over Chinese and Malabar rites. The Roman Church could scarcely be permitted to battle against customs defined as 'superstitious' in Europe and accept them in Asia, nor is it fortuitous that the Augustinians, who were most demanding in this area as it concerned Europe, were also the main opponents of the admission of Chinese and Malabar rites into Eastern Christianity.

There was more justification for their trying to complete this programme of conversion to the religious form of Western learned culture inside the ostensibly Christian countries. What we are see-ing, therefore, is a conscious, totalitarian desire for acculturation. The Renaissance, it is true, put the knowledge and power of the elites on a firmer foundation, thanks to classical authority and rapid economic and scientific development. Here it is as if the written, urban culture which was born of the encounter between Christianity, the achievements of the Middle Ages, and humanism was felt to be precarious, even threatened by a vast sea of oral, rural culture, the full extent of which could only now be assessed. Hence the aggressive reactions of those in power, and the deliberate desire to break down the culture which surrounded them. This would explain the witch trials that were held in Protestant and Catholic countries alike in the name of a demonology fabricated by judges and theologians,[49] the multiform battles against 'pagan' entertainments

---

[47] Carlo Ginzburg in *Storia d'Italia, I: I Caraterri Originali*, (Turin, 1972), pp. 656–8.
[48] C. Levi, *Christ Stopped at Eboli*, trans. F. Frenaye (London, 1948).
[49] See J. Sprenger and H. Institoris, *Malleus maleficarum*, trans. M. Summers (London, 1928, repr. 1948).

such as the Feast of Fools, Childermas, the torches of the first Sunday in Lent, *calendimaggio*, and sometimes the St John's Eve bonfires,[50] as well as the prosecutions for blasphemy and the vigorous steps taken to combat those sorts of moral behaviour which were not deemed tolerable in a Christian society. It also accounts for many aspects of the incarceration of the insane and the homeless which Foucault has described – not as a re-establishment of order but as the taming of a 'savage society' which had not yet been brought under control.[51]

Fear and repression were not the only elements in this acculturation process: education was also involved. The compelling assertion (which had little or nothing of the medieval about it) that religious ignorance led to damnation became an integral part of the outlook of the Christian elite. Indeed, on that point Luther and St Vincent de Paul, Calvin and St Charles Borromeo, were all in accord. The principal effort of the Western churches, from the moment the two competing but unrelated Reformations began to take concrete effect, was aimed at teaching Christian doctrine to the masses, particularly the peasants, who had hitherto been left to their own devices. Academies and seminaries were established to train a more worthy and competent priesthood; as a result, a new emphasis was laid on the weekly sermon, and those internal missions were despatched which covered the whole of Catholic Europe from the seventeenth to the twentieth century. It also led to a great increase in the number of schools, not only in Protestant areas but in the Catholic dioceses too – a fact which is often overlooked. It also led to the very great importance which now came to be placed on the Catechism, made readily available everywhere by the spread of printing. Recently, one of my colleagues drew a comparison between the Catechism and Mao's *Little Red Book*, and I hope he will permit me to borrow it here (with no sacrilege intended). Putting aside the differences in time and place, there was, I think, a comparable programme of indoctrination on the part of this Christian society: and it was a kind of indoctrination unknown in the Middle Ages, or, at least, unknown in that repetitious, didactic form.

The difficulty, then, was how to persuade hundreds of millions of people to embrace a severe moral and spiritual discipline of a sort which had never actually been demanded of their forebears, and how to make them accept that even the most secret aspects of their daily lives should thenceforth be saturated by a constant preoccupation

---

[50] J. Delumeau, *Le Catholicisme*, pp. 256–61.
[51] M. Foucault, *Folie et déraison. Histoire de la folie à l'âge classique* (Paris, 1961), partly trans. as *Madness and Civilisation* (London, 1961).

with things eternal. I shall respond to this by focusing on what occurred in Catholic areas; but my hypothesis, which I hope soon to demonstrate, is that, despite its variations, Protestant pedagogy was not fundamentally different from that which was practised by the Catholic Church. In Catholic Europe missionaries sought converts by inculcating a sense of guilt, by an obsessive emphasis on original sin and day-to-day transgressions, by the examination of conscience taken to scrupulous extremes,[52] by the constantly reiterated threat of hell, and by a ministry of fear. Where necessary the missionaries made their already frightening message even more melodramatic by preaching at night, or with a skull in their hand, or by using the actor's technique of a 'third tone' to cast a spell over the crowds. Yet there was far more to this than mere artifice and theatrical technique; the preachers themselves were clearly convinced of the reality of the threats they held out. Education through fear was implicit in the logic of the whole enterprise. So that whole populations, whose primary fears were of illness, famine, and war, could be raised above the level of their everyday concerns, the fears already in their hearts had to be replaced by a new kind of fear; they needed to be shown that the dangers faced on earth were as nothing compared with the perils of the after-life. In Catholic countries the confessional (that 'comically sinister' object, as Jacques Maritain called it), first mentioned in 1516,[53] became the symbol of this process of evangelization. In fact, in the seventeenth century there was one missionary who strolled from village to village in the Dauphiné with a portable confessional on his back.[54]

However, evocations of hellfire were not themselves enough to keep the masses under control. This new, relentlessly pervasive Christianity could only become universal if civil authorities provided constant support and reminders. Since the churches, after the Renaissance, were able to count on a state more powerfully constituted than before, both Reformations were able to survey the people of Europe more vigilantly and effectively than would have been conceivable a few centuries earlier. The result was that by 1700, after years of persevering effort, a situation had been achieved in which religion was presented as a personal choice, a decision of the heart and mind, a road to individual salvation, but in which everyone, or nearly everyone, was nevertheless involved in regular church attendance, with people showing a degree of punctuality

[52] E. Mounier, *Oeuvres, II, Traité du caractère* (Paris, 1961), pp. 694–5.
[53] At a council held that year at Seville.
[54] Paper given to my seminar by B. Dompnier.

never previously attained. This may at first sight seem impossibly paradoxical, but it is quantitatively and qualitatively the situation implied by contrast in the use of the word 'dechristianization'. The model of Christianity we normally use as a parameter is not the syncretism of the Middle Ages so much as the austere unanimist religion of the seventeenth century, which was far more concerned than the medieval church to transform prescription and regulation into reality at the popular level, and to turn the ideal of the few into the daily life of all. If it is indeed true that this model of Christianity underlies our current thinking about dechristianization, then we must conclude that the large-scale Christianization of Europe is a relatively recent phenomenon. The two Reformations, Protestant and Catholic, took the kind of religion and religious observances by which we assess the present situation out into the countryside, where the vast majority of the population lived.

If this comparison seems unconsciously familiar, even forms part of our general patterns of thought, this is not a coincidence. By using it we simply show how close, in terms of the time-scales of religion, we are to that period; we also indicate the importance of the results of that long process of acculturation; its effects are still with us. There can be few events in the earlier history of mankind which are of equivalent scope or profundity. The slow fertilization of the Middle Ages prepared the way for the conversion of millions to an exacting spirituality and the customs of a religious elite: a major transformation in the psychology of the masses in favour of a written culture, a message based on a Book, and a form of education which relied increasingly on print. Although this movement appeared to die away about 1750, it actually drew new life from the Enlightenment thinkers at the end of the century. Despite growing difficulties, the churches, on the eve of the Revolution and throughout the nineteenth century, continued the process of religious acculturation in Europe, and expanded their work overseas in a series of new efforts all conceived and executed within the framework established by the two sixteenth-century Reformations. Having identified and defined this continuity and its periodic renewals, we must discard the oversimplified linear explanation which sees the eighteenth century as initiating a uniform decline in all the Christian denominations.

There is a further point to be made in connection with this. Christian acculturation worked on the basis of guilt, and hypertrophied superegos were probably responsible for a few losses of balance on the part of some over-scrupulous individuals. But what effect did it have on Western civilization as a whole? A historical reflection on this problem brings to mind the writings of Carl Jung. For Jung, Freud's disciple and later his adversary, consciousness (and conscience) is deeply bound up with civilization. The process of awareness is what creates culture. Humanity emerges from unconsciousness by means of a profound, almost Promethean, impulse. It is conscious man who conquers the earth. Now it is quite clear that the activity of the Reformations created a previously unparalleled amount of surplus of conscience and consciousness, and also a substantial development in the sense of responsibility. Jung wrote, 'Nothing is more apt to provoke consciousness and awakening than internal disagreement. It is quite impossible to imagine a more effective means of arousing humanity from an irresponsible, sinless, semi-somnolent state in order to lead them to a state of conscious responsibility.'[55] If Jung is right, the guilt inculcated by Christianity was beneficial for Western civilization.

## THE LIMITS OF THE UNDERTAKING

An emphasis on the quantitative aspects of the acculturation achieved by both Reformations should not blind us to the fact that a very visible gap existed between pastoral ambitions and concrete results. Theoretical unanimity in fact masked a state of affairs which was much more complex, and it is to this that I wish to turn in the last section of this account. It is a pity we have no history of 'hypocrisy' in society. In the eighteenth century Madrid courtesans sold their clients letters of confession as Easter approached, enabling them to make their obligatory annual Communion.[56] Undoubtedly, instances less glaring than this caricatural manner of behaving exist which have yet to be brought to light. But I want to stress first that under the *ancien régime* a significant minority of 'delocalized' individuals (to use Le Lannou's word) lived outside the parish framework on which the whole system, whether Protestant or Catholic, rested. I am thinking here of the different sorts of 'travelling people' (pedlars, strolling players, soldiers, sailors, shepherds, emigrants, and convicts) and also of all the people pushed over the threshold of poverty by some unexpected misfortune, the temporary or permanent beggars, and often wanderers as well. For all intents and purposes these people lived outside the social framework, rootless and reputedly dangerous; there were always plenty of them in the towns

[55] C. G. Jung, *L'Ame et la vie* (Paris, 1965), p. 59.
[56] See B. Benassar, *L'Homme espagnol* (Paris, 1975), p. 78.

and on the high roads, and their numbers swelled at times of crisis. In Lyons in 1789–90 they may have accounted for between twenty and twenty-five thousand of the city's one hundred and fifty thousand inhabitants.[57] Authorities were well aware that this sub-proletariat lived on the fringes of Christianity. The *echevins* of Bruges commented on the presence in their city, in 1517, of a 'great multitude of poor people . . . knowing nothing of the articles of faith and the commandments of God. . . begging. . . in the town and the surrounding areas, and accompanied by a great number of children, whom they allow to grow up in utter wickedness and stupidity, and in ignorance of the Catholic faith'.[58] A hundred years later a Paris burgher recommended to Louis XIII the incarceration of the kingdom's poor, arguing that it would ensure the 'salvation of several millions of souls who would otherwise be lost for the want of instruction in the fear of God'.[59]

The logical implication of the authorities' belief that salvation and ignorance were incompatible was that there should be more schools. People could remember a Catechism more easily if they could read it or copy it out for themselves. Europe did indeed have more schools between the sixteenth and eighteenth centuries than it did in the Middle Ages; yet in France, at the end of the *ancien régime*, 53 per cent of men and 73 per cent of women were illiterate. Even in 1886 there were still 35 per cent and 42 per cent respectively.[60] There are two important historical consequences of Christianity's close bond with education and the Catechism. First, in Western Europe today, it is usually in the areas where there is a long history of written culture that religious faith seems best able to stand up to attack;[61] this basic connection links Christianity more to education than to wealth, although the two may be to some extent interconnected. Conversely, the most hard-hit of the country-dwellers who, with the coming of industrialization, left the overpopulated rural areas, represented the least catechized element in Europe at that time,[62] the people who remained for the most part outside the world of reading and, more importantly, of writing. Abruptly transplanted to the suburbs, with

---

[57] J.-P. Gutton, *La Société et les pauvres: l'exemple de la généralité de Lyon, 1534–1789* (Paris, 1971), p. 53; *La Société et les pauvres en Europe (XVIe–XVIIIe siècles)* (Paris, 1974).

[58] G. Van Severen, *Inventaire diplomatique des archives de l'ancienne école Bogaerde à Bruges* (Bruges, 1899), vol. I, p. 81.     [59] Gutton, *La société et les pauvres*, p. 317.

[60] M. Fleury and P. Valmary, 'Les Progrès de l'instruction en France de Louis XIV à Napoléon III', in *Population* (1957), 71–92; and F. Furet and W. Sachs, 'La Croissance de l'alphabétisation en France', in *Annales E.S.C.* (May–June 1974), 721.     [61] See E. Pin, *Pratiques religieuses et classes sociales* (Paris, 1956), pp. 213–19.

[62] See M. L. Fracart, *La Fin de l'Ancien Régime à Niort* (Paris, 1956), p. 79.

no parish to welcome them, they quickly forgot what little religion they knew. Thus the church did not lose the working class, as it had never actually won its allegiance.

We ought also to re-examine the results of the struggle waged by the Christian churches against 'superstition', the ecclesiastical concept which at that time embraced all beliefs and customs not endorsed by the authorities, including all those that concerned terrestrial anxieties. Some historians now believe that, as Tridentine Catholicism strengthened the measures it took against superstition, it encouraged dechristianization – in the long term – by creating a disembodied religious life, cut off from the soil in which it ought properly to have been rooted. I mention this interesting opinion, without for the time being taking a view of the matter, mainly to point out that if this analysis is advanced for Catholicism, it must also a fortiori apply to Protestantism. Yet this new religion, endeavouring increasingly to deal with spiritual matters only, with its emphasis on salvation in the after-life, was only partially successful in destroying the religion of magic, rooted as it was in the here and now. Recent and continuing investigations have shown that even in Protestant areas such as Germany,[63] England[64] and the Cévennes,[65] culture managed to survive the attacks by going underground or camouflaging itself in order to escape the attention of religious authorities. It is also quite clear that the Roman Catholic Church was prepared to accept local compromises, although more noticeably in Spain and Italy than in France or Germany, and more obviously in the country areas than in the towns. The consequence was that the split that occurred between the spiritual religion (modelled on that of the elites) and the continuation of medieval syncretism did not reflect the division between Protestant and Catholic countries, but happened within both. It is worth pointing out here that, in France, the Revolution and education under the Third Republic carried on the struggle against superstitious customs which the two Reformations had undertaken. The present situation is an indication of the partial failure of these attacks, and we are now witnessing a large-scale return of a neo-magism which has held out against religion and science.

The survival of magism should prompt more extensive investigations into the modes of collective resistance to the Reformations

---

[63] B. Vogler, *Vie religieuse en pays rhénan dans la seconde moitié du XVIe siècle (1556–1619)* (Lille III, reproduction services, 1974), vol. 2, pp. 815–39.
[64] K. Thomas, *Religion and the Decline of Magic* (London, 1971), pp. 70–4.
[65] P. Joutard, *La Légende des Camisards. Une sensibilité au passé* (Paris, 1977).

at the periods when they appeared most in control of their respective territories. As this will involve looking at a different level from that of intellectual formulations, we should expect to find opposition that is instinctive, intermittent, and passive rather than the conscious, continuous, and aggressive traits usually picked out in historiography. There is no doubt, for example, that post-Tridentine Catholicism and the Protestant Reformation sought to moralize everyday life, to purify language (the *précieux*, for example), and above all to bring sexual activity under strict control. This led to a kind of 'desexualization' of Western society, similar in some ways to what has happened in modern China. People married late, yet for a long time there were very few pre-marital pregnancies or illegitimate births. Statistically speaking, in France between 1650 and 1750 the church's demands seem to have been followed with a degree of obedience which must express, to some extent at least, the impact of the new clergy and their activity. It would be wrong to give absolute credence to those figures, however. Jean-Louis Flandrin is quite right when he says, 'Chastity cannot be expressed in statistics.'[66] The parish registers whose entries have been evaluated can tell us nothing about clandestine adultery of married women, or about masturbation. And the fact that confessors' manuals and many other texts lay so much stress on solitary practices also shows that not all young people sublimated their libido until they were twenty-six or twenty-seven. In addition (and this strikes me as fundamental), it is questionable whether the parish priest had the same concept of sin as most of his congregation. What did they own up to in the confessional? We need a history of auricular confession which approaches the subject not as a free individual act, but in terms of its public reception: people in general felt coerced. There is enough evidence from quite a wide variety of sources – priests' journals, confessors' manuals, accounts of missions, synodal decrees, and the like – to suggest that the average Catholic of the period only went to confession because he had to, and that moreover he disliked very strongly having to confess his faults to somebody he knew as well as his parish priest. As for the reasons for attendance at the offices or Communion, the priest J.-B. Thiers, writing at a time of general religious observance, said, 'People go to mass to finalize business arrangements, and pass on the latest news and gossip' and 'People take communion in order not to be thought rebellious or not to be

[66] J.-L. Flandrin, 'Mariage tardif et vie sexuelle', in *Annales E. S. C.* (November–December 1972), 1351–87.

made to look conspicuous',[67] which tells us something which for a long time has been left out of account, namely that a good many people would have stayed away from church, even at a period of unanimous Christianity, if they had been able to do so.

People did hold attitudes hostile to the obligatory religion of those days, attitudes whose importance has, I believe, been underestimated so far, and any broad-based investigation of them should include a survey of lists of proverbs, songs, swearwords and blasphemies (notably in Italy, Spain, and Quebec), and trials before ecclesiastical courts, as well as edicts and tracts put out by the authorities in an attempt to regulate pilgrimages, processions, and lenten fasts, and to enforce Sundays and holidays as days of rest. Any enquiry on these lines is bound to shatter the superficial appearance of religious unanimity. Plenty of people tried, in practice if not with conscious intention, to evade the strict framework imposed jointly by the church and the state. Sometimes, for as long as it took to let out a blasphemous oath, a vehement but short-lived opposition would break out and then would be almost immediately forgotten. Gabriel Le Bras pointed out that the hostility between the parish church and the tavern which was so pronounced in nineteenth- and early twentieth-century France was in existence long before the Revolution, and that the priests were not always successful in their attempts to ensure that drinking places were closed during divine service.[68] The internal missionaries of the seventeenth and eighteenth centuries speak of areas, even whole regions (especially in wine-growing districts and along the sides of rivers), where the inhabitants evinced what they called 'republican' attitudes, which meant that they were indifferent, or indeed hostile, to religion.[69] On the basis of these indications, there would appear to be a good case for trying to establish the history and geography of anticlericalism, which reached beyond the ecclesiastical institutions themselves, being in practice often aimed at official dogma and morality.

There can be no doubt, therefore, that the intensive process of Christianization which was carried out on new principles from the sixteenth century onwards achieved striking results, both quantitatively and qualitatively; but it cannot be denied, either, that under the superficial gloss of obligation and conformity there still existed the whole range of behaviour, from piety to indifference to

---

[67] J.-B. Thiers, *Traité des superstitions*, II, bk 3, chap. 9.
[68] G. Le Bras, *Etudes de sociologie religieuse*, vol. 1, pp. 66–7; and A. Molinier, *Une Paroisse du Bas-Languedoc: Sérignan, 1650–1792* (Montpellier, 1968), pp. 130–5.
[69] L. Perouas, *P. Fr. Hacquet*, pp. 28–66.

outright hostility. If there is any truth in the foregoing analysis, then any comparison between the religious situation today and that under the *ancien régime* is inapposite, since today's religion is expressed in terms of individual liberty, rather than in terms of authority and the masses. With this perspective, dechristianization becomes the disappearance in Western Europe of a political and religious system that required everybody to observe the same faith and perform actions which it was impossible, in theory, to evade.

However, dechristianization is obviously more complex than that. Historians need to look again at two sets of facts, both of which were in evidence before the Revolution. First, both catechizers and catechized sooner or later grew tired of the ministry of fear. One expression of this was the decline in requests for masses for the dead in the eighteenth-century wills studied by Michel Vovelle in Provence[70] and Pierre Chaunu in Paris.[71] St Charles Borromeo advised that Sunday should be used for meditation on the last things, and in his *Mémoires d'outre-tombe* Chateaubriand tells of the 'terrors' inspired in him when, as a child, he read a book called *Les Confessions mal faites*. 'Spectres dragging chains and vomiting flames', he wrote, 'threatened me with eternal torture for one sin concealed.'[72] To the extent that religion was closely bound up with fear of the hereafter, the weakening of the latter led to disaffection with the former, if not for Chateaubriand himself then certainly for very many others.

The other strand of explanation, which complements the first, is the fact that both Reformations greatly strengthened the parish structure, and placed greater emphasis – *de jure* or *de facto* – on the importance of priest and pastor. The religious authorities, better trained and more respectable than hitherto, were intended to be models of virtue and teachers of religion. In addition, they had some standing in the community. Priests, and to a lesser extent pastors, appeared to be set apart from other men. As long as there was still a gap between the knowledge of those teaching the faith and the ignorance of the people they taught, the redefined, restructured Christianity of the sixteenth century was able not only to hold its own but, as I have tried to show, to improve its real position considerably. But the civilization of Western Europe was far from static, and lay knowledge developed more rapidly than the increasingly defensive, hidebound, religious culture. This led to a threefold

[70] Vovelle, *Piété baroque.*
[71] P. Chaunu, *La Mort à Paris, XVI^e, XVII^e et XVIII^e siècles* (Paris, 1978).
[72] Chateaubriand, *Memoirs of François René, Vicomte de Chateaubriand*, translated by A. T. de Mattos (London, 1902), vol. 1, p. 53.

reversal of the situation that had emerged in the Middle Ages. First, the educated people tended more and more to be laymen; second, secular learning conquered an ever-larger area, worrying the orthodox, who by and large thought of stasis as good and change as bad; and thirdly, the towns, which were originally better religiously 'equipped' than the country, and which were the starting-point for both Reformations, became increasingly independent, in terms of learning and power, from the spokesmen of the Christian religions. From about 1630 or 1650 onwards the first serious signs of this conflict become visible: the trial of Galileo is one of them. As this movement grew, religion turned more and more for support to the rural areas which only a few centuries earlier had been seen as the repository of paganism, and began to regard with growing disquiet the lay, urban culture with which it had lost touch. (This loss of contact can be seen very clearly in the inventories of eighteenth-century ecclesiastical libraries studied by Jean Quéniart.)[73]

Yet it might well be argued that this secularization sprang from the deepest spirit of Christianity. An account must be written some day of the successive shifts in the boundary between sacred and secular in Christian history – by 'sacred' I mean here the separate domain in which, with the appropriate observances and taboos, the relationship between man and the divine unfolds; and by 'secular', everything outside this area. From its first page, the Bible teaches forcefully that neither the sea, nor the earth, nor the sun, nor the stars, are divine. The world is not God, and it is given to man. Furthermore, Judaism contrasted Yahweh, the one, personal god, with the many Baals whose altars peopled the countryside of Palestine. Then came Jesus, who seems to have carried out a fundamental desacralization of religious conduct by relativizing observances. He rejected the excessive requirements of sabbath prohibitions and ritual ablutions, subordinated the special status of the temple at Jerusalem to worship in truth and the spirit, refused to believe in the sacred punishments – of those born blind and the victims of the tower of Shiloh – and proclaimed salvation through charity. From that point on, as Father Chenu has pointed out,[74] everything secular or profane became sanctifiable, yet without ceasing to be profane. St

---

[73] J. Quéniart, 'Culture et societé urbaines dans la France de l'Ouest au XVIIIe siècle' (Thèse de doctorat d'Etat, Paris I, 1975), 4 vols., mimeo, with maps and graphs.

[74] M. D. Chenu, 'Consecratio mundi', in *Nouvelle Revue Théologique* (June 1964), 612. See also F. Bourdeau, 'Fin du sacré? Sainteté du profane', in *Forma Gregis*, 26th year, no. 1 (first quarter, 1974), 1–94, and 'Une sainteté séculière', in 26th year, no. 1 (second quarter, 1974), 97–144.

Paul in turn stressed justification by faith rather than by law – and therefore by the sacred. The first Christian communities were not ruled by a sacerdotal caste but by 'elders', a term borrowed from the secular vocabulary. As Origen said, responding to one of Celsus' accusations, 'we [Christians] avoid setting up altars and images and temples' except in a purely spiritual sense.[75] Thus Bouthoul can write that Christianity gave rise to 'the most large-scale and most radical shift between the sacred and profane',[76] and it is certainly not coincidental that it was in the Christian West that man succeeded in controlling his earthly destiny by means of science and technology.

However, having taken on after Constantine the government of an entire civilization, Christianity agreed to allow a place for pagan notions of the sacred, which varied according to period and location, and which included taboos, ceremonies of control, and a powerful hierarchy of priests. This tendency towards resacralization was attacked from time to time, and renewed arguments broke out, the most important being the Protestant revolution of the sixteenth century, although the Catholic Reformation did attempt to spiritualize the Sacraments and collective piety and to relativize the worship of the saints. The two Reformations also permitted substantial expansion of the neutral ground, outside of their direct influence. Calvinism shifted art outside the temple; Catholicism allowed secular music to develop and accepted the nude in painting and sculpture as long as they remained outside the churches. The Protestant abandonment of Latin, and the multiplication of vernacular canticles and religious works in Catholic countries, marked a move away from the sacred language of the Western Middle Ages; and the critical spirit whose rise enabled science itself to develop was to a great extent a product of Christianity reflecting on its own history. Humanist philology returned to the Bible and the Church Fathers to escape the toils of scholasticism; there were the Protestant disputations from Luther to Bayle; and the rigorous erudition of the Bollandists and the Maurists. Hence the current work on the Christian origins of the Enlightenment thinkers.[77] But because Christianity wanted to retain a particular area of life for itself, it found itself in conflict in the modern period with a secular culture which its own deepest dynamic had helped to create.

There is, in the end, no simple answer. Seen in contrast to the previous state of 'Christendom', in the seventeenth and eighteenth

[75] Origen, *Contra Celsum*, trans. H. Chadwick (Cambridge, 1953), VIII, 17, p. 464.
[76] G. Bouthoul, *Les Mentalités* (Paris, 1966), p. 100.
[77] Thesis by Jacques Solé, University of Lyon (unpublished).

centuries particularly, dechristianization appears first and foremost
as a quantitative phenomenon, a decline in the number of practising
Catholics once the period of compulsion, conformism, and hereditary
Christianity is over. The removal of a religion based on fear thus
inaugurates a process of declericalization and secularization. This
does not mean we need to extrapolate from these facts and conclude
that the death of Christianity is imminent.[78] It is more likely that
dechristianization is nothing but the withering away of one model of
Christianity, while another replaces it before our eyes. It is not the
job of a historian to predict the future. Rather, by refusing to accept
over-simplifications, he increases its possibilities.

[78] Cf. Joachim Wach, *Sociology of Religion* (Chicago, 1944), who writes that religious
experience should not be identified with any of its historical expressions, and who
thinks that 'religious creative energy is inexhaustible, ever aiming at new and
fuller realization', (p. 14).

◁ ════════════════════════════════════════════ ▷

# 5

# The 'new art of lying' : equivocation, mental reservation, and casuistry*

JOHANN P. SOMMERVILLE

The word 'casuistry' has two meanings. Firstly, it signifies 'the art or science of bringing general moral principles to bear upon particular cases'. Secondly, it means 'sophistical, equivocal, or specious reasoning'. The connection between the two is historical. Catholic casuists, and particularly Jesuits, were accused by their opponents in the sixteenth and seventeenth centuries of employing sophistry in support of lax and absurd moral conclusions. The mud stuck. Casuistry was the dominant form of moral theorizing in late medieval and early modern Europe. Yet Henry Sidgwick was content to give it short shrift in his *Outlines of the History of Ethics*. The Jesuits, he said, attempted to win back souls from Protestantism 'by accommodating ecclesiastico-moral law to worldly needs'. The excesses to which this laxity led were decisively 'revealed to the world in the immortal *Provincial Letters* of Pascal'.[1]

In Sidgwick's view, Catholic thinkers had been hampered not only by moral but also by intellectual failings. Scholasticism, he claimed, had shackled 'the renascent intellectual activity which it stimulated and exercised, by the double bondage to Aristotle and to the Church'. As long as thought remained the slave of authority, moral philosophy in its modern sense remained impossible. Similarly, William Whewell, in his *Lectures on the History of Moral Philosophy in England*, dismissed casuistry in a preliminary 'Note', and granted it that much space only because he was lecturing as Professor of Moral Theology or Casuistical Divinity. Whewell explained that the

---

* I am grateful to Mr W. P. Sommerville, jr., for discussions relating to aspects of this chapter, which was written in the summer of 1983.
[1] Hans Schär, 'A Protestant view of conscience', in the Curatorium of the C. G. Jung Institute, ed., *Conscience* (Evanston, 1970), pp. 111–30, at pp. 126–7, n. 4. Henry Sidgwick, *Outlines of the History of Ethics* (London, 1931), pp. 153–4.

Catholic casuists had merely amassed opinions from earlier writers: 'There was not in these books any attempt to lay down general principles, which might show that the decisions were right.' As long as blind obedience to the church had been the rule, he argued, there had been no point in providing justifications for its decisions: 'the lay disciple was supposed to be in entire dependence upon his spiritual teachers for the guidance of his conscience'.[2]

These two charges, that the casuists were lax in their practical teachings, watering down morality to suit the convenience of the immoral, and that they adhered blindly to authority, avoiding arguments from general principles, have consigned casuistry to an undeserved oblivion. In fact, neither charge holds up to scholarly examination. Nevertheless, it is true that the particular conclusions of the casuists were sometimes odd or even abhorrent. An example is the notorious doctrine of (strict) mental reservation, according to which it is not lying to make a spoken assertion which you believe to be false, and which you believe will deceive your hearer, provided that you add in thought some words which make the whole truthful. For instance, the English Catholic priest John Ward was asked by his Protestant captors in 1606 whether he was a priest and whether he had ever been across the seas. He replied 'no' to both questions, though in fact the correct answer was 'yes'. When evidence was produced that his answers were false, he claimed that he had not lied, for, in denying that he was a priest, he had mentally added 'of Apollo', and in saying that he had not been across the seas he had reserved 'Indian' before 'seas'. According to the views of a sizeable proportion of contemporary Catholic casuists, such action was neither lying nor wrong. They were not led to this conclusion by laxity, or by an unwillingness to reason from general principles. Rather, it was their rigid devotion to certain general principles and their single-minded insistence upon following these principles to their logical conclusions which gave birth to the doctrine of mental reservation. Let us examine in more detail the history of this most casuistical of the casuists' doctrines.[3]

The starting-point must be lying. In the first four centuries of Christianity there was little agreement on the question of whether

---

[2] Ibid., p. 156. William Whewell, *Lectures on the History of Moral Philosophy in England* (London, 1852), p. xxxi.

[3] *Calendar of State Papers Domestic, 1603–10*, p. 286. W. H. Frere, *The English Church in the Reigns of Elizabeth and James I* (London, 1904), pp. 328–9. Elliot Rose, *Cases of Conscience* (Cambridge, 1975), p. 90. Robert Abbot, *Antilogia adversus Apologiam Andreae Eudaemon-Ioannis Iesuitae* (London, 1613), f. 12a. Abbot adds similar examples in ibid., ff. 12a–13a.

lying could ever be justified. The Bible itself was not entirely clear on the subject, combining general prohibitions with examples of lying in a good cause. Such thinkers as Origen, Cassian, St Jerome, and St John Chrysostom maintained that it was lawful, perhaps even obligatory, to lie in special circumstances. Change came with St Augustine. Reacting against the followers of Priscillian, the first Christian martyred by Christians, who claimed that it was licit to lie in a just cause (for example, to safeguard Priscillianists from persecution), Augustine pronounced that lying was always wrong. His opinion triumphed, becoming the orthodox doctrine of Catholics. Aquinas summarized the conventional teaching, distinguishing between officious, jocose, and pernicious lies. Officious lies were intended to benefit someone; jocose lies were told in jest, and without an intention to benefit or harm; pernicious lies were intended to harm. Aquinas condemned all lying as sinful, but held that only pernicious lying was a mortal sin. Lying was invariably wrong, but 'the greater the good intended, the more is the sin of lying diminished in gravity'.[4]

Catholic casuists agreed in condemning all lying. There was also wide agreement on what lying was. 'A lie', wrote the Jesuit Toletus, 'may be described thus: a false statement intended to deceive.' He went on to explain that the statement did not have to be spoken, and that it had to be false only in the sense that the liar did not believe it to be true, 'for it is not saying something false that is telling a lie, but saying something other than you think to be true, whether or not it is in fact true'. The point was illustrated by a bogus Latin etymology: 'mentiri' ('to lie'), said Toletus, was derived from 'contra mentem ire', 'to go against one's mind'.[5]

[4] A survey of pre-Augustinian ideas on lying is in Kenneth E. Kirk, *Conscience and its Problems: an Introduction to Casuistry* (London, 1948), pp. 182–8. Augustine's views are set out in his two treatises *De mendacio* and *Contra mendacium*, important extracts from which are translated in Sissela Bok, *Lying: Moral Choice in Public and Private Life* (Hassocks, Sussex, 1978), pp. 250–5; cf. also several of Augustine's letters, translated in Philip Schaff, ed., *A Select Library of the Nicene and post-Nicene Fathers of the Christian Church*, first series, vol. 1 (Grand Rapids, 1974), pp. 251–3, 272–5, 349–60, 547–8. Aquinas' main discussion of lying is in *Summa theologiae*, 2a2ae, q. 110, art. 1–4, extracts from which are translated in Bok, *Lying*, pp. 255–61; the quotation in the text, from art. 2, is at p. 257.

[5] Franciscus Toletus (Francisco de Toledo, 1532–96; Spanish Jesuit), *Instructio sacerdotum, summam casuum conscientiae complectens* (Lyons, 1601), p. 922: 'Mendacium potest sic describi: Verbum falsum cum intentione fallendi . . . non est mendacium dicere, quod non ita est, sed dicere aliter quam homo putat, sive sit, sive non sit ita in re: ob id dicitur mentiri, quasi contra mentem ire.' I have translated Toletus' 'verbum' as 'statement'. It may be that to lie is to perform a different kind of speech act. Perhaps lies are not statements but assertions. Yet it would be ludicrous to attribute to Toletus and his contemporaries a sophistication on such matters which they did not possess.

Lies, then, were held to be statements which the speaker believed
to be untrue, and which he uttered with the intention of deceiving
his audience. It was generally recognized that lies could be expressed
through any acts to which convention had assigned meaning, and
not just through words. Non-verbal lying was termed simulation.
Not all statements which the speaker believed to be untrue were
construed as lies; the further necessary condition of lying was the
intention to deceive. Thus, such things as fables, jokes, and parables
did not count as lies if, as was often the case, the speaker did not
intend his hearers to believe that they were literally true. The
audience, 'through too great simplicity or stupidity', might in fact be
deceived into thinking that what they had heard was true. However,
unless the speaker had intended to produce this result, he would not
have lied. Again, it was not essential to lying that the intended
deception be successful. No deception might occur if the hearer
perceived that the speaker was lying, or if the liar's proposition was
in fact true, though he believed it to be false.[6]

Lying, as the casuists understood it, is and doubtless was the most
commonly practised form of intended deception. So it is easy
enough to see why it was singled out for special vituperation by
moralists. It is less clear that the traditional concept is much use in
serious moral analysis. Of the few modern philosophers who have
written on the subject, a number have preferred to abandon the old
usage. Raphael Demos, for example, noted that 'an odd consequence
of this usage is that B, in lying to C, may, in fact, induce a true belief
in C's mind', and, in his study of 'Lying to oneself', adopted a concept
of lying according to which lies always deceive. Frederick A. Siegler
observed the peculiarity of something being at once true and a lie,
and suggested that it might be profitable to distinguish between
'lying' and 'telling a lie'. In her pioneering book on Lying, Sissela Bok
also chose to redefine the concept: 'I shall define as a lie any
intentionally deceptive message which is stated.' On this definition,
intentionally deceptive statements which the speaker believes to be
true are lies – so I can say what I think is true, and what is in fact true,
and still be telling lies. The definition avowedly abolishes the

---

[6] Paul Laymann (1574–1635; Austrian Jesuit), *Theologia Moralis, in quinque libros
partita* (2 vols., Munich, 1626), ii. 164–5. An intention to deceive was standardly
regarded as a necessary condition of lying, though it had not been included as part
of the formal definition by Aquinas; see *Corpus Juris Canonici* (Paris, 1587), p. 269:
'Non mentitur, qui animum fallendi non habet' (*Decreti secunda pars*, causa xxii,
q. ii, c. v. ).

distinction between lies and other intentionally deceptive statements. Is there any point in retaining the distinction?[7]

According to R. M. Chisholm and T. D. Feehan there is indeed a clear distinction to be drawn: 'lying, unlike the other types of intended deception, is essentially a breach of faith', since it violates the right of the person to whom the lie is told to expect that the speaker believes what he asserts. A worry remains: is this right itself derived from the prohibition of intended deception? Employing the idea of a 'breach of faith', Chisholm and Feehan attempt to refurbish the traditional concept of lying in a way that will meet the exacting standards of modern philosophers of language. They hold that lies are *assertions*, and argue that the point of making an assertion 'is that of causing *justified* belief in the propositions (1) that the speaker accepts the *assertum* and (2) that he intends to convey his acceptance of the *assertum*'.[8]

On this analysis, a man does not lie unless he believes that the conditions under which he states a proposition are conditions that justify his hearer in believing that he, the speaker, accepts the proposition. One implication of this is that, if I believe that you will think I am lying, I cannot lie to you. Known liars will find it increasingly difficult to lie – a strange case of the punishment fitting the crime. Of course, the known liar could attempt to deceive his hearer by telling the truth. He would not be guilty of lying, but it is unclear that we would think his action any less immoral for that. We might also hold him guilty of committing a breach of faith, because he acted in a manner calculated to deceive.

If the traditional conception of lying was odd, the widely accepted notion that lying is always wrong was still odder. The casuists believed that it could be right to deceive someone knowingly. They also believed that it could be permissible to state what you believe to be false. Since lying was held to be nothing more than stating a falsehood with the intention of deceiving, it might seem that the question of whether I may lie would, in any particular case, dissolve into the question of whether I may perform both of the constituent acts involved in lying. Labouring under the weight of a tradition that had fossilized in the centuries after Augustine, the casuists refused

---

[7] Raphael Demos, 'Lying to oneself', in *Journal of Philosophy*, 57 (1960), 588–95, at p. 588. Frederick A. Siegler, 'Lying', in *American Philosophical Quarterly*, 3 (1966), 128–36, at p. 132. Bok, *Lying*, p. 13.

[8] Roderick M. Chisholm and Thomas D. Feehan, 'The intent to deceive', in *Journal of Philosophy*, 74 (1977), 143–59, at pp. 152–3.

to take this approach. No one, they declared, might state a falsehood with the intention of deceiving.

The task of the casuists was not merely to apply general principles to particular cases, but also to resolve conflicts between principles. What made a case of conscience problematical, and interesting, was precisely that it involved a conflict between commonly accepted moral rules. To simplify, these rules were of two basic kinds. Firstly, there were absolute duties, of which the duty not to lie is an example. Some of these duties were held to be set out in the Ten Commandments. Examples are the prohibitions of adultery and theft, while the ninth commandment ('Thou shalt not bear false witness') was construed as banning lying, amongst other things. Other equally binding rules derived their force from Revelation rather than from the natural law, and were only indirectly related to the Commandments. An example is the duty of a confessor to keep secret what he has learned in the confessional.

A second set of rules was directed towards the temporal good of mankind, and the fulfilment of God's purposes for man. The obligations to join together in civil society, to obey laws which had been made for the public good, and to keep secrets entrusted to us are examples. Characteristically, rules of this second sort lost their force in cases where their application would be contrary to the public interest. Rules of the first sort, by contrast, were regarded as binding whatever the consequences. For instance, a man would be obliged to reveal secrets, or betray confidences, if failure to do so would cause public harm. But a priest could not break the seal of the confessional in any circumstances. In short, some rules condemned or approved actions in themselves, while others were calculated to distinguish between actions according to their consequences in conferring or withholding benefits. Here, a rigid Augustinian deontology confronted the consequentialism inherent in Aquinas' world-view.

Several devices were employed to show that the two sets of rules were in fact compatible. Firstly, the Ten Commandments were standardly supposed to summarize the principles which it would be rational for men to follow if they were to obtain temporal felicity. If it were commonly practised, the argument ran, lying would undermine one man's faith in another's word, destroying commerce and eventually dissolving society. This line of approach served to explain why lying should not generally be practised, but not why it should always be avoided. Secondly, thinkers adopted the scriptural principle that evil should never be done, even with the intention of bringing about some greater good. A third notion was that doing evil could not, in fact, lead to good results, for God's providence would prevent this.

Providence, it was claimed, would inevitably frustrate a man's plans, however laudable, if he employed evil means to effect them. This argument was invoked with particular frequency against the ideas of Machiavelli. The Florentine was portrayed as not merely evil, for encouraging evil, but also foolish, for supposing that evil could bring about good consequences. Divine retribution would be wreaked upon the perpetrators of evil not only in the after-life but also here on earth. A tortured conscience, it was supposed, would be the inevitable but not the only penalty for wrongdoing. Like cancer, evil spread until it consumed the evil-doer. One infringement of God's decrees invariably led to others. Thus, new lies would be required to conceal earlier deceptions: 'when we have made one lie we must make twenty others to defend that one'.[9] Beginning with a single act, the impenitent wrongdoer would inevitably be driven to desperation' – a state of mind in which he was willing to flout all the laws of God and man, including, in the end, the law against suicide.[10]

This notion of a providential nexus between temporal welfare and rigid obedience to God's absolute commands underlay much contemporary literature, from pamphlets relating the miserable ends of murderers to the tragedies of the greatest dramatists. It received formal expression from Catholics as much as Protestants, from the Jesuit Thomas Fitzherbert and from his Protestant contemporary Christopher Lever, both of whom expended much energy in proving that disobedience to God's commandments could never be expedient, that honesty was the best policy.[11]

[9] Hugh Latimer, *Sermons*, ed. G. E. Corrie, (Cambridge, 1844), p. 503. Attitudes to providence in early modern England are discussed in Keith Thomas, *Religion and the Decline of Magic* (Harmondsworth, Middlesex, 1973), pp. 90–132. On Machiavelli's attitude towards providence and fortune, and its background in Italian Renaissance thought, see especially Quentin Skinner, *Foundations of Modern Political Thought* (2 vols., Cambridge, 1978), i. 95–8, 119–22, 145–6. The response of English casuists to Machiavellian ideas is discussed in G. L. Mosse, *The Holy Pretence: a Study in Christianity and Reason of State from William Perkins to John Winthrop* (Oxford, 1957), *passim*.

[10] Cf. e.g. Gervase Babington, *A verie faithfull exposition of the commandements*, in *Workes* (London, 1615), p. 109: 'The daily beggaries, discredits, shames, and deaths, strange and fearful of such as have made no conscience by false witness-bearing, to pollute their consciences ought mightily to move us, and very effectually to persuade us never to do it.'

[11] Thomas Fitzherbert, *The First Part of a Treatise concerning Policy and Religion* (Douai, 1606), and *The Second Part of a Treatise concerning Policy and Religion* (Douai, 1615), *passim*. Christopher Lever, *Heaven and Earth, Religion and Policy* (London, 1608), *passim*.

166 JOHANN P. SOMMERVILLE

Yet, in the sixteenth and seventeenth centuries the idea that God's providence worked in such a simple and easily comprehensible way was beginning to lose its hold. In reading the works of many of Machiavelli's critics one gets a sense that their authors did protest too much. Moreover, the principles of temporal advantage continued to exercise their fascination. Augustine himself had recognized, but ignored, the inhumanity of supposing that we should never tell a harmless lie even to secure some great good – for example, saving a life. The same problem troubled the casuists. As we shall see, they formally accepted the absolute ban on lying, but came increasingly to reject or evade the substance of the principle.

Few modern moral philosophers have been willing to follow Augustine and Kant in their doctrine that lying is always wrong. In the later Middle Ages and early modern period few allowed that it could ever be right. Some Protestants did, indeed, adopt this position, but more abided by Augustine's teaching, while a number took a third approach, redefining the concept to exclude acts of justified untruthful intended deception. In a similar way, certain acts of homicide and of taking another man's property were construed as falling outside the general prohibitions of these activities. For example, killing in self-defence or the killing of criminals by public authority were not held to be breaches of the sixth commandment. Again, it was widely acknowledged that you could take another man's goods in a case of extreme necessity – for example, to save yourself from starvation. Catholic casuists accepted these doctrines on killing and theft. Indeed, the Jesuit Lessius was taken to task by Pascal for allowing not only 'extreme necessity' but also mere 'grave necessity' to excuse acts of theft.[12] But the casuists refused to make a similar distinction in the case of lying. You could steal or kill to save your life, but never lie.

On the other hand, the casuists recognized that there were cases in which telling the truth could lead to disastrous consequences. If a killer asks me where his intended victim is, telling the truth could lead to murder. If a priest is asked what he has heard in the confessional, he is bound by an absolute duty to keep the confession secret. An obvious possibility in such cases is to remain silent. But silence itself, as much as speech, can convey a conventional meaning – for example, betokening assent. Moreover, the consequences of silence can be quite as dire as those of telling the truth. So the task of the casuists was to construct a means whereby a man could at once

[12] Blaise Pascal, *The Provincial Letters of Pascal*, ed. John de Soyres (Cambridge, 1880), p. 187.

avoid lying and prevent the harmful results which truth or silence would bring.

What proved of great help here was the ambiguity of language. As early as the thirteenth century Raymund of Pennafort argued that a man might deceive a murderer, to whose intended victim he had given refuge, by saying 'non est hic', which can mean either 'he is not here' or 'he is not eating here'.[13] All the casuists, and a good many of their opponents, agreed that such exploitation of equivocal terms was not lying, and that it could on occasion be justified, though Raymund's example did not meet with universal approval. It was out of the doctrine of verbal equivocation that the later theory of mental reservation grew. The theory relied on the assumption that verbal equivocation is not in fact lying. This is by no means obvious.

In essence, the proponents of verbal equivocation claimed that it is not lying to make a statement which possesses both true and false meanings, provided that it is true according to your sense (*sensus*) or meaning (*intentio*). It did not matter that you recognized that your words also bore a sense in which they were false. In Raymund's example the speaker is aware that his statement has a false meaning – 'he is not here' – and he hopes that his hearer will understand the words in this sense. This looks perilously close to saying that the speaker states what he believes to be false with the intention of deceiving, and so lies. The casuists mounted three separate arguments in order to evade the conclusion that verbal equivocation was lying. The first distinguished between the speaker's primary and secondary intentions. Where a man is unjustly questioned, the claim ran, and where 'the first and principal intention of the answerer is not to hurt or impugn others, but to defend and cover himself . . . it followeth evidently, that it can be no lie, nor deception on his part, though by his manner of answering they deceive themselves, which is not to be imputed to any fault of his'.[14] This argument could, of course, be extended to justify not only equivocation but also lying itself. In more recent times, a similar line of reasoning has some-times been used to show that those who die as a consequence of

[13] St Raymund of Pennafort (*c.* 1180–1275; Spanish Dominican), *Summa Sti. Raymundi de Peniafort* (Rome, 1603), p. 100. The example is discussed in Kirk, *Conscience*, p. 194.

[14] Robert Parsons, *A Treatise tending to Mitigation towardes Catholicke-Subiectes in England* (St Omer, 1607), p. 347. The claim that verbal ambiguity does not deceive the hearer but permits him to deceive himself was frequently made: see e.g. Laymann, *Theologia Moralis*, ii.165; Michael Bartholomew Salon (1538–1620; Spanish Augustinian), *Controversiae de Justitia et Jure . . . Tomus Primus* (Venice, 1608), i.527.

hunger strikes are not guilty of suicide, since their primary intention is not to kill themselves but to expose the iniquities of a tyrannical government.

The more sober casuists took a second approach. They concentrated upon the first component of lying – stating what you believe to be false, or going against your mind – rather than upon the intention to deceive. What counted, they said, was whether your statement did in fact have a true meaning and whether you meant it in the sense in which it was true. Meaning, they held, was a matter of convention and not, or not primarily, of intention. That is to say, the utterer's meaning might differ from the meaning which he intended his hearer to understand. This position was adopted not only by Catholics, but also by most Protestant casuists. If I am unjustly interrogated by someone who has no authority to question me, wrote the puritan Richard Baxter, 'I may lawfully answer him in such doubtful words as purposely are intended to deceive him, or leave him ignorant of my sense, so be it they be not lies or false in the ordinary usage of those words.'[15] A third argument similarly insisted that you did not lie if you believed what you meant, but left the conventional element out of meaning. In other words, you could say 'hot' and mean 'cold'. Once this argument was formulated, the theory of mental reservation had arrived. To see how this happened, we will need to delve a little deeper into the casuists' ideas on verbal ambiguity.

A statement, the casuists said, could be ambiguous in virtue of some equivocal term or grammatical construction which it contained. It could also acquire ambiguity from the circumstances in which it was expressed. For example, a defendant in an English court of law might say that he is 'not guilty'. Though ordinarily a profession of innocence, these words can take on a special significance when spoken as a plea in a court. They become less a statement of fact than a declaration of how you want your case to be tried.[16] Another

---

[15] Richard Baxter, *A Christian Directory: or a summ of practical theologie and cases of conscience* (London, 1673), p. 430. According to Laymann, *Theologia Moralis*, ii.167, words acquire meaning 'ex institutione et pacto hominum'. It is worth noting in passing that the Latin 'intentio' was used to signify both meaning and intention. The relationship between these two concepts has been much discussed by modern philosophers: see e.g. H. P. Grice, 'Utterer's meaning and intentions', in *Philosophical Review*, 78 (1969), 147–77; J. R. Searle, ed., *The Philosophy of Language* (Oxford, 1971), pp. 1–70; Mark de Bretton Platts, *Ways of Meaning: an Introduction to a Philosophy of Language* (London, 1979), *passim*, especially pp. 86–94.

[16] The Elizabethan Jesuit Henry Garnet drew attention to this in his *Treatise of Equivocation*, ed. David Jardine (London, 1851), p. 71. Significantly, Garnet retitled his work *A Treatise against Lying and Fraudulent Dissimulation*. Garnet's authorship is proved in A. F. Allison, 'The writings of Fr. Henry Garnet, S.J. (1555–1606)', in *Recusant History* (formerly *Biographical Studies*), 1 (1951), 7–21, at pp. 14–15.

instance, frequently used by the casuists, is the case of the confessor who is asked whether he knows something which he does know, but only through the confessional. In these circumstances, they argued, he could say 'no', meaning 'not in such a way that I can reveal it'. Here, 'no' takes on an unusual meaning because of a special fact about the speaker; namely that he is a priest bound by the seal of the confessional.[17] In other cases, the speaker's statement was held to acquire an added meaning because of some characteristic of his interlocutor, usually that this interlocutor was asking unjust or only partially just questions.

Truth-telling, the casuists admitted, was a socially useful institution. But so, too, was the preservation of secrets, especially, though not exclusively, from those who would put the information to evil use.[18] Equivocation, they argued, was justified whenever a man had no duty to tell the truth. Thus, equivocation could be employed by a defendant in a court of law – for example, if the judge questioned him on matters which were immaterial to the case in hand. As Martin de Azpilcueta put it, the accused was bound to reply only 'according to the intention which an upright, fair, and godly judge should have'.[19] This principle was often illustrated by the example of a traveller who, on arriving at the gates of a city, is asked by the guards whether he has come from some particular town which they believe to be infected by plague. The traveller knows that there is in fact no plague in the town, or, alternatively, he knows that though there is plague there, he has not contracted it. If he confesses that he has come from the town, the guards will not admit him. He has no duty to tell them where he has come from, but he does have a duty to satisfy them that his admission will not jeopardize the health and safety of their city. In these circumstances it was held to be permissible for the traveller to reply not to the guards' question itself but to their 'remote intention', as Sylvester termed it. In other words, what the guards really wanted to know and had the authority to ask was whether the traveller was carrying plague. If he was not, he could say 'no'. Given the circumstances, this reply was ambiguous, and, in his sense, truthful.[20]

[17] Laymann, *Theologia Moralis*, ii.167; Dominico Soto (1494–1560; Spanish Dominican), *De Justitia et Jure libri decem* (Salamanca, 1556), p. 458.
[18] Andreas Eudaemon-Joannes (1560–1625; Cretan Jesuit), *Ad Actionem proditoriam Edouardi Coqui, Apologia pro R.P. Henrico Garneto* (Cologne, 1610), p. 42.
[19] Martin de Azpilcueta (or Aspilcueta, 1493–1586; Spanish theologian, commonly known as Navarrus), *Commentarius in cap. humanae aures, XXII. Q. V.*, in *Commentaria*, 3 vols. (Venice, 1588), i. f. 221a: 'iuxta intentionem, quam ut rectus, aequus et sanctus iudex debebat habere'.
[20] Silvestro Mazzolini da Prierio, commonly known as Sylvester (1460–1523; Italian Dominican), *Summa Summarum quae Sylvestrina dicitur* (Strasburg, 1518), f. 275b: 'ad

Two ways were explored to explain why the defendant's 'not guilty', and the confessor's (or traveller's) 'no' were not lies. The first approach was to suggest that in the circumstances, and according to certain publicly accepted linguistic conventions, such statements could simply be true. If the speaker *meant* his statement in the sense in which it was true he did not lie, even if he intended it to be understood in the sense in which it was false. However, if, like Humpty Dumpty, he used words to mean just what he chose them to mean, the case would be altered. For, to believe that a statement is false is to disbelieve what you think the statement means, and this is defined by what you think are the publicly accepted linguistic conventions. The limits of permissible ambiguity, asserted the more conservative of the casuists, were circumscribed by these conventions. 'Although a man who is unjustly questioned is not bound to answer according to the intention of the questioner', wrote Pedro de Arragon, 'he is bound, in concealing what he wants to keep secret, to use words which are true in some sense accepted by the common people, or by the wise, for if he does not do so he lies, which is never permissible.' The Jesuit Azorius insisted that the use of words to mean what we believed they did not in fact mean was lying, and Laymann argued that Raymund of Pennafort's punning use of 'est' was a lie. In the circumstances of the case, 'est' could only mean 'is', 'as much according to the common manner of speaking as according to the wise'.[21]

A second approach to the problem was to argue that the confessor's 'no' was truthful because he construed it as meaning something like 'no, except under the seal of confession, which I may not break'. If the confessor had himself understood 'no' to mean 'in

intentionem ... remotam'. The same example was used by many other authors, e.g. Leonardus Lessius (1554–1623; Flemish Jesuit), *De Iustitia et Iure* (Antwerp, 1612), p. 621; C. Filiarchi, *De Officio Sacerdotis ... Tomus Primus* (Venice, 1597), p. 447; Garnet, *Treatise of Equivocation*, p. 80.

[21] Pedro de Arragon (d. 1595; Spanish Augustinian), *In Secundam Secundae D. Thomae Doct. Angelici Commentaria, De Iustitia et Iure* (Venice, 1595), p. 386: 'Nam quamvis, qui iniuste interrogatur, non teneatur respondere ad intentionem interrogantis, tenetur tamen eis verbis secretum celare, quae in aliquo sensu recepto apud vulgus, vel apud sapientes sint vera, alias mentietur, quod numquam licebit.' Joannes Azorius (Juan Azor, 1536–1603; Spanish Jesuit), *Institutionum Moralium ... Tomus Primus* (Rome, 1600), col. 1336. Laymann, *Theologia Moralis*, ii.171: 'tam secundum vulgarem loquendi modum quam secundum sapientes'. Cf. Genesius de Sepulveda (Juan Gines de Sepulveda, 1490–1573; Spanish theologian), *De ratione dicendi testimonium, in Opera Omnia*, vol. 4 (Madrid, 1780), pp. 375–413, especially at pp. 387–8. These authors derived the argument from Soto, *De Institia et Iure*, p. 458. A similar discussion is in Francis Hutcheson, *A System of Moral Philosophy* (2 vols., London, 1755), ii.35–8. Hutcheson very possibly derived his argument from Jeremy Taylor.

no way whatever', his statement would have been a lie, for he would have spoken against his mind. So, to prevent a deceptive and ambiguous statement which the speaker believes to be true in only one of its senses from being a lie, it was held to be necessary that he understood it in the sense in which he believed it was true. A man's understanding of a statement which he makes might, for convenience, be construed as a clause which he mentally added to his spoken words. In the confessor's case, the spoken part is 'no' and the mentally reserved clause is 'except under the seal of confession which I may not break'. The truthfulness of the whole statement was held to be dependent upon the truthfulness of the expressed words conjoined with the mental reservation, and not upon that of the expressed words alone.[22]

According to the conservative casuists, such as Soto, Sepulveda, Pedro de Arragon, Azorius, and Laymann, I believe that a statement is false if I believe that what it means is false. Its meaning is governed by public conventions. On this approach, a mental reservation served to explain why an ambiguous but possibly truthful statement was in fact truthful. It could never make an untruthful statement truthful. A consequence of this conservative line was that a man's ability to avoid lying while at the same time preventing some disaster could depend upon such arbitrary factors as whether a deceptive ambiguity was available, and whether the speaker had the linguistic skills needed to notice it. Dexterity at punning became a virtue. Again, if the unjust questioner suspected that he had received an equivocal and misleading answer, he might ask another question couched in terms intended to avoid further ambiguous responses. For instance, suppose that in Raymund of Pennafort's example the murderer has bothered to read the casuists. 'Non est hic' does not satisfy him. Instead of shrugging his shoulders, saying 'too bad', and trying the house next door, he continues the dialogue with 'I did not ask you whether he is eating here, but whether you have given him refuge in this house. Well, have you?' Having run out of ambiguous replies, you are faced once more with your original dilemma. Both silence and the truth will bring disaster. How can this be averted without lying?

To solve these problems some casuists took the momentous step of arguing that a false statement can be made true by the addition of an appropriate mental reservation. Not only ambiguous statements, but any statement whatever could become truthful if the speaker

---

[22] Cf. e.g. Azpilcueta, *Commentaria*, i. f. 218b–224a; Laymann, *Theologia Moralis*, ii.166–7; Garnet, *Treatise of Equivocation*, 10–11; Soto, *De Iustitia et Iure*, p. 458.

made judicious use of this casuist's stone. The effect of this notion was to revolutionize the moral theory of truthfulness and lying. The concept of lying was rendered virtually redundant, for there was little reason why a man should commit the sin of lying if he could avoid it by voicing exactly the same words with a suitable mental addition. This was the price which had to be paid for combining formal adherence to the rigid principle that lying was always wrong with a substantive belief in the priority of principles of human utility.

In his *Summa de casibus conscientiae*, published in 1488, Angelus de Clavasio claimed that an unjustly questioned man could reply by saying 'what is true according to his own meaning, even if it is false according to the understanding of his hearer'. Though Angelus did not make it clear whether he thought that the speaker might mean whatever he chose, later authors took this to be his argument.[23] In his *Summa summarum*, first printed in 1515, Sylvester more clearly adopted the theory of strict mental reservation. He considered the case of a man who has been waylaid by thieves. Not satisfied with their takings, they compel him to swear an oath promising to pay them a certain amount of money at a specified time and place. Is the man bound to pay the money? It all depended, said Sylvester, on what he had meant by his words. If, after speaking the words of the oath, he had mentally added some such clause as 'provided that I am indebted to you for that amount of money', he would not be obliged to pay, since they had not lent him the money.[24] Of course, the mental reservation in this case did not remove any ambiguity in the original words. Pure mental reservation had arrived.

The doctrine was countenanced by a number of casuists in the early sixteenth century, though the principles underlying it were rarely subjected to thorough scrutiny. In 1556 Dominico Soto displayed his familiarity with such ideas (which he rejected) in his *De Justitia et Jure*.[25] During the next fifty years pure mental reservation grew in popularity. Indeed, for a few decades on either side of 1600 it

---

[23] Angelus de Clavasio (*c*. 1411–95; Italian Franciscan), *Summa Angelica de casibus conscientiae* (Strasburg, 1515), f. 139a. Laymann, *Theologia Moralis*, ii.165. Azorius, *Institutionum Moralium ... Tomus Primus*, cols. 1334–5. There are intimations of mental reservation as early as St Raymund of Pennafort: see J. Brodie Brosnan, 'Mental restriction and equivocation', in *Irish Ecclesiastical Record*, 16 (1920), 461–9, at p. 461.

[24] Sylvester, *Summa summarum*, f. 276b: 'subaudiendo in animo suo, si debuero'.

[25] Soto, *De Iustitia et Iure*, pp. 457–9. Cf. the notes of Cajetan (Tommaso de Vio Gaetani, Cardinal Cajetan, 1469–1534; Italian Dominican) to Aquinas, *Summa Theologiae*, 2a2ae, q. 89, art. 7, in *Secunda Secundae Partis Summae* (Antwerp, 1567), p. 332.

was the dominant theory amongst Catholic casuists. The first full-scale defence of the doctrine was mounted by Martin de Azpilcueta in about 1575. He introduced into the discussion the notion of mixed propositions, derived from Aristotle. Statements could be expressed by means other than speech. Writing and signs were examples. So too, argued Azpilcueta, was thought. Moreover, statements could be expressed in a mixture of two or more of these manners. For instance, a man on his death-bed could say 'I give and bequeath unto Thomas Morton', then find that his voice had failed and write 'a thousand', then discover that his hand was shaking too much to write and point at a gold coin. His action could readily be understood as expressing a single sentence, though he had adopted a variety of means to do so. The truth of a mixed proposition did not depend upon the truth of any particular simple proposition that it contained. The parts might be true and the whole false, or, conversely, the whole might be true and the parts false. Azpilcueta claimed that there were innumerable instances in both sacred and profane writings of statements which were true only by virtue of some reserved clause. The first psalm, for example, stated that the wicked will not rise again on the day of judgment. Yet the Athanasian Creed affirmed that everyone will be resurrected on that day. What the psalm meant, said Azpilcueta, was that the wicked will not rise to eternal glory. The reserved clause made the statement true. A mixed proposition could contain reserved clauses, expressed only in the mind.[26]

Azpilcueta introduced into the discussion many elements which soon became standard. He told the story of St Francis who, when asked whether a certain fugitive had passed that way, put his hands in the sleeves of his cloak and replied that he had not passed that way – meaning through the sleeves. Christ himself, said Azpilcueta, had employed mental reservation. For instance, he had denied that he knew when the day of judgment would take place. Of course, being omniscient, he did know. He could not have lied, since that would have been evil. So he must have used mental reservation. Azpilcueta illustrated his arguments with the stock examples of the traveller coming from the plague-infected town, and the adulteress questioned by her husband on whether she has committed adultery. In the latter example, derived from Angelus de Clavasio, the wife will be killed by her irate husband if she either remains silent or admits adultery. Since her husband questions her unjustly, she can reply using mental

---

[26] Azpilcueta, *Commentaria*, i. f. 219a. The relevant passage from the first psalm is 'Non resurgent impii in iudicio.' Parsons, *Treatise tending to Mitigation*, pp. 326–7.

reservation. Azpilcueta, and other casuists, had no wish to encourage adultery, though their critics claimed that this was the effect of the principle.[27]

Amongst later authors who followed Azpilcueta were Suarez, Toletus, Lessius, Filiarchi, Salon, Valentia, and Sanchez.[28] Like Azpilcueta, these men singled out Soto as the opponent most worthy of serious consideration. Soto had argued that meaning is defined by public conventions. What I say is truthful if I believe what I think it means. Language, in short, is an instrument of communication, not a series of arbitrary noises signifying whatever the speaker fancies. His opponents agreed that it was a means of communication, instituted to further social intercourse. Their point was that language had not been set up to encourage the performance of unjust actions such as murder. If a murderer asks me whether I am giving refuge to his intended victim I have no duty to tell him the truth. Indeed, I have no duty to tell him anything at all. If I have no duty to answer him, then I have no duty to answer him in his language. If I choose, I may make noises which he takes to be English words but to which I attach an altogether different significance.

According to Lessius, for example, an unjustly questioned man has no duty to answer: 'He is not bound to lay open his mind on that matter about which he is questioned. So he is not bound to express all the words by which his mind would be laid open. He may, therefore, utter some of those words, and add the remainder silently.' In such circumstances 'he is no more bound externally to declare his thoughts to his interrogator than if he were on his own and speaking to himself'. But if he were speaking to himself he could truthfully retain part of his statement in his mind. So he might, without lying, deceive his interrogator by using mental reservation. Valentia argued similarly. A man who is speaking to himself, he claimed, may speak truthfully though he chooses to understand his words to mean something quite different from that which they usually signify. Provided that he believes that they are true in the sense in which he understands them, he speaks truthfully. Like Lessius, Valentia assimilated the case of a man who is unjustly

---

[27] Azpilcueta, *Commentaria*, i. f. 221b, 219b, 220a. Angelus de Clavasio, *Summa Angelica*, f. 139a. Abbot, *Antilogia*, f. 18b.

[28] More extensive lists are in Laymann, *Theologia Moralis*, ii.165–6, and Thomas Sanchez (1550–1610; Spanish Jesuit), *Opus morale in praecepta decalogi* (Antwerp, 1631), iii.350–9. It was one of Sanchez's propositions which Innocent XI condemned in 1679: D. Hughes, 'Mental reservation', in *New Catholic Encyclopedia*, vol. 9 (New York, 1967), p. 662. If we include pamphleteers, the number of authors who supported pure mental reservation is legion.

questioned to that of a man who is on his own. Someone who is unjustly questioned, he concluded, may use words to signify whatever he pleases.[29]

Though these casuists were interested primarily in cases where mental reservation was justified, their theory left open the possibility that people would use the device unjustifiably. According to the theory, truthful mental reservation was not lying, though it could in certain circumstances be unjustified. The casuists had, therefore, to invent a hitherto unknown sin, that of unjustifiable mental reservation. The old ban on lying had served the useful social function of promoting communication. The new device of mental reservation threatened to undermine the reliance on the words of others which binds society together. Valentia claimed that this threat was illusory: 'for although it is not, strictly speaking, lying to use words in your own sense in common conversation, since it does not infringe the negative precept that you ought not to lie, it is nevertheless a sin of omission against the positive precept of the virtue truthfulness'.[30] In other words, people were ordinarily bound to tell the truth. This was a positive precept, and not just a corollary of the ban on lying. Where the precept did not apply, you could use mental reservation. The rigid prohibition of lying was formally retained, but for all practical purposes it was replaced by two new precepts: a general precept obliging men to tell the truth, combined with a precept which in certain circumstances permitted or even obliged men to say what they believed to be deceptive falsehoods. The effect was to transform the traditional moral system, and to allow principles of human interest and utility – the principles according to which mental reservation was considered justifiable – to triumph.

[29] Lessius, *De Iustitia et Iure*, pp. 621–2: 'in his et similibus eventis non tenetur homo totam mentem suam circa rem de qua interrogatur aperire: ergo non tenetur omnia verba exprimere, quibus ea aperiatur. Poterit igitur partem exprimere, et partem tacitus addere. Confirmatur, Quia non magis tenetur totam mentem suam exterius declarare coram isto, quam dum solus agit et secum loquitur.' Gregorius de Valentia (c. 1549–1603; Spanish Jesuit), *Commentariorum Theologicorum Tomus Tertius* (Venice, 1598), col. 1041: if a man is alone, 'potest quod vult intelligere per quaecunque verba sine mendacio. Ergo etiam in casu quo inique interrogatur.'
[30] Ibid., cols. 1041–2: 'Nam quamvis verba usurpare ad aliquem sensum alienum significandum in conversatione communi, non esset mendacium proprie contra negativum praeceptum: esset tamen peccatum omissionis contra praeceptum affirmativum illius virtutis, Veritas.' Cf. Parsons, *Treatise tending to Mitigation*, pp. 424–5: unjustified equivocation, 'though it should not be properly the sin of lying . . . nor against the negative precept of truth; yet should it be an other sin against the public good of civil society, and consequently against the affirmative precept of truth'. The same argument is employed with regard to unjustifiable use of ambiguity by Laymann, *Theologia Moralis*, ii.171.

Mental reservation undermined traditional ideas not only on intentionally deceptive statements, but also on promises and oaths. By including a mental reservation in a promise, a man could evade the obligation to perform that which in spoken words he undertook to perform. As we saw, this was the position of Sylvester. Of course, if we follow Valentia in holding that there is a positive precept of truthfulness, we will regard a man who unjustifiably uses mental reservation in a promise as guilty of infringing the precept. But it looks as though such a man would still evade the obligation to perform what in spoken words he said he would perform. Suppose that I borrow £1,000 from a friend, promising to repay it on the first day of next month. There is no legal contract between me and my friend, so any obligation that I may have to obey the law is irrelevant. In making my promise I mentally reserve some such clause as 'provided that I choose to repay the money'. I ought not to make this reservation, but having done so I am under no obligation to return the money unless I choose to. Even if there is a legal contract, I may have no obligation to abide by it or to obey the law at all. If we regard political obligation as based on contract then, with suitable mental reservations, the contractors may evade this obligation too.

In order to avoid these consequences, the casuists argued that a man who unjustifiably employed mental reservation in a promise or promissory oath is nevertheless obliged to carry out what he undertook to do in his spoken words. Lessius, for example, acknowledged that 'by its own force' an oath or promise obliges the promiser to do only that which he promised to do – and this was defined by his mental reservations as well as by his spoken words. But if his spoken words intentionally created a legitimate expectation in the promisee, failure to carry out what he undertook in those words would harm the promisee and bring scandal upon the promiser. Since it was wrong to cause harm or bring oneself into disrepute the promiser was obliged to perform what he had promised in speech.[31]

The theory of mental reservation was concocted in order to reconcile the ban on lying with such duties as saving lives and preserving secrets. The casuists did indeed refer to the opinions of

[31] Lessius, *De Iustitia et Iure*, p. 621: 'vi sua'. Lessius says that the obligation arises 'ratione damni, vel scandali secuturi'. The point about promises was well made by Henry Mason, *The New Art of Lying, covered by the Iesuites under the Vaile of Equivocation* (London, 1624), pp. 105–6: 'And if he promises to pay me a sum of money, how can I tell that he keepeth not a reservation behind, that may disanull his promise aforehand; as that he will pay it, if himself shall think it necessary, or if he shall have so much to spare, or if he have nothing else to do with his money?'

earlier authors, but they did not blindly follow authority. Their disagreements with each other, and the fact that their doctrines changed over the centuries, bear witness to this. Moreover, they supported their decisions with reasons, even if the reasoning was sometimes sophistical. Again, the charge of laxity is difficult to sustain, at least in the case of their ideas on mental reservation. Their objective was not to pander to the worldly weaknesses of ordinary men and women, but to create a coherent moral theory which produced intuitively acceptable conclusions.

There may have been a more pressing practical reason for the popularity of the doctrine in the years around 1600. At that time, persecution of Catholics in Protestant countries was at its height. Catholic priests questioned by their religious opponents certainly found the doctrine convenient; but it was not for their benefit that it had been invented. The history of the doctrine proves this, and even in the post-Reformation period, the theory was usually discussed in contexts which had nothing to do with persecuted priests.

Yet it was the activities of equivocating priests which first brought the theory to public attention. In England the doctrine received widespread exposure in the wake of the trials for treason of two Jesuits, Robert Southwell (1595) and Henry Garnet (1606).[32] Hitherto most laymen, Catholic as well as Protestant, had been ignorant of mental reservation. Now they reacted to it with horror. Catholic vernacular writings, aimed at a lay audience, had inculcated the virtues of honesty and truthfulness, claiming that it was heretics who lied. To unsophisticated laymen, however, mental reservation itself seemed no more that downright lying or, worse still, lying of a new and devious variety. Ideas which were intended to solve knotty theoretical problems, and which had been buried in indigestible Latin tomes, were now laid open to the gaze of the unlearned. Theorists were soon made aware that the doctrine brought obloquy upon Catholicism, whatever its abstract merits.

As early as the 1590s, a manual of casuistry written for the use of Catholic priests on the mission to Protestant England warned that

---

[32] Southwell's case is discussed in Christopher Devlin, *The Life of R. Southwell* (London, 1956), pp. 311–14. The Protestant George Abbot exposed Southwell's equivocation in 1597: *Quaestiones sex totidem praelectionibus discussae* (Oxford, 1598), pp. 50–3. Mason, *New Art of Lying*, dedication, sig. (a)3a, calls Abbot 'the first writer that published those tricks in print to the world'. Garnet's alleged use of equivocation is recorded in *A True and Perfect Relation of the Whole Proceedings against the late most barbarous Traitors, Garnet a Iesuite, and his Confederats* (London, 1606), sig. Y3b. Shakespeare refers to the episode in *Macbeth*, act 2 scene 3 (*The Riverside Shakespeare*) (Boston, 1974), p. 1320; cf. Camille Wells Slights, *The Casuistical Tradition in Shakespeare, Donne, Herbert, and Milton* (Princeton, 1981), pp. 107–9.

deceptive statements should not be made to Protestant interrogators
in the presence of 'rude and simple' Catholic laymen, who 'being
ignorant of the difference between pretence and lying ... will
immediately think that the priest is denying the faith if he uses
pretence and ... will be confused and inwardly despair if they see a
priest do such a thing'.[33] Mental reservation might be justifiable, but
it should not be used if it led to bad publicity for the church and its
priests. When priests responded to Protestant criticisms of the
doctrine, their posture was defensive. After the trial of Southwell,
Garnet composed a treatise in English, justifying mental reservation
but admitting that 'this kind of doctrine seemeth strange both to
heretics and also to divers Catholics'. He insisted that the device
could be employed only in extreme circumstances and was at pains
to point out that Catholics detested lying.[34] The Jesuit Parsons went
still further, claiming that Catholic thinkers *permitted* but did not
*recommend* the use of mental reservation: they 'do allow and like far
better of simple, plain and resolute speech in all Catholics', but
tolerated mental reservation in a few cases since 'perfection is one
thing, and obligation is another'.[35] The doctrine had become an
embarrassment to Catholic publicists. It fell under heavy attack
from within as well as outside the church. Responding to this
pressure, Pope Innocent XI condemned it in 1679.[36]

During the seventeenth century, their enemies branded the
Jesuits as equivocators. Mental reservation was held to be a
peculiarly Jesuitical practice – a prime example of the Society's
immorality. The charge was unfair. Though some Jesuits wrote in
favour of the theory, others, including Azorius and Laymann,
shunned it. The Society's enemies found it handy to accuse the
Jesuits of all kinds of vice, but accusations of mental reservation
were particularly useful, since they undermined the credibility of
everything that Jesuits said. A Jesuit might swear that he was a loyal
and law-abiding citizen. His oaths, however, were unreliable, since it
was always possible that they included reservations.[37] In fact, there
was no distinctively Jesuitical moral code. The doctrine of mental

[33] P. J. Holmes, ed., *Elizabethan Casuistry* (n.p., Catholic Record Society, Record
Series 67, 1981), p. 64. On English Catholic attitudes to the subject see Rose, *Cases
of Conscience*, pp. 89–91, and especially Peter Holmes, *Resistance and Compromise: the
Political Thought of the Elizabethan Catholics* (Cambridge, 1982), pp. 121–4.
[34] Garnet, *Treatise of Equivocation*, pp. 4, 58.
[35] Parsons, *Treatise tending to Mitigation*, p. 274.
[36] H. Denzinger and C. Bannwart, eds., *Enchiridion Symbolorum, Definitionum et
Declarationum* (Freiburg-im-Breisgau, 1922), nos. 1176–8, p. 352.
[37] This point is made in the anonymous French pamphlet translated as *Anti-Coton, or a
refutation of Cottons Letter Declaratorie* (London, 1611), p. 21.

reservation was not grounded in any tenet peculiar to Jesuits. Indeed, divisions on equivocation bore little relationship to differences of opinion on other philosophical or theological questions.

The polemical assault on mental reservation cut across confessional boundaries. Such orthodox English Protestants as Thomas Morton or Henry Mason held religious views which were profoundly different from those of John Barnes, a Benedictine monk exiled in France. Yet all three adopted broadly the same position on equivocation. In essence, their case consisted of two propositions. Firstly, mental reservation was lying, and lying was wrong. Secondly, it was a devious, hypocritical, and Machiavellian doctrine.

Writing in 1606, Morton condemned mental reservation as 'this new-bred Hydra, and uglie Monster, which lurked a while in the invisible practice of the Equivocating sect', but had now thankfully been exposed. In his opinion, this kind of equivocation was merely lying. He admitted that it was sometimes legitimate to employ verbal ambiguity: 'we deny not but ambiguous words may sometime be used in common speech'. Yet even verbal equivocation was unlawful on oath or if there was no just cause. Mental reservation was always wrong, for it was lying. Those who distinguished between the two activities conjured up the absurd spectre of a society in which lying was impossible: 'if mental equivocation were lawful, and did qualify a false speech to free it from a lie, no man instructed in that Art would or could lie; and so we should seem to live in an Utopia, where men shall be convicted of the most manifest equivocating falsehood; only he shall be the liar, that giveth the convicted the lie'.[38]

Like Morton, Henry Mason drew a rigid distinction between verbal equivocation ('Logical Equivocation') and mental reservation ('Jesuitical Equivocation'). He had little quarrel with the former, 'which hitherto hath been received of all men, and now (for aught I know) is not rejected of any'. Jesuitical equivocation, by contrast, was 'an Art of falsehood and deceit, and such as the Scriptures do condemn under the name of lying'. The Jesuits styled the practice 'equivocation' only because 'they are ashamed to call it by its right name, which is, a lie'. Toletus defined a lie as a false speech intended to deceive; this definition obviously covered mental reservation.

[38] Thomas Morton, *A Full Satisfaction concerning a double romish Iniquitie; hainous Rebellion, and more then heathenish Aequivocation* (London, 1606), part 3, 47, 85, 64. Though most Protestants admitted that verbal ambiguity could sometimes lawfully be employed, William Ames rejected it as lying: *Conscience with the Power and Cases Thereof* (n.p., 1639), p. 271.

The notion that lies are distinct from mental reservations was absurd, since 'it impeacheth God of folly in making his laws against lying' and 'because it freeth the Devil from all just imputation of being a liar'. If the Jesuitical doctrine were true, 'no man can be convicted of the least lie unless himself will confess it'. Jesuits stressed the utility of mental reservation in affairs of state, but they did so only to conceal their own 'projects and plots'. Jesuitical equivocation – the 'new art of lying' – was essentially the same as the old art. Hypocrisy and deviousness were the only added elements.[39]

Mason's book was published in 1624. In the same year Barnes completed his *Dissertatio contra Aequivocationes*. He held that the Devil was the author of mental reservation, and asserted that all the arguments which had been cited in support of the practice worked equally well in favour of lying; indeed, lying was preferable, for it had ancient precedent and was an activity recognized by the Canon Law. Barnes had little time for liars. 'You should not lie', he said, 'even to save your life.' Direct divine commission provided the sole possible exception to this rule. Biblical liars had either acted wrongly, or had responded to God's immediate command, which alone could set in abeyance the general prohibition of lying. Barnes claimed that the Jesuitical doctrine was Machiavellian. Like the Florentine, proponents of mental reservation allowed evil to be done in order that good might result.[40]

---

[39] Mason, *New Art of Lying*, pp. 4, 88, 2, 12, 93, 100, 55.

[40] John Barnes, *Dissertatio contra Aequivocationes* (Paris, 1625), pp. 52, 218, 225, 243 ('non mentiendum ad salvandum vitam'), pp. 223–4, 106, 141, 504. A very different interpretation of the thought of Mason and Barnes is put forward in Mosse, *Holy Pretence*, pp. 45–7. Mosse argues that these authors permitted lying in a just and religious cause: 'The Jesuits are not attacked because they used equivocation, but because, not having true religion they used it solely for a secular end. As far as the Anglican parson was concerned, the Jesuits could not possibly have a "just cause" hallowed by God.' Where such a cause existed, Mosse argues, equivocation and even lying were regarded as permissible. Righteous intentions justified actions which were otherwise unlawful. He concludes that the moral theory of these writers was not far removed from that of the Jesuits, and uses this to illustrate his contention that both Protestant and Catholic thinkers accommodated traditional morality to Machiavellian 'policy'. Mosse's claims rest upon two mistaken assumptions: (1) that Mason's 'Logical Equivocation' was equivalent to equivocation in a just cause, while 'Jesuitical Equivocation' lacks such a cause; (2) that biblical examples of direct divine intervention setting aside the prohibition of lying on particular occasions are equivalent to a general dispensation in favour of those who have good intentions. In fact, Mason's 'Jesuitical Equivocation' was mental reservation (*New Art of Lying*, p. 4), while 'Logical Equivocation' was verbal ambiguity (ibid., pp. 4–6). He permitted the latter provided that it 'be not extended too far, or mis-applied to a wrong cause' (ibid., p. 7), but condemned the former absolutely, however good the cause might be (ibid., pp. 2, 12). Secondly, the fact that God had sometimes empowered biblical figures to depart from general rules did not show that mere good intentions (as distinct from direct divine

Were Jesuits in fact influenced by Machiavelli? Certainly they denied the charge. Protestants were the Florentine's true followers, said Eudaemon-Joannes, and he claimed that Queen Elizabeth had sent to Italy to seek out and reward Machiavelli's descendants. Nevertheless, Machiavellism was one of the commonest accusations levelled against the Society. Etienne Pasquier accused Loyola of using 'Machiavelisms ... to set his sect afloat'. John Donne portrayed Machiavelli as the Jesuits' schoolmaster, though the pupils had soon outstripped their teacher in all kinds of evil, and not least in their 'new art of equivocation', which 'raised to life again the language of the Tower of Babel, so long concealed, and brought us again from understanding one another'. According to the English Catholic Thomas Bluet, the Jesuits followed 'Machiavellian Rules'.

Such claims were often no more than routine jibes. Yet a serious point underlay them. True, Machiavelli permitted and indeed encouraged lying in the public interest, while the casuists pronounced all lying wrong. They did, nevertheless, allow deviations from veracity – in the shape of mental reservation – for the sake of promoting private interests and, overridingly, the public good. Barnes pounced on this point, convicting them of Machiavellism; and there was substance in his charge. Catholic casuists abhorred Machiavelli, the atheist politician; but working within a tradition quite separate from Renaissance 'reason of state', they reached conclusions not that far from the Florentine's.[41]

Barnes's book was approved by the Sorbonne. In France, popular misgivings about mental reservation were ruthlessly exploited by Gallican opponents of the Jesuits. Pascal's *Provincial Letters* of 1656–7 appealed to a venerable French tradition of anti-Jesuit polemic in the hope of eliciting sympathy for the Society's arch-enemies, the Jansenists. In England, the doctrine provided Protestants with a potent weapon in their campaign against popery. As late as 1864, J. H. Newman claimed that 'if there is one thing more than another which prejudices Englishmen against the Catholic Church, it is the doctrine of great authorities on the subject of equivocation'.

commission) justified the breach of divine or human law. To argue otherwise was to open the door to antinomianism – a position firmly rejected by virtually every moral theorist.
[41] Eudaemon-Joannes, *Apologia*, p. 225. Etienne Pasquier, *The Iesuites Catechisme* (n.p., 1602), f. 63b. John Donne, *Ignatius his Conclave*, in *Complete Poetry and Selected Prose*, ed. John Hayward (London, 1929), p. 370. William Watson (really Thomas Bluet), *Important Considerations* (1601), ed. Joseph Mendham (London, 1831), p. 37. Machiavelli, *The Prince*, tr. George Bull (Harmondsworth, Middlesex, 1961), pp. 99–101. A stimulating essay on the connections between casuistry and reason of state is Mosse's *Holy Pretence*.

Newman himself made clear his detestation not only of mental reservation but also of the use of ambiguity to deceive even an unjust questioner.[42] By then, mental reservation had long been condemned, and Catholic casuists were left with no alternative to silence or the truth except verbal equivocation – which sometimes took exotic forms.[43] The papal condemnation did something to save the church from bad publicity. It did less to solve the underlying problem which the doctrine had been designed to meet: what was to be done if silence or the truth led to disaster?

Protestants also confronted this dilemma. In its inception, Protestantism represented a break with the Roman Church on certain theological doctrines and on the question of papal authority. The status of other traditional Catholic teachings was left unclear, though it seemed conceivable that they too were erroneous. Augustine's doctrine on lying remained influential, but lost its old monopoly. We have seen that Protestants regarded mental reservation as lying. However, some of them came to argue that lying – and hence mental reservation, too – could be justified.

In England, the mid-sixteenth-century Reformer Roger Hutchinson argued that 'all lying is forbidden', and many agreed with him. His contemporary, Hugh Latimer, believed that lying was always wrong, even to promote God's cause. Both jesting and earnest lies, he thought, should studiously be avoided, for 'God is truth', and 'when we forsake the truth, we forsake God'. Latimer recommended that parents use coercive means to teach their offspring the wickedness of lies. 'When you hear one of your children to make a lie, take him up, and give him three or four good stripes, and tell him that it is naught: and when he maketh another lie, give him six or eight stripes; and I am sure when you serve him so, he will leave it.' Divine providence would, of course, reinforce the lesson of such social discipline by striking down liars. But Latimer felt it necessary to admit that this did not always occur as rapidly as the biblical story of Ananias and Sapphira might lead one to expect. The reason, he

---

[42] Pascal, *Provincial Letters of Pascal*, pp. 207–8. J. H. Newman, *Apologia pro vita sua*, in Wilfrid Ward, ed., *Newman's Apologia pro vita sua: the two versions of 1864 & 1865 Preceded by Newman's and Kingsley's pamphlets* (Oxford, 1913), p. 452. Newman's views are discussed in Josef L. Altholz, 'Truth and equivocation: Liguori's moral theology and Newman's *Apologia*', in *Church History*, 44 (1975), 73–84.

[43] There are a few exceptions to this rule, for some Catholic casuists came to allow that lying could be justified: see Newman, *Apologia pro vita sua*, pp. 456–7. A famous example of the verbal equivocations permitted by the eighteenth-century casuist St Alfonso de Liguori is 'I say, no' in reply to a question to which you believe the correct answer is 'yes'. 'I say, no' is truthful, since the speaker does in fact say 'no': cf. Altholz, 'Truth and equivocation', 74–7.

claimed, was that God 'would have us to repent', but 'if we will not repent, then he will come one day and make an end with us'. His words suggest an awareness that providence did not work in the simple rule-governed way assumed by tradition. Yet many Protestant theorists continued to abide by Augustine's line on lying. The Elizabethan casuist William Perkins held that the eighth commandment forbade all lies – every 'falsehood with purpose to deceive', 'be it for never so great a good to our neighbour'. As late as 1673 Richard Baxter declared that lying was 'absolutely forbidden of God'.[44]

Amongst some Protestant groups, however, different attitudes developed at an early date. The Swiss Reformer Henry Bullinger observed that 'very notable men have thought that Augustine was somewhat too stubbornly set against lying', though he did not commit himself on the subject. Calvin was equally cautious, condemning harmful lies, but maintaining silence on other varieties. Some Lutherans were more outspoken. William Tyndale, for example, bluntly declared that 'to lie also, and to dissemble, is not always sin'. It was 'the duty of charity, and no sin', he said, to 'tell a sick man . . . that wholesome bitter medicine is sweet', or to put a criminal off his victim's track by lying – and even by confirming the lie with an oath. Frederick Baldwin, Professor at Wittenberg in the early seventeenth century, and greatest of the Lutheran casuists, redefined lies to exclude those which were harmless. No one should lie, he asserted, but added that deceptions were not lies unless they were intended to harm our neighbour.[45]

Two major moral theorists of the seventeenth century, Hugo Grotius and Jeremy Taylor, adopted a similar line. Both were steeped in the learning of Catholic as well as Protestant casuists. Both exercised a great influence upon later moral thinking. Grotius argued that a man could not strictly be said to lie unless he infringed his interlocutor's rights, usually the right to be told the truth. This

---

[44] Roger Hutchinson, *The Works of Roger Hutchinson*, ed. John Bruce (Cambridge, 1842), p. 51. Latimer, *Sermons*, pp. 501–3. William Perkins, *Workes* (London, 1626), i.66–7. Baxter, *Christian Directory*, p. 424.

[45] Henry Bullinger, *The Decades of Henry Bullinger . . . the third decade*, ed. Thomas Harding (Cambridge, 1850), p. 116. John Calvin, *Institutio Religionis Christianae*, II, pp. 8, 47, in *Opera Omnia*, ed. G. Baum, E. Cunitz and E. Reuss, vol. 2 (Brunswick, 1864), p. 300; *Le Catéchisme de l'Eglise de Gèneve*, in ibid., vol. 6 (Brunswick, 1867), p. 73; cf. H. Zanchius, *Compendium praecipuorum capitum doctrinae Christianae* (Neustadt, 1598), p. 233 for a similar approach. William Tyndale, *Expositions and Notes on sundry portions of the Holy Scriptures*, ed. Henry Walter (Cambridge, 1849), pp. 57–8. Frederick Baldwin (Fridericus Balduinus), *Tractatus luculentus, posthumus, toti Reipublicae Christianae utilissimus, de materia rarissime antehac enucleata, Casibus nimirum Conscientiae* (Wittenberg, 1628), p. 1280. Luther himself held that lying could be justified: see Bok, *Lying*, p. 47.

right could be cancelled 'by the opposition of another right which, in the common judgement of all men, is much more cogent'. Taylor likewise employed the language of rights, while Catholic casuists spoke in terms of duties. The substantive difference is slight, since Grotius and Taylor held that the rights in question entail correlative duties. It does not much matter whether we talk of my having a duty to tell you the truth, or of you having a right to be told the truth by me. In essence, their notion of what justified lying, and the Catholic notion of what justified mental reservation, were identical.[46]

May we say that the two theories – justified lying and justified reservation – were themselves identical, and that the ideas of the Catholic casuists lived on in Protestant tradition? Perhaps so, if Taylor was right to claim that mental reservation is lying. He himself admitted that 'in the same cases in which it is lawful to tell a lie, in the same cases it is lawful to use a mental reservation'.[47] But perhaps mental reservation is not in fact lying. Certainly its opponents asserted rather than proved that it was. In this case it might be more fitting to follow the Catholic casuists, and retain, in name at least, a quaint old dogma – Augustine's rigid ban on lying.

---

[46] Hugo Grotius, *De Jure Belli ac Pacis*, 3.i.x–xv (Paris, 1625), pp. 564–9. Extracts are printed in Bok, *Lying*, pp. 263–7. Jeremy Taylor, *Ductor Dubitantium*, III.2.V, question 1, in *The Whole Works of Jeremy Taylor* (15 vols. London, 1839), xiii.351–74.

[47] Taylor, *Ductor*, III.2.V, question 2, in *Whole Works*, xiii.374.

# 6

◁ ═══════════════════════════════ ▷

## Kant and casuistry

### H.-D. KITTSTEINER

### GONE OUT OF FASHION

Towards the end of the eighteenth century, casuistry, which is so inseparably connected with the history of the Jesuit Order in Protestant and Enlightenment polemics, appears to have gone out of fashion completely. As early as 1733, Zedler's *Universal-Lexikon* contained only a short entry on casuists: 'Casuists are a kind of learned persons who investigate confused cases and scruples of conscience and present explications of the same in their writings.'[1] In the article on probabilists (1741) in the same lexicon we read: 'This is the name given to those Roman casuists who say that in deciding a question of conscience one can follow an opinion that is not probable and not certain.'[2] This is then relativized by the additional remark that even among the Jesuits the view was held that one ought 'always to follow the most probable and most certain opinion'; moreover, Pope Innocent XI had expressly condemned genuine probabilism in 1679.[3] A new German translation of Blaise Pascal's *Provincial Letters* published in 1773 justified itself by extending the concept 'Jesuit' in enlightened polemic: although the curtain is coming down on the Society of Jesus, which has played out its part in the world, nonetheless 'there are still too many Jesuits in the world for one to consider this Order to be exterminated – even if some are Protestant Jesuits'.[4] Those who rely on casuistry and probabilism are thus simply following an antiquated model of conduct.

---

[1] Johann Heinrich Zedler, *Großes vollständiges Universal-Lexikon* (Halle and Leipzig, 1732ff.) (Reprint Akademische Druck- u. Verlagsanstalt Graz-Austria, 1961) vol. 5, p. 1391.  [2] Ibid., vol. 29 (1741), pp. 618f.
[3] On the condemnation of lax moral principles by Alexander VII and Innocent XI, see Johann Joseph Ignaz von Döllinger and Franz Heinrich Reusch, *Geschichte der Moralstreitigkeiten in der römisch-katholischen Kirche seit dem 16. Jahrhundert* (2 vols., Nördlingen, 1889; Neudruck Scientia Verlag Aalen, 1968), pp. 38f.
[4] Blasius Paskal, *Provinzialbriefe über die Sittenlehre und Politik der Jesuiten*, tr. Friedrich Ludolf Lachmann (Legmo, 1773), introduction to part 2.

One can still feel reverberations of the consciousness of the surmounted danger for theology and moral philosophy in the presentation broadly laid out in Stäudlin's *History of Christian Morals since the Revival of the Sciences* (1808). Despite the forerunners of casuistry in antiquity and in early Christianity and in spite of the handbooks and confession-manuals of the thirteenth century introduced following the decrees of the Fourth Lateran Council (1215), which prescribed that all the faithful should confess their sins to a priest at least once a year,[5] the really pronounced form of casuistry is considered to be the 'probabilist' morals in the great post-Tridentine *casus conscientiae*.[6] As Stäudlin points out, one may not assume that the Jesuits had deliberately planned on corrupting all morals,[7] but their splitting and distorting of words, coupled with their Counter-Reformational thirst for power, drove them to nullify all basic moral principles.[8] The hero is Pascal, who delivered to casuistry in his *Provincial Letters* (1656–7) a hard blow from which it never recovered.[9]

With a shudder, Stäudlin quotes a casuistic apology from the time of the disputes between the Jesuits and the Jansenists: a monk who lays aside his monastic garb for a short time in order to indulge in debauchery should not be excommunicated; the Holy Bible, which one should certainly take as the guide for one's actions, is full of passages 'in which injury, even death, is wished on one's fellowman and implored from God'; young women had after all the right 'to dispose of their virginity against their parents' will, and those who misuse them are not sinning against justice if the girls have given their consent'.[10] But all of these moral–philosophical abominations are just historical reminiscences now – although even the Protestant moral theologian cannot help doing justice to casuistry and probabilism in a peculiar manner:

[5] Carl Friedrich Stäudlin, *Geschichte der christlichen Moral seit dem Wiederaufleben der Wissenschaften* (Göttingen, 1808), pp. 82ff.; Döllinger and Reusch, pp. 9ff.; Karl Bihlmeyer and Hermann Tüchle, *Kirchengeschichte*, 18th edition (Paderborn, 1982), vol. II, pp. 246ff.
[6] Döllinger and Reusch, pp. 19ff. On the concepts *Tutiorismus, Probabiliorismus, Aequiprobabilismus*, and *Probabilismus* see Döllinger and Reusch, pp. 4f. On the discussion of probabilism within the framework of modern philosophy of science see Benjamin Nelson, 'Probabilists, anti-probabilists, the quest for certitude in the 16th and 17th centuries' in *Actes du Xe Congrès international d'histoire des sciences* (Paris, Hermann, 1964).
[7] Stäudlin, *Geschichte der christlichen Moral*, p. 448.
[8] C. F. Stäudlin, *Geschichte der Lehre vom Gewissen* (Halle, 1824), p. 122.
[9] Stäudlin, *Geschichte der christlichen Moral*, pp. 542ff.; Pascal, *Lettres Provinciales*, ed. Louis Cognet (Paris, 1965); A. W. S. Baird, *Studies in Pascal's Ethics* (The Hague, 1975), pp. 26ff.  [10] Stäudlin, *Geschichte der christlichen Moral*, pp. 524f.

He who knows the world and has had much experience with people can easily have noticed that the same kind of moral judgments and opinions as the ones which the Jesuits propounded in their writings are often so ambiguously and sophistically spoken about, and immoral deeds so excused and justified by the circumstances, that an uncountable number of people lack solid moral principles . . . The real Jesuits brought this morality of everyday life into the books, and they dogmatized immorality.[11]

The bourgeois moral philosophy of the seventeenth and eighteenth centuries answered this 'dogmatizing of immorality' with a dogmatizing of morality. Of course it connects with the stricter tendencies in Catholicism and Protestantism;[12] but the crucial point is that the core of this new morality seems to have changed: the 'conscience' is no longer involved in the structure of casuistry, but asserts itself beyond casuistry as an independent object. When the translator of *Pascal's Letters* (1773), summing up in a note on probabilism, says, 'One can [thus] act against the voice of conscience without sinning',[13] casuistry and probabilism are located on one side and 'conscience' and its inner voice on the other. Casuistry goes out of fashion through a change in conscience itself. We will examine this event by considering three thinkers of the second half of the eighteenth century: Jean-Jacques Rousseau, Adam Smith, and Immanuel Kant.

'Conscience is the best casuist', said Rousseau in the 'Creed of a Savoyard priest' in the fourth book of *Emile*. In the vast labyrinth of human opinions, we have a reliable guide who tells us what is good and what is bad. We are relieved of the obligation to study morals in order to become moral. One doesn't argue with such an infallible conscience, because 'it is only when we haggle with conscience that we have recourse to the subtleties of argument'.[14] Understanding's predominance of control over actions is restricted: the acts of conscience are not logical judgments but rather feelings, or, to use Rousseau's more accurate definition, judgments grounded in

---

[11] Ibid., p. 463; cf. Benjamin Nelson's evaluation: 'The accommodation to the world that is allowed in casuistry becomes a "hedge around the law", making it proof against assault on the charge of being irrelevant to human needs and changing circumstances' (*Encyclopaedia Britannica* (1963), under 'Casuistry', p. 51).

[12] On Jansenism see Jean Delumeau, *Le Catholicisme entre Luther et Voltaire*, 2nd edition (Paris, 1979), pp. 165ff.; on the influence of the Jansenists and the Jesuits on the bourgeoisie, see Bernard Groethuysen, *The Bourgeois: Catholicism vs. Capitalism in Eighteenth-Century France* (New York, 1968), vol. II, chap. 3.

[13] Paskal, *Provinzialbriefe über die Sittenlehre und Politik der Jesuiten*, p. 303.

[14] Jean-Jacques Rousseau, *Emile*, tr. Barbara Foxley, with an introduction by André Boutet de Monvel (London, Dent, 1957), pp. 249, 254.

feelings.[15] As Kant would later say in *Religion within the Limits of Reason Alone*, this new practical conscience needs no other guide; conscience is the self-adjusting, self-arbitrating moral judgment, and for man it is enough to have such a faculty.[16]

At virtually the same time as Rousseau was working on the 'Creed of a Savoyard priest', Adam Smith laconically expressed his opinion on the same topic: 'Books of casuistry, therefore, are generally as useless as they are commonly tiresome.'[17]

This assertion is then explained: the casuists had futilely tried 'to direct by precise rules what it belongs to feeling and sentiment only to judge of'.[18] The casuists' rational apparatus of rules is here also invalidated by an anthropological faculty. If one has a moral feeling at one's disposal, then one no longer needs the advice and instruction of father confessors and scholarly pedants. This is because what they teach – at this point Smith also takes up the motif of 'quibbling' – is not merely useless, but is actually harmful, in particular to society. Many of these books had the effect, that is, 'to teach us to chicane with our own consciences, and by their vain subtilties serve to authorise innumerable evasive refinements with regard to the most essential articles of our duty'.[19] But the most important duty is the observance of justice, because a society cannot subsist 'unless the laws of justice are tolerably observed'.[20] Smith divides the virtues into the stricter, grammatically determinable ones, as it were, and the more elegant forms of behaviour which follow aesthetic rules.[21] The latter, in any case, only apply to the man of standing and culture; the coarse stuff out of which the mass of men are made would never

[15] 'The decrees of conscience are not judgments but feelings' (ibid., p. 253); and 'There is therefore at the bottom of our hearts an innate principle of justice and virtue, by which in spite of our maxims, we judge our own actions or those of others to be good or evil; and it is this principle that I call conscience' (ibid., p. 252). The decisive point in both cases is the opposition to intellectualism in the conception of the conscience and its functioning. Cf. Johannes Stelzenberger, *Syneidesis, conscientia, Gewissen. Studie zum Bedeutungswandel eines moraltheologischen Begriffes* (Paderborn, 1963), p. 109.

[16] 'The question here is not, how conscience ought to be guided (for conscience needs no guide; to have a conscience suffices), but how itself can service as a guide in the most perplexing moral decisions' (Immanuel Kant, *Religion within the Limits of Reason Alone*, translated by Theodore M. Greene and Hoyt H. Hudson (New York and Evanston, Harper and Row, 1960), pp. 173f.

[17] Adam Smith, *The Theory of Moral Sentiments* (ed. D. D. Raphael and A. L. Macfie), The Glasgow Edition of the Works and Correspondence of Adam Smith, second edition, vol. 1 (Oxford: Clarendon Press, 1979), p. 339. As Edmund Leites reports, casuistry in England can be considered overcome as early as the first half of the eighteenth century: Edmund Leites, 'Conscience, casuistry, and moral decision: some historical perspectives', *Journal of Chinese Philosophy,* 2 (1974), 54.

[18] Smith, *The Theory of Moral Sentiments,* p. 339.

[19] Ibid., p. 340.     [20] Ibid., p. 87.     [21] Ibid., p. 175.

allow such perfection. With strict discipline, however, one would be able to bring them at least to a tolerable level of decency, which would also include their showing a pious regard towards the general rules of social life. This, however, is based upon reciprocal justice, and that is why justice numbers among those virtues which must be strictly observed. Accordingly, the best man is the one who doggedly sticks to the general principles. As soon as someone even begins to intellectualize, to reason subtly, to twist and turn a case according to his own propensities, to give his wrongdoings the appearance of legitimacy, he is already on the way to become a scroundrel and a swindler.[22]

Finally, Kant, who read not only Rousseau but also the moral philosophy of Adam Smith,[23] turns against all probabilism in morals with the same resoluteness. The mere opinion that an action might very well be right is not nearly enough to justify it. In this connection, Kant replaces the old relationship between a law and an action which falls under the law with a new one:

Conscience does not pass judgment upon actions as cases which fall under the law; for this is what reason does so far as it is subjectively practical (hence the *casus conscientiae* and casuistry, as a kind of dialectic of conscience). Rather, reason here judges itself, as to whether it has really undertaken that appraisal of action (as to whether they are right or wrong) with all diligence, and it calls the man himself to witness *for* or *against* himself whether this diligent appraisal did or did not take place.[24]

The law as a self-given law has become a part of reason; at the same time, in the moral–practical feeling of 'respect for the moral law' this law is assigned an inner spring which is capable of influencing actions.[25] We cannot go more deeply into Kant's presentation of the doubling of the human ego here.[26] We are only concerned with the question of what Kant meant when he designated casuistry as a kind of dialectic of conscience.

---

[22] 'But it is otherwise with regard to justice: the man who in that refines the least, and adheres with the most obstinate steadfastness to the general rules themselves, is the most commendable, and the most to be depended upon ... A man often becomes a villain the moment he begins, even in his own heart, to chicane in this manner' (ibid., p. 175).

[23] See the letter from Marcus Herz to Kant, 9 July 1771, in *Briefe an Kant*, ed. Jürgen Zehbe (Göttingen, Vandenhoeck, 1971), p. 34.

[24] Kant, *Religion within the Limits of Reason Alone*, p. 174.

[25] Immanuel Kant, *Critique of Practical Reason*, translated with an introduction by Lewis White Beck (Indianapolis and New York, Bobbs-Merrill, 1956), pp. 78ff.

[26] See Rudolf Heinz, *Psychoanalyse und Kantianismus* (Würzburg, Königshausen & Neumann, 1981), pp. 70ff.

The concept of 'dialectic' does not mean here the transcendental dialectic in the sphere of the *Critique of Pure Reason*; nor does it mean 'the world's highest good' as the dialectic of the pure practical reason, which demands 'the absolute totality of conditions for a given conditioned thing'. Here a 'natural dialectic' is at work which rebels in the name of affects and desires against the ethical law and the categorical imperative.

Man feels in himself a powerful counterpoise against all commands of duty which reason presents to him as so deserving of respect; this counterpoise is his needs and inclinations, the complete satisfaction of which he sums up under the name of happiness. Now reason issues inexorable commands without promising anything to the inclinations. It disregards, as it were, and holds in contempt those claims which are so impetuous and yet so plausible, and which will not allow themselves to be abolished by any command. From this a natural dialectic arises, i.e., a propensity to argue against the stern laws of duty and their validity, or at least to place their purity and strictness in doubt and, when possible, to make them more accordant with our wishes and inclinations.[27]

These three statements from Rousseau, Smith, and Kant could be provisionally summarized as follows: casuistry has become obsolete because of the existence of a new connection between reason and moral feeling. Casuistry is now shown all the more clearly for what it is, for what it always was: the art of deliberate wrongdoing, the art of twisting the laws; it proceeds from the apparent justification of human propensities and from the special circumstances of each and every individual case, thereby ruining the general principle of social life. Casuistry is incompatible with the erection of a bourgeois society grounded in justice and morality.

## KANT'S DEPOSIT

Even Kant, however, does not do completely without casuistry – and his readers have partly resented him for this, partly smiled over his examples. His 'doctrine of virtue' in the *Metaphysics of Morals* is full of well-meant examples and odd cases of conscience. Kant questions whether or not the smallpox inoculation should be allowed, since one stakes one's life on something which is still uncertain in trying to meet the duty of preserving one's life.[28] He questions if it is morally

[27] Immanuel Kant, *Foundations of the Metaphysics of Morals*, tr. Lewis White Beck (Indianapolis and New York, Bobbs-Merrill, 1969), p. 25.
[28] Immanuel Kant, *The Metaphysical Principles of Virtue*. Part II of *The Metaphysics of Morals*, tr. James Ellington (Indianapolis and New York, Bobbs-Merrill, 1964), p. 85.

right to make use of woman's sexual characteristics when in so doing the intention of nature, the preservation of the human species, is parried in one way or another.[29] He ruminates whether or not the phrase 'most obedient servant' at the close of a letter can be let through as a mere politeness or if it has to be considered a lie, or if one may openly and directly tell an author that one doesn't like his work: 'An author asks one of his readers, "How do you like my work?" To be sure, the answer might be given in an illusory way inasmuch as one might jest concerning the captiousness of such a question. But who always has his wits about him? The slightest hesitation with the answer is already a mortification for the author. May one flatter him, then?'[30]

That such ethical micrology was seriously discussed is seen in the exasperated reaction of Friedrich Nicolai to this Kantian 'casuistry' – especially since Kant had very sternly expressed himself in an article of 1797, 'Concerning the supposed right to lie out of philanthropy': 'it is a holy, unconditionally governing obligation of reason, which is not to be restricted by any conveniences: to be truthful (honest) in all explanations'.[31] Nicolai tries to nail Kant firmly to the contradiction between the universal validity of the moral claim and the monstrousness of simply taking casuistry into account: 'Illusory answers, especially if they are witty, are allowed by the strict Kantian doctrine of virtue which makes truthfulness towards everyone a formal duty ... Can a virtuous man evade this duty? I would have sooner looked for such confusion of concepts in Escobar's ethics than in Kant's doctrine of virtue.'[32] To be sure, one has to make clear to oneself the status of casuistry within the framework of the Kantian doctrine of virtue. Casuistry does not belong to ethics considered as a science in so far as it is deducible from *a priori* principles of pure practical reason. Rather, it is concerned with the problem of applying those general statements in the throng of everyday moral decisions.[33] Where the question is posed how 'a maxim is to be used in individual cases', Kant distinguishes between the *doctrine of right* and the *doctrine of virtue* – a

[29] Ibid., p. 87.    [30] Ibid., pp. 92f.

[31] Immanuel Kant, 'Über ein vermeintliches Recht aus Menschenliebe zu lügen', in Immanuel Kant, *Gesammelte Schriften* (Königlich Preußische Akademie der Wissenschaften, Berlin, 1902–),vol. VIII, p. 427.

[32] Friedrich Nicolai, *Neun Gespräche zwischen Christian Wolff und einem Kantianer über Kants metaphysische Anfangsgründe der Rechtslehre und der Tugendlehre* (Berlin and Stettin, 1798; impression Anastaltique Culture et Civilisation, Brussels, 1968), p. 24.

[33] Willem Heubült, *Die Gewissenslehre Kants in ihrer Endform von 1797. Eine Anthroponomie* (Bonn, Bouvier Verlag Herbert Grundmann, 1980), p. 180.

distinction not at all dissimilar to the differentiation made by Adam Smith between duties which should be strictly observed and the forms of behaviour which are to be judged on more aesthetic grounds. The distinction is made since the question of casuistry only arises for an ethic that not only deals with duties in the strict sense but also with those that have to be more broadly interpreted. Casuistry is only added to the system, like the scholia. But above all, the doctrine of right knows nothing of casuistry; it does not need it, because it only deals with duties which are by nature strictly determining.[34]

Interestingly enough, Kant also furnished the strict duties of the doctrine of right with casuistic examples, as it were, and one of his most famous and most offensive examples is of this type: the question, namely, whether there are circumstances under which a deposit is allowed to be embezzled. Kant presents the case twice: first in the *Critique of Practical Reason* (1788) and then in the essay concerning the common expression, 'That may be right in theory, but doesn't work in practice' (1793). The inclusion of the individual case in the doctrine of right, in spite of the denial that individual cases are relevant to that doctrine, says considerably more about the fate of casuistry in the eighteenth century than does its continued influence, still bound within the traditional framework, in the spheres of appropriate, i.e. socially acceptable, behaviour in the doctrine of virtue.

Even before Kant formulates the basic law of pure practical reason in his second critique: 'So act that the maxim of your will could always hold at the same time as a principle establishing universal law',[35] he demonstrates its premise, that practical general laws always stipulate the determining basis of the will only formally, not materially. This he does by using the following relationship between a maxim and a law:

What form of a maxim makes it suitable for universal law-giving and what form does not do so can be distinguished without instruction by the most common understanding. I have, for example, made it my maxim to increase my property by every safe means. Now I have in my possession a deposit, the owner of which has died without leaving any record of it. Naturally, this case falls under my maxim. Now I want to know whether this maxim can hold as a universal practical law. I apply it, therefore, to the present case and ask if it could take the form of a law, and consequently whether I could, by the maxim, make the law that every man is allowed to deny that a deposit has

---

[34] Kant, *The Metaphysical Principles of Virtue*, pp. 70f.
[35] Kant, *Critique of Practical Reason*, p. 30.

been made when no one can prove the contrary. I immediately realize that taking such a principle as a law would annihilate itself, because its result would be that no one would make a deposit.[36]

The singular, presumptuous demand of raising my individual intent of action to a general law already betrays that this example does not deal at all with a case for traditional casuistry, in which a universally valid rule can indeed be modified under the aspect of individual conditions. Of course, Kant does not really want to consider whether or not the embezzlement of a deposit might be allowed under special circumstances; it is only supposed to be shown that in no case whatsoever is it permissible to tamper with the general law when coming from an individual maxim which is not identical to the general law. The 'natural dialectic', which rises up against the categorical imperative in the name of happiness, would only cause the form of a false generality to annihilate its own object: namely, bourgeois society itself, represented here in the form of the deposit and finally in the form of property.

'But if there were no deposit at all, what contradiction would lie therein?' Such is the young Hegel's comment on this case. What makes him distrustful is that the demand in which the maxim of a reasonable will must have the form of strict generality amounts to the deduction and legitimation of an empirical object. In the *Wissenschaftlichen Behandlungsarten des Naturrechts*, he endeavours to show that Kant does not posit absolutely the practical legislation of pure reason, but rather 'property'.[37] Karl Rosenkranz reports that Hegel had already critically surveyed Kant's doctrine of right and doctrine of virtue in the summer of 1798.

At that time, he was already striving to unite the legality of positive right and the morality of an inwardness which knows itself to be good or bad, in a higher concept which he often designated in these commentaries simply as 'Leben', later as 'Sittlichkeit'. He protested against the suppression of nature by Kant and against the dimemberment of man in the casuistry which developed through the absolutism of the concept of duty.[38]

It should be remembered that this is not the traditional casuistry which lived on as an appendix to the doctrine of virtue; this is the *negative casuistry* of the categorical imperative, in which all queries

[36] Ibid., pp. 26f.
[37] G. W. F. Hegel, *Über die wissenschaftlichen Behandlungsarten des Naturrechts*, in *Werke*, ed. E. Moldenhauer and K. M. Michel (20 vols., Frankfurt, Suhrkamp, 1969–77), vol. 2, p. 464.
[38] Karl Rosenkranz, *G. W. F. Hegels Leben* (1844; reprinted Darmstadt, Wissenschaftliche Buchgesellschaft, 1972), p. 87.

from the sphere of the special and individual are forever being answered with only the stereotypical: 'Handle so, daß die Maxime deines Willens jederzeit zugleich als Princip einer allgemeinen Gesetzgebung gelten könne.' Hegel espies here the heteronomy of the supposedly autonomous moral: it is precisely the ethical law's form of generality which leads to the harshest one-sidedness and suppression: 'Woe to the human relationships that do not exactly fit into the concept of duty which, if it is not merely the empty thought of generality but actually shows itself in an action, excludes or rules over all other relationships.'[39]

Kant was well aware of this one-sidedness and harshness. Accordingly, when he told the story of the deposit once again in 1793, he intensified the circumstances in such a manner that healthy common sense and enlightened popular philosophy became downright bewildered by his solution of the case:

Suppose, for instance, that someone is holding another's property in trust (a deposit) whose owner is dead, and that the owner's heirs do not know and can never hear about it. Present this case even to a child of eight or nine, and add that, through no fault of his, the trustee's fortunes are at their lowest ebb, that he sees a sad family around him, a wife and children disheartened by want. From all of this he would be instantly delivered by appropriating the deposit. And further that the man is kind and charitable, while those heirs are rich, loveless, extremely extravagant spendthrifts, so that this addition to their wealth might as well be thrown into the sea. And then ask whether under these circumstances it might be deemed permissible to convert the deposit to one's own use. Without doubt, anyone asked will answer 'No!' – and in lieu of grounds he can merely say: 'It is wrong!', i.e., it conflicts with duty.[40]

Everything here is now mobilized to set the rebelling 'natural dialectic' of casuistic thinking in motion. The most appalling circumstances (precisely according to the standards of value of the average enlightened understanding) are presupposed: the family man is an 'altruist', he has fallen into misfortune through no fault of his own, the heirs (beneficiaries) are a contemptible lot, and so on – and nevertheless this wonderful eight-year-old child is capable of clarifying the case if he just lets himself be guided by the feeling of duty. Even today, the reader senses that something is wrong here – before he finally yields to the judgment of that child. We want to try and clarify just what arouses this feeling of uneasiness by going back

[39] G.W.F. Hegel, *Der Geist des Christentums, Werke*, vol. 1, p. 323.
[40] Immanuel Kant, *On the Old Saw: That May be Right in Theory, but it Won't Work in Practice*, tr. E. B. Ashton (Philadelphia, University of Pennsylvania Press, 1974), p. 53.

a couple of steps in the moral theology of the German Enlightenment of the eighteenth century and in the Protestant casuistry of the seventeenth, thereafter coming forward again to Kant and to bourgeois society.

## MORAL THEOLOGY IN CASUISTIC INTENTION

Johann Peter Miller (1725–1789) was an Evangelical theologian and pedagogue, private tutor in Göttingen, school principal in Helmstedt and Halle, and finally theology professor in Göttingen. After Mosheim's death, Miller took up that author's immense unfinished *Ethics of the Holy Bible* (*Sittenlehre der Heiligen Schrift*) and saw it to completion. In his own *Complete Introduction to Theological Morals, of Mosheim in Particular* (*Vollständige Einleitung in die theologische Moral überhaupt und in die Mosheimische insbesondere*) (1772), he brings forward a case of conscience which one can confidently read as the fore-runner of the Kantian 'deposit', provided that one reduces the embezzlement of a deposited object to the general denominator of 'theft' – which is, to a certain degree, permissible in the tradition of the 'Carolina', the penal code of Emperor Karl the Fifth.[41]

A poor family man, whose eight children have been begging him in vain for bread while living on grass and roots for three days already, could think to himself: 'you certainly should not steal, but you should let neither yourself nor your children perish. Your rich but merciless neighbour, with his full granaries, will not notice it at all if you pilfer a few sacks of grain little by little' . . . He climbs in, is caught, and is punished as a thief. By rights? Yes. On what grounds? I answer: the culprit chose the greater of two moral evils. His example would have immensely bad consequences for society itself. So should he have died a slow death with his family instead? Yes, and that way become a martyr and victim of the common good and of his fear of God . . . But in that case would he still have chosen a moral evil?[42]

Everything which Kant can no longer consider at all is still brought forward here as a serious objection. Of course, Miller also answers that the culprit has to be punished because otherwise bourgeois society could not exist; the decisive difference, however, is that the

---

[41] Paragraph 170 of the 'Carolina' fixes the same penalty for the embezzlement of goods entrusted or deposited as it does for theft: *Die Peinliche Gerichtsordnung Kaiser Karls V. von 1532* (Carolina), ed. Gustav Radbruch, 5th edition (Stuttgart, Reclam, 1980), p. 108. On the discussion carried out around 1800 on the relationship of embezzlement and theft, see Carl Klien, *Revision der Grundsätze über das Verbrechen des Diebstahls* (Nordhausen, Johann Adolf Nitzsche, 1806), pp. 156ff.

[42] J. P. Miller, *Vollständige Einleitung in die theologische Moral überhaupt und in die Mosheimische insbesondere* (Leipzig, 1772), p. 387.

story is told by Miller within a completely different systematic framework. This is an instance not of a law which no casuistry tolerates alongside itself, but rather of a collision between two laws. The case can be compared with the famous example from antiquity which gives one the choice after a shipwreck of either perishing oneself or pushing another person away from the life-saving plank: 'The commandment here reads: "Save your life", and the prohibition: "thou shalt not kill".'[43]

Command and prohibition are not of bourgeois but of biblical origin, and the entire story is found in the supplement to a paragraph which deals with the 'Surest conduct in doubtful cases'; not only that, but there is the further complication that there is no time left for long deliberations and consultations. Now it is presumed that, if an action includes trespassing on a divine command, it must be completely abstained from, 'since every action which is expressly contrary to a prohibition is literally a sin; hence, it is also a moral evil. Now one certainly may choose the lesser of two physical evils, but never of two moral evils; because every sin is repugnant to God's love, and one may not offend God under any circumstances.'[44]

God, who is weakened to a mere idea of reason by Kant and has to find his support in the 'moral law',[45] is still in the foreground for Miller. Although he gives much to the claims of bourgeois society, his case of conscience is nevertheless ultimately oriented towards the concept of 'sin' and towards offence against the divinity. It is ultimately God, too, who frees the unfortunate family man from the dilemma of having to choose between *two moral evils*: if he gives precedence to the command 'Thou shalt not steal' and dies of hunger together with wife and children, then he has not violated the colliding command of having to preserve his God-given life. His suicide, which had to be taken into the bargain, was a

necessary action if he did not want to sin. He submitted himself to the will of God. If, accordingly, God himself makes it impossible for us, whenever we neither are allowed nor want to commit a greater evil in order to prevent the less harmful one: then the latter, under consideration of our weaknesses, changes from a moral evil into a mere physical evil.[46]

As if it were a particular in theodicy, the entire weight of a very difficult case of conscience is thrown upon God. He also sees with the eyes of bourgeois society and decides what is the greater and the lesser evil here. Kant wriggles himself out of the whole affair in

[43] Ibid., p. 387.    [44] Ibid., pp. 383f.
[45] Kant, *Critique of Practical Reason*, p. 3.    [46] Miller, *Vollständige Einleitung*, p. 387.

another way. Actually, he too should talk about the dutiful citizen's death by starvation, but he doesn't. On the contrary, he has embellished the example in such a manner that the embezzlement of the deposit would not help *in any case*. If it is used as a way out of misfortune too rashly, then the man brings suspicion upon himself; if it is taken into account too slowly, then the misfortune has already become so great that all help arrives too late.[47] All of these considerations are meant to counter the objections of the Breslau popular philosopher Christian Garve; according to these objections, a concept of duty totally cleansed of the concept of happiness is incapable of being applied in practice. Kant wants to show to the contrary that such a concept and only such a concept is really applicable. But what is to become now of the man and his family? Kant does not give a direct answer to the question; but it can be inferred from the framework of his essay, *That May be Right in Theory, but it Won't Work in Practice*.[48] A new entity absorbs the fate of the virtuous man: it is no longer God, but rather history – more precisely, it is history interpreted in view of a philosophy of history that takes over the systematic place of the former theodicy.[49] Kant knows that, up to now, historical experience has not yet proved the success of the doctrine of virtue;[50] that does not, however, speak against the pure 'idea of duty', but only against the hitherto existing state constitutions and their development. Just as man grasps hold of pure moral intention, there is 'the revelation of divine tendencies within himself deep enough to fill him with sacred awe, as it were, at the magnitude and sublimity of his true destiny'.[51] This newly felt dignity of man cannot be contrary to the development of history. In the debate with Moses Mendelssohn, Kant firmly rejects the view that man, although making a little progress towards the better here and there, does so only to fall back again afterwards into his old condition with twice the speed.[52] A God conceived of in terms of philosophical ethics watches as it were the inner battle of the family man torn between duty and inclination:

[47] Kant, *On the Old Saw: That May be Right in Theory, but it Won't Work in Practice*, p. 54.
[48] Kant starts with a problem in moral philosophy, extends the discussion to constitutional law, and then closes the essay with the question characteristic of his philosophy of history, namely, whether the human race as a whole is making moral progress.
[49] Heinz-Dieter Kittsteiner, *Naturabsicht und Unsichtbare Hand. Zur Kritik des geschichts-philosophischen Denkens* (Frankfurt-on-Main, Berlin, Vienna, Ullstein, 1980), p. 158.
[50] Kant, *On the Old Saw: That May be Right in Theory, but it Won't Work in Practice*, p. 55.    [51] Ibid., p. 54.
[52] Ibid., p. 76. Cf. Kittsteiner, *Naturabsicht und Unsichtbare Hand*, pp. 90ff.

If it is a sight fit for a god to see a virtuous man wrestle with tribulations and temptations and yet stand firm, it is a sight most unfit, I will not say for a god, but for the commonest man of good will to see the human race from period to period take upward steps toward virtue, only to see it soon after relapsing just as deeply into vice and misery. To watch this tragedy for a while may perhaps be toughing and instructive, but eventually the curtain has to fall.[53]

The curtain will fall over the previous course of history; the moral conduct of the family man obtains a world-historical dimension: viewing him lays open the hope, for without the prospect of 'better times the human heart would never have been warmed by a serious desire to do something useful for the common good'.[54]

Our man is supposed to be prevailed upon to hope for a general betterment of the conditions of the human race – a hope which is connected with sacrifices – by a feeling of 'regard', which the moral law itself pours into him, independently of all maxims of happiness and prosperity.[55] It is this subjective side of the downfall of casuistry which will now occupy our attention. The arguments which Kant brings forward for the practicability of this felt concept of duty appear to be plausible. Conscience as grounded in morality resolves its 'cases' fast and unequivocally. That makes for a great advantage over a will which sways according to the maxims of happiness. This will has a considerably difficult task to master, 'for it considers the outcome, and that is most uncertain: one must have a good head on his shoulders to disentangle himself from the jumble of arguments and counterarguments and not to deceive himself in the tally'.[56] It is obviously one thing to let oneself be guided by regard for the moral law and another thing to sort out reasons and counter-reasons for a decision by using an operation of the understanding. It appears that, behind the scientific categories 'enlightened moral philosophy of the eighteenth century' and 'casuistry of the seventeenth century' there stand entirely different views about what this 'conscience' actually is to which each is referring.

## CONSCIENCE AS SYLLOGISM

Kant was right: a mastery of casuistry requires a 'good brain'; and it requires an even better brain the less tightly the general rule is formulated whose application is being dealt with – that is, the more that equally strong or even contradictory considerations and

---

[53] Kant, *On the Old Saw: That May be Right in Theory, but it Won't Work in Practice*, p. 76.    [54] Ibid., p. 77.    [55] Ibid., p. 49.    [56] Ibid., p. 54.

objections enter into the judgment. Although the general law already dominates unequivocally in the work of J. P. Miller, it does not carry along with it a practical, unconsciously working 'inner spring' which effects a feeling of respect for the moral law; instead, considerable hermeneutic and logical operations are necessary if it is to be guaranteed that one acts rightly in a difficult situation. Rightful actions result exclusively from the application of a divine law upon a certain situation. Carrying out this application is the task of conscience: 'Since the entire prestige of conscience is dependent upon the law alone, it follows that conscience is actually binding only when it is really in accordance with the divine will and with divine satisfaction, or when it explains to us what the law is asserting; that is, only true or *right* conscience is actually binding, because it alone can make an action rightful.'[57] In order to make an action a rightful one, the following presuppositions are therefore necessary:

1. The basic principle which we use as a rule has to be a divine law.
2. It has to be not only a divine law but also a law that fits and is applicable to the given case.
3. The law has to be correctly and precisely interpreted and understood.
4. Finally, it must also correctly 'be applied to the case both *materialiter* and *formaliter* (both according to the object and the case and according to all circumstances and moral determinations in general) and also *extensive* and *intensive* (that is, to the whole extent and in the right amount, so that one does neither more nor less than God the Wisest Himself has prescribed.'[58]

'If, on the other hand, just one of these requirements is missing, then the judgment of conscience is always wrong.'[59] It is obvious that a conscience structured in this way is constantly in danger of doing something wrong. All of the well-known phenomena of casuistry – the erring conscience, the doubting conscience, the merely probable conscience, the scrupulous conscience, even the sleeping conscience, result from this problem of having to apply a given, revealed law to a specific situation.[60]

---

[57] Miller, *Vollständige Einleitung*, p. 374.    [58] Ibid., pp. 374f.    [59] Ibid., p. 375.
[60] These figures of conscience appear from Friedrich Balduin, one of the first Protestant casuists (see Stäudlin, *Geschichte der christlichen Moral*, pp. 228f.) until J. P. Miller, one of the last Lutheran moral theologians of the eighteenth century, who was still influenced by scholastic doctrines (see Johannes Stelzenberger, *Syneidesis im Neuen Testament* (Paderborn, Schöningh, 1961), p. 15. Balduin (1628) distinguishes the Conscientia Recta, Erronea, Dubia, Opinabilis et Scrupulosa. The right conscience consists in agreement with divine commands; the erring conscience applies these commands falsely: 'approbans falsa pro veris, et vera pro falsis; certa pro incertis, incerta pro certis', etc. (Friedrich Balduin, *Tractatus Luculentus, Posthumus, Toti Reipublicae Christianae Utilissimus, de Materia rarissme antehac enueleata, Casibus nimirum Conscientiae* (Frankfurt, 1654), pp. 10ff. The major problem always consists in the fact that the conscience does not judge and pledge

Consequently, since conscience itself is nothing but 'a logical
conclusion of intention of the will to check and examine our deeds
according to the law in order to see if these comply with the latter',[61]
it is also organized in such a fashion that it can execute this task.
Conscience is divided – and with this, J. P. Miller places himself
entirely within the scholastic tradition – namely, into the areas of
*syneidesis* and *conscientia*:

The Greek word *syneidesis* and the Latin word *conscientia* strongly indicate
that man, if he is acting with common sense, is aware of the action as well as
the morality of his action, or of this action's relationship to the law. In
respect to that empirical knowledge which every man can and should have of
his individual action, conscience is called a *witness*, and in relation to its
judgment, it is called a judge; in accordance with the syllogistic form, this
judge takes in the major premise the general rule of the law as the basis, but
in the minor premise, the action as the basis, and if everything else has
proceeded normally in *materia* and *forma*, he then makes a correct, either
sanctioning or condemning, deduction from those premises.[62]

This overly intellectual view of conscience is worked out by St
Thomas Aquinas,[63] and it also determines via Melanchthon –
'Conscientia est syllogismus practicus in intellectu, in quo maior
propositio est Lex Dei seu verbum Dei. Minor vero et conclusio sunt
applicatio approbans recte factum vel condemnans delictum, quam
approbationem in corde sequitur laetitia et condemnationem
dolor'[64]– the tradition of early Lutheran–Protestant casuistry since

out of its own sovereign power, but rather according to pre-given guidelines:
'Obligat autem conscientia non per se, sed ratione legis, quae aliquid praecipit vel
prohibit. Legis enim proprie est obligare: Conscientia autem est praeco legis'
(ibid., p. 9). Just as the herald is subordinated to the judge, so too is the conscience
subordinated to the divine command. Consistently, Balduin equates 'conscience-
lessness' with atheism (p. 1) – on the corresponding forms of conscience in Miller,
see Miller, *Vollständige Einleitung*, pp. 379ff.

[61] Johann Lorenz v. Mosheim, *Sitten-Lehre der Heiligen Schrift*, 3rd edition,
(Helmstadt, 1742–70), 2nd edition (1749), vol. 3 p. 234.
[62] Miller, *Vollständige Einleitung*, p. 371.
[63] Thomas Aquinas, *S. Th.* 1 q. 79 a. 13. Cf. Johannes Stelzenberger, *Syneidesis,
conscientia, Gewissen. Studie zum Bedeutungswandel eines moraltheologischen Begriffes*,
pp. 90ff.
[64] *Melanchthons Werke*, ed. Robert Stupperich, vol. II/2, *Loci praecipui theologici* (1559)
(C. Bertelsmann Verlag, 1953), p. 790. As opposed to Luther, who quite early
abandoned the scholastic concept of *synteresis* which he had at first taken up (see
Emmanuel Hirsch, *Lutherstudien*, vol. I (Gütersloh, 1954), pp. 109ff.), and for
whom the conscience is, on the one hand, the tormenting place of the awareness of
remoteness from God and of divine wrath and, on the other hand, the place of
redemption through faith in Jesus Christ (*Lutherstudien*, vol. I, pp. 130ff.),
Melanchthon remains more closely bound to the Catholic–medieval tradition
because of his synergistic moral teaching (Ottmar Dittrich, *Geschichte der Ethik. Die
Systeme der Moral vom Altertum bis zur Gegenwart* (Leipzig, 1932; reprinted Aalen,
1964), vol. 4, pp. 98f.

Balduin. The higher faculty of conscience, the *syneidesis* or *synteresis*, is here also considered as a knowledge of divine laws that has not been corrupted by the fall of man.[65] The *con-scientia*, the actual awareness of our actions, ascertains the fact of what has occurred and places it in relation to the major premise. An orderly deductive procedure is run through which Balduin illustrates with the following example: 'In hoc syllogismo propositio maior est ex lumine naturae vel Scripturae, e.g. qui sanguinem humanum effundit, ejus sanguis etiam effundetur, ut scriptura docet Gen. 9. Conscientia homicidae subsumit: Tu sanguinem humanum effudisti: Hinc concludit sibiipsi sententiam dicens homo: Ergo sanguis tuus etiam est effundendus.'[66]

These operations of the conscience are repeated in the casuistic tradition with innumerable variations and sub-divisions; as the example in J. P. Miller shows, the idea is still alive at the end of the eighteenth century. Conscience is not simply an entity *in* us; rather, as revealed, divine law it is just as much an entity *outside* us.[67] Since it is – with the described complications – always a matter of applying this divine law properly to the case at hand, it is no surprise that Miller, too, advises the faithful Christian that, whenever he falls into doubt about his decision from conscience, he should turn to men who are more experienced in thinking and in morals, 'who check our

[65] Balduin, *Tractatus Luculentus*, pp. 7ff. (De discrimine conscientiae et syntereseos); cf. Hans Emil Weber, *Reformation, Orthodoxie und Rationalismus*, vol. 2: *Der Geist der Orthodoxie* (Darmstadt, Wissenschaftliche Buchgesellschaft, 1966), pp. 60ff.

[66] Balduin, *Tractatus Luculentus*, p. 3; and on the example of the seventh commandment, 'Thou shalt not steal', p. 6.

[67] Stelzenberger points out that the Franciscan conception of *synteresis* – coined by Bonaventura – as an affective, driving potency of the will was pushed back by the Thomist intellectualist view and was only revitalized with the rise of 'moral-sense' philosophy (Stelzenberger, *Syneidesis, conscientia, Gewissen*, pp. 87, 93, 109f.). That a purely intellectualistic view cannot steadfastly be held can be seen from the example of William Ames (cf. Melanchthon, n. 64 above). Although he, too, defines conscience as a judgment and ascribes it to the understanding and not to the will, he makes the qualification that this practical judgment of the understanding is linked to an inclination of the will that distinguishes it from a merely cognitive act (Guiljelmus Amesius, *De Conscientia et eius iure, vel Casibus libri quinque* (Amstelodami, 1654), pp. 1f.). However, even for Ames, conscience retains the form of the syllogism (p. 3), the major premise of which is posited by the revealed will of God ('Hinc lex dei sola obligat conscientiam hominis', p. 5). J. P. Miller, who already deals with Shaftesbury, Hutcheson, and the theory of 'moral sentiment', is prepared to apply the new doctrine in a subsidiary manner: the appeal to (an acquired rather than innate) moral sentiment is supposed to put to shame those who will no longer heed the demand for obedience to divine laws (Miller, *Vollständige Einleitung*, pp. 157 and 369); in doubtful cases, however, he falls back on the secure knowledge of the law and its logically exact application (pp. 370ff.).

examination and our reasons'.[68] It is a view of conscience which
Schopenhauer later describes in the following manner:

Religious people of every faith very often understand *conscience* to be nothing
but the dogmas and prescripts of their religion and the self-examination
undertaken in respect to these: the expressions 'moral constraint' and
'freedom of conscience' are also taken in this sense The theologians,
schoolmen, and casuists of the middle and later period also took it in this
sense: everything that one knows about statutes and prescripts of the
church, along with the intention of believing and complying with it,
constituted one's *conscience*.[69]

## CONCERNING THE SOCIAL FUNCTION OF CASUISTRY

Schopenhauer said – and he was completely justified in doing so –
that for *religious* people, conscience is bound to the dogmas and
prescripts of the respective laws considered divine. Was the bulk of
the population of the Middle Ages, of the Reformation, or of the
seventeenth century 'religious' in this sense, then? We have good
reason to doubt this. In *Un chemin d'histoire. Chrétienté et christianisation*,
Jean Delumeau refers to the 'religious ignorance' and to a pre-
domination of 'magical mentality' into which religious thinking is
carried by the churches, very gradually, with the Reformation and
the Counter-Reformation in a universal process of the 'inner
mission'.[70] And even if religious ways of thinking begin asserting
themselves in the battle against the magical ways of thinking
brought forth and maintained by the supremacy of nature and by the
domination of undisclosed societal relationships, it is by no means
settled which magical relicts remain preserved in the new, accepted
forms, for example in 'prayer'.[71] 'Conscience' is also in a bad way in
so far as it is really dependent upon the 'knowledge' of the biblical

[68] Miller, *Vollständige Einleitung*, p. 383. However, Miller warns against outdated
theological evaluations and advice; one ought not to go further back than Spender
(1635–1705) and Baumgarten (1706–57). In general, the doubtful cases would be
fewer if one expounded and studied morals more systematically (p. 385).
[69] Arthur Schopenhauer, *Sämtliche Werke*, ed. Julius Frauenstädt, 2nd edition
(Leipzig, 1922), vol. 4, p. 192 (Preisschrift über die Grundlage der Moral).
[70] Jean Delumeau, *Un chemin d'histoire. Chrétienté et christianisation* (Paris, Fayard,
1981), pp. 115ff. and 154ff. See also Delumeau, *Le Catholicisme entre Luther et
Voltaire*, 2nd edition (Paris, Presses Universitaires de France, 1979), pp. 237ff.
[71] See Keith Thomas, *Religion and the Decline of Magic: Studies in Popular Beliefs in
Sixteenth- and Seventeenth Century England*, 3rd edition (Harmondsworth, Middlesex,
Penguin, 1978), pp. 301ff. Cf. Leander Petzold, ed., *Magie und Religion. Beiträge zu
einer Theorie der Magie* (Darmstadt, Wissenschaftliche Buchgesellschaft, 1973). For
an example of the amalgamation of magic words with Christian sayings, see Ulrich
Jahn, *Hexenwesen und Zauberei in Pommern* (1886; reprinted Wiesbaden, Dr. Martin
Sändig, 1970).

Commandments. Many penitents – as one preacher complains in the
*Theologia Pastoralis Practica* of 1739/40 – set their hearts on the
absolution in a 'very superstitious manner'. They do not have a
literal, let along a 'living knowledge' of Christianity: 'For example,
they know of no awakening of conscience, of no feeling of sin and of
divine wrath; they have no true desire for the Grace of God in Christ,
know of no inner burden of conscience and soul, are not troubled
and afflicted; but they nevertheless want to be spiritually acquitted
and absolved.'[72]

What then does their trust rest on? They go every quarter of a year, or
however often they are told to, to penance, to confess their sins, even
counting off certain vices, deporting themselves in a melancholy manner at
the same time, and listen to the absolution. And afterwards, even though
they have never entertained the thought of leading an entirely different life,
they still firmly imagine themselves as leaving the confessional as free of sin
on the strength of the absolution and the laying of hands upon them as if
they had never committed any sins. Then the wrongdoings start up again;
until the next quarter term comes around.[73]

That such a penitent (as far as he can read at all) takes a casuistic
summa in his hands in order to check over his actions by using the
syllogistic procedure appears unthinkable; that he asks an expert for
advice, appears improbable. The extent to which the moral
theologians themselves are scrupulous becomes evident from the
fact that it is precisely in the Protestant tradition that a distinction is
drawn between an average 'conscience' and the conscience of
someone 'born again'.[74] It is only in the person who has been born

[72] 'Zufällige Gedancken, vom Mißbrauch und Verbesserung des Beicht-Stuhls,
sonderlich unter dem unwissenden Land-Volk, entworfen, von einem, unter
vielen Gewissens-Unruhe, nach des Beicht-Wesens Verbesserung seufzendem
Prediger', in: *Theologia Pastoralis Practica*, vol. 2 (Nr. 9–16) (1739/40), 305.
[73] Ernst Christian Philippi, *Wohl-gegründetes Zeugniß der Wahrheit von denen vornehmsten
und gemeinesten Mängeln bey dem Beicht-Wesen in der Evangelischen Kirche* (Halle, 1720),
p. 24.
[74] Max Weber's general evaluation, 'In consequence of its doctrine of Grace in
particular, Lutheranism lacked the psychological impulse to systematization in
the conduct of life that forces its methodical rationalization' (Max Weber, *Die
protestantische Ethik I. Eine Aufsatzsammlung*, ed. Johannes Winckelmann, 6th edition
(Gütersloh, Gütersloher Verlagshaus Mohn, 1981)), p. 143, must be modified, as
Weber himself implies with regard to Pietism. As soon as it is a question of the
'visible effect in holy conduct of Grace acquired through penance' (p. 148) it
becomes clear that the subjects of the theological ethic can only be those born
again who concern themselves with the preservation of their 'state of Grace' (H. E.
Weber, *Reformation, Orthodoxie und Rationalismus*, pp. 53ff.). From this there arises in
the eighteenth century the interpretation of justification typical of the Enlightenment, for which 'faith' no longer means the freely given Grace of God but rather
one's own step towards 'virtue', which can be maintained by constant self-control.
See Otto Hermann Pesch and Albrecht Peters, *Einführung in die Lehre von Gnade und
Rechtfertigung* (Darmstadt, Wissenschaftliche Buchgesellschaft, 1981), pp. 248ff.

again that a conscience is at work – not through one's own merit but through the Grace of God – as an

upright will which does not undertake anything important without first checking if and to what extent it is allowed by the law and which does not daily examine whatever has occurred without a sufficient check-up to see if it is according to the law or not. This intention cannot be lacking in anyone who has truly renounced his sins and has surrendered himself to the Lord. Hence, all pious men have a conscience: all of them are conscientious.[75]

Conscience is at work here as the preservation of a 'state of Grace' once obtained from God; as such, it presupposes faith in Jesus Christ's act of redemption. Furthermore, it presupposes a belief in the otherworldly compensation of good and bad with reward and punishment. Where this is not present, where the children of the world – as one Evangelical chaplain in 1685 complained, using Ecclesiastes 3.18 – would rather see 'that they lived and died, nevermore to rise from the dead, the same as the beasts without the faculty of reason',[76] then every starting-point is lacking for a theological–moral renewal of the mode of life.

In this light it seems justified to consider the great casuistic summas of the seventeenth century as a constituent part of the *inner mission*, as an attempt to introduce biblical norms into the interpretation of daily conduct.[77] Naturally, the mode of life of the bulk of the population is not generally unscrupulous. To be sure, the norms of real conduct – for example, endeavours to preserve professional honour – conflict under circumstances with religious commandments and prohibitions. There are, however, situations in

[75] Mosheim, however, makes the restriction that, wherever the judgment of self-examination is too harsh, the 'born again or holy person' can console himself in faith in the merits of the Redeemer: J. L. Mosheim, *Sitten-Lehre*, vol. 3, p. 254. The difference between a sensitized and an 'ordinary' conscience also becomes clear through the fact that many of the cases of conscience mentioned in pastoral theological writings deal not with the 'conscience' of the parish members but rather with the conscience of the minister in the lights of the activities and conduct of his parish.

[76] David Trommer, *Die Seligste Land- und Bauer-Weißheit* (Leipzig, 1685), p. 668.

[77] The fact that a zealous minister to a certain extent creates his 'sinful' parish himself in the first place can be seen from a report from the first half of the eighteenth century: 'As far as my audience are concerned, they seemed to me at first to be quite bourgeois and honourable, so that I had the hope that the widespread bad reputation of the community for heinous conduct would have no basis.' Only when – in Luther's words – in his sermons he poured 'water on the unslaked lime' did 'the seething fire of their evil [rise] up that lay hidden beneath the outward semblance of honourableness'. 'Oh, how much did it pain the old man (= Adam), that this knife was put to his throat, and everything in which they had before found enjoyment unhindered was made condemnable sin' (Herrn Christoph Matthias Seidels Nachricht von der Gemeinde zu Schönborn, in *Theologia Pastoralis Practica*, vol. 3 (nr. 17–24) (1740), pp. 231, 361).

which the 'sleeping conscience' itself sometimes awakens: for example, when there are wars, sickness, and famines. There is hardly a preacher who lets the opportunity slip by of despatching from the pulpit a sermon of thunder and atonement after a heavy storm. Only to the extent that the idea can be fortified in faith that at least at the end of life a situation could arise for which it is worthwhile to have preserved one's 'conscience' and in which it will hardly be sufficient to take leave of this world with a fleeting 'God be merciful to my soul' if one wants to obtain eternal life,[78] only to that extent is a foothold gained from which casuistry can start. We can observe the structure of such a counsel of conscience by examining a collection from the middle of the seventeenth century, Andreas Kesler's *Theologia Casuum Conscientiae* of 1658, and we will choose the case of conscience in such a manner that it remains comparable to the treatment of embezzlement and theft in Kant and in J. P. Miller. In chapter 59 of his casuistry, Kesler discusses the question 'whether or not a man sins against the seventh commandment who makes use of something belonging to his neighbour without the latter's knowledge or consent in order to preserve his own life during a great famine'. Although Kesler begins with the obligatory delimitation of his position from the Catholic 'Casistas', at the same time he refers to Thomas Aquinas, who, against the severity of the laws, does actually argue (*S. Th.* 2, 2 q. 66 a.7) that human law has to take a back seat to the divine law and the natural law and that, in the case of misery, the goods ordained by God for subsistence have to be accessible to everyone.

Kesler also refers to Luther, who in the *Exhortation of the Ministers to Preach against Usury* says: 'Famine and good times are very different / they also constitute very dissimilar periods and persons / what is right outside of misery / is not right in misery / and again / he who takes bread from the baker's store without there being famine / is a thief / if he does this while there is a famine / then he is doing the right thing / because one is obligated to give to him.'[79] One has to interpret the commandments of the second tablet (hence, the seventh commandment as well) to include the love of God and one's

---

[78] Since the proverb from Eccles. 11.3, 'In the place where the tree falleth, there it shall be', was quite well known in connection with the hour of death, ministers could make an impression on the country folk with the representation of 'how wretched they would be if they were overtaken by death while drinking, dancing, playing cards' (ibid., p. 362).

[79] Andreas Kesler, *Theologia Casuum Conscientiae, Das ist: Schrifftmäßige und Außführliche Erörterung unterschiedlicher (. . .) Gewissens-Fragen*, ed. Joh. Christ. Seldius (Wittenberg, 1658), pp. 340f.

neighbour. 'Hence, if you cannot preserve your life during the period of your greatest distress in hunger by any other means / than that you take something to refresh yourself from the tilled land of your neighbour / who is not present / then you are acting in accordance with the love of God, / who does not wish that you deliberately die of hunger.' And finally, he also presents the following case: 'When two wanderers are travelling in the country / and the one becomes weak / so that he cannot go on / then it is not contrary to the commandment and will of God that the fresh and healthy wanderer / seizes the resources nearest at hand / and takes the same / wherever he finds it in his distress / because there is no opportunity and no time to buy or beg for something / and refreshes his companion. This is according to the love of God and neighbour / and thus happens in good conscience.'[80]

'And thus happens in good conscience' – and that, even though what could constitute the 'resources nearest at hand' to which the wanderer is justified in laying hold of is left unspecified. Certainly, it has to be made clear which conscience one is talking about here. If the man takes something and is caught in the process, there arises a wide spectrum of possibilities, as a glance in the 'Carolina' confirms: stealing out of real distress in hunger (§166) is to be distinguished from food theft, where once again it depends if the theft is committed at night and is considerable or if it is done during the day and occurs without much loss to the owner (§167). It becomes more difficult when the theft occurs 'by means of breaking and entering' (§159), or when the stolen goods exceed the value of 5 Gulden (§160). But in all cases – in Kesler as well as in Kant's second deposit case and also in J. P. Miller's breaking into the granary – §166 would come into consideration, of which the penal code says: 'If someone were caused to steal some food because of real distress in hunger from which he, his wife, or his children are suffering, where then the said theft was "tapffer groß und kündlich", then the judge and the jury consult each other once again.' So such a case should receive special deliberation. On the other hand, if the theft is not 'tapffer groß und kündlich', that is if it is relatively insignificant, then the culprit – according to the commentary from G. Radbruch[81] – is, without further ado, to be considered exempt from punishment. Even the 'penal code' judges this case mildly – always, of course, on condition that the culprit is caught at all, and, what with the in-

[80] Ibid., p. 344.
[81] *Die Peinliche Gerichtsordnung Kaiser Karls V*, p. 147. For the mitigation of penalties for theft done out of real starvation in the 'Bambergensis', see Erik Wolf, *Große Rechtsdenker der deutschen Geistesgeschichte*, 3rd edn (Tübingen, 1951), p. 120.

efficiency of the police power in precapitalist society, this was generally not the rule.[82] Accordingly, if he is not caught, and if this offence weighs upon his conscience when he finds himself in a fearful situation or on his death bed, then even the casuist of the seventeenth century will tell him that he has 'preserved' his conscience well with this act and that he need not be afraid of being punished for it with the eternal death of hell.

## THE EXCEPTION AND THE RULE

Both worldly jurisdiction and theological casuistry are, in extreme situations, inclined to allow exceptions to the rule – that much at least is evident from the examples presented. The major premise of the syllogism of conscience does not dominate to such an absolute extent that considerable modifications would not be possible in judging the 'deed', that is, the real occurrence. Basically, the general commandment 'Thou shalt not steal' is sacrificed in Kesler to the action done out of hunger or during a famine. For Miller, somewhat more than one hundred years later, the same constellation already results in the conflict between two laws, with the tendency of subordinating the individual situation to the security guaranteed by law in a bourgeois society. Finally, for Kant, the mere consideration of such a casuistic dialectic is impossible in questions occurring within the juridical area.

Once the historical perspective is reversed and, instead of looking out from the eighteenth century into the seventeenth, one views bourgeois moral philosophy from the standpoint of the old casuists, Kant takes himself into a sensitive area with his strict treatment of the question of the 'deposit' (especially in the second version of 1793). The whole cluster of problems becomes even more difficult when we see that one of the first examples which he notes for the formula of the categorical imperative is, of all things, a granary theft: 'Assume that I am preparing to go and steal the grain belonging to another. Because I do not know any man who, on condition that he be robbed himself, wants to gain the goods of another, I will

---

[82] Richard J. Evans, 'Öffentlichkeit und Autorität. Zur Geschichte der Einrichtungen in Deutschland vom Allgemeinen Landrecht bis zum Dritten Reich', in Heinz Reif (ed.), *Räuber, Volk und Obrigkeit. Studien zur Geschichte der Kriminalität in Deutschland seit dem 18. Jahrhundert* (Frankfurt, Suhrkamp, 1984), pp. 192f. and Carsten Küther, 'Räuber, Volk und Obrigkeit. Zur Wirkungsweise und Funktion staatlicher Strafverfolgung im 18. Jahrhundert', in Reif (ed.), *Räuber, Volk und Obrigkeit*, pp. 17ff.

something which I do not will for the generality.'[83] To be sure, the situation 'distress in hunger' is not given here as a condition, but it is quite obvious that Kant chooses the example of food theft in order to make clear that the thinking which has come down in the categories of natural desires should capitulate to the severity of the moral law.[84] The basic categories of bourgeois society – property and the exchange of property – would be invalidated if the thief could raise his maxim to a law. The trick of the Kantian argumentation consists on the whole – as already mentioned – in demanding of the thief that he consider what would happen if his conduct were to be elevated to a general law. The thief thinks along totally different lines. Far from wanting to generalize his maxim, he sets a small piece of casuistry to work in which, as Adam Smith very nicely points out, it is not the concepts 'law' and 'crime' but rather 'poor' and 'rich' which appear: 'The thief imagines he does no evil, when he steals from the rich, what he supposes they may easily want, and what possibly they may never even know has been stolen from them.'[85] He does not think juridically but rather economically, and for him that means in the categories of securing subsistence. He does not say: 'Thou shalt not steal', but rather: 'If I steal, would it do me more good than it would harm the person stolen from?' How much this casuistic thinking fell into discredit among the moral philosophers influenced by Kant is shown in an example from F. V. Reinhard from the year 1801. The same pattern of casuistical reasoning to which Pascal objected in his struggle against calumny is transformed to become an example of casuistical reasoning in matters of property rights, which Reinhard wishes strictly to secure:

Certainly one should *not slander any man*; however, if he is a malicious *enemy*, a *heretic*, he is an *infidel*, and one wants to cause him to lose his credit; with such people, an exception is made. One should *never appropriate something belonging to another's property in an unlawful manner*; however, the one with the advantages is a *rich* man who does not even notice the trifle one has taken from him; he himself has *not acquired* what he has *by the best means*; consequently, he cannot

---

[83] Dieter Henrich, 'Ethik und Autonomie', in Henrich, *Selbstverhältnisse. Gedanken und Auslegungen zu den Grundlagen der klassischen deutschen Philosophie* (Stuttgart, Reclam, 1982), pp. 20f.; Kant, *Gesammelte Schriften*, Preußische Akademie der Wissenschaften edn (Berlin, 1902–83), vol. 20, p. 161.

[84] It must of course be taken into consideration that a mitigation of penalties was carried out in the eighteenth century according to the principle of the proportionality of punishments. For instance, in 1743 the death penalty for theft was abolished in Prussia, even for repeated theft, as long as it was committed without violence: Carl Ludwig von Bar, *Geschichte des deutschen Strafrechts und der Strafrechtstheorien* (Berlin 1882; reprint Scientia Verlag Aalen, 1974), p. 157.

[85] Smith, *The Theory of Moral Sentiments*, p. 175.

complain if the right of recompense is exercised on him; and shouldn't one be allowed to withdraw from another what the latter *can easily forgo*, if one *requires* it oneself for desperately needed essentials?[86]

There would be nothing special about this result if it were only supposed to verify that the economic ethics in Thomas Aquinas or Luther[87] was different from that in Adam Smith or Kant. But it has to do with something else: namely, with the question how these socio-philosophical and socio-theological premises affect the structure of casuistry. As H. Weber notes, casuistry mediated between an ethos of redemption and a philosophic–sociological world ethic; it connected *life in its 'givenness'* with the question concerning the right way to salvation.[88] Its cases of conscience emerge out of this bipolarity; although it is a syllogism, its form is flexible enough to place both areas – according to the changing situations – in an appropriate relationship. In our case, in pre-capitalist societies, the difference between 'normal' times and times of distress was so great, and the times of distress were so frequent, that regulated theoretical and practical precautions had to be taken.[89] To demonstrate this, using an apparently trivial example from A. Kesler's casuistry: in good harvest years, a Christian might in good conscience wear starched collars; in those days, starch was made from wheat which God – and here is the problem – allowed to grow not so that man could dress lavishly but so that he would have bread to eat. But if enough grain was available, one could starch one's collars without any misgivings, so that one did not go about 'sloppy' around the neck. However, if times were hard and prices high, all use of wheat for spirits, starch, paste, and so on should be prohibited. In such years, the Christian would burden his conscience if he continued to insist on starched collars. Kesler hopes, by the way, that other

[86] Franz Volkmar Reinhard, *Über den Kleinigkeitsgeist in der Sittenlehre* (Meissen, 1801), p. 126.
[87] Ernst Troeltsch, *Die Soziallehren der christlichen Kirchen und Gruppen*, 2nd edn (Tübingen, J. C. B. Mohr, 1919), pp. 349 and 573.
[88] H. E. Weber, *Reformation, Orthodoxie und Rationalismus*, pp. 59ff.
[89] On the problem of the constancy of the living conditions in feudalism as compared to capitalism, Witold Kula makes the following remark: 'Finally, we might risk a generalization: in precapitalist societies many economic indexes are subject to great fluctuations in the short run and only to very slow change in the direction of the trend; in industrial societies, however, the range of short-run fluctuations is reduced, but the trend of changes in direction is accelerated' (Witold Kula, *An Economic Theory of the Feudal System. Towards a model of the Polish Economy (1500–1800)* (London, NLB, 1976), p. 181). On the economics of the poor as a subsidiary system in crises and times of rising prices, see Edward P. Thompson, 'The Moral Economy of the English Crowd in the 18th Century', in *Past and Present*, no. 50, pp. 76–136.

materials for starching collars would soon be invented so that, along the way of progress, the world could be rid of the problem of misusing God-given grain.[90]

Viewed from the standpoint of the individual who seeks advice because he wants to 'preserve his conscience', the information with which casuistry provides him seems to be a possibility of establishing a practical relationship between worldly and religious life. But even if someone submits himself to ecclesiastical advice, it still holds for him that 'The mode of life is not in this case a systematizing from within and out from a centre which the individual has achieved himself; rather, it feeds itself out of a centre lying outside of itself.'[91] This balancing act between the world and religious scruple is gradually shifted in Protestant casuistry in favour of an emphasis on and strengthening of the *general principle* (which does not generally state a permission, as in the last case, but a prohibition) and against the interpretation which gives pre-eminent consideration to the special circumstances. This may very well be connected with the fact that – as is emphasized in all of the polemics against Jesuitic casuistry – the highest norm for conduct is always taken to be the Holy Bible and never human statutes such as papal decrees.[92] Accordingly, more weight is given to the syllogistic major premise right from the start – and its weight increases with the reception of the in any case severer Anglican-Reformed or even Calvinist casuistry in the area of the so-called Lutheran Reformorthodoxy around the end of the seventeenth century.[93] At this point, one is no longer merely asking whether every action contemplated is right or necessary. Instead, the practical application of Christian moral principles is supposed to guide all men on the way to moral perfection.[94]

In the process of the internal transference of casuistry into moral philosophy, the Enlightenment is just taking another, and final, step. For one thing, it explains the ordinary casuistic conscience that is oriented towards the individual statutes of revealed religion as superstitious. Kant talks of the 'man-traps' that are set on the path of

[90] Kesler, *Theologia Casuum Conscientiae*, pp. 36ff.
[91] Max Weber, *Wirtschaft und Gesellschaft. Grundriß der verstehenden Soziologie*, ed. Johannes Winckelmann, vol. 1, part 1, p. 437.
[92] In his polemic against the papal 'Casistas', Balduin wrote: 'In caeteris decisionibus suis graviter aberrant, quia non verbi divini (quod solum confirmare potest conscientias,) sed Papalium decretorum ductum sequebantur' (Balduin, *Tractatus, Luculentus, Posthumus*, preface).
[93] Hans Leube, *Die Reformideen in der Deutschen Lutherischen Kirche zuc Zeit der Orthodoxie* (Leipzig, Dörffling and Franke, 1924), pp. 162ff.
[94] Thomas Wood, *English Casuistical Divinity during the Seventeenth Century, with Special Reference to Jeremy Taylor* (London, 1952), p. 65.

life of such 'fantastically virtuous' men,[95] and F. V. Reinhard, full of
comical abhorrence, reports of an Italian woman strictly observing
the religious customs 'who, although having impermissible relationships with more than one lover, ate, for heaven's sake, no meat on
feastdays and allowed none of her admirers any new freedoms before
she had balanced accounts with heaven from time to time by
receiving absolution'.[96]

The 'grovelling religious madness' to which Kant and Reinhard
objected offered up to God everything possible except moral
intention. This, however, is just what in their view would be 'well
pleasing to God' and would furthermore be in agreement with 'the
world's highest good' ('Weltbesten').[97] Here we reach a second stage
of the critique on casuistry. The orientation of conscience has
shifted from the question concerning the justification before God to
the problem of responsibility towards society.[98] Morality has thus
taken the outer form of legality, but with the intensifying addendum
that the observance of ethical duties no longer needs outer coercion;[99] at this point, the 'idea of duty' alone should suffice to serve
as the 'inner spring' of conduct. Kant defines this inner spring as an
'unusual feeling' that is comparable to none of the already known
pathological feelings – a 'positive feeling' that, all the same, can be
known *a priori*.[100]

---

[95] Kant, The *Metaphysical Principles of Virtue*, p. 69.
[96] Franz Volkmar Reinhard, *Über den Kleinigkeitsgeist in der Sittenlehre*, p. 124.
[97] Immanuel Kant, *Religion within the Limits of Reason Alone*, tr. Theodore M. Greene
and Hoyt H. Hudson (New York: Harper and Row, 1960), pp. 160f.
[98] Bernhard Groethuysen, *The Bourgeois. Catholics vs. Capitalism in Eighteenth-Century
France*, vol. I, chapt. 4, section 2.
[99] Kant, *The Metaphysical Principles of Virtue*, p. 19: 'Accordingly, the legislation that
promises must be kept is contained in *jus* and not in ethics. Ethics teaches only that
if the incentive which juridical legislation connects with that duty, namely,
external constraint, were absent, the idea of duty alone would still be sufficient as
an incentive.'
[100] Kant, *Critique of Practical Reason*, p. 76. This 'kind of feeling, (even) under the name
of a practical or moral feeling' (ibid., p. 77) 'is so far from being a feeling of
pleasure that one only reluctantly gives way to it as regards a man' (ibid., p. 80).
However, this feeling doesn't only humiliate men – it compensates humiliation 'on
the sensuous side' with an 'elevation of the moral' one (ibid., p. 81); it is the feeling
of the 'higher vocation in men'. It is quite different from the religious kind of
conscience which according to Kant is in essence fed by fear: 'Sclavisch ist ein
Gewissen, das sich im Urtheilen selbst schrecken läßt. Wenn aber des Gewissens
urtheil sich auf Glauben gründet, dieser aber auf Schrecken' (Kant, Akadamie-
Ausgabe, 6576, 91).
    In the old Protestant form this fright of conscience could be overcome only by
faith and the Grace of God and not by moral self-control. See Hans Schär, 'Das
Gewissen in protestantischer Sicht', in *Das Gewissen. Studien aus dem C. G. Jung-
Institut*, VII (Zurich, Rascher Verlag, 1959), p. 132. In the new type of conscience

This simultaneous secularizing and psychologizing of the centre of morality, the withdrawal of morality from transcendency, and its anchorage in society and in the felt regard for the moral law – all this could not explain the good conscience with which, in a counter-move against casuistry, the individual is neglected in favour of the general. There is a third consideration. The moral law does not simply represent bourgeois society as it is, but rather constructs from its elements a society *as it should be*. Let us keep in mind that casuistry originally operated within a static view of the world and tried to bring the realities of the world into harmony with religious demands that stood in relation to heaven. It then turns out that the crucial difference in the bourgeois moral philosophy of the final third of the eighteenth century consists in its not wanting to leave the world as it is at all.

The neglect of the individual,[101] and the demand that the maxim of action be elevated to the general law, postulates the individual's

of the eighteenth century the consoling function of conscience is triggered by moral action. It already functions according to the model that Freud describes as follows: 'While, however, instinctual renunciation for external reasons is only painful renunciation for internal reasons, in obedience to the demands of the Super-ego, it has another economic effect. It brings besides the inevitable pain a gain in pleasure to the Ego – as it were, a substitutive satisfaction. The Ego feels uplifted; it is proud of the renunciation as of a valuable achievement' (Sigmund Freud, *Moses and Monotheism*, tr. Katharine Jones (New York, Knopf, 1939), pp. 183f. Freud connects the genesis of this feeling of human dignity to the 'love' that the individual experienced as a child: 'When the Ego has made the sacrifice to the Super-ego of renouncing an instinctual satisfaction, it expects to be rewarded by being loved all the more. The consciousness of deserving this love is felt as pride. At the time when the authority was not yet internalized as Super-ego the relation between the threatened loss of love and the instinctual demand would have been the same. A feeling of security and satisfaction results if out of love to one's parents one achieves an instinctual renunciation' (ibid., p. 184). Recent work on the history of education and child rearing and on the role of father and mother stresses that a process of ego-building corresponding to the model drafted by psychoanalysis can be assumed as early as the family grounded on 'love' of the educated bourgeoisie at the end of the eighteenth century. See Jürgen Schlumbohm, '"Traditionale" Kollektivität und "moderne" Individualität: einige Fragen und Thesen für eine historische Sozialisationsforschung', in Rudolf Vierhaus (ed.), *Bürger und Bürgerlichkeit im Zeitalter der Aufklärung*, Wolfenbütteler Studien zur Aufklärung, 7 (Heidelberg, Schneider, 1981), p. 280.

[101] Of course, the bourgeois system too developed methods for the individual evaluation of the individual case. They are, however, different from the procedure of casuistry. Whereas casuistry decided according to the 'external circumstances' and the 'intention', now psychological and sociological knowledge come to the fore. See Michel Foucault, *Überwachen und Strafen. Die Geburt des Gefängnisses*, 3rd edition (Frankfurt, Suhrkamp, 1977), p. 127. Typical of the new questions are, for instance, the court expert-testimonies in the case of the murderer Woyzeck from the 1820s. See H. D. Kittsteiner and Helmut Lethen, 'Ich-Losigkeit, Entbürgerlichung und Zeiterfahrung. Über die Gleichgültigkeit zur "Geschichte" in Büchners "Woyzeck"', in *Georg Büchner Jahrbuch* 3 (1983), 244ff.

concordance with the idea of the whole of society: of a moral union of reasonable world-citizens, considered as possible.[102] Such conduct is no longer directed towards particular goals but towards a 'principle of humanity and of every rational creature as an end in itself.[103] It thus stands in opposition to society as it still is, in which 'the *designs* of men start with the parts . . . The whole as such is too large for men; they can extend their ideas to it, but not their influence.'[104] For the time being, a responsible command over history can only be expected from a being of the highest wisdom and its providence; however, in order to be allowed to think this idea at all, moral conduct has to be presupposed. With that, the moral law in Kant obtains a teleological orientation with respect to a philosophy of history. Kant determines this moral teleology by setting it off from the teleologically reflecting faculty of judgment as follows:

Teleology considers nature as a realm of ends; morals regards a possible realm of ends as a realm of nature. In the former the realm of ends is a theoretical idea for the explanation of what actually is. In the latter it is a practical idea for bringing about that which is not actually real but which can become real through our conduct, and which is in accordance with this idea.[105]

Within the categorical imperative, there reposes – equipped with a temporal index in regard to a philosophy of history – the hope of a better future society, and the severity of the moral law is only understandable against this background: the downfall of casuistry was caused by this unity of moral philosophy and a philosophy of history.

---

[102] Kant, 'Idea for a universal history from a cosmopolitan point of view', in *On History*, ed. Lewis White Beck (Indianapolis, Bobbs-Merrill Co., 1963), p. 14.
[103] Kant, *Foundations of the Metaphysics of Morals*, p. 49.
[104] Kant, *On the Old Saw: That May be Right in Theory*, p. 78.
[105] Kant, *Foundations of the Metaphysics of Morals*, p. 55. The fact that for Kant all teleology (and thus the teleological view of history too) is grounded in the claims of moral philosophy can be seen in the introduction to the *Critique of Judgment*: 'Now even if an immensurable gulf is fixed between the sensible realm of the concept of nature and the supersensible realm of the concept of freedom, so that no transition is possible from the first to the second (by means of the theoretical use of reason), just as if they were two different worlds of which the first could have no influence upon the second, yet the second is *meant* to have an influence upon the first. The concept of freedom is meant to actualize in the world of sense the purpose proposed by its laws, and consequently nature must be so thought of that the conformity to law of its form at least harmonizes with the possibility of the purposes to be effected in it according to laws of freedom' (Kant, *Critique of Judgment*, tr. J. H. Bernard (New York/London, Hafner Press/Collier Macmillan Publishers, 1951), p. 12.

# 7

◁ ══════════════════════════════════════ ▷

## Moral arithmetic:
## Seven Sins into Ten Commandments

JOHN BOSSY

And God spake all these words, saying,

I am the Lord thy God, which have brought thee out of the land of Egypt, out of the house of bondage.

Thou shalt have no other gods before me.

Thou shalt not make unto thee any graven image, or any likeness of any thing that is in heaven above, or that is in the earth beneath, or that is in the water under the earth:

Thou shalt not bow down thyself to them, nor serve them: for I the Lord thy God am a jealous God, visiting the iniquity of the fathers upon the children unto the third and fourth generation of them that hate me;

And shewing mercy unto thousands of them that love me, and keep my commandments.

Thou shalt not take the name of the Lord thy God in vain: for the Lord will not hold him guiltless that taketh his name in vain.

Remember the sabbath day, to keep it holy.

Six days shalt thou labour, and do all thy work:

But the seventh day is the sabbath of the Lord thy God: in it thou shalt not do any work, thou nor thy son, nor thy daughter, nor thy manservant, nor thy maidservant, nor thy cattle, nor the stranger that is within thy gates . . .

Honour thy father and thy mother: that thy days may be long upon the land which the Lord thy God giveth thee.

Thou shalt not kill.

Thou shalt not commit adultery.

Thou shalt not steal.

Thou shalt not bear false witness against thy neighbour.

Thou shalt not covet thy neighbour's house, thou shalt not covet

214

thy neighbour's wife, nor his manservant, nor his maidservant, nor his ox, nor his ass, nor any thing that is thy neighbour's.

Exodus 201–17 (Authorized Version)

For most people, for most of the Middle Ages, the moral system which was taught in Western Christianity was constituted by the Seven Deadly or Capital Sins: Pride, Envy, Wrath, Avarice, Gluttony, Sloth, and Lechery, usually in that order. The list was not Christian, but Greek and possibly astrological in origin. In its medieval form it had been given authority by Pope Gregory the Great, and systematized as part of a larger system of septenary forms of instruction during the twelfth century. It was related to the moral teaching of the New Testament by being treated as a negative exposition of the two commandments of the Gospel, the love of God and the love of one's neighbour. Among various methods of rationalizing the sequence which were tried, the most satisfactory was to expound it as a kind of moral spectrum showing sins of the spirit at one end and sins of the flesh at the other; the first were held to be graver than the second.[1] The main advantage of this moral system was that, in an age when the passions of hostility were probably the most vigorous of natural sentiments, it provided a useful set of categories under which people could identify these as un-Christian: it taught fairly effectively a social or community ethics. Its main weaknesses were that it made little of obligations to God, as compared with obligations to one's neighbour; and that it had no scriptural authority. It may be that, directed to the average Christian, it implied that holiness was not his business, but the business of special categories of Christians like 'religious' men and women.

After the sixteenth century, a different moral system was universally taught in the West: the scriptural (though not New Testament) catalogue of the Ten Commandments. It may seem odd to suggest that, for the average person, the Decalogue was in 1600 a relative novelty, but so it was. In the early church it seems to have been treated as part of the old law from which Christians were anxious to distance themselves. St Augustine, for reasons arising out of his conflict with the Manicheans, had asserted its fundamental validity for Christians, and sought to make it the base of Christian

---

[1] Morton W. Bloomfield, *The Seven Deadly Sins* (Michigan, 1952).

moral teaching; but until the thirteenth century he had not been widely followed. From that point, as we shall see, the Commandments began to make headway, but it was not until the universal diffusion of the Catechism in the sixteenth century and after that their dominance of the moral scene was established.[2]

Thereafter all mainstream denominations taught the Commandments as the Christian moral code, though there were two schools of thought about what they actually were. Catholics and Lutherans accepted the order adopted by St Augustine, who had included the prohibition of graven images under the first commandment and divided, in the last two, the coveting of wives from the coveting of goods. Calvinists and Anglicans had adopted a numbering which had better authority in Greek and Hebrew tradition and separated the prohibition of graven images as a second commandment, while combining the two forms of coveting in the tenth. The two schools also differed in using the complete scriptural text, or a boiled-down version of it, as the form in which to convey the Decalogue to the masses. There was also, of course, much difference in the interpretation of individual commandments. But, with very marginal exceptions, everybody was now using the Decalogue as the system of Christian ethics.

The main substantive difference between the two systems was the greater importance given in the Decalogue to offences against God. True, the first table contained only three commandments (or four in the reformed version), as against the seven (or six) of the second, which concerned one's neighbour; but the first commandment, against worshipping strange gods, was fundamental to the whole system in a way that the equivalent deadly sin, pride, could not be. The rationale of the Decalogue was the prohibition of idolatry; it was a ritual as well as a moral code; its purpose was to keep the people of Israel in holiness, and thereby ensure the perpetuity of their alliance with God; its strategy was the fear of the Lord. Its character could be tempered by Christian expositors, but not radically changed.

---

[2] *Dictionnaire de théologie catholique*, ed. A. Vacant, E. Mangenot, E. Amann (15 vols., Paris, 1923–50) (hereafter *D. T. C.*), *s.v.* Décalogue, Catéchisme. Though I have not pursued the topic in this paper, I am very greatly indebted to Margaret Aston's work on the theology of images and iconoclasm, and in particular to chapter vii, 'The sin of idolatry: the teaching of the Decalogue', of her forthcoming book, which she has been kind enough to let me read; for recent writing on the Commandments, see her nn. 78ff. For the moment, see 'Lollards and images', in her *Lollards and Reformers: Images and Literacy in Late Mediaeval Religion* (London, 1984), pp. 135–92.

The main formal difference was that the Commandments were very much more precise: commands or prohibitions of fairly exactly described actions or, in the case of the last two (or one), dispositions. It is true that the Deadly Sins had been construed, mainly, as implications of the command to love one's neighbour as oneself. But a command to love one's neighbour is not quite the same sort of thing as a command to keep the sabbath holy, or to avoid adultery. What is commanded is a feeling of some generality: to translate it into suitable acts requires interpretation and invites some initiative, either on the part of the recipient or on the part of some authorized interpreter like the church. Even with such an interpreter, the Seven Sins were more a system of indicative moral planning than a code. Of course, the Commandments required some interpretation too, even in the most literally minded Christian traditions: the gravamen of the second (or second part of the first: images) was a matter of intense dispute; everybody interpreted the fourth (fifth), in some degree, as requiring obedience to metaphorical as well as to actual parents; I do not think anyone supposed that the commandment against coveting did not also forbid women to covet their neighbours' husbands. Nevertheless it remained true that, in exchanging the Seven Sins for the Ten Commandments, Christians had acquired a moral code which was stronger on obligations to God, somewhat narrower on obligations to the neighbour, and in both directions more precise, more penetrative, and more binding. The Decalogue was truly a law, in a way that the alternative system had not been.

This was an event in the moral history of Europe, not so far as I know discussed by historians, which nevertheless had important consequences in a number of areas which have traditionally been the subject of historical investigation. Why had it happened? The obvious answer might be that it was a consequence of the Reformation, which had replaced a non-scriptural code by a scriptural one. Reformers had indeed universally adopted the Decalogue, with some misgivings in Luther's case; but so had the Church of Rome in the *Catechism of the Council of Trent*. This was not simply to keep up with the Reformers, since in quite a lot of the West the transition had occurred before the Reformation. Though I am not a medieval historian, and medieval history is not the subject of this book, I think it important for the moral history of early modern Europe to try and explain how the transition had occurred.

The story seems to begin with the scholastic theologians of the thirteenth century. Though they admitted the traditional authority of the Seven Sins, they had been sufficiently impressed by the scriptural and patristic evidence to build their treatments of Christian ethics around the Decalogue. In this they were followed by a number of contemporary pastoral authorities. The Franciscan Archbishop of Canterbury, John Pecham, in his Council of Lambeth of 1281, required his clergy to know and teach the Decalogue, after the Creed but before the Seven Sins. He also gave them a hand by providing an exposition of it, which was widely diffused. His scheme was imitated by others, and by the numerous manuals which enlarged on the instructions of thirteenth-century bishops for the benefit of fourteenth-century priests; notably by William of Pagula in his classic *Oculus Sacerdotis*, written in the 1320s.[3] If the clergy had followed these instructions, the average Englishman would by the end of the fourteenth century have been well acquainted with the Commandments and, in so far as he sought to lead a Christian life, would have governed his actions in accordance with them.

It seems reasonably clear that he was not, and did not, though this was not entirely the clergy's fault. If England is a good example, the evidence suggests that they had made an effort to do what was required of them but, faced with alternative moral systems, had found the Seven Sins more manageable for themselves and more persuasive to their hearers. Some authors of manuals followed Pecham's lead by giving roughly the same attention to the Sins and the Commandments; others left the discussion of the Commandments in a more or less elementary form, while they concentrated on elaborating and subdividing the Sins. By 1400 authors of the second type seem to have dominated the field, and the multiplying process had acquired a life of its own. They wrote in Latin; in vernacular works of the period, which were often in verse for memorizing, the Commandments played a modest role, the Sins a dominant one. This was still more the case in the writings of secular poets who wrote on or used the themes of the manuals: Langland, Chaucer, and Gower had a great deal to say about the Seven Sins (Chaucer, about 1390, concluded the *Canterbury Tales* with a straightforward exposition of them), but seem scarcely to have heard of the Commandments. It

[3] *Councils and Synods [of] the English Church, ii (1205–1313)*, ed. F. M. Powicke and C. R. Cheney (2 vols., Oxford, 1964), ii. pp. 900ff; also pp. 1059ff., and index under *Commandments*. D. L. Douie, *Archbishop Pecham* (Oxford, 1952), pp. 134, 138, 140f., 142; W. A. Pantin, *The English Church in the Fourteenth Century* (Cambridge, 1955), chaps. ix and x, and Appendix II. *The Lay Folks' Catechism*, ed. T. F. Simmons and H. E. Nolloth (Early English Text Society, o.s. vol. cxviii, London, 1901), contains the republication and vernacular translation of Pecham's instructions by Archbishop Thoresby of York in 1357.

was the same story, we are told, in Germany; in France, the (clumsier) equivalent of Pecham's corpus of Christian knowledge, a vernacular work of the late thirteenth century known as the *Somme-le-Roy*, was a compilation of the second type, where the precedence given to the Commandments was largely honorific. Chaucer's parson seems to have summed up the attitude of the fourteenth-century laity and their teachers when, after his painstaking account of the Seven Sins, he declared himself unable to expound the Commandments. 'So heigh a doctrine I lete to divines.'[4]

One of the reasons for this hiatus must be the dominant position occupied in the later medieval moral scene by the institution of sacramental penance. Pecham's instructions about the Command-ments were intended as part of a programme conveying general knowledge (as much to priests as to the laity), to be pursued by parish priests throughout the year; whether or not they were generally observed, they seem in any case rather remote from the crunch of a parishioner's moral experience, his annual confession before Easter. Until 1400 the general feeling was that, in communi-cations between the clergy and the laity directly related to confession – that is, in discussion or interrogation between the priest and penitent, and in the Lenten preaching which preceded it, not to mention the Carnival proceedings which often preceded that – the Commandments did not offer a very satisfactory alternative to the Sins.[5] Familiar, flexible, covering remedy as well as disease, the Sins were a more serviceable slate on which, guided by the priest, one might perform an annual calculation of the moral account or annual moral check-up; their prominence in the penitential season cast its shadow over the rest of the year.

---

[4] Pantin, pp. 225f.; note his doubt, concerning Henry of Lancaster, the one con-tributor to his series of vernacular writers who was neither a priest nor a pro-fessional author, 'whether he had ever heard of . . . Pecham's constitutions'. L. W. Spitz, 'Further lines of inquiry for the study of "Reformation and pedagogy" ', in H. A. Oberman and C. Trinkaus (eds.), *The Pursuit of Holiness in Late Mediaeval and Renaissance Religion* (Leiden, 1974), pp. 295ff.; citing work by 'Professor Oberlin of Strasburg' which I have not seen. For the *Somme-le-Roy*, see *D.T.C., s.v.* Catéchisme, col. 1900; there is an abstract of it in Ch. V. Langlois (ed.), *La Vie en France au moyen âge: iv, La Vie Spirituelle* (Paris, 1928), pp. 142–98. *The Works of Geoffrey Chaucer*, ed. F.N. Robinson (London, 1957), p. 260.

[5] This is my deduction from the discussion of confession manuals in P. Michaud-Quantin, *Sommes de casuistique et manuels de confession au moyen âge* (Louvain, etc., 1962), especially pp. 43, 49f. on the much-used *Confessionale* (*c.* 1295) of the Dominican John of Freiburg; also p. 66 (Italy); cf. Aston, 'The sin of idolatry', n. 9. For some contrary evidence, see Michaud-Quantin, pp. 54–7; *Councils and Synods*, pp. 1062ff. (Bishop Quivel or Quinel of Exeter, *c.* 1287). I am extremely grateful to my colleague Peter Biller for help with the subject of this and the previous note; he is not responsible for my conclusions.

Strictly in the field of expository teaching, too, there were difficulties about the Commandments, partly practical and partly theoretical. Even if one omits the elaborations, like those concerning the sabbath, the Commandments are rather a mouthful, and not easy to remember. As the sixteenth-century catechist Robert Bellarmine wisely remarked, it is difficult to remember more than seven of anything; it is particularly difficult, perhaps impossible, when the series is being conveyed by word of mouth.[6] Apart from their brevity, the Sins had the advantage of fitting into, the Commandments the disadvantage of disrupting, a whole string of septenary classifications: the seven Sacraments, the seven works of mercy, the seven petitions of the Paternoster, and so on. Teachers with a knowledge of their flocks were sensibly anxious to integrate their moral teaching as tightly as possible with these other *memoranda*, and though they sometimes overdid it, their concern was realistic. Finally, though it is not actually impossible to represent the Commandments visually, they lack the obvious facility with which the Sins could be represented in visual, symbolic, or allegorical form (for example, as animals).[7] This was an important matter when the visual image was a powerful teaching medium.

On the theoretical side the difficulties seem as follows. Since the Comandments were not, as such, binding upon Christians, it had to be explained why they were being taught. The theological explanation was that they were the elaboration, authorized (more or less) by Christ as recorded by St Matthew, of the two commandments of the Gospel.[8] The first table codified the obligations of the love of God, the second, the obligations of the love of your neighbour. This was Aquinas' view, and it had been followed by the thirteenth-century synods and fourteenth-century manuals, which had required people to learn these two commandments as well as the ten of the old law: this was confusing, and an additional strain on the memory. One way

---

[6] J.-C. Dhotel, *Les Origines du catéchisme moderne* (Paris, 1967), p. 37. For two examples of this, consider the 'hash' made by the author of the play of Christ and the Doctors in the Chester cycle (A. C. Cawley, 'Middle English versions of the Decalogue, with reference to the English Corpus Christi cycles', Leeds Studies in English, n.s. viii (1975), 140) when trying to cite the Commandments from memory: and Langland's (Latin) citation of the wrong one in *The Vision of Piers Plowman* (B-text, ed. A. V. C. Schmidt (London, 1978), Passus x, l. 364).
[7] Bloomfield, *The Seven Deadly Sins*, pp. 245–9; but cf. Cawley, n. 43, for a spirited set of Commandment windows in Ludlow parish church: 'a thief is quietly cutting the purse-strings of a man who gazes devoutly upon the words "Thou shalt not steal"'; other cases below, nn. 17 and 20.
[8] Matthew 19. 16–19, where Christ does not actually recommend the first table; 22. 35–40.

round the problem was to smuggle the two commandments of the Gospel into the Decalogue itself, by substituting them for the first two, or by otherwise juggling with the series. This was, eventually, the procedure of the authors of the mystery plays, when facing the problem of producing a version of the Commandments which could be expounded by the youthful Christ to the doctors in the temple, and properly contrasted with the original version which had already been proclaimed by Moses at the bottom of Mount Sinai. It was a respectable ambition to turn the Commandments into a Gospel of love, but without extremely skilful guidance the result was likely to be a muddle. Langland, who produced the Tables of the Law, but wrote upon them the Commandments of the Gospel, had a more convincing solution.[9] Finally, there was the problem that, in his Aristotelian mood, Aquinas had also held that the Commandments were a compendium of natural law having force prior to their enactment or to Christ's confirmation of them. Although this view was to be confirmed by the *Catechism of the Council of Trent*, it seems both theologically awkward and difficult to teach.[10] If we dismiss this as an excessively theoretical question, we may be doing an injustice to the intelligence, or at least to the argumentativeness, of late medieval audiences.

To sum up: besides the particular problems presented by certain items in the Decalogue, its diffusion as a generally accepted system of Christian ethics had been inhibited, during the thirteenth and fourteenth centuries, by the practice of the Sacrament of penance and by a number of practical and theoretical difficulties. Penitential arrangements and practical difficulties had led priests to prefer moral exposition according to the Seven Sins. The theoretical difficulties had led theologians, during the fourteenth century, to propose an alternative rationale.

Scholastic authorities after Aquinas found his attempted moral synthesis unconvincing, and were particularly offended by its naturalistic aspect. Scotus with caution, and William of Ockham with perfect confidence, concluded that it was an inadmissible interference with God's sovereignty and freedom to bind his decisions within a normative system of good which would need to be envisaged as somehow outside or apart from himself. If something

---

[9] *D.T.C., s.v.* Décalogue, col. 170; *Councils and Synods*, p. 903; Cawley, 129–45, a reference for which I am once more indebted to Margaret Aston; *Piers Plowman*, B-text, ed. Schmidt, Passus x, ll. 344–68, xvii, ll. 1–16, pp. 112f., 207f.

[10] *Catechism of the Council of Trent*, chap. 28, sections i–ii (I have used the French version of 1923, repr. Paris, 1969).

was good, or conducive to human salvation, it was because God had
sovereignly willed it so, not vice versa; he might have willed
differently from, or the opposite of, what he actually had willed.
Hence there was no method by which Christians could determine
what was good or bad, except by discovering what God had actually
commanded to be done or avoided. Ethics was a matter of faith, not
of reason.[11] This pointed to the Decalogue as the only comprehensive
moral code available to or authoritative for Christians, and not as a
summary of what was naturally so, but as a free, ungrounded,
specific expression of God's legislative will.

Ockham was not always the most acceptable of scholastic
authorities, but in this case the genuine force of his argument carried
the day, at least for the time being. By the end of the fourteenth
century he seems to have convinced most theologians who were not
constitutionally required to follow Aquinas (and some who were); in
particular he had converted the theology faculty of Paris, whose
dominant master towards the close of the century, Cardinal Pierre
d'Ailly, gave the doctrine the stamp of his authority, and passed it on
to his pupil Jean Gerson.[12]

Gerson, who was no friend to scholastic speculation as such, took
the doctrine not as a theoretical statement but as a charter for
pastoral activity; and since, at least in northern Europe, he was much
the most influential doctor of the Christian life during the century
before the Reformation, his was a conversion of importance. He was
not the first to write an extended commentary on the Commandments,
but the general agreement that he launched a new departure in the
teaching of Christianity seems well founded. He did this by treating
the Commandments as the rock of Christian ethics, by establishing a
tradition of effective vernacular exposition, and by integrating this
into a larger theological position and into a general scheme of
Catholic piety which included the practice of confession.

---

[11] F. C. Copleston, *A History of Philosophy*, ii (London, 1950), pp. 545–50 (Scotus); iii
(1953), pp. 103–10 (Ockham).
[12] *D. T. C.*, *s.v.* Gerson, cols. 1322–4, quoting D'Ailly: 'Nullum est ex se peccatum sed
praecise quia lege prohibitum.' Gerson, *Liber de vita spirituali animae*, *De consolatione
theologiae*, and *Regulae morales* in *Opera omnia*, ed L. Ellies du Pin (5 vols., Amsterdam,
*vere* Antwerp, 1706), cols. 13 (where he states the opinion as only 'probable', but
draws d'Ailly's conclusion above), 147; col. 78; cf. T. F. Tentler, *Sin and Confession on
the Eve of the Reformation* (Princeton, N.J., 1977), p. 146 (Gerson on mortal sins; and
see n. 16 below). Gerson did not identify God's commandments with the
Decalogue, but he obviously considered it the handiest compendium of them: cf.
the citation in H. A. Oberman, *The Harvest of Mediaeval Theology* (Cambridge, Mass.,
1963), p. 337, n. 46: 'Lex Christi sufficienter data est in praeceptis decalogi.'

Gerson's French expositions of the Commandments are contained in their simplest form in his *ABC des Simples Gens*, in their most extended form in the *Miroir de l'ame*, the first part of his guide to Christian piety, the *Opus tripartitum*, and in the versified version beginning 'Ung seul Dieu . . . '. All these were extremely popular and long-lived works, notably the last, which has had an extraordinarily long career in French catechetical teaching – not, admittedly, in Gerson's own form, which was somewhat cumbersome, but in the simpler form to which it had been reduced by the time it was printed in an encyclopedia of popular knowledge, the *Compost et kalendrier des Bergers*, in 1491. It had also by this time acquired a tune, and children learned it by singing it, which was rather a breakthrough.[13] Three characteristics of his exposition seem worth remark. First, he was concerned, even at the simplest level, to justify his scheme theologically: in the *ABC*, which actually begins with the Seven Sins, he explained that the Commandments (unlike the Sins, he silently implied) had been 'révélés de Dieu et monstrés clairement en la lumière de vraie foy dedans les âmes des saintes et dévotes personnes'. Second, his treatment of the text of the Commandments was fairly free: he made no mention of images whatever. It also differed in different versions. Thus the first commandment is, in the *ABC*, 'Tu n'adoreras non les ydoles ni plusieurs dieux'; in the *Miroir*, 'Tu aimeras Dieu de tout ton cuer'; in his own verse version, 'Ung seul Dieu de tout creatour / Croyras, craindras et serviras / Sur toutes choses nuyt et jour / T'amour, force et pansée mectras'; and in the version given in the *Compost*, 'Ung seul Dieu tu adoreras / Et aymeras parfaitement.'

His difficulties here are as obvious as everyone else's, but his solution was more elegant than most. By holding on to the scriptural text as far as possible, by renouncing the attempt to construct an alternative version, and by allowing the commandments of the Gospel (like those of the church, which I discuss below) to influence the text but not compete with it, he produced something coherent, persuasive, and reasonably memorable. The price to be paid for this, it seems to me, was that in his version the Decalogue retained somewhat the character of an Old Testament code. If not on fear, the stress seems finally to fall more upon worship than upon love.

[13] Gerson, *Oeuvres complètes*, ed. P. Glorieux (10 vols., Paris, 1960–73), vii (1966), pp. 154ff., 193ff., 423ff; *D.T.C.*, *s.v.* Décalogue, col. 173, *s.v.* Catéchisme, cols. 1902f; Dhotel, *Les Origines du catéchisme moderne*, p. 34. I have used the reprint of a late edition of the *Compost* (Troyes, *c.* 1520): *Le Grant kalendrier et compost des bergiers*, ed. B. Guégan (Paris, 1926).

His injunction, in the *Miroir de l'ame*, that the way to love God is to keep his Commandments seems to distribute the emphasis differently from Aquinas; his concluding statement that the Commandments *were* the mirror of the soul, which looks innocuous enough, turned out to have some alarming implications.[14]

There was also, for a Catholic expositor, the problem that the Commandments did not obviously impose any obligation of obedience to the instructions of the church about religious observance, on which legislation had been accumulating since the fourth Lateran Council of 1215. (This was, of course, also true of the Seven Sins, which treated this obligation rather unsatisfactorily under Sloth.) The Ockhamite position was usually that the church was the authoritative interpreter of divine commands, and that its own commands were to be treated as the commands of God. Gerson was not happy about this view, and made a strong distinction between divine commandments and human ones; one of his motives for sticking to the Decalogue was to inhibit an unauthorized multiplication of sins. He extracted a moderate doctrine of obedience to the church from the Commandments themselves, interpreting the fourth as a general commandment of obedience to spiritual and temporal authorities, and the third as a commandment to obey the church's instructions about Sundays and holy days.[15] But the stronger line prevailed after him, and it became the custom during the fifteenth century to stick to a fairly literal exposition of the Commandments, but to attach to them a series of additional commandments about religious observance which were described as the Commandments of the Church. In the *Compost et kalendrier des bergers* there were five of these, concerning Sunday observance, annual confession and communion, feast-days and fasting; they were embodied in five couplets which followed the ten of the Decalogue, and were stated to be equally binding; in transmitting Gerson's work to their clergy, French bishops often added them. This became

---

[14] *Oeuvres complètes*, vii, pp. 196, 203; cf. below, p. 231. I should say that Gerson did not abandon or, so far as I know, deprecate the use of the Seven Sins; the second part of the *Opus tripartitum* gives a method of confession according to them, and says that this is sufficient for the self-examination of the average person (cf. Tentler, *Sin and Confession*, pp. 137f., and 139, n.5). His method was to expound the Sins as sources of temptation to disobey the Commandments, a line followed in another popular compilation, the *Grand ordinaire des Chrétiens* (1464) (Dhotel, *Origines du catéchisme*, p. 36); or used in confessional enquiry about the circumstances of sin (Tentler, *Sin and Confession*, pp. 146f). He also preached at length on the Sins: *Oeuvres complètes*, vii, pp. 793–932. None of this seems to reduce the genuine originality of his scheme of popular moral instruction.

[15] *Opera omnia*, i., cols. 15ff.; *Oeuvres complètes*, vii, 197–9; Tentler, *Sin and Confession*, pp. 146f., 159.

standard procedure in the Catholic catechisms of the sixteenth century, though more of a distinction was usually made between the two sorts of commandments.[16] The Christian code was achieving a formidable comprehensiveness.

One region where Gerson's innovation proved decisive was Germany. Here, in the century between Gerson and Luther, there was a visible shift to the exposition of Christian behaviour through the Commandments. This was particularly true of the innumerable guides to confession which were composed, especially for children, during the period. The invention of the printing-press gave them a considerable boost, and they were perhaps one of the main driving-forces behind its diffusion: they were frequently illustrated. Gerson was translated, imitated, and expanded by a string of German disciples from the south German Dominican Johannes Nider (*Praeceptorium legis sive expositio decalogi, c.* 1440) to the secular preacher of Strasburg, Johann Geiler of Kaisersberg. Schemes for interrogating the laity at confession according to their observance of the Commandments came in all shapes and sizes, and modern scholars have commented, with reason, on the excessive character of many of them.[17]

Outside Germany the innovation met with much inertia and some opposition. In France Gerson's influence does not seem to have been dominant until the end of the century, when the *Opus tripartitum* began to get a sort of *imprimatur* from the bishops: the *Compost et kalendrier*, which included the versified Commandments, had also included a huge elaboration of the Seven Sins.[18] The great authority in Italy was St Antonino of Florence, a Thomist whose *Confessionale* and *Summa theologica*, where his moral doctrine was expounded, went

[16] *D.T.C.*, *s.v.* Commandements de l'Eglise, Catéchisme, cols. 1903–5; A. Villien, *Histoire des commandements de l'Eglise* (Paris, 1909), pp. 1–19; S. E. Ozment, *The Reformation in the Cities* (New Haven and London, 1975), p. 29. *The Table Talk of Martin Luther*, ed. J. Aurifaber, tr. W. C. Hazlitt (London, 1883), no. cccxliii recorded his gratitude to Gerson for teaching that it was *not* a mortal sin to neglect the Commandments of the Church.

[17] The essential work here is Johannes Geffcken, *Der Bilderkatechismus des fünfzehnten Jahrhunderts* (Leipzig, 1855); cf. Ozment, *Reformation in the Cities*, pp. 16–17, and woodcuts of the first two commandments reproduced from it in Aston, *Lollards and Reformers*, illustrations 12 and 13. For the general point, see Ozment, *Reformation in the Cities*, pp. 22–9; *D.T.C.*, *s.v.* Catéchisme, cols. 1905–6; Tentler, *Sin and Confession*, pp. 45, 145f., 159, 242 (Gerson and Nider); J. Connolly, *John Gerson, Reformer and Mystic* (Louvain, 1928), pp. 371–4 (Gerson, Nider, Geiler).

[18] J. Delumeau, *Le Péché et la peur* (Paris, 1983), p. 229 (this does not appear in the version of the *Compost* which I have used (n. 13 above); cf. Tentler, *Sin and Confession*, p. 132, for the two-page spread of the tree of sins in Jan Mombaer's influential *Rosetum*. Olivier Maillard (Tentler, *Sin and Confession*, p. 139) and the *Grand ordinaire des Chrétiens* (n. 14 above) seem to be Gersonian in this respect.

through innumerable editions. He gave the Commandments and the Sins equal time, but seems on the whole to have preferred the Sins; this was probably because he was much concerned with business morality, and found it simpler to expound this under Avarice, which he placed first.[19] Artists, who rarely found the Commandments much of an inspiration, depicted the Seven Sins with more vigour than ever before: the genre reached a climax in the early and mid sixteenth century in the Netherlands with Hieronymus Bosch, whose tableau of the Sins was used as a standing *memento* by Philip II of Spain, and the elder Bruegel.[20] In two countries with important unorthodox traditions, Bohemia and England, there was actual opposition to the Commandments, though for opposite reasons. The dissident Czech Unity of Brothers rejected the Old Testament as a moral authority altogether, as they rejected the death penalty in secular law, as breathing a spirit of vengeance incompatible with Christian brotherhood.[21] Their example was to be followed among the English sectarians of the seventeenth century, but at the time the ethical scene in England was dominated by the assertions of John Wycliffe and the Lollards. These affirmed the absolute supremacy of a textually complete version of the Commandments, interpreted with particular reference to the prohibition of idolatry, images, and the veneration of saints. The orthodox reaction of the fifteenth century consequently identified the teaching of the Commandments in English with heretical opinions, and it seems to have remained in bad odour almost until the Reformation. The substantial orthodox exposition of the Commandments, *Dives and Pauper*, written in the 1400s, was honest enough about difficulties to be thought heretical by some, and founded no tradition; nor did the acerbic Reginald Pecock, who disapproved of both the Sins and the Commandments and tried to establish a system of his own. On the eve of the Reformation, the moral universe represented by pillars of orthodoxy like Sir Thomas More and the Scottish poet William Dunbar was still the universe of the Seven Sins, which indeed still

[19] Bloomfield, *The Seven Deadly Sins*, p. 91; Delumeau, *Le Péché et la peur*, pp. 246, 260; Ozment, *Reformation in the Cities*, p. 24. I have used the edition of the *Confessionale* (Paris: Jean Petit, n.d.) bound with Nider's *De lepra morali* (? Paris, Raulin Gautier, s.d.) and other works in Bodleian Douce C.76.

[20] Delumeau, *Le Péché et la peur*, pp. 265ff.; cf. Spitz, in *The Pursuit of Holiness* (n. 4 above), p. 298, for illustrations of the Commandments by Baldung Grien and Cranach, and n. 17 above.

[21] P. Brock, *The Political and Social Doctrines of the Unity of Czech Brethren* (The Hague, 1957), pp. 86, 89.

had some life in them in the Elizabethan age. The Reformer Hugh Latimer was probably right in suggesting that the average unreformed English layman knew no other system.[22]

Hence it is not quite true that the Reformation introduced the Commandments as the effective moral system of Christianity; what is true is that its insistence on a scriptural ethics caused all resistance to collapse. Luther himself was a surprising vehicle for this triumph, since he might more naturally have fitted among the resisters. A child of late-medieval Catholicism, he had grown up with the Commandments, and the hardening of Christian moral obligations which they represented was certainly something to do with the panic about salvation which dogged his earlier years. In his interpretation of St Paul's Epistle to the Romans he took the view, against Erasmus and medieval tradition, that in rejecting 'the works of the law' as a means of salvation, the apostle had not only been excluding Jewish ritual practices, but Jewish moral law as well. Nonetheless in his teaching he continued to use them, and in roughly the form which Gerson had transmitted to the Germans; in his paradoxical or dialectical way he managed to give them even greater prominence by arguing that, in their function not of saving the soul but of revealing sin (as in Gerson's mirror) they were a necessary preliminary to the knowledge of Grace provided by the Creed, the Lord's Prayer, and the Sacraments. They *must*, therefore, in any programme of basic Christian teaching, be inculcated first; this was the method of his own classic catechisms, and of all subsequent Lutheran examples. In his attitude to their content he resembled Gerson in explaining that they were to instill the love as well as the fear of God (he concealed from German children, though others did not, his conviction that they were impossible to fulfil), and in his free treatment of the scriptural text. He differed, not so much from Gerson as from his German Catholic followers, in the simplicity, warmth, and positive direction he gave them. He also differed by clearing away as rubbish all alternative or additional systems: from a very early date, perhaps from before his breach with Rome, he had abandoned the Seven

[22] Aston, *Lollards and Reformers*, especially pp. 147–8, 208, 210; J. A. F. Thomson, *The Later Lollards, 1414–1520* (London, 1965), pp. 74f., 116, 126, 162, 245; *Dives and Pauper*, ed. P. H. Barnum (part 1, Early English Text Society, no. 275, London, 1976), especially pp. 54f., 65f.; Bloomfield, *The Seven Deadly Sins*, pp. 224–6 (Pecock) and notes (n. 162 for Latimer), 236, 240; William Dunbar, 'The Dance of the Seven Deadly Sins', in *The Poems of William Dunbar*, ed. W. McKay Mackenzie (Edinburgh 1932), pp. 120–3, and cf. pp. 163–7.

Sins, and the Commandments of the Church were, in effect, translated into commandments of secular authority.[23]

Luther's attitude to the Commandments was therefore scriptural but not textual. In this he differed from most other Reformers, including his disciple William Tyndale, who conveyed his gospel to the English. Tyndale believed (like Aquinas) that the Commandments were the 'law natural', and (like the Lollards) that they were the essential item in the written communications from God to man which, against More, he considered the only reliable vehicle of truth. He launched the process whereby, from 1547 onwards, the Commandments in their extended, textual form became for the English one of the three requisites of Christian knowledge. In practice they achieved a pre-eminence over the Creed and the Lord's Prayer by being painted up, in all their admonitory fulness, above the denuded altars of English churches, dramatically replacing the Host, lights, images, and sacramental paraphernalia of the old regime. There, until the nineteenth century, as Thomas Hardy put it in *Jude the Obscure*, 'the tables of the Jewish Law towered sternly over the utensils of Christian grace'.[24] Considering the previous history of the Commandments in England, this was a traumatic shift, and I doubt if it did English Christianity much good. By this time, furthermore, the scholarship of Bucer and Calvin had determined that the Greek tradition of numbering was more authoritative than Augustine's: hence the prohibition of graven images now stood out nakedly as the first consequent of the prohibition of worshipping false gods. The first table had achieved an extra commandment and, at least in wording to be remembered, primacy over the second.

Faced by this scriptural onslaught, and already half-converted anyway, the Church of Rome finally went over to its own version of the Commandments as the sole vehicle of its moral teaching. In

[23] G. Strauss, *Luther's House of Learning* (Baltimore and London, 1978), pp. 151–75, 203–14; and his 'Reformation and Pedagogy', in *The Pursuit of Holiness*, pp. 290ff. Luther, 'Autobiographical fragment' and 'The Freedom of a Christian', in *Martin Luther: Selections from his Writings*, ed. J. Dillenberger (Garden City, N.Y., 1961), pp. 10f. (*justitia Dei*), 57; Letter to George Spalatin, 19 October 1516, in *Luther's Works*, ed. J. Pelikan and H. T. Lehmann (55 vols., Philadelphia, 1955– ), vol. xlviii, pp. 23f. (Luther and Erasmus: for the mediaeval tradition on this point, see Oberman, *Harvest of Mediaeval Theology*, pp. 113–19); *Shorter Catechism* (1529), in *Documents of the Continental Reformation*, ed. B. J. Kidd (Oxford, 1914; repr. 1967), pp. 209–11; Spitz, in *The Pursuit of Holiness*, p. 296.

[24] Here, and in particular for the last quotation (*Jude the Obscure*, part V, section 6), I am dependent on Aston, 'The sin of idolatry' ('Catechizing and the Decalogue'); Thomas More, *The Confutation of Tyndale's Answer*, i (1532), in *The Complete Works of St Thomas More*, viii, part 1 (New Haven and London, 1973), e.g. pp. 5, 273f.

England, in the reign of Queen Mary, Bishop Bonner even adopted the reformed numbering in his attempt to reconvert the English to Catholicism; though I do not think anyone else went as far as that, the *Catechism of the Council of Trent* (1566) endorsed the view that the Decalogue comprehended the entire moral obligation of Christians. This view governed the structure of Catholic catechisms thereafter: earlier attempts, like those of Peter Canisius in Germany, had kept a place for the Seven Sins, but from now on it became a mere vestige. For Catholics as for Protestants, the age of catechism was an age of the Commandments.[25]

In sketching some historical consequences of this event, we can distinguish between the consequences of adopting as a moral system any particular version of the Commandments, and the consequences of adopting the Commandments in general. Under the first heading we can put the effect of the separation of the ban on images as a second commandment in inspiring in Reformed enthusiasts the iconoclastic passion which, so far as it could, destroyed a whole epoch of European visual culture; and also the interpretation of the third/fourth commandment as a charter for strict sabbatarianism, which came to characterize the Calvinist tradition from the close of the sixteenth century. I shall take such particular consequences for granted, as I shall the extremely general consequences of the transition from the Seven Sins which have already been mentioned: the supremacy of the first table over the second, the characterization of Christian behaviour as obedience to the commands of the Divine Legislator, and the primacy of explicitly verbalized over other forms of moral awareness. Between the two, there seems to be an area where some concrete effects of the transition from the moral universe of the Sins to that of the Commandments can be detected. I choose one from each table.

It was a universal consequence of Decalogue ethics to treat idolatry, or false worship or 'religion', as the primary offence of Christians, and other offences as contingent upon that: this was as true of Gerson as of the Reformers. Among the consequences of the adoption of an ethics founded on worship was a change in the status of the Devil. Under the old moral regime the Devil had been an anti-type of Christ, teaching universal hatred where Christ taught love: he was the Fiend. Under the new regime he became the anti-type of

[25] Aston, 'The sin of idolatry', citing Edmund Bonner, *A profitable and necessary doctrine* (1554); *Catechism of the Council of Trent*, part iii; Dhotel, *Les Origines du catéchisme moderne*, pp. 70–3, and cf. pp. 18f.

the Father, the source and object of idolatry and false worship. Norman Cohn has remarked that in the course of the fifteenth century the Devil acquired in the popular mind a grandeur and formidable character which he had not hitherto possessed, and I doubt if we need to look much beyond the Gersonian reform of ethics to explain why this enhancement occurred. The most obvious effect of the new dispensation was a change, universally recognized to have occurred during the fifteenth century, in the character attributed to the offence of witchcraft. Under the regime of the Sins, witchcraft had been the offence of causing by occult means malicious harm to the body or goods of one's neighbour or, in the more sensational cases, of procuring the death of political enemies by such means; in Chaucer's exposition it was dealt with, rather loosely, under Wrath. In the new regime it was an offence against the first commandment, that is, an offence of false worship inferior, in Gerson's *Miroir*, only to heresy and idolatry.[26] The developments which inspired the early-modern witch-craze – the attribution of all occult effects, except those produced by the rituals of the church, to a pact between the offender and the Devil, and the erection of a towering superstructure identifying the witch as a practitioner of Devil-worship – were a lurid elaboration of this original step. the more the Commandments became established as the reigning system of Christian ethics, the more persuasive the spell of the witch-syndrome proved.

This is, I think, a novel view of the subject, but three pieces of evidence can be cited in favour of it. *First*: it has been long recognized that a decision of the theological faculty of the University of Paris in 1398 had an important effect in launching the judicial persecution of witches, in particular their pursuit by inquisitors concerned with heresy. The decision put a sharp edge on an opinion which had been held or implied by theologians since Aquinas, as part of a more general truth about superstition, and embodied in the teaching of the Commandments, without being given much precision or regarded as a charter for action. It arose from a case where a group of people had performed a spirit-raising ritual in order to find some buried treasure, and stated that such behavour, all strictly maleficent witchcraft, and all seemingly beneficent counter-witchcraft were to be treated as idolatrous, since they entailed,

---

[26] N. Cohn, *Europe's Inner Demons* (London, 1975), pp. 232f.; Gerson, *Oeuvres complètes*, vii, pp. 195, 196.

explicitly or implicitly, apostasy from the Christian faith and an agreement to serve the Devil. As Chancellor of the University, Gerson presided over the meeting which came to the decision; as such he appears at the beginning of it, and I think it is clear that he wrote it himself.[27] *Second*: the intellectual fathers of the witch-syndrome seem to be found among Gerson's German disciples. Johannes Nider, the most faithful of them, was the first to collect empirical evidence about the doings of witches, in his *Formicarius* of *c.* 1435; he passed the habit on to his fellow Dominicans, the authors of the *Malleus Maleficarum*.[28] *Third*: it is not difficult to detect Gerson's sequence of thought still actively present behind the moral engineering attempted in Lutheran catechisms. Here is the Nuremberg Reformer Andreas Osiander, *Catechismus oder Kinderpredig* (1533): the Decalogue is the beginning of wisdom, because it shows us sin ('as in a polished mirror', another Lutheran catechist put it); sin is rebellion against the word of God (i.e. the Decalogue); those who disobey the law get a bad conscience and go into a decline; the Devil tempts them, 'and from this temptation follow idolatry, sorcery, heresy and error'; the multitude of such persons creates a population riddled with envy, hatred, slander, murder, and so on. Here moral instruction according to the Commandments, designed expressly for children, brought the new-model witch on to the scene at a very early stage in moral indoctrination: he (or more usually she) was a type of disobedience to God, surrender to Satan, idolatry, and false religion, and all this prior to the production of any maleficent

---

[27] *Chartularium universitatis Parisiensis*, ed. H. Denifle and E. Chatelain (4 vols., Paris, 1891–9; repr. Brussels, 1964), iv, pp. 32–6; cf. R. Kieckhefer, *European Witchtrials: their Foundations in Popular and Learned Culture, 1300–1500* (London, 1976), p. 22. Besides Gerson's presence as 'cancellarius Parisiensis' in the text, and the content of the decision itself, there is a sign of Gerson's authorship in the silent emendation of a quotation from St Jerome to show that a quotation which Jerome himself was using was actually from Horace (*Chartularium*, p. 35, n. 3). There is a commentary on the decision by Gerson in *Oeuvres Complètes*, x (1973), pp. 77–86. For the history of the idea, see J.-B. Thiers, *Traité des superstitions qui regardent tous les sacremens* (4 vols., Paris, 1704 edition), i, pp. 3–7, 79ff.; H. C. E. Midelfort, *Witch-hunting in South-West Germany* (Stanford, Cal., 1972), p. 17f.

[28] I can find no evidence of Gerson's influence in the *Formicarius* (Douai, 1602 edition consulted), where the main modern authority is Aquinas; but in both the *Praeceptorium* (Nuremberg, 1496 edition) and *De lepra morali* there is a crucial citation of Gerson on the idea of 'contempt of God'; H. C. Lea, *Materials towards a History of Witchcraft* (3 vols., New York and London, 1957), i, pp. 260–72, prints extracts from the *Formicarius* and *Praeceptorium*. Kieckhefer, *European Witchtrials*, pp. 20, 23, 81f.; C. Ginzburg, *I Benandanti: Stregoneria e culti agrari tra Cinquecento e Seicento* (Turin, 1974 edition), pp. 66–9; E. Delaruelle, *L'Eglise au temps du Grand Schisme et de la crise conciliaire* (Fliche-Martin, *Histoire de l'Eglise*, vol. xiv, part 2, Paris, 1964), p. 833.

effects.[29] Luther's moral strategy had only given theological or psychological foundation to what had happened in practice under Gerson's fifteenth-century scheme; it is no surprise that Lutherans were persuaded of the reality of the fearful images revealed in Gerson's mirror. The geographical extension of the witch-syndrome, which captured the imagination in Germany and France while failing to make much headway in, say, England or Spain, surely points rather strongly to the effect of Gerson.[30]

The exposition of the second table was a less controversial matter than that of the first, and for the most part entailed only a rearrangement of the moral teaching conveyed by the Seven Sins. The exception was the first item in the table, the commandment to honour one's father and mother, for this introduced an obligation which had not received much notice in the exposition of the Sins. Under Lechery, much had been made of the obligations of wives and husbands, albeit of a fairly crude kind; very little had been made of the mutual obligations of children and parents. There is indeed probably a case to be made out that the transition to the Commandments had an important effect in helping to fix the notion of childhood in the European mind: it is at least extremely interesting that Gerson should be a principal figure in the 'discovery' of childhood attributed by Philippe Ariès to the fifteenth century, and that Luther should have discovered an exceptional talent in the Christian instruction of children. Here I shall evade the temptations of the history of childhood, and stick to that of parenthood. Exponents of the Commandments generally held that the fourth/fifth had in the second table the same kind of primacy as the first in the first table; hence, as Luther said, it was to be regarded as the corner-stone of the entire edifice of Christian social obligation. The *Catechism of the Council of Trent*, though more sensitive to

[29] Strauss, *Luther's House of Learning*, pp. 209–10; Aston, 'The sin of idolatry', demonstrates the direct succession of teaching on this point from the fourteenth century to Luther and other Reformers; she also shows that the effect of renumbering the Commandments was to divert attention somewhat from witch-idolatry to image-idolatry (see especially n. 186). It seems to me extremely likely that there is a connection between the sensitivity of late-medieval Commandment-teaching about images and the cultivation of the witch-syndrome: I mean that people found it awkward to talk about images and talked about witches instead.

[30] From the description of the first English witchcraft statute (1542) given in K. Thomas, *Religion and the Decline of Magic* (London, 1971 edition), p. 525, it looks as if whoever drafted it was familiar with the Sorbonne decision of 1398: note the reference to buried treasure. For the development of the doctrine in England, see ibid., pp. 521ff.

the empirical likelihood of conflict between the commands of parents and those of God, took substantially the same view. Obedience to parents and other authorities, though in itself a lesser obligation than those of the first table, was in a special way the symbol of obedience to the first commandment; the promise of eternal life was attached to it. In a startling addition to the Gospel, the *Catechism* enquired rhetorically how, if we do not duly honour our parents, whom we see continually, we shall honour God, the supreme Father, whom we do not see? It would have been hard to state more clearly than this a moral transition from fraternity to paternity.[31]

Gerson, Luther, and the authors of the Roman Catechism may be thought to be professionals of morality, whose thoughts were of little relevance to the rest of mankind. To suggest that this is not so, I conclude with two examples of sixteenth-century men to whom the objection cannot apply. One is a great figure in the intellectual history of Europe; the other a modest contemporary living in a remote part of northern Italy, unknown until rescued from oblivion a few years ago.

Since Jean Bodin, born in Angers in 1529 or 1530, grew up under the wing of the bishop of that city, he must surely have been weaned on Gerson's version of the Commandments; by his maturity he had developed a cult of them, as God's supreme law, so intense as apparently to have converted him from Catholicism to Judaism. For present purposes this had two important consequences. The first was the structure of political and moral obligation expounded in the *Six Livres de la République* (1576), and the second was the theory of witchcraft described in the *Démonomanie des Sorciers* (1580). His commonwealth was a morally imperative system consisting of a single, irresistible, inviolable sovereign legislator governing a corpus of families ruled by the equally imperative authority of the *paterfamilias*. I am persuaded by the suggestion that the model for this construction was the two tables of the Decalogue, though Bodin avoided presenting it as such and thus established his position as the founder of modern political thought. In the *Démonomanie* he took as self-evident the view that witchcraft meant idolatry, and therefore accepted as compelling the evidence for diabolic worship among witches which had been accumulating since the time of the *Malleus Maleficarum*; he insisted on the binding character of the Old

---

[31] P. Ariès, *Centuries of Childhood* (London, 1962), pp. 106ff. for Gerson; *The Table Talk of Martin Luther*, p. 157; *Catechism of the Council of Trent*, chap. 32, introduction.

Testament command to put them to death.[32] By this time, most human legislators had come to agree with the divine legislator on the subject.

The second example is the Friulian miller Domenico Scandella *alias* Menocchio, burned as a relapsed heretic in 1600, the story of whose encounters with the Roman Inquisition has recently been written by Carlo Ginzburg. In the course of his interrogation in 1584, Menocchio had expressed a number of opinions taken by his inquisitor as contrary to Catholic orthodoxy. Among them was the view that blasphemy was not a serious sin. He defended his opinion on the grounds, in effect, that Christian ethics consisted in the avoidance of the Seven Sins, and that the object of this code was the love of one's neighbour; offences against God were a less serious matter than offences against your neighbour, since they could be forgiven by simple contrition, while offences against your neighbour called for a tiresome process of penance, compensation, or resti- tution. The inquisitor then asked him whether he knew the Com- mandments; he said he had never heard of them. Since he had been born in the 1530s, at a time when in Italy the tradition of the Seven Sins was still in possession of the moral field and the catechisms of the Counter-Reformation had not yet been composed, this was quite probably true. On the other hand, he knew very well the two commandments of the Gospel, so it may be that he did know the Decalogue but, with good Christian tradition behind him, rejected its authority.[33] In either case he is a witness to a moral transition of considerable historical significance, and (though he had other dif- ficulties with post-Reformation Catholicism) might even be claimed as a martyr to it.

[32] Christopher Baxter, 'Jean Bodin's *De la Démonomanie des Sorciers*: the logic of persecution', in S. Anglo (ed.), *The Damned Art* (London, 1977), pp. 76–105; Bodin, *Six Books of the Commonwealth*, abridged and tr. by M. J. Tooley (Oxford, n.d.), pp. 1–36, especially pp. 12, 36. Bodin placed at the beginning of his *Démonomanie* the Sorbonne decision of 1398. On the death penalty, compare the views of the Unity of Brothers: n. 21 above.

[33] C. Ginzburg, *The Cheese and the Worms* (London, 1980), pp. 37–40, 88f.

# 8

◁ ══════════════════════════════════════════════ ▷

## Optics and sceptics: the philosophical foundations of Hobbes's political thought

### RICHARD TUCK

When moral philosophers at the end of the seventeenth century began for the first time to write the history of their discipline, they accepted as self-evident a particular account of the origins of a modern 'science of morality'. According to Jean Barbeyrac, the most systematic and interesting of these writers, all moral philosophy up to the time of Hugo Grotius had been almost worthless. Aristotle, the most influential classical writer on ethics, had contaminated the subject by his unsystematic and local opinions about such things as the virtues and the possibility of natural slavery; Cicero's *De officiis* was the best ancient ethical treatise, but even that was flawed in many ways. The Church Fathers were equally unsatisfactory, while the medieval scholastics produced a confused mix of Aristotelian ideas. But once Hugo Grotius 'broke the ice', a true science of morality became possible, and his insights were exploited and systematized by a number of followers: John Selden, Thomas Hobbes, Richard Cumberland, and finally Samuel Pufendorf and John Locke. By a 'science' of morality, these historians of course understood an *episteme* – a systematic body of knowledge deduced from a set of necessary principles.[1]

This is on the surface a strange history, and it has usually been disregarded by modern (i.e. post-Kantian) historians of the subject (I myself in my *Natural Rights Theories* thought it clearly mistaken in some fundamental matters).[2] It is not, in fact, as odd as it might

---

[1] The first statement of this history that I know of was by Samuel Pufendorf in his *Specimen Controversiarum circa Jus Naturale ipsi nuper Motarum* (Lund, 1678). Barbeyrac's account forms the preface to his translation of Pufendorf's *De Iure Naturae et Gentium* into French (Paris, 1709), and was translated into English as *A Historical and Critical Account of the Science of Morality*, as a preface to the fifth English language edition of Pufendorf (London, 1749).

[2] R. Tuck, *Natural Rights Theories* (Cambridge, 1979), p. 176.

seem. Barbeyrac made clear why he thought no true science of morality had been possible until Grotius when he took, in the introduction to his *History*, the late sixteenth-century French writer Pierre Charron as the figure whose views had to be repudiated if a moral science was to be established – for Charron was the most thoughtful and coherent modern *sceptic*. What Barbeyrac and the others had perceived was that there was no self-conscious and high-level reply to the ethical sceptic before the early seventeenth century: no classical text survives in which a representative of another school formally and effectively answers the Pyrrhonian or Academic sceptic; and no medieval writers (not even the Ockhamists) took classical scepticism seriously as something to be either advocated or attacked. But Grotius *did* take it seriously, and so (in other fields) did most of the interesting philosophers of the seventeenth century. If a 'science of morality' was made such by the effectiveness of its answer to the sceptic, then indeed there was no such thing until the early seventeenth century.

Moreover, the post-Grotian part of this history is also plausible. The connection between Grotius and Pufendorf is clear and well known; but it is striking how many of Hobbes's early opponents took it as obvious that he and Grotius were engaged in the same enterprise.[3] Modern writers on Hobbes have to some degree lost this sense; Hobbes is commonly seen as creating some new science of the moral world, intimately linked to his metaphysics. What I intend to do in this chapter is to restore the seventeenth-century view of Hobbes as, to some extent, a philosophical associate of Grotius. Both were members of a group whose common concern was a philosophically sensitive response to the scepticism of both classical antiquity and modern Europe. In this chapter I shall concentrate on Hobbes; in another and related paper I have attempted to give a fuller account of Grotius' work than is possible here.[4]

If the late seventeenth- and early eighteenth-century account of the history of morality is true, then we can see more clearly the character of the relationship between the 'modern' moral science based on a set of natural laws, and its scholastic predecessor within which most casuistical discussion of moral issues took place. There is a critical break in the history of a scientific and systematic

---

[3] See e.g. Robert Filmer, both in *Patriarcha* and in *Observations Concerning the Originall of Government* (in P. Laslett, ed., *Patriarcha and Other Political Works of Sir Robert Filmer* (Oxford, 1949)), and Roger Coke, *Justice vindicated from the false focus put upon it by Thomas White Gent., Mr. Thomas Hobbes, and Hugo Grotius* (London, 1661).

[4] R. Tuck, 'Grotius, Carneades and Hobbes', *Grotiana*, new series 4 (1983), 43–62.

approach to ethical matters, signalled by the emergence of a tradition which took the avowedly anti-scientific and sceptical views of some Renaissance humanists seriously. The similarity in (some) terminology and (some) issues between late medieval Aristotelians and seventeenth-century natural law writers should not blind us to the absolutely crucial differences.

Let us begin not from any major text of Hobbes, but from one of the most familiar, though usually overlooked, facts about his biography. Between 1628 and 1651, the years which on any account (except the Straussian) were formative in his intellectual development, he spent only six years in England. The remaining seventeen were spent largely in France, and particularly (from 1634 onwards) in Paris. In Paris, as he himself freely confessed in his two Latin autobiographies, the centre of his intellectual life was the household of Marin Mersenne, where his closest associate seems to have been the philosopher Pierre Gassendi.[5] Hobbes's philosophy belongs as much or more to the intellectual history of France as to that of England, and if we are to look anywhere for its origins, it must be in the Mersenne circle. Mersenne encouraged the publication of *De Cive*, the first theoretical work of Hobbes to appear in print, in 1642, while Hobbes's general philosophy in fact first appeared in print in the form of a treatise on optics printed in Mersenne's *Ballistica* of 1644 and a report by Mersenne about his theories in the preface to that work.

The role of Mersenne has often been misunderstood in histories of the period. He has been described, for example, as 'the heart of the contemporary republic of letters',[6] with the implication that he had a kind of eclectic interest in talent; and certainly, his championship of the apparently diverse figures of Hobbes, Gassendi, and Descartes seems to point that way. However, Mersenne appears to have had a definite programme in view, and his adoption and publication of these three philosophers (and of other more minor figures) was part of that programme. It was adumbrated in 1625, when he published *La Verité des Sciences. Contre les Sceptiques ou Pyrrhoniens.* That work was an attempt at a refutation of the various arguments advanced by the sceptics of both the ancient and modern worlds in order to show the

[5] Hobbes, *Latin Works*, ed. W. Molesworth (London, 1839–1845), I, pp. xiv–xv, xc–xci.
[6] W. von Leyden, *Seventeenth-Century Metaphysics* (Oxford, 1968), p. 38, quoting Baillet's *Life of Descartes*. There are useful accounts of Mersenne in R. Pintard, *Le Libertinage erudit* (Paris, 1943), pp. 348ff., and in the incomparable study of this whole area, R. H. Popkin, *The History of Scepticism from Erasmus to Spinoza* (Berkeley, 1979), pp. 130–41.

indeterminate character of human knowledge, a refutation which took the arguments seriously and sought to meet the sceptics on their own ground. Mersenne perceived that almost all the basic arguments in favour of scepticism depended on some claim about the fallibility of the senses, and in particular, he observes, 'virtually all of them depended on Optics';[7] it was the fallibility of the sense of sight, the 'noblest' of the senses, which gave force to the sceptics' case.

Mersenne made no attempt to defend the non-illusory character of perception; instead, he argued that each science had at its heart a set of *a priori* principles which were indisputable and upon which a science could be based despite the inadequacy of the senses. This was true even of physics.

> Physics, which seems to be one of the sciences most infected by doubt, has its known subject-matter: for who can deny that there are bodies and motions? Are there not light, quantities, causes, and a thousand other things which are available to the senses, and of which Physics treats? It does not matter that there are such different opinions concerning the principles of nature, for all contain something true, even though they have not considered all the causes, circumstances and effects.[8]

It was even true of Ethics – 'just as it is true that *a material body is mobile*, . . . it is no less true that *evil is to be avoided, and good sought*, whatever the character of good and evil are taken to be'.[9] Although Mersenne failed to go deeply into the nature of these *a priori* principles and to discuss how they could be used as the basis of a recognizable science, he had promulgated a programme for the refutation of scepticism which *accepted* the basic sceptical arguments and then sought to transcend them. Descartes, Gassendi, and – I shall argue – Hobbes were all recruited into this campaign, since

---

[7] 'Ce 6. fondement, aussi bien que les precedens, & presque tous les autres, dependent de l'Optique.' M. Mersenne, *La Verité des Sciences. Contre les Septiques [sic] ou Pyrrhoniens* (Paris, 1625), p. 148.

[8] 'La Physique laquelle semble entre la plus douteuse, a son object cognu, car qui peut nier qu'il n'y ait des corps, & des mouvements? n'y a-il pas de la lumiere, des quantites, des causes, & mille autres choses, qui tombent sous les sens, desquelles elle traicte? N'importe qu'il y ait tant de diverses opinions touchant les principes de la nature, car tous ont secu quelque choses de veritable, bien qu'ils n'ont pas considere toutes les causes, les circonstances, & les effets.' Ibid., p. 54.

[9] 'car s'il est vray que *corpus naturale mobile est*; . . . il n'est pas moins veritable que *malum fugiendum, & bonum amplectendum . . .*'. Ibid., p. 56. This account of Mersenne is based very much on his *La Verité des Sciences*; elsewhere, as Popkin (p. 137) points out, Mersenne has less confidence in the possibility of a prioristic science. But it was notorious among his friends that he both respected the sceptical arguments and disliked the conclusions, an attitude which he appears to have shared with Descartes, Gassendi, and Hobbes. See Popkin, p. 138.

each seemed to provide both, in general, an answer of this kind to scepticism (though, of course, a different one in each case), and, in particular, a new theory of optics which did the work Mersenne expected. Moreover, Mersenne seems not to have been mistaken in his sense of their work: each of them as far as we can now tell *did* share his ambitions.

The character of the scepticism which seemed so potent a movement in the early seventeenth century is (as Barbeyrac observed) best illustrated in Pierre Charron's best-selling *Of Wisdom*. This first appeared in French in 1601, and was reissued at least twelve times between 1601 and 1663; it was soon translated into English, and ran through eight editions between 1608 and 1670. There were important elements of this scepticism present from the very beginnings of the Renaissance, but it was Montaigne and Charron who were generally seen as the originators of modern scepticism, and Charron who came closest to defining a sceptical system.

The essence of this modern scepticism was firstly its anti-Aristotelian character. Aristotelian physics worked on the assumption that entities in nature possessed real properties which could be seen veridically by a human observer. In the *De anima*, for example, Aristotle argued that we simply cannot be mistaken in our perceptions, at least to a degree– it must be the case that something is white if it appears to us to be white. [10] A common-sense view of the world was thus at the heart of Aristotelian physics, as well as expressed in such things as its cosmology, and it was precisely this view which scepticism put under suspicion. Charron said of Aristotle that he 'hath uttered more grosse absurdities than [all philosophers], and is at no agreement with himself, neither doth he know many times where he is; witnesse his Treatises of the Soule of man, of the Eternitie of the world, of the Generation of winds and waters, and so forth . . .'. [11] The sceptics were in the vanguard of late sixteenth-century anti-Aristotelianism.

In place of Aristotle's account of perception as the reception by sense organs of a veridical representation of the thing perceived (like a piece of wax receiving the imprint of a seal), Charron insisted on the relativity of perception. 'The eie pressed downe and shut, seeth otherwise than in ordinary state; the eare stopt, receiveth the objects otherwise than when it is open: an infant seeth, knoweth, tasteth,

[10] Aristotle, *De anima* 418a11–16. See W. K. C. Guthrie, *A History of Greek Philosophy*, VI (Cambridge, 1981), pp. 294–5.
[11] P. Charron, *Of Wisdome* (London, n.d. (before 1612)), sig. a7v.

otherwise than a man; a man than an olde man; a sound than a sicke; a wise than a foole. In this great diversitie and contrarietie what shall we hold for certain?' [12] He recognized that perception was modified by the understanding; but the understanding for him was enmeshed in the material substance of a man's body (though he was careful to avoid saying that there was no incorporeal soul) and influenced by all the organic changes that came over it. Moreover, it was an uncontrolled and uncontrollable power. He mocked the conventional picture of man's spirit, and the notion that

there is nothing great upon the earth but man, nothing great in man but his spirit; if a man ascend to it, he ascendeth above the heavens. These are all pleasing and plausible words whereof the Schooles do ring. But I desire that after all this we come to sound and to study how to know this spirit, for wee shall finde after all this, that it is both to it selfe and to another a dangerous instrument, a ferret that is to be feared, a little trouble-feast, a tedious and importunate parasite, and which as a Iugler and plaier at fast and loose, under the shadow of some gentle motion, subtile and smiling, forgeth, inventeth, and causeth all the mischiefs of the world: and the truth is, without it there are none. [13]

Because of this, according to the sceptic, there was no criterion available to determine which perception of the world was the correct one. So the right course of action for the wise man was to suspend judgment. It is important to stress that this suspension of judgment followed from the assumption that *in principle* one view of the world was correct; but which one it was was indeterminate. The sceptic did not deny that knowledge of the world would take the form of a veridical perception, to be distinguished from a false perception, but simply denied that we can know that we know. As Charron said,

veritie is not a thing of our owne invention and purchase, and when it yeelds it selfe into our hands, we have nothing in our selves whereby we may challenge it, possesse it, or assure our selves of it; That truth and falsehood enter into us by one and the same gate, and there hold the same place and credit, and maintaine themselves by the same meanes; That there is no opinion held by all, or currant in all places, none that is not debated and disputed, that hath not another held and maintained quite contrarie unto it . . . [14]

The same suspension of judgment was called for in ethics and politics. There is an enormous variety of moral beliefs, and we cannot tell which is correct, so the wise man will not choose his actions according to some universal canon of rectitude but will use a lower-level principle – substantially, obedience to the customs and

---

[12] Ibid., p. 42.     [13] Ibid., pp. 55–6.     [14] Ibid., pp. 237–8.

laws of his own society. In politics this attitude was usually linked to an enthusiasm for the works of Machiavelli or the theorists of a quasi-Machiavellian 'political science' such as Lipsius. The wise man, according to the sceptics, was wholly a prudent man; although Aristotle had recognized the role of prudence in moral thinking, he was mistaken in believing that there was any wisdom beyond it.

The impossibility of true and definite knowledge put a great weight on the avowedly uncertain and non-theoretical maxims which made up the prudential tradition of political science, since they constituted an appropriate set of principles by which a sceptic could live; and a sceptical prince, at least in Charron's eyes, turned out to be very close to a Machiavellian prince. For example, discussing the rule of law, he remarked, 'to dispatch and secretly to put to death, or otherwise without forme of iustice, some certaine man that is troublesome and dangerous to the state, and who well deserveth death, but yet cannot without trouble and danger be enterprised and repressed by an ordinarie course; herein there is nothing violated but the forme. And the prince, is he not above formes?'[15]

In theology, to consider the last feature of late-sixteenth-century scepticism relevant to my theme, the sceptic was led naturally to what is usually termed a 'fideistic' position; namely, that there are no rational grounds for a belief in any religion. As Charron said in one of his most famous phrases, 'all religions have this in them, that they are strange and horrible to the common sense'.[16] But just as the wise man was not free to pick any moral beliefs he chose, so he was not free to pick any religious beliefs; in another work Charron argued that there were important political and prudential reasons for maintaining religious beliefs in a community, and that, in general, Christianity (and specifically *Catholic* Christianity) was the best bet. Still there could be no rational proof of the existence of God: 'every deity who can be proved and established by reason . . . is a false and not a true deity'.[17] This view became surprisingly popular among Catholics, and Popkin has argued that even Bellarmine endorsed it.[18]

We can summarize this sceptical philosophy by saying that it denied the existence of secure criteria for establishing the truth of any proposition (and the rejection of the *criterion* became a standard trope in scepticism). Epistemology, narrowly defined, was only one among several issues which concerned the sixteenth-century scep-

---

[15] Ibid., p. 362.    [16] Ibid., p. 277.
[17] 'Toute Deite, qui se prouve & s'establit par raison, . . . est false & non vraye Deite.' P. Charron, *Les Trois Veritez* (2nd edition, Bordeaux, 1595), sig. B2.
[18] Popkin, pp. 68–73.

tic: the relativity of morals was as important, and it was not argued
for directly on the basis of epistemological considerations. It could,
for example, have been the case that all men in fact believed the
same moral propositions and acted in the same way, and this would
have radically weakened the sceptic's case for moral relativism
without in any way affecting his epistemological arguments.[19] But
the refutation of scepticism involved the refutation of each bit of the
sceptical package.

Most of the interesting philosophers of early seventeenth-century
Europe agreed that the sceptical attack on Aristotelianism had succeeded. They also agreed that scepticism itself had to be refuted in
some way, a way which involved accepting the validity of the points
the sceptics had made against Aristotle, but which would transcend
them and recover the notion of truth. The belief that this was possible seems to have received two encouragements in the 1620s and
1630s. One was provided by Galilean physics, for what Galileo
showed was that while naive realism was indeed misleading, a persuasive physics was still possible. Observation alone could not in
principle determine whether, for example, the earth rotated; so the
sceptic was right to cast doubt on the sufficiency of observation as a
means to knowledge of the truth. Moreover, the telescope showed
that familiar observational methods in physics might lead to misleading or false results. Yet it was possible to have theories which
were consistent with any possible observations and which met other
criteria such as simplicity.

The other form of encouragement was provided by Grotius'
invention of a new kind of natural law theory. Grotius not only
attacked Aristotle in his *De Iure Belli ac Pacis* (1625); he also directed
his enormous learning against Carneades, the famous Academic
sceptic (and indeed in the context of early seventeenth-century
Europe, he had to signal by some such device that his anti-
Aristotelianism was not sceptical in character).[20] According to
Grotius, if we look carefully enough at the ethical beliefs men have
held at different times and places, and the moral practices they have
countenanced, we can see that they have, in fact, a universal though
minimal core. All men have acknowledged the legitimacy of self-

[19] The same could be said of the ancient scepticism on which this modern scepticism
drew. For the ancients, see M. F. Burnyeat, 'Can the sceptic live his scepticism', in
M. Schofield, M. Burnyeat, and J. Barnes, eds., *Doubt and Dogmatism* (Oxford,
1980).
[20] Grotius singled out Carneades for attack in the Prolegomena V of *De Iure Belli ac
Pacis*. For a full discussion of this, see my paper 'Grotius, Carneades and
Hobbes'.

defence, and the defence of the material objects necessary for one's existence, and they have also acknowledged the illegitimacy of wantonly injuring another – though depriving them of possessions or even life if one's own life is in danger is not necessarily wrong. This is as far as the common ethical core goes: benevolence, for example, as we customarily understand the notion, is not universal and natural, but a product of developed civil life. But all societies, according to Grotius, must exhibit the two universal principles, or else they cannot subsist.

Grotius was thus able to articulate a new moral and political science, in which the 'natural' life of men, prior to civil society, was depicted as governed by these universal principles, and in which civil life was represented as the superaddition to the natural law of local beliefs and practices. In its structure this resembled pre-Renaissance theories, but in the minimalism of its laws of nature and its explicitly anti-sceptical thrust it was a wholly new phenomenon. Grotius did not, however, provide it with any extensive philosophical underpinning, any more than Galileo did his physics; these fragments of anti-Aristotelian, post-sceptical sciences had yet to be put into the kind of comprehensive *organon* into which Aristotle had integrated his own sciences. It was this task which seventeenth-century philosophers, and particularly those of the Mersenne 'circle', seem to have set themselves.

The first attempt was made by Pierre Gassendi. He began with what up to then was the most comprehensive statement of the sceptical case against Aristotelian epistemology and the physics based upon it. The final section of his *Paradoxical Essays Against the Aristotelians* (1625) began with the ringing claim, 'there is no science, particularly of an Aristotelian kind'.[21] In fact, the work set out the conditions which any future science would have to meet. There could be no real knowledge of externals, but there could be knowledge of one's own sensations; there could be no mistake that one felt pain or had a particular visual perception. Accordingly, the only appropriate philosophy had to be a version of *nominalism*. Earlier writers such as Charron had gestured towards this,[22] but Gassendi was the first to make the connection clear. There could be no true propositions about universals, since universals could not be the

---

[21] 'Quod nulla sit scientia, & maxime Aristotelea'. P. Gassendi, *Opera*, III (Lyons, 1658), p. 192. For Gassendi, see O. R. Bloch, *La Philosophie de Gassendi* (The Hague, 1971); R. Pintard, *Le Libertinage erudit* (Paris, 1943) especially pp. 147–55, 477–504, and idem., *La Mothe le Vayer, Gassendi, Guy Patin* (Paris, 1943).
[22] Charron, p. 54.

objects of perception; nor could there be any meaningful statements about essences. Even mathematical demonstration, he argued in the *Essays*, was demonstration not of universal truths but of features of a precept which we have not yet had drawn to our attention.[23] The fact that Gassendi could derive his nominalism straightforwardly and explicitly from scepticism should alert us to the fact that Hobbes's very similar nominalism might derive from the same source.

Between 1625 and 1641 Gassendi developed a comprehensive post-sceptical philosophy. In Epicurus he discovered someone who had also used the indubitability of sensation to refut the sceptic, and he devoted the rest of his life to a reconstruction of Epicureanism in a modern form. Although this became a vast enterprise, at its heart was a simple argument. Questions of truth and falsehood do not arise in relation to sensations and perceptions: the sceptic is mistaken in his belief that one among the variety of disparate views of the world is the correct one; but we lack the criteria to determine which. All sensations are equally veridical; the only things which can be false are the propositions which relate mental occurrences (which Gassendi termed *phantasiae*) either to external objects or to other mental events. What determines whether such a proposition is true is whether it is a valid prediction about the occurrence of a perception.

This theory can be used elegantly to underpin modern, post-Galilean physics. For example, when we look at the Milky Way, we see a continuous, faint band of light. It is legitimate for us to say that what we are *really* seeing is a multitude of separate stars – but only because we can in principle have such a new and more detailed perception, with the aid of the telescope.[24] Strictly speaking, our first notion of the galaxy was no less 'real' than our subsequent one; it is as true that things very far away appear indistinct as that things nearby appear distinct, and the idea that they have some kind of 'real' size or shape is a mistaken one. But we can talk loosely about deception and illusion provided that we are aware that our language is only a shorthand for the ideal language referring exclusively to sensation. Gassendi developed an elaborate theory of 'signs' to capture the relationship between actual and possible perceptions; thus the faint band of light in the sky is the sign of a galaxy, but only in so far as we can subsequently perceive the separate stars. Physical theories about the connection between a sign and the as-yet-unknown thing which is signified must be provisional and hypothetical.

[23] Gassendi, *Opera*, 111, p. 208.     [24] Gassendi, *Opera*, I, p. 82.

Such a position leads rather naturally to atomism, as Epicurus had found. For if we cannot talk about the real structure of anything unless it is in principle capable of being directly apprehended, and if human beings (however equipped with microscopes, and so forth) cannot perceive infinitesimal increments, then the only real entities with which science can deal are atoms. The position also leads to a kind of natural theology, and during the 1640s Gassendi abandoned his earlier sceptical fideism and began to take natural theology seriously:[25] the world is a sign of some manufacturing intelligence at work, and it is conceivable that we could perceive such an intelligence directly. This change in his theology has occasioned much debate, but it does not seem particularly puzzling.

Part of Gassendi's excitement about Epicurus seems to have been caused by the fact that Epicurus had provided a *comprehensive* theory, in which logic, physics, and ethics all found a place. Epicurus' ethical theory, moreover, was peculiarly well fitted to underpin a moral science of the Grotian kind, just as his physics could underpin Galileo: for like Grotius, Epicurus refuted the sceptic by insisting on the universality of self-interest as a foundation for ethics, combined with the irrationality of wantonly attacking one's fellow men. In Epicurus' grave words, 'he who best knew how to meet fear of external foes made into one family all the creatures he could; and those he could not, he at any rate did not treat as aliens; and when he found even this impossible, he avoided all intercourse, and so far as was expedient, kept them at a distance'.[26] All civil laws, in Epicurus' eyes, were designed to foster this kind of security from one's fellow men, and since this was the point of justice, all civil laws were *ipso facto* just. So the relativist was right to insist on the variety of possible moral beliefs and practices, but wrong to conclude from this variety that there could be no universal ethics. This is precisely the kind of response to scepticism which Grotius had employed, and it is not surprising to find Gassendi building on his Epicurean foundations a fully developed theory of rights in a state of nature which are bargained away by self-interested men following the law of nature in order to create a multiplicity of civil societies.[27] This is a seventeenth-century structure which Epicurus would have been astonished to find reared upon his philosophy.

[25] See his reply to Descartes's *Meditations*, in Descartes, *The Philosophical Works*, tr. E. S. Haldane and G. R. T. Ross (Cambridge, 1931), II, p. 175.
[26] Diogenes Laertius, *Lives of Eminent Philosophers* X.154, tr. R. D. Hicks, Loeb Classical Library (London, 1925), II, p. 677.
[27] See e.g. Gassendi, *Opera*, II, pp. 783ff. originally published in 1649. A proper study of Gassendi's moral theory and its relationship to Hobbes is urgently needed.

Gassendi provides a fine example of the Mersenne 'programme'. He abandoned nothing of his early scepticism, but used what even sceptics would accept in order to create a new kind of science. But his efforts were directed against the arguments which the sceptics of the previous generation had used, and when in 1637 Descartes published his *Discourse on the Method*, his attention was drawn to a new extension of those arguments. This was Descartes's famous 'hyperbolical doubt', the possibility that there is no material world at all and that all our perceptions are like the sensations we have when dreaming. This was not an argument which had been used at all extensively by either ancient or modern sceptics, and although it was in a way a natural adjunct to their position, it could not be met by a theory like Gassendi's.

The sceptic had assumed that *some* perceptions were veridical, but we do not know which; Gassendi replied that strictly speaking, *all* perceptions are veridical. Descartes now pointed out that a sceptic could reply that *no* perceptions are veridical; none correspond to anything in the world at all. This observation clearly gave Gassendi a great deal of trouble, and when in 1641 he replied to Descartes's *Meditations*, he could only remark feebly that 'since we wake and dream alternately as long as we are alive, deception may occur owing to a dream, because things appear in the dream to be present which are not present. Nevertheless, neither do we always dream, nor, when we are really awake, can we doubt whether we are awake or dreaming.'[28] Gassendi was not so worried by Descartes's brand of hypothetical scepticism that he abandoned his own enterprise. As he pointed out, unlike traditional scepticism, Cartesian doubt was not a principle anyone could actually and honestly live by. It thus did not need refuting in the same manner.

But Gassendi's failure to answer to Descartes showed that the Mersenne programme had not yet been fulfilled; that is, if we assume (as most of his contemporaries did) that Descartes had also failed to answer his own doubt. His theory is well enough known for it to need little explication here. He founded his canon of truth on a combination of the *cogito* argument and his 'proof' of God's existence. The crucial remark comes in his *Discourse on the Method* of 1637, during his discussion of the apparent fallibility of sense-impressions:

[28] Descartes, *Philosophical Works*, II, p. 193. See also Gassendi's reply to Descartes's response, *Opera*, III, pp. 388–90. This consists simply of the point that it is as reasonable to suppose that the material world exists as that it does not.

Though we see the sun very clearly, we should not for that reason judge that it is of the size of which it appears to be . . . For Reason does not insist that whatever we see or imagine thus is a truth, but it tells us clearly that all our ideas or notions must have some *foundation of truth* [my italics]. For otherwise it could not be possible that God, who is all perfection and truth, should have placed them within us.[29]

The reality of external objects, and even the truth of many laws of nature (such as the laws of motion) is deducible from these premises alone: the world, according to Descartes, is going to be *roughly* what it seems, provided that we are careful about accumulating plenty of evidence about what it *does* seem like before pronouncing. God has given us (so to speak) both the image of the Milky Way in the naked eye and in the telescope, and we have to work out a theory of galaxies which takes account of both these gifts. In the end, Descartes's physics were not very far removed from Gassendi's, for both accepted that a closer look at something will change our ideas about it; but they put forward very different grounds for believing that what we see at any one point is how the world is.

Two problems remained about Descartes's reply to the sceptic. The first was that even if his argument against his own hyperbolical doubt was accepted, it was not clear how far it met the *ancient* sceptical case, which had after all not been based on the hyperbolical doubt. Moral relativism in particular seemed on the face of it to be untouched by Descartes's argument, for as we have seen, in ancient scepticism it was wholly independent of any epistemological doubt. That is why there is, as is well known, no developed moral theory in Descartes's *oeuvre*, though he did say that his programme might eventually, and in some unspecified way, issue in one. Because of the absence of any such theory, we find in general in his writings only the sceptical premises, and not the anti-sceptical conclusions drawn from them which we might have expected, and which Descartes intended to draw one day.

In the *Discourse on the Method* he stressed that his premise of hyperbolical doubt was not sufficient to prevent him from living as sceptics like Montaigne and Charron had always urged, namely as a law-abiding citizen of his country who was nevertheless not prepared to act on any assumptions about a moral reality. In particular, Descartes remarked that he was not willing to be bound voluntarily by contractual agreements. 'Because I saw nothing in all the world

---

[29] Descartes, *Philosophical Works*, I, p. 106. For the Cartesian enterprise in general, see E. M. Curley, *Descartes Against the Sceptics* (Oxford, 1978).

remaining constant, and because for my own part I promised myself gradually to get my judgements to grow better and never to grow worse, I should have thought that I had committed a serious sin against commonsense if, because I approved of something at one time, I was obliged to regard it similarly at a later time . . .'[30] The hyperbolical doubt did not touch these sceptical commitments, nor did its resolution in itself remove them: there was nothing in our assured knowledge of the physical world which could tell us anything about the moral world, despite Descartes's hope that the link could be made. So he remained a pretty pure sceptic in these matters, a point underlined by the fact that the only political philosopher he was at all drawn to was Machiavelli,[31] just as Charron and the others had been.

The second of the two problems mentioned above was, of course, that his argument against the hyperbolical doubt was notoriously unconvincing. Once Descartes had let the genie out of the bottle, however, there was no putting it back: henceforward any serious refutation of scepticism had to deal with both Pyrrho or Carneades *and* Descartes. Hobbes seems to have regarded as his major triumph the fact that his theory at least ostensibly did this.

Given what we have now seen, the fact that so much of Hobbes's early philosophical work was on *optics* takes on a new significance: if we had no other indication about what kind of enterprise he was engaged on, that would be sufficient to alert us; but in fact he tells us himself what his fundamental concern was, and tries to tell us what his fundamental insight was. In his verse autobiography, written when he was eighty-four (perhaps his great age explains the obscurity of the passage's syntax; I apologize for the oddity of my deliberately literal translation), he recorded that during his travels on the Continent between 1634 and 1637

I thought continually about the nature of things, whether I was travelling by boat or coach, or on horseback. And it seemed to me that there was only one true thing in the whole world, though falsified in many ways: one true thing, which is the basis of all those phenomena which we wrongly say are something (such as we get fleetingly in sleep, or with the aid of lenses can multiply as we choose) – the phenomena of sense-impressions, which are offsprings of our skull, with nothing external. And in those internal regions, there could be nothing but *motion*.[32]

[30] Descartes, *Philosophical Works*, I, p. 96.
[31] See G. Rodis-Lewis, *La Morale de Descartes* (Paris, 1957), pp. 100–5.
[32] 'Ast ego perpetuo naturam cogito rerum, / Seu rate, seu curru, sive ferebar equo. / Et mihi visa quidem est toto res unica Mundo / Vera. Licit multis falsificata modis. / Unica vera quidem, sed quae sit basis earum / Rerum quas falso dicimus esse aliquid; / Qualia somnus habet fugitiva, et qualia vitris, /

This passage is not at all clear about *what* he took to be the 'one true thing', but it does make clear that it was the search for truth in a world of uncertainty which absorbed Hobbes; in other words, precisely the enterprise upon which Gassendi and Descartes were also engaged. It is not surprising that towards the end of his stay Hobbes should have communicated his discoveries to Mersenne.

Although we can rely on this as an account of what the central concern in the Hobbesian enterprise was, we must take Hobbes's dating of his insight with some caution. Hobbes persistently claimed that his own ideas were independent of those of Gassendi and, particularly, of Descartes – a claim which in itself reveals that Hobbes was aware of the broad similarity between their concerns. We have no direct evidence concerning what Hobbes thought on any philosophical topic before he had read the *Discourse on the Method*, with the possible exception of a Harleian manuscript known as the *Short Tract on First Principles* which Toennies dated to *c.* 1630 and which connected with Hobbes's reminiscence about a discussion on optics with the Earl of Newcastle in that year. This manuscript differs from Hobbes's later ideas in a number of important ways; in particular, it espouses an atomism very similar to Gassendi's. It is among the papers of Charles Cavendish, who was a friend and correspondent of both Hobbes and Gassendi; it is not in Hobbes's hand, but seems to be in the hand of Robert Payne, who was himself a distinguished mathematician and (apparently) philosopher, and friend of both Cavendish and Hobbes.[33] Until its authorship and date are properly established, it is wise to ignore it in discussions of Hobbes's intellectual development.

We do have some indirect evidence about what Hobbes thought before he read Descartes, in letters exchanged between Cavendish,

Arbitrio possum multiplicare meo. / Phantasiae, nostri soboles cerebri, nihil extra, / Partibus internis nil nisi motus inest' (Hobbes, *Vita authore seipso* (London, 1679)). (I would like to thank Noel Malcolm for pointing out that the first edition of the *Vita* differs in a number of respects from that printed in Molesworth's edition, though this passage is not seriously affected. The translation is my own, though a contemporary translation was published only a fortnight after the *Vita*.)

[33] The MS is Harl. 6796ff. 297–308. Toennies' dating is in his edition of the *Elements of Law* (2nd edition, London, 1969), p. xii (original pagination). For Cavendish, see J. Jacquot, 'Un amateur de science', *Thales*, 6 (1949–50), 81–8, and idem., 'Sir Charles Cavendish and his learned friends', *Annals of Science*, 8 (1952), 13–27 and 175–91. There is no readily accessible study of Payne, but the basic facts of his life are in Foster's *Alumni Oxonienses* and Walker's *Sufferings of the Clergy*, while a remarkable set of letters written by him to Gilbert Sheldon (many about Hobbes) give a sense of his activities and interests *c.* 1650. They are printed from a Harleian MS by W. N. Clarke, 'Illustrations of the state of the church during the Great Rebellion', *The Theologian and Ecclesiastic*, 6 (1848), 161–75, 212–24.

Payne and the optical theorist of an earlier generation, William
Warner, and in some letters from Hobbes himself to the Earl of
Newcastle, all between 1634 and 1636.[34] In them, Hobbes expresses
scepticism over the optical theories of Warner (he later noted that
he had told Warner that 'light and colour were but fancy'), and in
general appears as a critical commentator on the ideas of his friends.
In a letter to Newcastle in July 1636, Hobbes stressed the uncertain
character of physical knowledge:

> in thinges that are not demonstrable, of which kind is the greatest part of
> naturall philosophy, as dependinge upon the motion of bodies so subtile as
> they are invisible, such as are ayre and spirits, the most that can be atteyned
> unto is to have such opinions, as no certayne experience can confute, and
> from which can be deduced by lawfull argumentation, no absurdity . . .[35]

In October he was equally ready to admit doubt. In another letter to
Newcastle, concerned with the passage of light off a wall and into a
*camera obscura,* he remarked

> whereas I use the phrases, the light passes, or the coulor passes or diffuseth
> itselfe, my meaning is that the motion is onely in the medium, and light and
> coulor are but the effects of that motion in the brayne. But if one should
> aske me what kind of motion I can imagine in the medium or ayre that
> touches the wall, which should beget such motion in the wall or parts of it, as
> should move the ayre again, every way, that I can not answer. This
> proposition so true, and so well received, *simile generat sibi simile,* is too hard
> to be demonstrated, and too manifest to be denyed.[36]

His position on the eve of reading Descartes seems to have been one
of far more doubt and scepticism than his later writings display; the
intense conviction of those writings that he could reconstruct the
sciences on a post-sceptical foundation seems to have developed
after his exposure to the Cartesian enterprise.

We have plenty of evidence about what Hobbes thought in the
period between 1637 and the publication of his general philosophy
to the world in Mersenne's *Ballistica* of 1644. We have the *Tractatus
Opticus,* which deals with Descartes's *Dioptrics* and which Toennies
dated to shortly after 1637, the *Elements of Law* (1640), his letters to
Mersenne and answers to Descartes's *Meditations* (1641), *De Cive*
(1642), and his *Critique of Thomas White's De Mundo* (1643), discovered
in the Bibliothèque Nationale in 1952 by Jean Jacquot. In these
works we find the outlines of the general theory which Hobbes spent

---

[34] See J. Halliwell (ed.), *A Collection of Letters Illustrative of the Progress of Science*
(London, 1841), pp. 65–9; HMC Portland MSS App. II, pp. 124–31 (MSS at
Welbeck).    [35] HMC Portland MSS App. II, p. 128.    [36] Ibid., p. 130.

the rest of his life polishing and refining. The first two chapters of
the *Elements* contain the fullest statement of it, and they make it clear
that his starting-point was a set of familiar sceptical arguments.

For example, chapter 2 is devoted to a sceptical refutation of
Aristotelian physics – 'because the image in vision consisting in
colour and shape is the knowledge we have of the qualities of the
object of that sense; it is no hard matter for a man to fall into this
opinion, that the same colour and shape are the very qualities
themselves. . . And this opinion hath been so long received, that the
contrary must needs appear a great paradox.' (Remember Gassendi's
*Paradoxical Essays against Aristotelianism*.) This Aristotelian position
Hobbes refuted in the standard sceptical manner; for example,
'every man hath so much experience as to have seen the sun and
other visible objects by reflection in the water and in glasses, and this
alone is sufficient for this conclusion: that colour and image may be
there when the thing seen is not'.[37] He summed it up neatly: 'whatsoever accidents or qualities our senses make us think there be in the
world, they are not there, but seemings and apparitions only'.[38]
Moreover, Hobbes even endorsed Descartes's hyperbolical doubt
about dreaming:

nor is it impossible for a man to be so far deceived, as when his dream is past,
to think it real: for if he dream of such things as are ordinarily in his mind,
and in such order as he useth to do waking, and withal that he laid him down
to sleep in the place where he findeth himself when he awaketh (all which
may happen) I know no κριτήριον [the technical term of scepticism] or mark
by which he can discover whether it were a dream or not.[39]

But the possibility of such fundamental deception is compatible
according to Hobbes with a demonstration of the existence of
material objects; there are some 'things' which 'really are in the
world without us', namely 'those motions by which these seemings
are caused'.[40] Hobbes clearly believed that his reconciliation of these
sceptical doubts with the demonstrable existence of material
objects was his major contribution to philosophy, and allowed him
to succeed where both Gassendi and Descartes had failed; his
argument did indeed depend upon *motion*, for he perceived that the
knowledge of *change* which we possess gives us an additional
epistemological lever. The theories of both Gassendi and Descartes
would be as plausible in a world without change as in one with it, but
this is not so for Hobbes.

[37] Hobbes, *Elements of Law*, pp. 3 and 4.
[38] Ibid., p. 7.   [39] Ibid., p. 12.   [40] Ibid., p. 7.

Before we consider how Hobbes effected this reconciliation, it must be emphasized that his argument was what a later philosopher would have termed a transcendental argument: that is, it was not merely a physical theory which served to explain perception and illusion, but an argument which sought to show how the world *must* be conceived by any being constructed like a human being. In the *Critique* he remarked that we can talk about necessity not because the world is necessarily as it is, but because of the way *we* are constructed.[41] It is true that most versions of empiricism have been underpinned by more-or-less transcendental arguments, but Hobbes's use of them is particularly striking, and so extensive that it might call into question the extent to which he was genuinely an empiricist.

Hobbes always distinguished between mere physical theories and necessarily true assertions. The distinction is best expressed in the *Tractatus Opticus*, though it had been present as early as 1636 in his letter to Newcastle:

The natural sciences differ greatly from the other sciences. In the latter, nothing is needed or admitted as a foundation or primary principle of demonstration other than the definition of terms, by which ambiguity is excluded. They are first truths; every definition is a true and primary proposition because we make it true ourselves by defining it, that is, by agreeing about the meaning of the words. Thus if it pleases us to call this a Triangle, then it is true that this figure is a Triangle. But in the explanation of natural phenomena, another kind of procedure must be followed, which is termed Hypothesis or supposition. Suppose a question is raised about the efficient cause of any event which is obvious to the senses, the sort of thing which we usually term a Phenomenon. Any answer will consist standardly in the designation or description of some motion, to which the Phenomenon is necessarily consequent; and since it is not impossible for dissimilar motions to produce the same Phenomenon, it is possible for the effect to be correctly demonstrated using the hypothetical motion, even though the hypothesis may be untrue. Nothing further is required in Physics, therefore, than that the motions we suppose or imagine are conceivable, that the necessity of the Phenomenon can be demonstrated from them, and that nothing false can be derived from them.[42]

---

[41] 'Illud igitur *non posse aliter concipere*, non est rerum incapacitas, sed nostra.' Hobbes, *Critique du De mundo de Thomas White*, ed. J. Jacquot and H. V. Jones (Paris, 1973), p. 337 (f. 320).

[42] 'Rerum naturalium tractatio a caetarum scientiarum tractatione plurimum differt. In caeteris enim fundamenta sive principia prima demonstrandi alia neque requiruntur, neque admittentur, quam definitiones vocabulorum, quibus excludatur Amphibologia. Eae primae veritates sunt, est enim definitio omnis, vera propositio; a prima; propterea quod definiendo, id est consentiendo circa vocabulorum usum, ipsi inter nos veram esse facimus. Siquidem enim nobis inter nos libuerit figuram hanc Triangulum appellare, verum erit, figura illa est Triangulum. Sed in explicatione Causarum naturalium, aliud genus principiorum

The demonstration that motion is the only reality was part of the first kind of science mentioned in this passage, that concerned (in Hobbes's eyes) with necessary truths, of which we can be assured. In the *Elements of Law* he outlined this science as follows:

The first principle of knowledge ... is, that we have such and such conceptions; the second, that we have thus and thus named the things whereof they are conceptions; the third is, that we have joined those names in such manner, as to make true propositions; the fourth and last is, that we have joined those propositions in such manner as they be concluding.[43]

Thus like Gassendi, he believed that – because of the force of the sceptical arguments – we could have true demonstration only if we restricted ourselves to propositions about how the world *seems* to us. It is possible for us (in Hobbes's terminology) to 'mark' for our own use or 'signify' for other people's use particular perceptions – 'seemings', 'phenomena', 'phantasies' or 'ideas' – and to express relationships between them. Both the nuclear and the more complex statements are necessarily true because the subject-matter, the 'seeming', is an object of direct acquaintance and cannot be doubted. It was a science based on these necessary propositions which Hobbes seems to have sought to construct from the late 1630s onwards. But of course, as Gassendi had found, the necessary truth of such statements is not enough to give us confidence in the reality of hypothetical motions which *cause* sense-impressions, and thus to answer the Cartesian doubt about the existence of a material world. This is where Hobbes's originality lay, and it is shown most clearly perhaps in the arguments which Hobbes used against White in 1643. The same arguments appear in a condensed form (though sometimes virtually word-for-word) in the preface to Mersenne's *Ballistica* of 1644. Essentially, Hobbes argued three things which in his opinion were *a priori* truths to be established using the method outlined above, which even a sceptic must accept. First, any alteration or mutation in anything is to be understood as motion: 'it is not

necessario adhibendum est, quod vocatur Hypothesis sive suppositio. Cum enim quaestio instituta sit, de alicuius eventus sensibus manifesti (quod Phaenomenon appellari solet) causa efficiente, quae consistit plerumque in designatione seu descriptione alicuius motus, quem tale Phaenomenon necessario consequatur; cumque dissimilibus motibus produci Phaenomena similia non sit impossibile; potest fieri ut ex motu supposito, effectus recte demonstretur, ut tamen ipsa suppositio non sit vera. Amplius igitur a Physico non exigitur, quam ut quos supponit vel fingit motus, sint imaginabiles, et per eos concessos necessitas demonstretur Phaenomeni; et denique ut nihil inde falsi derivari possit' (F. Alessio, 'Thomas Hobbes: Tractatus Opticus (Harley MSS 6796, ff. 193–216)', *Rivista critica di storia della filosofia*, 18 (1963), 147).
[43] Hobbes, *Elements of Law*, p. 26.

conceivable for any body to change into something without motion,
[and therefore] all action which can be conceived is motion'.[44]
Second (though this is usually taken for granted, not unreasonably,
rather than spelled out), we perceive the world as changing, or, more
precisely, our perceptions of the world themselves exhibit continuous
change. Third, and the point which Hobbes hammered home
repeatedly in all his writings, all motion is only conceivable as the
operation of one body upon another. As he said, all philosophers
have attributed motion only to bodies, 'for what moves, travels from
place to place, and what is in any place, is accommodated to the
dimensions of the place, and therefore is a body'.[45] Moreover, it is
only conceivable for one body to move if it is affected by another
body outside itself – we cannot understand what it could be for a
body to move itself. 'The reason for this can be easily given, for a
body which now begins to move, has in itself everything necessary
for the motion. Whence it follows, that if now it moves of itself, it
must have moved earlier, because it has everything in itself
necessary for the movement.'[46]

The first two premises entailed the reality of motion, for we
cannot be mistaken that our sensations are changing, and change
can only be understood as motion. Since motion can only be
understood as the operation of bodies upon each other, it follows
that there must be bodies, and that our sensations are corporeal. It
does *not* follow, of course, that the world is *actually* as it is perceived:
according to Hobbes, as to Gassendi, we simply have no way of
knowing what it is 'really' like. All we have is a direct and veridical
acquaintance with caused movements within our minds, and though
we can conjecture or hypothesize about *what* causes them, we cannot
be *certain* about it.

That is why there can be no definite criterion for distinguishing
dreaming from waking, for in each case we experience a procession
of ideas which have been caused by something, and it can only be a
matter of conjecture whether they have been caused by an object
present simultaneously with the experience or previous to it.

---

[44] 'non conceptibile esse quomodo unum corpus aliud mutare possit sine motu . . .
omnis actio (quae quidem concipi potest) est motus' (Hobbes, *Critique*, p. 320 (MS
f. 301)). There is a translation of the *Critique* by H. W. Jones, Bradford 19, but I
have used my own translations.

[45] 'quod movetur enim transit a loco in locum, quod autem in loco est, loci
dimensionibus accomodatur, et proinde corpus est' (ibid., p. 409 (f. 417)).

[46] 'Ratio cuius rei ut breviter dicam ea est, quod corpus quod nunc incipit moveri,
habet in se nunc omnia quae necessaria sunt ad motum. Unde sequitur, si modo
moveri incipit a seipso, quod haberet in se omnia necessaria ad motum, antequam
moveretur' (ibid., pp. 251–2 (f. 211v)).

Although he did not discuss the issue, Hobbes would presumably have accepted that Descartes's demon could be a possible cause of our sensations – but only because he is an actual material demon with direct inputs into our brain, and thus a physical hypothesis on the same level as other more reasonable hypotheses.

However, Hobbes did propose a method for distinguishing between most dreams or idle imaginings and conscious, rational thought, a method of great importance in his theory. It rested on the fact that a sequence of ideas can be either *ordered* and *purposive* or not.

*Discourse*, or a series of imaginings, is either *ordered* or *disordered* – what we might call fortuitous. The latter occurs when someone wanders in their thoughts from Pythagoras to a bean [*faba*, the cult vegetable of the Pythagoreans], from a bean to a fable, and from a fable to Aesop, and that is what you get in dreams or delirium. An ordered series is regulated by some end which the person wishes to follow and towards which he tends.[47]

This distinction does not, of course, permit a *strong* disjunction between dreams and rational thought, for it is, as Hobbes pointed out, perfectly possible to have an ordered dream.

In the *Critique*, Hobbes emphasized that the elements of each series stand in different causal relationships, but both series are to be understood in terms of cause and effect. In an ordered sequence, the person remembers things as standing in a previously observed causal relationship, and his memory of that observation is what leads him to recapitulate the sequence mentally. In a disordered sequence, the person's 'imagining' or conception directly causes him to have another conception, without the mediation of an act of remembrance. Of course, even the sequence Pythagoras – bean – fable – Aesop can figure as an 'ordered' series if, say, a brain scientist is interested in the causal relations between different notions in the mind. He could then bring it about that a patient thinks of Aesop by starting him in suitable circumstances on thinking about Pythagoras. It will be the case for the scientist as well as the patient that their thinking 'Pythagoras' brings it about that they think 'Aesop', but the explanation of *why* thinking about Pythagoras causes someone to think about Aesop will be different in each case; for the scientist knows that one notion causes the other, and his knowledge of how

[47] '*discursus* his (sive imaginationum seies) quandoque ordinatus, quandoque inordinatus. Inordinatus est veluti fortuitus, ut si quis a *pycsagora*, ad fabam, a faba ad fabulam, a fabula ad Aesopum cogitando vagaretur, cuiusmodi est discursus somnantium, deliramtiumque; ordinatus est qui regitur ab aliquo fine sive scopo, quam quis cupit assequi' (ibid., p. 352 (f. 341)).

they stand in a causal relation to each other causes his sequence of thoughts, whereas the patient has no knowledge (necessarily) of any causal connection between his own conceptions. It is important to stress, as Hobbes did both in the *Critique* and later in his debates with Bramhall, that rational discourse on this account is as much *caused* as irrational discourse: in neither case does any traditional notion of free will get any purchase, since one cannot choose freely and rationally to *be* rational – it merely happens that on some occasions one is led to think in an ordered way and on others in a disordered way.[48]

Rational or ordered discourse, for Hobbes, thus represents a series of concepts which are taken by the agent himself to stand in a causal relationship. As we have seen above, for Hobbes all causal relations are fundamentally a matter of the interaction of corporeal bodies – for all change is motion, and motion can only be conceived as brought about by 'propulsion or traction'. The only science is thus (at the deepest level) ballistics. (This science even underlay, in Hobbes's view, the purest of existing sciences, that of geometry itself; for a line was definable as the path of a moving body, a plane as the area swept by a moving line, and a volume as the space swept by a moving plane.)[49] The sequence of cause and effect embodied in rational discourse did not have to represent the *actual* sequence in the real world which brought about the effect: the actual sequence might be (as we have seen) unknowable. It was sufficient (as the passage quoted above from the *Tractatus Opticus* shows) that the effect could conceivably be brought about by the ascribed cause, and that it would bring about nothing that was not the case. Rational discourse for Hobbes was thus essentially corrigible in the light of any *a priori* inconsistency or observational inadequacy; but in principle a science relating cause to effect and therefore means to ends was possible.

An example of the difference between rational and irrational discourse and conduct is provided by Hobbes's account of how to control the passions. This, the theme of so much seventeenth-century moral philosophy, might seem particularly alien to Hobbes, but embedded in the *Elements of Law* and the *Critique* is a theory of emotions which permits their rational control; in *De Homine* (published in 1658) this theory is made completely explicit.[50] The

[48] See the *Critique*, chap. XXXVII *passim*, especially para. 13 (p. 411, f. 421); Hobbes, *English Works*, ed. W. Molesworth (London, 1839–45), IV, pp. 254–5.
[49] See Hobbes's *Notes pour le De Corpore*, dating from the mid 1640s, and *Critique*, p. 478.    [50] Hobbes, *English Works*, II, pp. 103–4.

first part of the theory rested on Hobbes's claim that he had shown how

conceptions or apparitions are nothing really, but motion in some internal substance of the head; which motion not stopping there, but proceeding to the heart, of necessity must there either help or hinder that motion which is called vital; when it helpeth, it is called DELIGHT... but when such motion weakeneth or hindereth the vital motion, then it is called PAIN[51]

This physiological picture is clearly hypothetical, but it captures the important logical point that emotion and perception are connected: there is on Hobbes's account the same kind of causal relationship between a concept and an emotion as between the relevant bit of the external world and a concept. Different perceptions bring about different emotions, and in chapter 9 of the *Elements* he analyses each passion in terms of the perception which causes it. It follows that if rational or ordered discourse produces a different set of conceptions in the mind from that produced by disordered discourse, then the corresponding emotions will be different also.

In particular, a man who passionately desires something may be brought to change his attitude towards it by a demonstration that the object of his passion stands in a causal relationship with something which he greatly dislikes. In this process he is not a free agent, any more than he is in the anterior process of changing his conceptions, since his desires are still caused by external phenomena. He is not choosing as a pure act of free will to desire something else, but he may be said to be causing himself to desire something else, simply by virtue of the fact that he happens now to be thinking rationally rather than irrationally. But there is clearly no scope in Hobbes's theory for altering a man's desires by any technique other than a demonstration of an inconsistency between them and other desires which he might have.

Hobbes had thus provided an answer to both Pyrrho and Descartes. To Descartes, he was able to say that it was inconceivable that a material world did not exist, while to Pyrrho he was able to demonstrate that there could be at least one science. But of course a central feature of his response to the sceptic, just as it had been of Gassendi's or Descartes's own, was that much of what the sceptic argued was to be accepted. The fallibility of perception and therefore the impossibility of an Aristotelian physical science was true; the radical subjectivity of moral beliefs and the consequent impossibility of Aristotelian ethics was also true. So Hobbes

---

[51] Hobbes, *Elements of Law*, p. 28.

258          RICHARD TUCK

concluded his account of the passions by drawing a crisply anti-
realist ethical conclusion: 'every man, for his own part, calleth that
which pleaseth, and is delightful to himself, GOOD; and that EVIL,
which displeaseth him ... Nor is there any such thing as
ἀγαθὸν ἀπλῶς, that is to say, simply good'.[52]

But just as the fallibility of perception was compatible with a
physics reconstructed as ballistics, so the subjectivity of morals was
compatible, Hobbes believed, with an ethical science. To meet his
purpose, this had to be a *true* science: Machiavellianism, of the kind
endorsed by Charron and Descartes, was insufficient, since it was
avowedly (in Aristotelian terms) a *practical* and not a *theoretical* way of
thinking about ethics and politics. The Machiavellian maxims were
not elements in a deductive system analogous to a Galilean physics,
and although later writers, notably Spinoza, believed that they could
be transformed to play this role, Hobbes seems to have been too
conscious of the connection between Machiavellianism and the
moral subjectivity of the sceptics. His passionate denunciation of
the false political science of antiquity, and of its role in fomenting
moral and political conflict,[53] meant that he could not use his new
epistemology to underpin a moral science of that kind.

But as we have seen, there was available to him a moral science
which appeared to meet his requirements, being avowedly both anti-
Aristotelian *and* anti-sceptical, while accepting the force of much of
what the sceptics had argued. This was Grotius' theory as outlined in
*De Iure Belli ac Pacis* (and to a limited degree in *Mare Liberum*; the more
extensive discussion contained in *De Iure Praedae* was not available to
any contemporary readers). This was a theory which used not the
vocabulary of *interests* but the vocabulary of *rights* and *duties*, thus
clearly differentiating itself from the Machiavellian tradition; but it
did so without restricting itself to the limited and local moral
principles of the Aristotelian. What Grotius argued, to summarize it
once again, was that the moral relativist was correct in pointing to
the enormous variety of moral beliefs and practices as evidence for
the invalidity of Aristotelianism, but that this variety was compatible
with universal rights and duties of a *minimalist* kind. All societies
recognize that an individual has the right to protect himself from
others if attacked, and to secure the material goods necessary for his
existence; they also all recognize that no one has the right wontonly
or unnecessarily to attack others – necessity being represented by

[52] Ibid., p. 29.
[53] The most eloquent expression of this is in *Leviathan*, chap. 21 (ed.
C. B. Macpherson (Harmondsworth, Middlesex, 1968), pp. 266–8), but intimations
of it are to be found earlier, e.g. in the *Elements of Law*, p. 177.

the imminent likelihood of loss of life or legitimate possessions. This right of self-defence entails a right of pre-emptive action, but not, in Grotius' eyes, a right to attack on the mere off-chance that someone else may be a threat to our well-being. Thus he remarked at one point,

if I cannot otherwise save my Life, I may, by any Force whatever, repel him who attempts it, tho', perhaps, he who does so is not any ways to blame. Because this Right does not properly arise from the other's Crime, but from that Prerogative with which Nature has invested me, of defending myself. By which also I am impowered to invade and seize upon what belongs to another, without considering whether he be in fault or no, whenever what is his threatens me with any imminent Danger . . .[54]

But at another point he asserted that

to pretend to have a Right to injure another, merely from a Possibility that he may injure me, is repugnant to all the Justice in the World: For such is the Condition of the present Life, that we can never be in perfect Security. It is not in the Way of Force, but in the Protection of Providence, and in innocent Precautions, that we are to seek for Relief against uncertain Fear.[55]

Because these are universal rights and duties, they can be used not only to analyse what kinds of civil constitutions all societies must have (for according to Grotius, no society could subsist for long which did not acknowledge these principles), but also to depict the moral relations of men outside civil society, and in particular in the sphere of international relations. Grotius thus used not only the vocabulary of rights and duties, but also the imagery of the states of nature and civil society.

It is clear that Hobbes believed that any worthwhile moral science would take broadly this form, and that his use of juridical concepts around which to structure his science is most readily to be explained by the apparent success of the Grotian model. Like Grotius, he combined an acceptance of the fundamental claim of the moral relativist – that all social practices are in some sense equally good – with the belief that there are minimal but universal rights and duties. The equal rectitude of all customs and laws is a familiar Hobbesian theme: 'no civil law whatsoever, which tends not to a reproach of the Deity . . ., can possibly be against the law of nature'.[56] But this does

[54] This is from the great English translation of Barbeyrac's edition of Grotius' *De Iure Belli ac Pacis, The Rights of War and Peace* (London, 1738), p. 517 (III.1.2).
[55] Ibid., p. 141 (II.1.17).
[56] Hobbes, *Philosophical Rudiments Concerning Government and Society* (his translation of the second edition (1646) of *De Cive*), in B. Gert (ed.), *Man and Citizen* (n.p., 1972), p. 278 (XIV.10).

not represent a sceptical position, because Hobbes was always able to combine it with his account of the natural rights and laws of mankind.

Moreover, the fundamental picture of man's moral status in Hobbes is not very different from Grotius', for Hobbes too believed that we have a natural right to defend ourselves but not *wantonly* to attack our fellow men. That a man's right in the state of nature against his fellows extends in Hobbes only to actions necessary for his self-preservation is well enough known, but is still worth documenting. It is put clearly enough in the *Elements of Law*:

> It is a proverbial saying, *inter arma silent leges*. There is little therefore to be said concerning the laws that men are to observe towards one another in time of war, wherein every man's being and well-being is the rule of his actions. Yet thus much the law of nature commandeth in war: that men satiate not the cruelty of their present passions, whereby in their own consciences they foresee no benefit to come. For that betrayeth not a necessity, but a disposition of the mind to war, which is against the law of nature ... For nothing but fear can justify the taking away of another's life.[57]

Hobbes presented this qualified right as the natural expression of his account of rational conduct. As he said in the *Elements*,

> Forasmuch as necessity of nature maketh men to will and desire *bonum sibi*, that which is good for themselves, and to avoid that which is hurtful; but most of all that terrible enemy of nature, death, from whom we expect both the loss of all power, and also the greatest of bodily pains in the losing; it is not against reason that a man doth all he can to preserve his own body and limbs, both from death and pain. And that which is not against reason, men call *RIGHT*, or *jus*, or blameless liberty of using our own natural power and ability.[58]

In fact, as most commentators have been, albeit vaguely, aware, while Hobbes's account of the human psychology shows why we should fear death more than anything else, it does not show why we should not be as concerned to seek minor benefits (if they can be had without great costs) as to seek the major benefit of self-preservation. Hobbes's psychology, as has been frequently observed (for example by Plamenatz)[59] could be the basis of a kind of utilitarianism, but what Hobbes actually used it for was to support a much more limited moral doctrine, in which *only* self-preservation is truly a right. This

---

[57] Hobbes, *Elements of Law*, p. 100. This point is emphasized by A. G. Wernham in his introduction to Spinoza's *Political Works* (Oxford, 1958), pp. 12–14.

[58] Hobbes, *Elements of Law*, p. 71.

[59] J. Plamenatz, *The English Utilitarians* (Oxford, 1958), pp. 12ff.

limitation seems to me to spring naturally from his overall purpose –
if it was, as I have suggested, the underpinning of a pre-existing
modern moral science.

Hobbes introduced two corrections to the Grotian scheme at this
point, which were sufficient to make his work unacceptable to
Grotius when he read it in 1645. First, he asserted that the right of
self-preservation implied a right to all things outside civil society,
and a radical instability in the life which men were able to lead in
nature. It did so not because we are in nature entitled to everything
(as the quotation above shows), but because our judgment concerning
what is necessary for our own self-preservation is unstable, and there
is no general category of actions which cannot be seen as conducing
to self-preservation. This is not, in fact, such a dramatic departure
from Grotius' account as it might seem, for Grotius had accepted
that in a warlike situation both sides may in some cases act
legitimately, because of the difficulty of securing genuine agreement
over the facts of the case. What he said was that

In the particular Acceptation of the Word, and as it regards the Action itself,
War cannot be just on both Sides, nor can any Law Suit be so, because the
very Nature of the Thing does not permit one to have a moral Power, or true
Right, to two contrary Things, as suppose *to do a Thing, and to hinder the doing of
it*. But it may happen that neither of the Parties in War acts unjustly. For no
Man acts unjustly, but he who is conscious that what he does is unjust; and
this is what many are ignorant of. So People may justly, that is, may honestly
and fairly go to War. Because Men are very frequently unacquainted with
several Things, both as to Matter of Right, and as to the Fact, from whence
Right proceeds.[60]

Second, Hobbes argued that the right of self-preservation applied
even though a man has endangered his life through an action against
the law of nature, which he had no right to perform. The important
specific case of this is a criminal who has broken the social contract –
something which, in society, is against the law of nature. In *De Iure
Belli ac Pacis* Grotius was quite clear that this was not so; he criticized
those jurists who had claimed about wars that

even those who have given just Cause to take up Arms against them, may
lawfully defend themselves; because, say they, there are few who are content
only to proportion their Revenge to the Injuries they receive. But such a
Suspicion of what is uncertain, gives no Man a Right to oppose Force to a
just Attack, no more than a Criminal can plead a Right of defending himself
against the public Officers of Justice, who would apprehend him, by order of

---

[60] Grotius, *The Rights of War and Peace*, p. 490 (II.23.13).

the Magistrate, on a Pretence that his Punishment may be greater than his Crimes deserve.[61]

We can contrast this remark with Hobbes's observation in *De Cive* that

they who are threatened either with death (which is the greatest evil to nature), or wounds, or some other bodily hurts, and are not stout enough to bear them, are not obliged to endure them. Furthermore, he that is tied by contract is trusted; for faith only is the bond of contracts; but they who are brought to punishment, either capital or more gentle, are fettered or strongly guarded; which is a most certain sign that they seemed not sufficiently bound from non-resistance by their contracts.[62]

For an astonishing number of individual arguments in Hobbes we can find clear parallels somewhere in Grotius, but the idea that criminals are entitled to resist punishment was something which Grotius was never prepared to countenance.

It should be said that Hobbes, too, found difficulty in countenancing it at first. Although he made his position on the matter clear in *De Cive*, as I have shown in my *Natural Rights Theories*, the *Elements of Law* was much more equivocal. There, Hobbes claimed that a civil sovereign could be created by men renouncing their right to defend themselves against it; he was vaguely aware that this created problems for his psychological arguments, and in the successive drafts of the *Elements* he tried to sort the problem out, before abandoning it altogether and revising his theory for *De Cive*.[63] This change in his theory suggests that the absolute right of resistance possessed even by criminals was not a fundamental feature of Hobbes's enterprise from the beginning.

The point of these corrections – and particularly of the first, if, as I have just suggested, the second was less crucial in Hobbes's original theory – was, it is reasonable to assume, to take more seriously than Grotius had done the force not just of sceptical moral relativism, but of sceptical *epistemology*. The state of nature in Hobbes is the world as seen by the sceptic, both in ethics and physics: not only is there fundamental disagreement about most moral principles, but even where there is an ethical consensus, there is radical disagreement about how to apply the principles to the real world, and about what *actually* conduces to any individual's self-preservation. If Hobbes's epistemological arguments were right, the facts of the matter in this

[61] Ibid., p. 141 (II.1.17).
[62] Hobbes, *Philosophical Rudiments*, p. 130 (II.18).
[63] Tuck, *Natural Rights Theories*, pp. 122, 124.

context, like all facts about the material world, were to be rather laboriously worked-out; they were not open to direct observation or the simple exercise of a 'rational faculty'. Thus, until the practical implications of the fundamental laws and rights of nature had been learned, a state of nature like Grotius' was impossible; and once they had been learned, it would *ipso facto* be superseded by civil society.

This is of course a valid criticism of Grotius, and one which arises naturally from the fact that Grotius had not deeply considered the *general* character of the sceptical enterprise, but only its moral relativism. But it was by no means sufficient to lead Hobbes to abandon the broad Grotian model of a moral science, any more than the same weaknesses, highlighted by Hobbes's disturbing corrections, led to its abandonment by Selden, Pufendorf, or Locke. The sense that Barbeyrac and the other historians of moral science at the end of the seventeenth century had, that Hobbes and Grotius were engaged in a common enterprise, and that the keynote of that enterprise was its critique of scepticism, seems to have been fully justified.

# INDEX